Militant Islam in Southeast Asia

Militant Islam in Southeast Asia

Crucible of Terror

Zachary Abuza

BOULDER
LONDON

Published in the United States of America in 2003 by
Lynne Rienner Publishers, Inc.
1800 30th Street, Boulder, Colorado 80301
www.rienner.com

and in the United Kingdom by
Lynne Rienner Publishers, Inc.
3 Henrietta Street, Covent Garden, London WC2E 8LU

Library of Congress Cataloging-in-Publication Data
Abuza, Zachary.
Militant Islam in Southeast Asia : crucible of terror / by Zachary Abuza.
p. cm.
Includes bibliographical references and index.
ISBN 1-58826-212-X (hc : alk. paper) — ISBN 1-58826-237-5 (pbk. : alk. paper)
1. Terrorism—Asia, Southeastern. 2. Islam and terrorism—Asia, Southeastern. 3. War on Terrorism, 2001– 4. Qaida (Organization) 5. Islam and politics—Asia, Southeastern. 6. Asia, Southeastern—Politics and government—1945– I. Title.

HV6433.A785A28 2003
303.6'25'0959—dc21

2003047046

British Cataloguing in Publication Data
A Cataloguing in Publication record for this book
is available from the British Library.

Printed and bound in the United States of America

∞ The paper used in this publication meets the requirements of the American National Standard for Permanence of Paper for Printed Library Materials Z39.48-1992.

5 4 3

Contents

Tables and Figures

Tables

Figures

Acknowledgments

A BOOK THAT COVERS SUCH A RANGE OF COMPLEX ISSUES IN SO MANY COUNTRIES IS only the result of the time, assistance, and knowledge of many people. Most of the government officials whom I interviewed and spoke with requested anonymity. They hail from the United States, Australia, Canada, Singapore, Malaysia, Indonesia, the Philippines, Brunei, Thailand, India, Switzerland, and Germany. They know who they are and how grateful I am for their assistance.

In the Philippines, I am grateful to former president Fidel Ramos and his staff, especially Norman C. Legaspi. Former national security adviser Jose Almonte provided invaluable advice and background. I would also like to thank members of the "other side" who went out of their way to meet with me and share their perspectives. Although most requested anonymity, they include Abod Lingga and Eid Kabalu of the Moro Islamic Liberation Front, Abu Bakar Ba'asyir, as well as several members of the Mujahidin Council of Indonesia and Jemaah Islamiya.

The thoughts and insights of members of the Institute of Strategic and International Studies (ISIS) network in the region were invaluable, in particular those of Kusnanto Angoro in Jakarta, Kusuma Snitwongse in Bangkok, and Dato' Mohamed Jawhar bin Hassan, director general of the ISIS, Malaysia. In Singapore I would first like to thank several people at the Institute of Defense and Strategic Studies in Singapore who hosted the conference "After Bali" in January 2003. They are Andrew Tan, Rohan Gunaratna, Moshahid Ali, Kumar Ramakrishna, and Chong Kwa. I would also like to thank Derek DaCunha of the Institute of Southeast Asian Studies for his editing of an article based on an early draft of this book. Outside the region I would like to thank General Hank Stackpole and Paul Smith of the Asia Pacific Center for Security Studies in Honolulu for inviting me to their two conferences. At the National Bureau of Asian Research, I would like to thank Richard Ellings and Michael Wills. I would also like to acknowledge the help and encouragement of Matthew Levitt at the Washington Institute for Near East Policy.

I owe an enormous debt of gratitude to my friends in the Fourth Estate from around the region. It is these individuals who shared ideas, exchanged information and analysis, and encouraged my research. They were the first to seriously address the threat of terror in the region and did a very professional job in their coverage. In no particular order they are Simon Elegant, Michael Elliott, and Jason Tedjasumana of *Time;* Dan Murphy of the *Christian Science Monitor;* Maria Ressa of CNN; Carlos Conde of the *Philippine Daily Inquirer;* Ellen Nakashima and Allen Sipress of the *Washington Post;* Leslie Lopez and Barry Wain of the *Asian Wall Street Journal;* Michael Sullivan of NPR; Derwin Pereira and Shefali Rekhi of the *Straits Times;* Jo Puccini, Sally Neighbor, and Margot O'Neil of the Australian Broadcast Corporation; Marianne Wilkinson and Tony Parkinson of the *Age;* Moritz Klein-Brockhoff; Kavi Chong Kittavorn of the *Nation;* and Carsten Oblaender, Peter Bergen, and Vicky Mathews from Storyhouse Productions.

At Simmons College, I am truly grateful to my department chair, Cheryl Welch, and my colleague Kirk Beattie, who covered for me during my trips to the region. I would also like to thank Dean Diane Raymond, Jon Kimball, and the Freeman Foundation, whose support helped pay for a portion of the research. I owe a large debt of gratitude to Jessica Robash, the department administrator, for all of her work.

I am always grateful for the continued support from my mentors, W. Scott Thompson and Carl Thayer. They have promoted my work, provided invaluable insight and advice, and opened doors for me.

Leanne Anderson was a great (tough) editor at Lynne Rienner, who went out of her way to address my thoughts and concerns. I would also like to thank the anonymous reviewers of this book for their helpful comments and suggestions.

I would like to thank my family—my wife, Junko, and my twins, Taeko and Charlie—who have had to put up with months of absence, constant travel, and my frenetic schedule. I appreciate their love, support, and understanding.

Finally, my dear friend Dana Laird was in the process of editing this manuscript for me when she was tragically killed in July 2002. A brilliant mind, firm critic, and a live spirit, it is to her memory that I dedicate this book.

—Zachary Abuza

Militant Islam in Southeast Asia

CHAPTER 1

Al-Qaida and Radical Islam in Southeast Asia

ISLAM IN SOUTHEAST ASIA HAS ALWAYS BEEN DEFINED BY TOLERANCE, MODERATION, and pluralism. Most of the Muslim inhabitants of Southeast Asia support the secular state and eschew the violence and literal interpretations of Islam that have plagued their South Asian and Middle Eastern co-religionists. Only a small minority advocates the establishment of Islamic regimes governed by *sharia,* law based on the Quran. There have always been Muslim militants in the region, but the conventional wisdom holds that these militants were focused on their own domestic agenda. As one of the most noted U.S. scholars on Southeast Asian security wrote: "Southeast Asian terrorist groups are essentially home grown and not part of an international terrorist network, although individual members may have trained with Al-Qaida in Afghanistan."[1] That analysis is naïve and underestimates the degree to which radical Islamists in Southeast Asia have linked up with transnational terrorist organizations like Al-Qaida. Academics and policymakers have been loath to come to terms with the growing threat of radical Islamicism in Southeast Asia. The devastating attack on a Balinese nightclub on October 12, 2002, in which some 202 people (mainly Australian tourists) were killed, was a wake-up call to governments in denial and skeptics in the region. The attack was Al-Qaida's second most deadly after the September 11, 2001, attacks on the United States and drove home the point that Al-Qaida and its regional arms pose an enormous threat to the safety and well-being of states. Although these militants represent a distinct minority of the population, their ability to cause political and economic instability means that we have to take them seriously. To date there has been no study of militant Islam in Southeast Asia, nor an appreciation of Al-Qaida's links to the region.

The Impact of September 11 on the Region

The impact of the September 11 terrorist attacks on the governments of Southeast Asia was enormous, forcing them to confront a radically changed security environment. It elicited an unprecedented and robust Japanese commitment to the U.S. effort, the deployment of Japanese military forces abroad, and potentially a constitutional amendment eliminating Article 9, which makes foreign deployment of Japanese forces illegal. It also raised questions of China's role. On the one hand, China has its own problems with Muslim radicals and Uighur separatists now linked to Al-Qaida by the United States. On the other hand, China remains critical of the unilateral use of force by the United States. To date, China has cooperated fully with the United States, but in return it expects a greater role in international security issues. More important to Southeast Asian states is the question of Chinese aggression in the region if the United States becomes embroiled in a drawn-out war against terrorism. One should have taken note of how quickly the Philippines, which recently has had territory seized by the Chinese, offered the United States transit and supply facilities in its former naval and air bases and allowed more than 1,000 U.S. troops to train Philippine forces. Many Southeast Asian countries are concerned that if the United States becomes disengaged from the region, China will try to fill the strategic vacuum. Questions now exist in all Asian countries about the future of national missile defense, which could have a hugely destabilizing impact on the Asia-Pacific region.

The long- and short-term effects on already fragile economies, whose recovery since the 1997 economic crisis is uncertain and overly based on export-led growth, will be enormous. If the U.S. economy continues to slow, leading to declining imports, the impact across Asia will be profound. The oil-producing states in Southeast Asia have a compensating factor, but certainly not enough to make up for a global economic downturn. In a recent report, the World Bank revised its forecast for export growth in the region, from 3.6 to 1 percent in 2001.[2] Across the region, growth estimates for 2001 were slashed: Singapore revised its gross domestic product (GDP) estimates from 3.5 to 5.5 percent downward to 0.5 to 1.5 percent. The Philippines lowered theirs from 4 to 2.5 percent. Thailand's fell from 4.5 to 2 percent. Indonesia's estimate fell from 5 to 2.5 percent. Although Asian countries, excluding Japan, received a record amount of foreign investment in 2000, some $143 billion, only 10 percent, went to Southeast Asian nations, down from 30 percent in the mid-1990s. China is far more appealing to international investors, with its huge internal market and its cheap labor force.[3] However, with war in Iraq, the amount of foreign investment moving into Southeast Asia declined further, with considerable impact on the region's economies.

Like everywhere else, the regional airline industry was particularly hard hit. The manufacturing industries in Southeast Asia, with their focus in electronics, are very vulnerable to global slowdowns. Sixty percent of Malaysia's exports come from the electronics industry; in Singapore, exports, mainly in the electronic sector, account for 153 percent of GDP. In the Philippines and Thailand, where exports account for 50 percent and 65 percent of GDP, respectively, there was a palpable sense of alarm as exports slowed. Unemployment was already a problem in the region.

The Southeast Asian economies remain vulnerable to external forces, and they are highly vulnerable to terrorism. The October 2002 bombing of the Sari Nightclub in Bali led to an immediate 10 percent drop in the Jakarta Stock Exchange, as traders contemplated the bombing's effect on the $5 billion a year tourist industry. Indonesian GDP for 2002 fell to 3.4 percent, down nearly 1 percent due to the bombing.[4] The outbreak of SARS (severe acute respiratory syndrome) has further hurt regional tourism.

Yet the most profound impact on the region will be felt politically. Every country in Southeast Asia has a Muslim community: 5 percent of the Philippines, 5 percent of Thailand, 5 percent of Cambodia, 65 percent of Malaysia, and 85 to 90 percent of Indonesia. Indeed, Indonesia is the world's largest Muslim country, with some 180 million Muslims.

Southeast Asia was always considered the "Islamic fringe," home to mostly secular Muslims who shunned the radical variants of Islam found in the Middle East. Studies reinforced the notion that unlike in the Middle East, Islam in Southeast Asia facilitated the development of civil society and democracy. Across the region, there has been an Islamic resurgence in the past few decades.[5] Spectacular economic growth from the mid-1970s to the mid-1990s led to two contradictory pressures for an Islamic revival. On the one hand, the rapid pace of industrialization, urbanization, and the decline in traditional village life created a spiritual vacuum. Change is destabilizing, and people often turn to religion to make sense of their changed lives. Development led to the introduction, and in some cases saturation, of Western values into the region, threatening the traditional elites. And the influence of the Iranian Revolution on the entire Muslim world was profound. On the other hand, Islamization of Southeast Asia was also the direct result of sustained economic growth. For many in Indonesia and Malaysia, it was proof that one could be modern, industrial, and urban while still being a devout Muslim. Muslim moderates rejected the idea that Islam held the country in a state of underdevelopment.

All of the governments of Southeast Asia are secular. Extremists represent a miniscule proportion of the populations, and the potential for any Southeast Asian state to be taken over by a fundamentalist regime is small. The resounding defeat of the inclusion of *sharia* law into Indonesia's constitution by the parliament is evidence of this. But Islamic fundamentalism has been growing steadily since the early 1970s, and many in the region are beginning to at least acknowledge that they share the extremists' grievances, if not methods. In some countries, it has even become politically incorrect or politically foolhardy to stand up to the extremists. Governments, especially in Malaysia and Indonesia, used Islam as a legitimizing force to varying degrees in the past, though both governments have always been wary of the independence of the ulamas, Muslim scholars trained in Islamic law.

For the most part, the grievances of radical Muslims across Southeast Asia are local in nature. However, since the early 1990s, there has been a noticeable expansion of both radical Islamists and their transnational activities. Such groups are now operating out of foreign countries, where there are fewer political and law enforcement constraints on their activities than at home. In that process, the radical Muslims are beginning to establish relationships with other extremist groups. It is not uncommon now for groups from one country to train and coordinate their activities and assist one another.

That militant and extremist groups are gaining strength throughout the region is alarming. Yet an even greater cause for concern is that radical Islamists—those who are trying to establish an Islamic state governed by *sharia* through violence and extralegal means—are increasingly relying on each other in different states for assistance, financing, and training. Domestic groups with domestic grievances are now forming international alliances in pursuit of their goals—if not the furtherance of those goals.

There is one final cause for concern, the linkages between the loosely affiliated terrorist network known as Al-Qaida, run by Osama bin Laden, and local Islamic groupings, insurgencies, and cells. There has clearly been deep penetration of Southeast Asia by Al-Qaida, with cells in Indonesia, Malaysia, the Philippines, Thailand, Myanmar (Burma), Cambodia, and Singapore. Following the loss of its secure bases in Afghanistan in late 2001–early 2002, Al-Qaida became a more dispersed and diffuse organization, and Southeast Asia emerged as one of its major operational hubs. In a sense, the defeat of the Taliban has increased the threat to Southeast Asia.

Al-Qaida

There is a growing body of literature on Osama bin Laden and the Al-Qaida network.[6] For our purposes here, we need not delve into the organization's history. The scion of Saudi Arabia's largest construction magnate, bin Laden was one of fifty children. In many ways, he was always the outsider: Unlike many of his brothers, he was educated in Saudi Arabia, not Europe or the United States; he was born to a Syrian mother while his father was a Yemeni; and he joined the family concern, the Bin Laden Group, but it was firmly in the control of his elder brothers. It was not until he joined the mujahidin in Afghanistan that he found his calling.

In Afghanistan, bin Laden was deeply influenced by three individuals: Abdullah Azzam, Prince Turki bin Faisal bin Abdelaziz, and Ayman al-Zawahiri. Azzam was the founder of the Maktab al Khidmat lil-Mujahidin al-Arab (MaK), known as the Afghan Bureau. The MaK was established around 1985 and was based as an organization on the life of the Prophet Mohammed. It was responsible for coordinating the recruitment of "Arab volunteers" to the mujahidin. Bin Laden became the organization's principal funder and coordinated fund-raising in the Gulf region. Prince Turki, the head of Saudi intelligence, was the key conduit of weapons and money to the mujahidin (usually through the Pakistani Inter-Service Agency—the Pakistani Intelligence Service, ISI). Prince Turki saw to the establishment of two banks and nongovernmental organizations (NGOs) under the World Muslim League umbrella, to funnel money to the mujahidin. Ayman al-Zawahiri was the head of the Egyptian Islamic Jihad, responsible for the assassination of Egyptian President Anwar Sadat. Al-Zawahiri became bin Laden's spiritual mentor.[7]

Abdullah Azzam, himself a member of the Muslim Brotherhood, was the Vladimir Lenin of radical Islam. He believed that jihad had to be led by an organization. And that organization had to be based on the life of the Prophet Mohammed. To that end, the organization would have four phases: *hijra* (emigrate/withdrawal), *tarbiyyah* (recruitment and training), *qital* (fighting the enemies of Allah), and *sharia* (implementing Islamic law and creating an Islamic state). Upon the completion of this cycle, the organization would then move on to the next jihad.[8] Al-Qaida has implemented this cycle around the world.

Historically Al-Qaida was not a terrorist organization but a network designed to assist foreigners to join and fight alongside the mujahidin in their war against the Soviets. Bin Laden established Al-Qaida (literally the "Base") in 1988, with help from the head of Saudi Arabian intelligence in order to organize Arabic recruiting for the mujahidin; in reality, he was engaged in this work from 1984. In this context, he has always been involved in international networking. He spent $25,000 a month from his own personal fortune to support the 17,000-strong Arab brigade.

With the Soviets' defeat, Bin Laden moved Al-Qaida to Khartoum, Sudan, where he developed a more international vision and thought of the possibilities of waging little jihads all over the world. Although he was probably still receiving some funding from Saudi intelligence and individual Saudi patrons, he wanted financial independence. He opened several businesses that served as fronts and the financial backing of his terrorist operations. He has often been called the "Ford Foundation" of terrorists; groups and cells have come to him for financial support, expertise, networking, and logistical planning. Under pressure from the United States, the Sudanese government expelled bin Laden in 1996, when he returned to Afghanistan. He ingratiated himself to the country's new and radical Islamic leadership, the Taliban, donating millions of dollars to the diplomatically and economically isolated regime. It is estimated that bin Laden and Al-Qaida funneled upward to $100 million per year to the Taliban, two times their official budget. He engaged in construction projects and road building, while at the same time establishing a network of forty terrorist training camps in Afghanistan.

The central leadership of Al-Qaida is a small organization, perhaps thirty senior officials; its strength is derived from its international network with cells in some sixty countries. Al-Qaida is thought to have between 5,000 and 12,000 members (Figure 1.1). As John Arquilla notes:

> Terrorist networks develop along the lines of "diverse, dispersed nodes" who share a set of ideas and interests and who are arrayed to act in a fully internetted "all-channel" manner. . . . Ideally there is no central leadership, command, or headquarters—no precise heart or head that can be targeted. The network as a whole (but not necessarily each node) has little to no hierarchy, and there may be multiple leaders. Decision-making and operations are decentralized, allowing for local initiative and autonomy. Thus the design may appear acephalous (headless), and at other times polycephalous (hydra-headed).[9]

Bin Laden has several lieutenants, beneath which is the *shura majlis,* or the consultative council. Four specialized committees—military, religious-legal, finance, and media—report to bin Laden and the *shura majlis*. "Vertically, Al-Qaida is organized with Bin Laden, the emir-general, at the top, followed by other Al-Qaida leaders and leaders of the constituent groups. Horizontally, it is integrated with 24 constituent groups. The vertical integration is formal, the horizontal integration, informal."[10] Al-Qaida is highly compartmentalized. "These groups share the principles of the networked organization—relatively flat hierarchies, decentralization and delegation of decision-making authority and loose lateral ties among dispersed groups and individuals."[11] These networks are not easy to maintain.

> The capacity of this design for effective performance over time may depend on the presence of shared principles, interests, and goals—at best, an overarching doctrine or ideology that spans all nodes and to which the members wholeheartedly subscribe . . . [providing] a central ideational, strategic and operational coherence that allows for tactical decentralization. It can set boundaries and provide guidelines for decisions and actions so that the members do not have to resort to a hierarchy—"they know what they have to do." . . . But when communication is needed, the network's members must be able to disseminate information promptly and as broadly as desired within the network and to outside audiences.[12]

Al-Qaida is thought to control roughly eighty front companies and includes a fleet of ocean-going cargo vessels. For the most part, the front

Figure 1.1 Arquilla's Terrorist Network Models

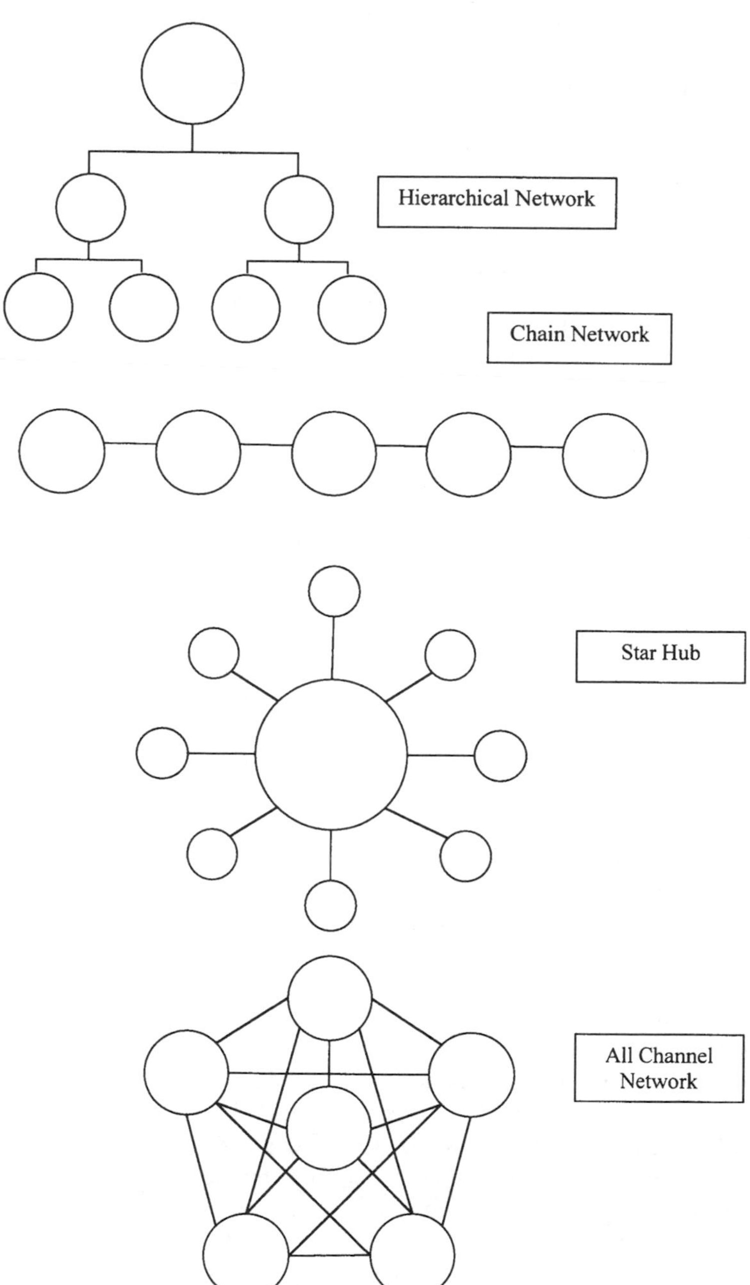

companies have been commercial failures. But Al-Qaida is known to provide only start-up costs for cells and operations, and it expects cells to become financially self-sustaining. Al-Qaida's financial network is very sophisticated and complex, dating back to the late 1980s to early 1990s. Osama bin Laden set out to establish an organization that would be self-sustaining over time: one part self-reliant, another part reliant on the *umah*—the Muslim community. Built on "layers and redundancies,"

> Al-Qaida's financial backbone was built from the foundation of charities, nongovernmental organizations, mosques, websites, fund-raisers, intermediaries, facilitators, and banks and other financial institutions that helped finance the *mujahidin* throughout the 1980s. This network extended to all corners of the Muslim world. [13]

Although most of the money from Islamic charities goes to legitimate social work, some of the money is diverted to clandestine activities.

It is not known how many extremists trained at the camps bin Laden established in Afghanistan, but German police have estimated that number to be as many as 70,000 people. The U.S. Central Intelligence Agency (CIA) has placed this number between 15,000 and 20,000. Clearly there were two generations of "Afghan veterans," a pool of some 50,000 potential supporters. So what happened to them and how did they become members of Al-Qaida?

Most became foot soldiers in an international brigade, also referred to as the Arab brigade, that fought alongside the Taliban, which included individuals from Southeast Asia. There were about 6,000 members of this brigade. The international brigade comprised up to one-third of Taliban forces. What is clear is that the brigade contained the fiercest and most disciplined fighters of the Taliban, and they displayed the most resistance to the Northern Alliance and U.S. forces in the Afghan War in the fall of 2001 through early 2003. Many were killed in the fighting, but many also disappeared, either returning to their home countries of simply regrouping. The capture of Abu Zubaydah in April 2002 and Khalid Sheikh Mohammed in March 2003, the operational chiefs, were serious setbacks.

Al-Qaida used the basic military training at the camps to select promising individuals for advanced training in establishing cells and combat. These camps were not run gratis. Groups and individuals paid either through a donation to Al-Qaida or through personnel. Al-Qaida got its choice of individuals who trained at the camps. Some were brought directly into the Al-Qaida organization and became operational agents while others were sent home as sleeper agents who were responsible for establishing independent cells.

Al-Qaida agents look to bin Laden and the other senior Al-Qaida leaders for guidance, a "blessing," funding, and help in establishing contact with other cells that they operate independently. Although most maintain operational autonomy, they are part of the network. As Richard Schultz notes, "They [Al-Qaida operatives] are not micro-managed, but that does not mean they are not connected."[14] The links are personal, rarely structured, and amorphous. As Bruce Hoffman of the Rand Corporation notes: "Al Qaida works on multiple levels, which is what makes it such a formidable opponent. Sometimes it operates top-down, with orders coming from the CEO, and sometimes it is a venture-capitalist operation, from the bottom up, when the terrorists come to ask for finance from bin Laden."[15]

In addition to establishing independent cells, Al-Qaida has been brilliant in its co-option of other groups, those with a narrow domestic agenda and bringing them into the Al-Qaida network. In short, bin Laden tries to "align with local militant groups with country-specific grievances to increase his reach and influence."[16] It is an amalgam of organizations. "They have not been subsumed into Al-Qaida," said one British analyst, but "they work with Al-Qaida," giving the organization "a degree of rootedness in their countries."[17] Associates, who pledge *bayat,* a form of allegiance to Osama bin Laden, share intelligence, money, equipment, and recruitment.[18] Although independently the cells are too small to make an impact, their strength lies in the network itself. Al-Qaida is able to graft itself on radical groups in the region or establish new cells from scratch; and increasingly, those cells are using the Al-Qaida network to coordinate their activities.

In several cases bin Laden took over these domestic groups and networks slowly. This was clear in the case of the Algerian Armed Islamic Group's (GIA) network in Europe. Senior GIA leader Antar Zouabri and Hassan Hattab, a leader of a GIA faction, were both brought into the Al-Qaida fold, and by 1997–1998, Al-Qaida had co-opted much of the radical Algerian network in Europe.[19] As Rohan Gunaratna notes, "Over time Al Qaida gradually absorbed Jemaah Islamiya (JI) into its wider structure, just as it has absorbed Egyptian Islamic Jihad and the Islamic groups of Egypt. And just as the Algerian Islamist groups were co-opted to work for Al Qaida in Europe, JI members were similarly co-opted in Southeast Asia."[20] JI put itself at the disposal of Al-Qaida; in return for funding and training, it coordinated attacks and supported Al-Qaida operations in the region.

For the purposes of this book, it's important to understand that Al-Qaida is a global network of small, independent, self-sustaining cells. As Reuel Marc Gerecht put it, "Bin Laden's greatest achievement—the creation of a worldwide network of warrior cells—will outlive bin Laden unless the United States physically eliminates al Qaida's entire command structure."[21]

Al-Qaida's Ties to Southeast Asia

Southeast Asia has become a major center of operations for Al-Qaida operatives for three primary reasons: the Afghan connection to Middle Eastern extremists, the growth of Islamic grievances within Southeast Asian states since the 1970s for socioeconomic and political reasons, and, most important, that Southeast Asian states are "countries of convenience" for international terrorists. One of the aspects that made Southeast Asia so appealing to the Al-Qaida leadership in the first place was the network of Islamic charities, the spread of poorly regulated Islamic banks, business-friendly environments, and economies that already had records of extensive money laundering. It is the contention of this book that Al-Qaida saw the region, first and foremost, as a back office for its activities (especially to set up front companies, fund-raise, recruit, forge documents, and purchase weapons), and only later became a theater of operations in its own right as its affiliate organization in Southeast Asia, the Jemaah Islamiya, developed its own capabilities.

Up to a thousand Southeast Asian Muslims fought with the mujahidin the 1980s, and there is an Afghan connection to most of the radical Islamic groups. Beginning in 1982, the Pakistani Intelligence Service began to "recruit radical Muslims from around the world to come to Pakistan and fight with the Afghan Mujahidin."[22] Others disagree with this assertion. In the *Bear Trap*, the authors, senior ISI officials, contend that they simply tolerated the foreign jihadis.[23] Between 1982 and1992, some 35,000 Muslim radicals from thirty-five countries joined the mujahidin—17,000 from Saudi Arabia alone. When bin Laden set up training camps in Afghanistan, he continued to recruit Islamic militants from around the world. Whether they returned home, or whether they joined Al-Qaida, the veteran mujahidin were able to rely on the network. One cannot underestimate how crucial the Afghan connection is: It was the basis for the Al-Qaida network around the world. As Peter Bergen wrote:

> Still, in the grand scheme of things the Afghan Arabs were no more than extras in the Afghan holy war. It was the lessons they learned from the jihad, rather than their contribution to it, that proved significant. They rubbed shoulders with militants from dozens of countries and were indoctrinated in the most extreme ideas concerning jihad. They received at least some sort of military training, and in some cases battlefield experiences. Those who had had their [tickets] punched in the Afghan conflict went back to their countries with the ultimate credential for later holy wars. And they believed their exertions had defeated a superpower.[24]

Undeniably, the Afghanistan experience was the formative experience in the lives of Southeast Asian jihadis. In Indonesia, there was the Group 272 of returned veterans, and the key leaders of radical groups in the region are all veterans of the mujahidin: Jafar Umar Thalib, Riduan Isamuddin (Hambali), Mohammed Iqbal Rahman (Abu Jibril), Nik Aziz Nik Adli, Abdurajak Janjalani, and others. As one regional intelligence official recounted, they were miserably homesick, spoke poor Arabic, were unaccustomed to the harshness of their surroundings and the weather, hated the food, and experienced "diarrhea as a way of life."[25] Nonetheless, they were driven by the call to jihad and their experience in Afghanistan was the catalyst for radical activities in Southeast Asia.

By December 2001, there were an estimated 200 undocumented Filipinos in Afghanistan and 600 Islamic scholars in Pakistan.[26] Of those scholars in Pakistan, only 70 percent were studying Islam and some 200 were "missing," according to the Philippine Embassy in Pakistan. The whereabouts of those students were unknown.[27] According to a Russian report given to the Philippine government, "at least 50 Filipinos were recently trained in one of the 55 camps and bases being maintained in Afghanistan by Osama bin Laden" and who fought in the Taliban's 8th Division, which included fighters from across the Muslim world. With the rout of Taliban forces in November 2001, intelligence analysts estimated that some fifty Filipino militants had already returned to the southern Philippines.[28]

More extensive and influential were the networks of *madrasas,* or Islamic schools, that were established in the 1980s by President Zia-ul-Haq to train refugees and young Pakistanis whose secular school system was beginning to crumble. The *madrasas* were the ideological front line against the Soviets, the primary socialization vehicle and recruitment organ for jihad. The *madrasas* teach only Quranic studies and Arabic—no modern or secular studies. The products of *madrasas* are radical Muslims who believe that their life mission is jihad. As Simon Reeve put it, "They leave the schools with only a rudimentary knowledge of the world, but a fanatical belief in the supremacy of Islam and their responsibility to fight and ensure its spread."[29] Once the Soviets were defeated, the *madrasas* stayed open, often funded by radical political parties or wealthy patrons. And as Pakistan slumped into economic malaise, the *madrasas* filled an important void in the country's crumbling educational system. By 2000 there were some 10,000 *madrasas* that had almost 1.5 million students. During the 1980s, up to 100,000 foreigners attended *madrasas* in Pakistan where they came into contact with the jihad and established transnational networks. The World Bank found that 15 to 20 percent of Pakistani *madrasas,* to some degree, had a military training component. In early 2002, Pakistani president Pervez Musharraf announced that he would implement new policies to oversee the 10,000 *madrasas,* which "propagate hatred and violence" and "produce semi-literate religious scholars."[30] Pakistan has recently pledged to reduce the number of foreign students attending Pakistani *madrasas* by 60 percent.[31]

Most Southeast Asians returned and set about committing themselves to running jihads at home, recruiting followers, in an attempt to create Islamic states governed by *sharia* law. Since the mujahidin, tens of thousands of Southeast Asian Muslims have traveled to the Middle East to study in Islamic universities, including those in Egypt, Syria, Yemen, and Pakistan. Thousands of Southeast Asians have studied in the Pakistani *madrasas* that gave rise to the radical Taliban regime.[32] In the 1990s the CIA tried to keep track of some 700 to 1,500 Indonesian students who went to Egypt, Syria, and Iran for study. According to a retired CIA officer, "We figured 30–40 percent of them never showed up. We don't know where they went."[33] None of the countries in Southeast Asia has an accurate fix on how many of their nationals studied in *madrasas* in the past or are currently studying now. There are an unknown number of Malaysian students studying in other Islamic universities and *madrasas* in Pakistan, as the government keeps no records on privately funded students studying abroad.[34] One Malaysian official recounted to me how its embassy in Islamabad, Pakistan, believed there were 5 to 10 Malaysians studying at a certain *madrasa* in Pakistan; there turned out to be 150. In the Philippines, some 1,600 *madrasas* have been established, unsupervised by state educational authorities, and almost entirely funded by contributions from the Middle East.[35] Forty-four Indonesian students were expelled from Yemeni *madrasas* in February 2002 alone. The Indonesian government has no idea how many Indonesians are studying in Egypt, Pakistan, or elsewhere. In addition to the Pakistani *madrasas*, many Southeast Asians have attended Egypt's Al-Azhar University, the foremost Islamic university in the world, and Yemen's Al Imam University, both of which teach rigid Wahhabi interpretations of Islam and have produced the most radical firebrands in the Muslim world, such as Abdel Meguid al Zindani, and have been key recruiting grounds for Al-Qaida. At Egypt's Al-Azhar University, there are some 6,000 Malaysian students alone. Each of the nine state governments on the Malaysian peninsula rents a block of apartments for the students that it sponsors. Although most of these students will return and join the government's Islamic bureaucracy, and not turn militant, some students return committed to turning Malaysia into an Islamic state. This was brought to the government's attention in February to March 2002, when twelve Malaysian students were arrested in Yemen in a crackdown on radical Islamic *madrasas*. Though released after they were found to not have terrorist connections, Malaysia agreed to repatriate the 250 to 300 privately funded students in Yemen.[36]

The very strict and orthodox Wahhabi brand of Islam is a literal interpretation of the Quran. This puritanical sect was founded by Muhammad Ibn al-Wahhab (c. 1703–1791) and rejects all Islamic practices adopted after the third century of the Muslim era (approximately 950 C.E.). Wahhab considered it a duty to conquer all other "heretical" sects of Islam practiced among the Saudi tribes. He allied himself with one clan, the Saud, in 1744. In the mid-1760s the Saud completed their conquest of Saudi Arabia, and ever since, there have been close links between the House of Saud and the Wahhabi sect.

The growth of the Wahhabi sect around the world can be explained by two reasons. First, the sect markets itself as the "purest" brand of Islam. Second, it has been patronized by the Saudi royal family, the Saudi Arabian government, and especially Saudi-based charities, which have financed thousands of Islamic schools around the world as well as new mosque construction. The financial power of Saudi Arabia has ensured that its predominant Islamic sect has been able to propagate itself, including in places like Southeast Asia that have always had very tolerant and undoctrinaire interpretations of Islam. Even in devoutly Buddhist Cambodia nearly 15 percent of Cham Buddhists are Wahhabi, the result of Saudi aid and scholarships.

The Pakistani *madrasas* blended rigid Wahhabism with Deobandism, an authoritarian and pan-Islamic sect that emerged in the subcontinent in the nineteenth century. Deobandists wanted to create a pan-Islamic movement to combat British and other European colonial rule.[37] This is noteworthy because if one studies the language of bin Laden, he evokes the idea of the caliphate. As Gerecht explained, "For many fundamentalists, as least sentimentally, the ideal geopolitical expression of Muslim universalism [is] an empire free of Westernized nation-states, where the sharia, the holy law, reigns supreme, thus guaranteeing the union of the church and state and the brotherhood and strength of the faithful."[38] This is important because increasingly in Southeast Asia, radical groups, such as the Kampulan Mujahidin Malaysia and the JI, are beginning to reconceive precolonial notions of pan-Islamicism.

Madrasas are not just a Middle Eastern phenomenon. In their pursuit of the creation of Islamic states, many Southeast Asian jihadis established Islamic schools to indoctrinate, propagate, and recruit. The leaders of many militant groups in Southeast Asia, including the Laskar Jihad, Kampulan Mujahidin Malaysia, and Jemaah Islamiya, returned from Afghanistan and established a network of *madrasas* as the base of their operations and recruitment.

And *madrasas* are increasingly beyond state control. Of the 37,362 *madrasas* in Indonesia, only 3,226 (8.6 percent) are run by the state; and 81 percent of the 5.6 million students enrolled in *madrasa* attend privately funded and run Islamic schools. In the Philippines only thirty-five of 1,600 are controlled by the state, with alarming consequences. As one education official put it, the privately funded *madrasas* "tailor their curricula to the wishes of whoever subsidizes them."[39]

The *madrasas* and *pesentren,* or Muslim boarding schools, in Southeast Asia that have been set up since the late 1980s, have advocated a stricter, more intolerant brand of Islam and condemn the secular nation-state. They are the core of a growing and powerful radical Islamic movement and have established networks within the region and with the Middle East. There is now a critical mass of students studying in Islamic universities and *madrasas* who are reinforced in their conviction that Malaysia, Indonesia, and Mindanao must become Islamic states in order to overcome the myriad socioeconomic and political woes that secularism has wrought. They believe that in Islam there is no separation between church and state, that Islam is a complete way of life, and that *sharia*, not man's positive laws, can be the only ordering principle in society. This radical fringe will continue to grow, as modernization leaves people more isolated and the political process leaves people more disenfranchised. The Islamists and their supporters will continue to gain in power unless the more secular Muslim community again provides a successful model of tolerant and modernist Islam that it has done fairly successfully for forty years.

The vast majority of Southeast Asian Muslims do not attend *madrasas* and *pesentren;* they are the products of secular education. Yet they are attending prayers at mosques in increasing numbers, more children are being educated in Islamic schools, and there has been a surge in interest in Arabic studies. Many parents lament that their children are unable to read the Quran in Arabic. *Pesentren* also provide room and board, in addition to education, which is not insignificant in the context of a prolonged economic downturn and declining public investment in public education in the region. But parents are increasingly sending their children to *pesentren* because of their discipline, the failure of states to provide adequate schooling, and the protection of their children from the vices of secular, urban education: the decline of Islamic values, drug use, and teenage pregnancy. In Malaysia's Kelantan State, for example, there are some 40,000 students enrolled in ninety-two *madrasas;* 50 percent of those come from other states. Moreover, since 1994, the passing rate for the government's secondary school examination for students in Kelantan's *pesentren* has been 90 percent, higher than the national average.[40] *Madrasas* in Pakistan and elsewhere in the Middle East are increasingly appealing to Malaysians, Moro Filipinos, and Indonesians for several reasons: They were a cheap source of education that gave the student and their family status in their communities; they were a hedge against the growing political clout of Islamic hardliners; and finally, in uncertain economic times, graduates of *madrasas* could always find work as clerks in mosques or *sharia* courts.

Although many of the recruits into the ranks of militant Islamic groups in Southeast Asia came from *madrasas*, one of the hallmarks of Al-Qaida is its ability to recruit and radicalize students from Western secular education, especially those with technical training. In Southeast Asia, many of the leading operatives in Jemaah Islamiya were trained or teachers in technical universities, notably the University of Technology Malaysia and Bandung Institute of Technology. Both have traditionally been hotbeds of radical Islamic activities.

In addition to prayers, which are shown on TV in Malaysia, Indonesia, Singapore, and the southern Philippines five times a day, there are Arabic language lessons on television focusing solely on the reading of the Quran across the region.

There is also the Yemeni connection. The traders who spread Islam to Indonesia and Southeast Asia from the Arabian Peninsula hailed in particular from what is now Yemen. Osama bin Laden, though formerly a Saudi national, is actually from a south Yemeni clan from Hadramaut. Hadramauts were seafaring traders who migrated en masse to Southeast Asia and were instrumental in spreading Islam. The British actively encouraged Yemeni and Arab migration to their colonies in Singapore and Malaya. Even in the predominantly Muslim states of Malaysia and Indonesia, there were distinct Arab minorities who constituted a powerful economic and social force. The fact that they came from the land of the Prophet accorded them special status: "As nominal countrymen of the prophet, Arabs came to be respected as scholars of the writ and as judicial authorities in matters of the Islamic faith."[41] As Peter H. Riddell put it, "Their influence as traders and authorities in the religious sphere should be seen as inextricably interlinked; it is likely that the authority accorded to them in the religious domain at times seemed to provide them with preferential trading circumstances."[42] And there continued to be considerable flows between the communities throughout the twentieth century. Riddell notes considerable Malay Arab and Singaporean Arab communities in Hadramaut and Mecca. Both Indonesia and Malaysia have sizeable Arab minority communities. The vast network of Yemenis in the region is not a tangential point. Bin Laden, as with Al-Qaida, relies on personal networks, and Yemen's clan-based society transcends the oceans and has spread to Southeast Asia. The single largest Yemeni industrialist, Hail Saeed, had extensive investments throughout the region, as does the Binladen Group itself.[43] These corporate conglomerates have always relied on the vast network of Yemeni traders and businessmen in the region as business partners. And Yemen itself has become a key operational base for Al-Qaida agents as well as a site for attacks, such as the bombing of the USS *Cole* or the French oil tanker in October 2002. Yemenis are major investors in Southeast Asia, and they operate many joint ventures that we now know were fronts for Al-Qaida.

The second reason that Al-Qaida has looked to Southeast Asia is that the Islamic resurgence in the region has occurred because of long-standing disputes with the secular governments. Many of the Islamic movements in Southeast Asia have legitimate grievances, whether they have been repressed or whether they clamor for autonomy or simply greater religious freedom. Economically speaking, in all Southeast Asian countries, the Muslim *pribumi* or *bumiputera* communities are less well off.[44] Indeed, Malaysia had to implement a reverse-affirmative action program in the early 1970s following race riots in 1969 to give the ethnic majority a greater share of the nation's wealth. The goal of the New Economic Policy (NEP), as it was titled, was to ensure that Malays (who make up two-thirds of the population) were able to account for one-third of economic assets. Now, more than thirty years later, the original goals of the NEP still have not been met, despite significant improvements in the socioeconomic position of Malays. There are considerable socioeconomic inequalities that exist across the region between the different religious communities that have only been exacerbated by the Asian economic crisis since 1997. In Indonesia, anti-Chinese riots in May 1998, though provoked by a faction within the military, were the clearest manifestation of popular grievances toward the commercially advantaged Chinese community. In Indonesia, there is a stronger sense that the economy has still not recovered than in any other Southeast Asian state: 58 percent argued that it is harder to find work, 56 percent believed that working conditions are getting worse, 74 percent believed that the gap between the rich and poor is getting worse, and 44 percent attributed that to globalization.[45]

The growth of Islamic extremism around the world since the Iranian Revolution of 1979 has less to do with theology and a lot to do with the failure of the domestic political economies of their respective countries. Increasing gaps between the rich and poor, unemployment, corruption, a lack of economic diversity, and the lack of a viable political alternative have all given rise to Islamic extremism. People literally become so desperate that they have nowhere to turn but to extremist religious politics. The Iranian Revolution, which took place in the most secular state in the region, was clearly a catalyst. The most secular governments in the Muslim world were Malaysia and Indonesia, two of the fastest growing economies from the mid-1970s to the mid-1990s. Once their economies slowed and became mired in the Asian economic crisis, which saw the value of their currencies collapse and public and private debt soar, causing mass unemployment, Islamic extremism was able to take hold and enter the mainstream, whereas before it was on the fringes of society. Clerics were able to veil their political criticisms in Friday prayer sermons.

In some countries, notably Malaysia and Indonesia, rather than being aggrieved by minority status, Islam became more radical because authoritarian secular governments repressed it for so long. Secular leaders never gave political space to religious elites and religious-based political parties, even when they relied on them in their own ascension to power. Religious elites and parties felt that they had been, at best, ignored or marginalized, and, at worst, repressed by governments who feared the Islamization of politics.

The jailed former Malaysian deputy prime minister, Anwar Ibrahim, contends that the lack of democracy and civil society is the root cause of Islamic fundamentalism in the country. Without a free press and a truly democratic system where people can blow off steam, radical Islamists provide one of the only viable alternatives to the ruling coalition. In a well-publicized essay entitled "Who Hijacked Islam?" Anwar made a compelling, though implicit, argument that the government's authoritarian policies and the lack of democracy were only going to serve as a catalyst for Islamic fundamentalism:

> Bin Laden and his protégés are the children of desperation; they come from countries where political struggle through peaceful means is futile. In many Muslim countries, political dissent is simply illegal. Yet, year by year, the size of the educated class and the number of young professionals continues to increase. These people need space to express their political and social concerns. . . .

> The need for Muslim societies to address their internal social and political development has become more urgent than ever. Economic development alone is clearly insufficient: it creates its own tensions in the social and political spheres, which must be addressed.[46]

At the same time, these governments have often turned to religion as a legitimizing force for their rule. For example, the Malaysian and Indonesian governments began to actively facilitate the *haj,* the pilgrimage to Mecca. By the 1980s, more than 80,000 Indonesians and 15,000 Malays went to Mecca annually, all with the support of their governments.[47] In short, across the region, socioeconomic and political issues have created a large body of people who are turning to Islam to change the status quo, which they believe has kept them poor and disenfranchised. Governments often turn to religion in times of political and economic crisis to shore up their domestic legitimacy, as Indonesian president Suharto did in the early 1990s. Although governments try to keep religion in check, this is never easy to do. For example, the mosques are often the focal points of antigovernment resistance and propaganda, as the Iranian Revolution drove home in 1979.

The growth of radical groups in Southeast Asia must also be seen in the context of religious and political leaders who were kept out of an elite status and used Islam to manipulate sectarian issues for their own political purpose. As Michael Davis said in his study of the Laskar Jihad in Indonesia, radical groups must be militant and confrontational: "This derives from basic self-interest: No conflict, no Laskar Jihad—only the maintenance of hostilities legitimates the group's position."[48] In part, Islamic hardliners have been able to do this because of the spread of democracy in the region. This is the irony of the "illiberal democracy." On the one hand, the lack of democratic institutions (political parties, freedom of assembly, and free speech) permitted Islamic extremism to spread. Only in the mosques in veiled language could there be political dissent. Yet the spread of democracy has now sanctioned the extremists, giving them political platforms to express their pent-up grievances. For example, in Indonesia, since the fall of Suharto in May 1998, nearly 25 percent of the political parties have an Islamic affiliation or identity. There is a crisis in the belief of democracy's efficacy in Indonesia. The percentage of people who believed that Western-style democracy works in Indonesia fell from 64 percent in 2002 to 41 percent in 2003, a trend that favors the less democratic Islamic parties.[49] The fact is, we have to let this run its course.

The breakdown of secular institutions, especially the educational and legal systems in the wake of the Asian economic crisis, has created a vacuum in which nonsecular institutions emerge to fill the void. Increasingly parents are turning to *pesentren* and *madrasas* to educate their children as state funding for the educational sector collapses. Likewise, in a recent column, the

Malaysian intellectual Farish Noor contended that *sharia* courts were becoming more prominent because of the absolute failure of the secular court system in adapting itself to changes in the political-economy of a "globalized" world.[50]

Finally, we cannot underestimate the influence of the ongoing conflict in the Middle East, which has a surprisingly large impact on popular opinion in the region. While the Palestinian issue is primarily a national struggle cloaked in religion, it strikes a chord in Southeast Asia. The injustices suffered by the Palestinians become a metaphor for the injustices of all Muslims, while the Americans, already scapegoats for the region's economic woes, are implicated again. It does not help matters that Singapore, whose Chinese population is mistrusted and maligned by the larger populations of Indonesia and Malaysia, is a very close ally of Israel.

What is so evident is that radical Islam is spreading very quickly across the region, and the once secular states are becoming more Islamic as a result. Moderate Muslims who embrace tolerance and cohabitation with ethnic and religious minorities are still the majority of the population, but they are being overshadowed by a more radical and outspoken group that is bent on establishing Islamic states. The radical right is dictating the national agendas and forcing the governments to adopt policies to protect themselves against the accusation of not protecting the rights and interests of the Muslim communities. What is more, secular politicians in the region are increasingly unwilling to confront the Islamic parties; to do so now is becoming a political liability.

Countries of Convenience

In addition to having a receptive population and being a large source of recruits, many of the countries in Southeast Asia are "countries of convenience" that make them attractive to terrorist cells. Terrorism differs from transnational crime in that there is no profit motive driving terrorism. Yet if one takes away the terrorist act itself, one sees that terrorist groups rely on the same infrastructure upon which transnational criminals rely.

Al-Qaida first came to Southeast Asia not as a theater of operations but as a back office for its terrorist infrastructure. Each country in Southeast Asia has its own comparative advantage, in the terrorists' eyes. First, while some states are strong, such as Malaysia and Singapore, with strong political institutions and legal infrastructures, most states in the region are weak, characterized by weak political institutions, decentralized politics, poor resources, and plagued by endemic corruption. Indonesian central authority broke down, especially in the outer islands, following the collapse of the new order regime in 1998. This has been compounded by abolishing the *dwi fungsi* principle of the Indonesian armed forces (TNI), which gave them a civil-administrative function in the provinces. The lack of strong central government control has always attracted Al-Qaida. That Jakarta was unaware of seven terrorist camps in Sulawesi is indicative of the tenuous control they have over the provinces.

Thus, terrorists are able to operate and plan attacks with little concern for their own security. Terrorists need to plan attacks meticulously because their acts must have a large impact. Often the terrorists have more resources at their disposal than the governments that they confront. "We lack the infrastructure," one Philippine police intelligence official complained to me. "We have no computerized immigration or tax data bases. It is easy for foreigners to marry Filipinas and change their names." He said that to break up the Ramzi Yousef cell, which was planning spectacular crimes, he only had two teams of twenty men. They simply could not keep up with the terrorists, not to mention all the other domestic insurgent groups: the Moro Islamic Liberation Front (MILF), the Moro National Liberation Front (MNLF), the Abu Sayyaf Group (ASG), the New People's Army (NPA), and all the factions thereof. There has been some training of Philippine intelligence and security personnel with U.S. intelligence agencies that seem more determined to upgrade the technical capabilities of their Philippine counterparts.

Moreover, despite large intelligence and internal security apparati in the region, in general Southeast Asian nations were not focused on the threat of international terrorism. Even Singapore, which has the region's most well-funded and robust security services, was caught completely by surprise by the network of Islamic militants because it has always focused its attention on other threats. Further, the intelligence services in Southeast Asia are often overly politicized and engaged in fierce bureaucratic infighting. Security forces in the region, when looking beyond their own borders, were confronting a host of other transnational threats: organized crime, people smuggling, drug smuggling and money laundering.[51]

So often, security services in weak states are plagued by endemic corruption. For example, in the Philippines, in the summer of 2000 and again on June 2, 2001, Abu Sayyaf forces were surrounded but escaped amid allegations that field commanders were on the take. Abu Sayyaf hostages recounted hearing rebel leaders conferring with local military commanders about the time and direction of attacks, while the governor of Basilan, himself a former guerilla, Wahab Akbar, was seen meeting an Abu Sayyaf leader and sending truckloads of supplies to their camp.[52] In both Indonesia and Thailand there is significant rivalry between the army and police forces over turf and illegal business empires, as most police and militaries in Southeast Asia rely on extra-budgetary sources of income to finance their operations. In September 2002 in Indonesia, a fire fight broke out between army and police forces over a drug-smuggling venture that left eight police dead. Even if they are not corrupt, these forces are underequipped and confronted by well-armed rebels.

Second, Southeast Asia is convenient for terrorists because the importance of tourism on Southeast Asian economies resulted in lax immigration procedures and easy access visas. And there are huge exchanges of people between Southeast Asia and the Middle East. Malaysia and Indonesia are attractive destinations for people from the Middle East, exotic and liberal, yet still Muslim. Until recently Malaysia did not have any visa requirements for citizens of other Muslim states, while the Philippines had no computerized immigration database, thus facilitating the laundering of identities. No alarms were raised when people departing the country used a passport that was not used to enter the country. Thailand has some of the laxest visa requirements of any nation, although no visa requirements exist for more than 100 countries around the world. Moreover, the borders in Southeast Asia, especially the archipelagic states of Indonesia and the Philippines, are incredibly porous. It is simply not possible to police the maritime borders of these states.

Two other immigration issues are pervasive in Southeast Asia: document theft and forgery, and human smuggling networks. Thailand has always been the regional hub of people smuggling and document forging, whereas Malaysian passports repeatedly turn up in cases of alleged terrorist associates of Osama bin Laden. In February 1999, a man wanted for the killing of fifty-eight tourists in Egypt in 1997, Said Hazan al Mohammed, and two other Al-Qaida operatives were detained in Uruguay for using a forged Malaysian passport.[53] Several of the operatives in the above-mentioned plot either used Malaysian travel documents or Malaysia as a transit point to the region. Indonesia has been at the center of smuggling rings transporting migrants from Afghanistan and Pakistan to Australia.[54]

Third, there are considerable financial links between the region and the Middle East to facilitate the thriving trade between the two regions. Southeast Asia is a business-friendly environment, where the establishment of shell or front companies is simple to accomplish. Malaysia is one of the world's pre-eminent Islamic banking centers,[55] with strong and deep financial ties to Middle Eastern businesses, banks, charities, and other financial institutions. Al-Fadl, a former member of the Al-Qaida network who turned himself in to the Americans and testified against Ramzi Yousef in the U.S. Embassy bombings case, said Osama bin Laden frequently used Islamic banks in Malaysia.[56] As the Binladen Group has had extensive dealings and investments in Malaysia,[57] it is apparent that Osama bin Laden, himself a former financier (though no longer a member of the Binladen Group), was cognizant of Malaysian financial institutions and banking regulations and entered into many joint ventures with Malaysian and Yemeni businessmen.

Thailand has grown into a major international banking center. Islamic banking is also taking hold in Indonesia, whose banking system is already ruinously underregulated. In 1992, there was only one Islamic bank in Indonesia; there are now five and roughly eighty local *sharia* banks. Beginning in the late 1990s, Brunei emerged as a center for Islamic banking, though without any legal and regulatory framework. Islamic banks, themselves, are not conspiratorial funders of terrorist acts. It is that many Islamic banks happen to be in countries with weak financial oversight and lax supervision. Their religious nature also accords them a greater degree of autonomy. As Islamic banks were established to circumvent the practice of paying and charging interest, they often commingle funds to create investment vehicles, "creating ready opportunities for anonymous money transfers and settlements."[58]

Across the region, with the exception of Singapore, the banking and financial sectors are poorly regulated, which makes transfers and money laundering easier. Three states—the Philippines, Indonesia, and Myanmar—are on the Office for Economic Cooperation and Development's (OECD's) Financial Action Task Force's blacklist for money laundering states. However, most terrorists do not transfer large amounts of funds through the banking sector, preferring smaller transfers through the unregulated remittance system. The Chinese have had a system known as *feiqian,* literally "flying money," in place to facilitate commerce for thousands of years. In the Middle East, this informal banking system is known as the *hawala,* or "trust" system, in which no money is ever wired, no names or accounts of senders or receivers are used, and no records are kept.[59] With commissions of only 1 to 2 percent, compared to average bank transfer fees of up to 15 percent, they are the transfer system of choice. In Pakistan, for example, of the $6 billion in foreign exchange that is remitted to the country annually, only $1.2 billion arrives through the banking system.[60] This type of system is common throughout Southeast Asia and used extensively in Malaysia, Singapore, and the Philippines, which has considerable financial exchanges due to the 1.4 million guest workers in the Middle East. In downtown Manila's Ermita District, there are blocks upon blocks of *hawala* shops. Over $6 billion is remitted annually to the Philippines, mainly through the *hawala* system, and there are some 1.35 million Filipino laborers in the Middle East alone. Overseas workers, who represent 10 percent of the labor force, have literally kept the Philippine economy afloat since the early 1980s. In 2000, they remitted some $6 billion, and in 2001, $5.4 billion.[61] Although overall remittances from overseas foreign workers dropped by 13 percent in the first half of 2001, compared to the first half of 2000, from $3.1 billion to $2.7 billion, receipts from the Middle East actually rose in that period, from $270 million to $352 million, up 30.3 percent.[62] The Philippines has a weak banking sector, with little regulatory oversight, especially over the flow of remittances, so it is easy to make fund transfers. Money wired from the Middle East, even to small post office accounts in the villages, do not raise eyebrows. As one Singaporean *hawala* said, "My company does not question the amount or the purpose of sending the money. They trust us, and I don't ask questions. Why would I, when I have a license to operate?"[63]

Hawala become even more important in countries that have currency controls. For example, in the fall of 1998, when the Malaysian government imposed capital controls and stopped the conversion of the ringgit in order to prevent capital flight, the *hawala* system was one of the few sources of foreign exchange.[64] Likewise, after the Philippines abolished exchange controls in 1992, remittances through the legal and regulated banking sector quadrupled.[65]

Much of Al-Qaida's funding is thought to come from charities, either unwittingly or intentionally siphoned off, because Al-Qaida inserted top operatives in Southeast Asia into leadership positions in several charities. Indonesian intelligence officials have estimated that 15 to 20 percent of Islamic charity funds are diverted to politically motivated groups and terrorists. In the Philippines, estimates range from 50 to 60 percent, according to regional intelligence officials.

In Islamic culture, Muslims are expected to donate 2.5 percent of their net revenue to charity, known as *zakat*.[66] "In many communities, the *zakat* is often provided in cash to prominent, trusted community leaders or institutions, who then commingle and disperse the donated moneys to persons and charities they determine to be worthy."[67] This practice is unregulated, unaudited, and thus leads to terrible abuse by groups such as Al-Qaida. There are some 200 private charities in Saudi Arabia alone, including 20 established by Saudi intelligence to fund the mujahidin who send $250 million a year to Islamic causes abroad. It is estimated that $1.6 million per day is donated by wealthy Saudis alone.[68] More disturbing, a Canadian intelligence report concluded that Saudi charities alone were funneling between $1 million to $2 million annually to Al-Qaida's coffers.[69] The Council on Foreign Relations, which published one of the most authoritative accounts of the problems facing the war against terrorist funding, concluded that Saudi individuals and charities are "the most important source of funds for Al Qaida."[70]

The four most important of these charities are the Islamic International Relief Organization (IIRO), which is part of the Muslim World League, a fully Saudi state-funded organization whose assets were frozen by the U.S. Treasury; the Al-Haramain Islamic Foundation, also based in Saudi Arabia; Medical Emergency Relief Charity (MER-C); and the World Assembly of Muslim Youth.[71] Although most of the money goes to legitimate charitable work, albeit to win political support, such as mosque construction, charities, cultural centers, and NGOs, a significant amount is diverted to terrorist and paramilitary activities.

Zakat taxes are common throughout Southeast Asia; indeed in late 2001, the Indonesian government agreed to make *zakat* tax deductible in order to encourage charitable donations. In addition to the obligatory *zakat* donations, there are also nonobligatory *infaq* and *shadaqah* donations (voluntary and made depending on the circumstance). Yet unlike the West, where NGOs and charities are closely regulated and audited, they are almost completely unregulated in Southeast Asia, allowing for egregious financial mismanagement and the diversion of funds to terrorist cells. For this reason, Osama bin

Laden's initial foray into the region came in the form of charities run by his brother-in-law in the Philippines, including a branch of the IIRO.

Fourth, Al-Qaida is interesting in one other respect: its use of Western technology to defeat the West. Al-Qaida operatives are very techno-savvy, and this meshes well with Southeast Asia, which comprises very wired societies. Southeast Asia is home to a large percentage of the world's hardware and software manufacturing. Its workers are high tech, well educated, and sophisticated computer users. Al-Qaida-linked websites have operated out of Malaysia and are currently under investigation.[72] Al-Qaida recruited extensively from the technical universities that have proliferated in the region.

Fifth, the region is awash in weapons, and there is not a terrorist organization or insurgent army that has not availed itself of the Southeast Asian arms markets. The Tamil Tigers, for example, had an office in Thailand for years just to purchase weapons. Every state within the Association of Southeast Asian Nations (ASEAN), with the exception of Laos and Brunei, produces small arms and ammunition.[73] Singapore, Thailand, and Hong Kong are also home to several leading arms brokers who exploit legal loopholes, negligent government supervision, official corruption, or even government complicity in the sale of weapons from legal sources (government-owned or -contracted firms). There are huge stockpiles of weapons in the region—both legal and illegal. For instance, in 1998, Philippine police identified almost 330,000 weapons outside of government control.[74] Likewise, Indonesian security forces were under pressure to conduct an audit of their arsenal in 2002, following revelations of TNI weapons being used by Acehnese guerrillas and robbers.[75] Weapons are either cascaded—that is, when new weapons enter service, the replacements are sold off—or they can be sold by corrupt officials. Thailand has been surrounded by civil wars and insurgencies and has a reputation for being one of the world's hottest black markets for weapons. In the summer of 2002 alone, there were discoveries of M-60s bound for Burma and M-16s, AK-47s, and ammunition bound for Aceh and the Tamil Tigers. Three countries in the region, the Philippines, Thailand, and Singapore, have also come under international scrutiny for disturbing arms transfers of weapons imported from abroad, mainly the United States, Canada, and Germany, and South Africa in the case of Singapore.[76] The breakdown of law and order and incipient corruption led to a loss of control over state arsenals—particularly in Thailand, the Philippines, and Indonesia. Indonesia, which has only five naval vessels to patrol the Malacca Straits and the Acehnese coastline, for example, simply cannot match the resources of the smugglers. One senior Indonesian intelligence official complained to me that smugglers and militants use speedboats that are manufactured in a state-subsidized shipyard, while the Indonesian police and navy did not have the budget to purchase the same boats.

Finally, there is a more hospitable environment in the region for terrorists and radicals to operate. The sheer number of radical groups operating with impunity outside of the legal political system is cause enough for alarm, even without having ties to Al-Qaida. These groups have conducted sweeps and threatened to attack U.S. interests. One group, the Indonesian Islamic Youth Movement (GPI), registered youths for a jihad after the United States began its war in Afghanistan.[77] Although the Youth Movement claims to have no ties to bin Laden or his organization, some youths have already gone to Afghanistan out of "Muslim solidarity." More than 300 went to fight in Afghanistan in the two weeks after the United States began its bombing campaign.[78] The Defenders of Islam (FPI) likewise recruited for a jihad to fight the Americans in Afghanistan and then to fight in Iraq in early 2003. The FPI's chairman, Habib Rizieq Shihab, told *Tempo,* "The FPI has held a *jihad* account filled by donors from all over Indonesia. Several Islamic businessmen are also ready to give large sums of money to send forces to Afghanistan."[79] The FPI organized massive demonstrations of up to 10,000 people to demonstrate against U.S. actions in Afghanistan in mid-October 2001; Habib himself went to Iraq. Although many analysts disregard him, he is one of the most inflammatory and anti-Western orators in Indonesia with a growing following. In Malaysia, the Kampulan Mujahidin is only one of many radical organizations; others include the Al-Ma'unah, Kampung Medan, and older groups such as the Islamic Revolution Cooperative Brigade (Koperasi Angkatan Revolusi Islam).[80]

One especially alarming trend was reflected in an online survey conducted by the daily newspaper *Media Indonesia:* A majority of the 2,400 respondents believed that bin Laden was a "justice fighter," and fewer than 35 percent considered him a terrorist. Nearly half of the respondents were university graduates, so clearly bin Laden is able to tap into a growing sentiment across the Muslim world. Indonesians surveyed in the Pew poll ranked Osama bin Laden third in a list of world leaders who could be trusted to do the right thing.[81] What is particularly troubling is that secular middle-class Indonesians are also turning against the United States, which they feel is unilateral, arrogant, and aggressive. As Harold Crouch warns, the "outrage expressed by the radicals against the United States is widely shared by the moderate Muslim majority, as well as by secular groups."[82] What happens when we no longer have to confront Al-Qaida as an organization but as an ideology?

In short, most Southeast Asian states have terrorist cells working in them. Although they are for the most part independent and focused on political and social issues within their own states, increasingly they are forming networks and engaging in transnational actions. We now know the importance that Al-Qaida placed on the role of sleeper agents, and Southeast Asia has been used extensively as a base since the early 1990s.

The War on Terrorism

The Taliban's collapse in Afghanistan was a serious blow for Al-Qaida. But now, instead of having one place to plan and train, Al-Qaida has diversified. Today, there are nodes of Al-Qaida cells that can conduct operations around the world, of which Southeast Asia is one. Were bin Laden and other senior members of Al-Qaida to be captured or killed, the organization would suffer a blow. However, it is dangerous to believe that either will end terrorism. Bin Laden's capture or death will only make a martyr out of him, and in his own words, he will be replaced by a 1,000 new martyrs. Despite nearly one year of investigations around the world, only some 3,000 Al-Qaida members and suspects have been detained, meaning that some 50 to 60 percent of Al-Qaida operatives remain at large around the world, and more than likely many are in Southeast Asia. As CIA director George Tenet warned, despite "disrupting terrorist operations, I repeat, Al-Qaida has not yet been destroyed. It and like-minded groups remain willing and able to strike at us. Al-Qaida's leaders are still at large, working to reconstitute the organization and resume its terrorist organizations." The October 2002 bombing in Bali, like the May 2003 bombings in Riyadh Saudi Arabia and Morocco, is evidence of a more dispersed Al-Qaida that is focusing on attacking softer economic targets in order to maximize economic and political instability. As Osama bin Laden warned in an October 2002 audiotape, the "young men of Islam are preparing for you something which will fill your hearts with terror and will target the nodes of your economy until either you cease your injustice and aggression or the quicker of us dies."

If we are truly going to fight a "war on terrorism," then we have to understand both its global reach and its root causes. We have to learn how terrorists plot against the secular states by operating across their borders; how they recruit, plan, and operate in different countries; and how they are able to find local communities to support their operations, or as pools of recruitment. To that end, this book has four main goals.

The first goal is to analyze the emergence of radical Islamic groups in the region and provide a brief historical context to understand why extremism was able to grow and take hold. Al-Qaida did not simply arrive in the region and establish a network from scratch, but rather it found groups, who had already been established and had legitimate grievances, that had been fighting their respective states for a prolonged period of time. They were brought into Al-Qaida or co-opted. The historical roots of militant Islam are not new in the region, but the links to international terrorist groups are. Al-Qaida was able to graft onto existing movements as well as establish independent cells. More important, it was able to link these organizations to create a complex network throughout the region. What were government policies in the region until September 10, 2001? Did they have a role in creating the conditions for terrorism? The September 11 attacks and the ensuing war on terrorism allows us to go back and examine the growth of Islamic fundamentalism in the region, to understand the underlying root causes. Only by taking a broader, more long-term historical and political-economic look can we understand the penetration of Al-Qaida into the region. This is the subject of Chapter 2.

This raises a larger question about how local radicals were brought into the Al-Qaida organization. How did individuals go from being parochial jihadis, concerned with narrow political agendas in their own state, to "internationalists"? What caused that transformation? Thus, the second goal of this book is to examine some of the linkages between Al-Qaida and Islamic extremists in Southeast Asia and, perhaps more important, the growing relationship among these groups themselves. To what degree has Al-Qaida penetrated the region? To what degree did it set up cells or graft on or form alliances with preexisting groups? Although these groups have been covered in the national presses, they are relatively unknown in the United States, and their ties to each other have been woefully unreported. Increasingly these groups are working together, operating across borders in pursuit of their own domestic political agendas, training together, providing intelligence and safe havens. A pan-Islamic movement in Southeast Asia is unlikely, but in the process, it has the capacity to wreak economic and political havoc. To this end, there are two chapters dedicated to the development of Al-Qaida in Southeast Asia. Chapter 3 analyzes the period from 1991 to 1995, when Al-Qaida's base of operations was in the Philippines, both to support terrorist acts against the United States, but also to liaise with Muslim militants in the southern island of Mindanao. Chapter 4 studies the development of the Jemaah Islamiya, Al-Qaida's regional arm that was founded between 1993 and 1994 and established a network of cells throughout the region.

The third goal of this book is to analyze the reactions of the regional governments to the September 11 attacks and the U.S. war on terrorism. The reactions and policies have been diverse and largely driven by each country's political and foreign policy goals. Chapter 5 seeks to understand (1) what the states are doing to confront Al-Qaida and prevent their territories from being penetrated by international terrorists, and (2) what the policy responses are to rising fundamentalism and addressing the legitimate grievances of the Muslim communities. Are states ready to confront Al-Qaida not as an organization but as an ideology? These are very different objectives, and it is yet to be seen how well the various governments respond to both of them. These governments are constrained politically as to how much they can and are willing to do, at the risk of alienating constituencies or galvanizing political opposition against them. How they respond to the war on terrorism has much more to do with domestic political considerations, and we must be aware of the domestic pressures that these regimes face.

The focus of Chapter 6, and the fourth goal of the book, is to analyze the six pitfalls (listed below) in defeating terrorism in Southeast Asia.

1. Despite considerable success in dismantling the Al-Qaida organization, it is still far from defeated. It is a fluid organization with an uncanny ability to recruit, indoctrinate, and reconstitute itself. It is a more diffuse organization, and Southeast Asia will be an important theater of operation for it in the coming years.
2. Despite the ongoing threat posed by terrorism in the region, there are uni-, bi-, and multilateral obstacles to effectively fighting terrorist groups. In addition to resource issues and bureaucratic competition, states will continue to react and cooperate only in their immediate short-term political, economic, and diplomatic interests.
3. Whereas ASEAN is the appropriate venue for a multilateral effort to fight terrorism, it is a much weakened organization and its efficacy in combating terrorism will be limited.
4. The war on terror is important in that it has reengaged the United States in the region. However, U.S. and regional governments' agendas will not always converge.
5. The war on terror cannot come at the expense of human rights in the region.
6. The threat posed to human rights could alienate secular nationalists and moderates who can project a viable alternative to the radical Islamists and whose cooperation is essential to their state's counterterrorism goals, by projecting a viable alternative to the radical Islamists. Can one be an Islamist without becoming a jihadist?

In the future, the United States will have to pay far more attention to the region because there is a growing awareness that "there has been a concerted effort by bin Laden and his people to expand their activities in East Asia, not only in the Philippines, but in Malaysia and Indonesia."[83] The United States can no longer distance itself from the region much less abandon it as it was accused of doing during the Asian economic crisis. There is a growing realization that the region's continued economic slide will have dire national security implications for the United States. As Michael Armacost put it, "Now no one in Washington can ignore Southeast Asia because there are large Muslim populations in Indonesia and the Philippines, and these countries are taking a real hit in the global downturn."[84]

Terrorism and the spread of radical Islam are global issues. If we are really intent on fighting terrorism, we have to understand its reach and its roots. The war in Afghanistan is important in denying Al-Qaida a base of operations, yet how many have already returned from the training camps ready to wage a jihad in Southeast Asia? The devastating impact of the attack on a Balinese nightclub, in which 202 people were killed, will have repercussions for the region. And governments, such as Indonesia's, which denied the presence of terrorist cells or Al-Qaida's presence for over a year, are now confronted with the reality that terrorists have set up large networks within their borders, able to conduct small-scale attacks that will have devastating impacts on their political and economic situations.

Notes

1. Sheldon W. Simon, "Southeast Asia and the US War on Terrorism," *NBR Analysis*, 13, no. 4 (July 2002): 37.

2. Michael Richardson, "Attacks Seen Stalling Asia's Recovery," *International Herald Tribune* (*IHT*), October 18, 2001, 11.

3. Chinese manufacturing employees earn, on average, $90 a month, compared with $117 in the Philippines and $137 in Thailand. Moreover, with an unemployment rate in China of 10 to 15 percent, there is little upward pressure on wages.

4. Estimates of the bombing's impact were that tourism revenue would drop from over $5 billion in 2001 to $3.4 billion in 2002 and between $2.7 billion and $3.2 billion in 2003. The number of foreigners expected to visit Indonesia in 2003 is approximately 4 million, down from 5.15 million in 2001.

5. See Robert W. Heffner, *Civil Islam* (Princeton: Princeton University Press, 2000); Robert W. Heffner and Patricia Horvatich, eds., *Islam in the Era of Nation States* (Manoa: University of Hawaii Press, 1997); and Mitsuo Nakamura, Siddique and Bajunid, *Islam and Civil Society in Southeast Asia* (Singapore: Institute of Southeast Asian Studies, 2001).

6. The best history and accounts of Al-Qaida are Peter Bergen, *Holy War Inc.: Inside the Secret World of Osama bin Laden* (New York: The Free Press, 2001); and Rohan Gunaratna, *Inside Al Qaeda* (New York: Columbia University Press, 2002).

7. Phil Hirschkorn, Rohan Gunaratna, Ed Blanche, and Stefan Leader, "Blowback: The Origins of Al-Qaeda," *Janes Intelligence Review* 13, no. 8 (August 2001).

8. Elena Pavlova, "An Ideological Response to Islamist Terrorism: Theoretical and Operational Overview," in Rohan Gunaratna, ed., *Terrorism in the Asia Pacific: Threat and Response* (Singapore: Eastern Universities Press, 2003), 30–46.

9. John Arquilla, David Ronfeldt, and Michele Zanini, "Networks, Netwar, and Information-Age Terrorism," in Ian O. Lesser et al., *Countering the New Terrorism* (Washington: Rand Corporation, 1999), 49, 51.

10. Hirschkorn et al., "Blowback."

11. Arquilla, "Networks, Netwar, and Information-Age Terrorism," 61.

12. Ibid., 51.

13. *Terrorist Financing: Report of an Independent Task Force Sponsored by the Council on Foreign Relations* (New York: Council on Foreign Relations, October 2002), 7.

14. Peter Ford, "Al Qaeda's Veil Begins to Lift," *Christian Science Monitor*, December 20, 2001.

15. Ibid.

16. Richard Engel, "Inside Al-Qaeda: A Window into the World of Militant Islam and the Afghani Alumni," Janes Online, September 28, 2001.

17. Ford, "Al Qaeda's Veil Begins to Lift."

18. Yonah Alexander and Michael S. Swetnam, *Usama bin Laden's al-Qaida: Profile of a Terrorist Network* (Ardsley, N.Y.: Transnational Publishers, 2001), 20.

19. Hirschkorn et al., "Blowback."

20. Gunaratna, *Inside Al Qaeda*, 194.

21. Reuel Marc Gerecht, "The Gospel According to Osama bin Laden," *The Atlantic Monthly* (January 2002): 46.

22. This policy was supported by the CIA from the start. See Ahmed Rashid, *Taliban: Militant Islam, Oil, and Fundamentalism in Central Asia* (New Haven: Yale University Press, 2000), 129. According to Rashid, for Pakistan this policy cemented Islamic unity and turned Pakistan into a leader of the Islamic world. For the United States it served as propaganda to demonstrate that the entire Muslim world was against the Soviet Union.

23. Mark Adkin and Muhammed Yousaf, *Afghanistan—The Bear Trap: Defeat of a Superpower* (London: Casemate Publishers, 2001).

24. Bergen, *Holy War Inc.*, 56.

25. Interview No. 25, Singapore, June 20, 2002.

26. Rasheed Abou Alsamh, "Why OFWs Are Safe in the Middle East," *Philippine Daily Inquirer* (*PDI*), September 28, 2001.

27. Lira Lalangin, "Bin Laden Seen Recruiting Ex-MILF," *PDI*, October 24, 2001.

28. "Filipino 'Terrorist Trainees' Return," *Straits Times* (*ST*), November 19, 2001.

29. Simon Reeve, *The New Jackals: Ramzi Yousef, Osama bin Laden, and the Future of Terrorism* (Boston: Northeast University Press, 1999), 226.

30. Michael Richardson. "Asians Taking a Closer Look at Islamic Schools," *IHT*, February 12, 2002.

31. The law requires *madrasas* to register with the government, disclose their sources of funding, and register foreign students. It also encourages the voluntary integration of mathematics and sciences into the *madrasa* curriculum. The government promised that those *madrasas* that did expand their course offerings would receive state aid, additional teachers, and textbooks. Most *madrasas* have rejected the law and have refused to comply. The government has not dedicated the resources to fully implement the law leading to charges of "cosmetic changes" to appease the Bush administration. See John Lancaster, "Room for Reform," *Washington Post Weekly*, July 22–28, 2002, 16; Douglas Jehl, "Pakistan to Expel Foreign Religious Students," *New York Times* (*NYT*), March 9, 2002, A8.

32. Rashid, *Taliban*, 17–30.

33. John McBeth, "The Danger Within," *Far Eastern Economic Review* (*FEER*), September 27, 2001, 21.

34. "KL to Require Students Going Abroad to Register," *ST*, October 13, 2001.

35. Only thirty-five of the 1,600 *madrasas* were integrated into the national educational system with government oversight. Beginning in June 2002, the Arroyo administration has begun to integrate the *madrasas* into the national curriculum.

36. Kean Wong, "A Malaysian Vision in Cairo," *New Straits Times* (*NST*) November 7, 2001; "12 Malaysian Students Arrested in Yemen," *ST*, February 28, 2002.

37. Robert Kaplan, *Soldiers of God* (New York: Vintage, 2001), 236.

38. Gerecht, "The Gospel According to Osama Bin Laden," 46.

39. "Philippine Madrasahs Spread North," *ST*, August 5, 2002.

40. Leslie Lopez, "Islamic Schools Flourish in Malaysia," *Asian Wall Street Journal* (*AWSJ*), October 23, 2001.

41. J. M. van der Kroef, "The Indonesian Arabs," *Civilisations* 5, no. 13 (1955): 15–23, esp. 16.

42. Peter R. Riddell, "Arab Migrants and Islamization in the Malay World During the Colonial Period," *Indonesia and the Malay World* 29, no. 84 (July 2001): 117.

43. The Hail Saeed Group of Companies is the largest private industrial concern in Yemen with vast interests overseas. In 1995 the Hail Saeed Anam Charity Society was established to carry out Saeed's philanthropic works. The charity receives 10 percent of the profits from the Hail Saeed Group of Companies and is primarily involved in the construction of mosques, health centers, and water projects.

44. *Pribumi* is the Indonesian term for a native Muslim. *Bumiputra*, literally "son of the soil" is the term for indigenous Muslim Malays. The distinction is mainly aimed at the ethnic Chinese minorities in those two countries. In Malaysia, Chinese constitute approximately 20 percent of the population; in Indonesia, they account for roughly 5 percent. Yet in both cases they control a disproportionate amount of their respective country's wealth.

45. Only 54 percent believed that they are better off living in a market economy. Pew Global Attitudes Project, *Views of a Changing World* (Washington, DC: Pew Research Center, 2003): 80, 84, 104.

46. Anwar Ibrahim, "Who Hijacked Islam?" *Time Asia*, October 14, 2001.

47. Paul Stange, "Religious Change in Contemporary Southeast Asia," in Nicholas Tarling, ed., *The Cambridge History of Southeast Asia, Vol. 2, Part 2, From World War II to the Present* (New York: Cambridge University Press, 1999), 229.

48. Michael Davis, "Laskar Jihad and the Political Position of Conservative Islam in Indonesia," *Contemporary Southeast Asia* 24, no. 1 (April 2002): 23.

49. There is also a growing sentimental yearning for strongman rule in Indonesia. Although 65 percent of the respondents argued that the country should be ruled by a democratic regime, 32 percent cited the need for a strong leader. And 69 percent believed that a strong economy was more important than a strong democracy. *Views of a Changing World*: 7, 65.

50. Farish Noor, "Negotiating Islamic Law," *FEER*, September 19, 2002, 23.

51. Alan Dupont, *East Asia Imperilled: Transnational Challenges to Security* (New York: Cambridge University Press, 2001).

52. On June 2, 2001, the Abu Sayyaf Group was surrounded in a walled hospital compound on Basilan Island. The ASG and hostages slipped through a hole in army lines when they were ordered repositioned; the army attacked eight hours later. Three captives, who had paid $500,000 walked free; it is alleged that much of the ransom went to bribe local army commanders to allow the ASG to escape. In October 2001, Abu Sayyaf rebels were again surrounded and then mysteriously broke through a military cordon. See Indira Lakshmanan, "Amid the Deaths, Tales of Collusion," *The Boston Globe*, February 3, 2002; Luz Baguioro, "Abu Sayyaf Slips Past Military Cordon—Again," *ST*, October 11, 2001.

53. Alexander and Swetnam, *Usama bin Laden's al-Qaida*, 43.

54. The illegal trafficking of individuals is a $7 billion a year industry. Bertil Lintner, "The Crime of Flight," *FEER*, July 18, 2002, 18–20.

55. By June 2001, "total Islamic banking assets stood at RM51.97 billion, or 7.3 percent of overall banking assets." Between 1994 and 2000, Islamic banking assets increased by 64 percent. For more see, Baidura Ahmad, "Strong Growth Seen for Islamic Banking and Takaful," *NST*, October 2, 2001.

56. Dafna Linzer, "From New York to Kabul and Back: Star Witness at the Embassy Bombing Trial Revealed bin Laden's World," AP, in *IHT*, October 1, 2001.

57. Reme Ahmad, "Osama Family Did Projects in Malaysia," *ST*, September 30, 2001.

58. *Terrorist Financing,* 10.

59. Douglas Frantz, "Secretive Money Moving System Scrutinized For bin Laden Funds," *IHT*, October 3, 2001. It is estimated that between $2 billion and $5 billion passes through the informal *hawala* system in Pakistan alone each year.

60. "Cheap and Trusted," *The Economist*, November 24, 2001, 71.

61. Luz Baguioro, "Overseas Filipinos Feel Pinch of Global Slump," *ST*, December 14, 2001. Also see "An Anthropology of Happiness," *The Economist*, December 22, 2001, 42–43.

62. "Filipinos Send Less Money Home Due to Global Insecurity," *ST*, November 1, 2001.

63. Michelle Cottle, "Eastern Union: Hawala v. the War on Terrorism," *New Republic*, October 24, 2001, 24–28, esp. 27.

64. Ibid.

65."Cheap and Trusted," *The Economist,* 71.

66. During the war against the Soviets, the Saudis established three charities, the Islamic International Relief Organization, Al-Haramain Foundation, and the Islamic Relief Agency. Al-Qaida has established many more since then. Mark Hubard, "Bankrolling Bin Laden," *Financial Times (FT)*, November 28, 2001.

67. *Terrorist Financing,* 7.

68. Jeff Garth and Judith Miller, "Threats and Responses: The Money Trail," *NYT*, November 28, 2001; Mark Hubard, "Bankrolling Bin Laden."

69. Edward Alden, "The Money Trail: How a Crackdown on Suspect Charities Is Failing to Stem the Flow of Funds to Al Qaeda," *FT*, October 18, 2002.

70. *Terrorist Financing,* 7.

71. MER-C played a facilitating role in the 1998 bombings of the U.S. embassies in Kenya and Tanzania. See Matthew Levitt, "The Political Economy of Middle East Terrorism," *Middle East Review of International Affairs* 6, no. 4 (December 2002): 56. The president of the World Assembly of Muslim Youth is Shaikh Saleh al-Shaikh, the Saudi minister of Islamic affairs. He is also the superintendent of all foundation activities for Al-Haramain. See Matthew Levitt, "Combating Terrorist Financing, Despite the Saudis," Washington Institute for Near East Policy, Policy Watch #673, November 1, 2002.

72. "KL Joins FBI Probe on Al-Qaeda Website," *ST,* July 10, 2002.

73. Keith Krause, ed., *Small Arms Survey 2001: Profiling the Problem* (New York: Oxford University Press, 2001), 20.

74. Ibid., 86. Also see Merliza Makinano and Alfred Lubang, "Disarmament, Demobilization, and Reintegration: The Mindanao Experience" (paper presented at the RCSS conference, Colombo, Sri Lanka, 2000).

75. Devi Asmarani, "Jakarta Groups Call for Audit of Military and Police Weapons," *ST*, July 25, 2002.

76. Krause, *Small Arms Survey 2001,* 155.

77. The GPI registered hundreds of people to join a jihad in Bosnia in 1994, though in the end it sent only eight. Those eight have returned to Indonesia and now serve as jihad instructors for the GPI along with fifteen veterans from Afghanistan, according to the head of the GPI Brigade, Handriansyah. For more, see Edy Budiyarso, "Indonesia's Afghan-Trained Mujiheddin," *Tempo Weekly*, October 2–8, 2001; and Vaudine England, "Indonesian Groups Respond to Growing Calls for Jihad," *South China Morning Post*, September 28, 2001.

78. Abu Hanifah, "Government in Dark About Indonesian Fighters in Afghanistan," *Jakarta Post*, November 15, 2001.

79. Wicaksono, Ardi Bramantyo, Adi Prasetya, and Agus Hidayat, "Jihad Jive," *Tempo Weekly*, October 2–8, 2001.

80. Hayati Hayatudin, "Most KMM Members Are Opposition Party Members Operating in Terengganu, Kelantan," *NST*, October 14, 2001.

81. Bin Laden ranked behind PLO leader Yassir Arafat and Saudi Crown Prince Abdallah. *Views of a Changing World*: 3.

82. Crouch, "Qaeda in Indonesia? The Evidence Doesn't Support Worries," *IHT*, October 23, 2002.

83. Johnathan Weiner, "American Action Is Held Likely in the Philippines and in Indonesia," *NYT*, October 10, 2001, A1.

84. James Hookway, "Just Say 'No' to U.S. Troops," *FEER*, December 6, 2001, 24.

CHAPTER 2

Islamic Politics, Grievances, and Militancy

ISLAM HAS ALWAYS HAD A POLITICAL COMPONENT TO IT IN SOUTHEAST ASIA. IT arrived in Southeast Asia between the twelfth and thirteenth centuries and was able to superimpose itself on the local political culture. Before the arrival of Europeans, there was a considerable pan-Islamic movement in the region: a network of Islamic sultanates bound by blood and marriage that extended from peninsular Malaya to the Sulu Archipelago in the Philippines. Islam became an important locus of anticolonial struggle and nation building but over time became marginalized by the development-oriented secular states, which denied Islam political space.

This chapter will provide the reader with a historical overview of Islamic politics in the region and an understanding of why more fundamental and radical Islam emerged. It will also introduce the reader to Islamic insurgencies and separatist movements and will identify their grievances.

Philippines

The Islamic Revolt in Mindanao

Widespread sectarian conflict erupted in the southern island of Mindanao in the 1970s. Some 120,000 people have been killed in Mindanao Province alone, while tens of thousands of people have become refugees in Malaysia in three decades of war. As a religious minority in the overwhelmingly Catholic Philippines, Muslims have been ignored by the central government. By every measure of human development, the inhabitants of the southern Philippines lag behind their compatriots. There are legitimate grievances for the 5-million-strong Muslim community.

Several different insurgent groups have fought for a Muslim homeland in the southern Philippines. The first was the Philippine Muslim National League, established in 1967. Out of that emerged the Moro National Liberation Front, the Moro Islamic Liberation Front, and later the Abu Sayyaf. Plagued by factional infighting and tribal conflict, the latter two groups broke away from the MNLF. The avowed goal of all three of these groups is to create an independent state for the Muslims in the Moro region in the southern Philippines, yet they are often plagued by internecine conflict.

Historical Roots

The Philippines has a 400-year-old secessionist movement in the southern islands around Mindanao led by an aggrieved Muslim minority. The Muslim-dominated territory includes western Mindanao, Tawi-Tawi, Basilan, and the Sulu Archipelago.[1] Today, thirteen of the country's sixty-seven provinces have significant, if not majority, Muslim populations.

Muslim separatists use the term *Bangsamoro*, or "the Moro nation." However, this is a historical misnomer. Thomas McKenna contends that there is no Moro nation.[2] Rather, there are three major linguistic and ten minor linguistic groups—and distinct ethnic differences. The term *Moro,* which derives from the Spanish word *Moor,* was meant to connote all of the various Muslim tribes that the Spanish were unable to effectively dominate. Moro as a concept of a nation, or Bangsamoro, was an artificial construct, which partially explains why the different insurgent groups are so ridden with factionalism. As one Filipino academic put it: "Total peace is unlikely because there seems to be no short-term solution to the conflict among three major Muslim tribes: the Mananaos, Maguindanaos and Tausogs."[3]

Islam first came to the Moro region of the Philippines almost 300 years before Ferdinand Magellan's arrival and the introduction of Christianity in 1521. In 1619, three sultanates were united into the Sultanate of Maguindanao.[4] Neither the Spanish nor the Americans were ever able to fully control the Moro region. Spanish conquest of the northern Philippines in the 1600s and their aggressive Christianization of the population effectively blocked the northward spread of Islam, confining it to the Sulu Archipelago and western Mindanao. The Spanish wars against the Moro and Sulu sultans were bloody, but largely ineffectual, and only in the 1850s did the Sulu Sultanate begin to submit to Spanish control; even then, the Spanish tended to rely on indirect rule with *datus,* or local leaders.

The wars were also exacerbated by European rivalry: The British, who were in the process of establishing colonies and trading posts on Sabah in Borneo, favored the establishment of a strong and independent Sulu Sultanate and did not formally acknowledge Spanish claims to the southern Philippines until a protocol was signed in 1877.[5]

Following its acquisition of the Philippines in 1898, after the Spanish-

American War, the United States, too, had trouble imposing law and order in the south, despite a treaty with the sultan of Sulu in 1899 that allowed for a degree of local autonomy and accepted *adat*, or local customary law.[6] U.S. forces allied themselves with powerful *datus*, and in return for economic privileges and the conferring of political power, the *datus* accepted U.S. overlordship. Nevertheless, President Theodore Roosevelt unilaterally declared the treaty null and void in 1904 and imposed direct rule and control over the Moro islands.[7] Direct rule was never that strong, though, owing to the U.S. predilection for decentralized rule, and the United States still relied on the *datus* as the source of local power. As the United States prepared the Philippines for independence, the *datus* who supported the government became the democratic leaders. McKenna contends that there was no Moro identity during the period of Spanish colonization but that it was forged during the colonial period. The U.S. colonial administrators found that the local population was surprisingly nonreligious and promoted the use of religion and Moro identity as a force for development: "The American colonial rulers encouraged the development of a self-conscious Philippine Muslim identity among a generation of educated Muslim elites who were otherwise divided by significant linguistic, geographic, and, to some extent, cultural barriers."[8]

Yet relations with Muslims soured for two reasons in the mid-1930s. First, in 1936, the Philippine government failed to recognize the successor of the sultan of Sulu, Jamal-ul-Kiram, who had died, thus the Sulu court lost its recognition or rights as an independent entity. Second, U.S. rulers encouraged the mass migration of landless peasants from Luzon, in the Christian north, to Mindanao. "This was seen as a neat way of side-stepping land reform while diluting the Islamic population with a steady influx of Christians, and it continued under [Ferdinand] Marcos despite the Muslims' growing unrest at what they saw as a Christian plot to grab their lands and submerge their culture."[9] Though a large-scale revolt was never organized, there were sporadic and small-scale outbursts against Christian rule. The United States was able to contain the insurgency but never eliminate it. One Muslim leader told me that Christians were commonly referred to as the "Ilongo Land Grabbers' Association."

The 1936 elections for constitutional convention delegates included representatives from the Moros who had hoped to use the democratic process to protect their indigenous rights. Although the majority of the population in the Moros accepted the new constitution in a referendum, Muslim leaders assert that the majority were Christian migrants who had shifted the demographic balance.[10]

The Growth of Islamic Consciousness

Following World War II, the United States gave the Philippines independence, including all rights and claims in the Moro islands, though some Muslims wanted to establish a separate Moro homeland at that time. Muslim resentment grew, as there was a mass influx of Christian settlers, the unintended consequence of the peace process between the government and insurgent communist Huks. As part of the peace agreement, the central government gave landless peasants land titles in Mindanao. Whereby it solved one insurgency, it unwittingly sowed the seeds of a new one.

In 1957 the Philippine Congress created the Commission on National Integration to address the grievances of the Muslim community. However, in the 1950s to the early 1960s, there was not much resistance to Manila for one fascinating reason: Differences in trading regimes and the degree of protectionism among the Philippines, Malaysia, and Indonesia made smuggling, especially of U.S. cigarettes, hugely profitable. "Thus the early post-war era saw the emergence and growth of a vast illegal economy in the southern Philippines, with local politicians in the Muslim provinces (and elsewhere) evolving into 'smuggling lords' thanks to their control over law enforcement."[11] In essence, the local Muslim political elite benefited from the status quo and had no desire to threaten their livelihoods by pushing for independence.

At the mass level, however, Muslim consciousness grew for several reasons. Internally, anger was growing because of continued Christian migration to the region, the Muslims' single greatest grievance. In 1968, some local politicians in Cotabato and Lanao provinces established the Moro Islamic Movement (MIM), which began to engage in small-scale violence against Christian settlers and vigilante groups known as the "black shirts." The MIM's formal goal was to secede and form an Islamic state, but there was little popular support for secession.

Another reason for the growth of Muslim consciousness had to do with two changes in the educational system. The government, in an attempt to bring Muslims into the mainstream of Philippine society, began offering scholarships and investing in education in the south. The government gave large numbers of scholarships to Moro students to study at the secondary and postsecondary levels. Between 1957 and 1967, 8,000 students studied in Manila, and there were 1,391 college graduates.[12] These graduates returned to the south and began to challenge the political status quo and, in particular, the dominance of the local *datus*, whom the students considered to be collaborators. There was also a rapid growth of Islamic education due to increased contacts with Egyptian president Gamal Nasser's pan-nationalist policy between 1955 and 1978. This led to scholarships for more than 200 Moro students to study at Egypt's Al-Azhar University, while Egyptian Islamic teachers and Indonesian graduates of Al-Azhar were sent to the Philippines for two-year stints.[13] The inflow of foreign aid also helped to fund Islamic education centers and *madrasas*, where the Al-Azhar graduates preached and taught. In 1950, the first *madrasa* was established, and in 1952 the first foreign teacher was sent there, an Indonesian cleric, Abdul Ghani Sindang.[14] Starting in 1971, Libya began to provide funds for the construction of mosques and *madrasas*.

The Organization of the Islamic Conference (OIC) funded the construction of thirteen new mosques in the south and the repair of many others. Libya and Saudi Arabia funded local imams (Muslim preachers) and ulamas (Muslim scholars), effectively paying their salaries.[15] As a result, the study of Arabic began at a larger scale in the 1970s.

There was a key external factor as well. The Moro issue became important again with the Sabah conflict between the Philippines and Malaysia. The new state of Malaysia was the amalgamation of peninsular Malaya (which gained independence in 1957), Singapore, and two other British colonies on Borneo, Sabah and Sarawak, in 1963. Based on a historical claim, the Philippines claimed that Sabah had actually been ceded to the sultan of Jolo by his relative, the sultan of Brunei, in the seventeenth century. The territory was "leased" by the British North Borneo Company in 1798, and in 1946 it fell under direct British control. The Philippine government, the successor to the Jolo Sultanate, formally claimed Sabah in 1962. The Malayan government, however, claimed that the territory was purchased outright by the British North Borneo Company. In 1963 the Cobold Commission conducted a referendum in Sabah in which the people overwhelmingly decided to join the Federation of Malaysia, which they formally did on September 16, 1963. Angered, the Philippine government broke off diplomatic relations with Malaysia twice. Indonesia also failed to recognize Malaysia and soon after began its policy of *konfrontasi* (confrontation).[16] In 1966, the new Philippine president, Ferdinand Marcos, recognized Malaysia, though he continued to press the claim to the Sabah at the diplomatic level.

At the same time, Marcos was also preparing to launch covert operations in Sabah. In 1968 a group of fourteen to twenty-eight Muslim commandos in the Philippine armed forces—though under the nominal command of the Civil Affairs Office—were killed in mysterious circumstances on Corregidor Island, an incident known as the Jabidah Massacre. There are alternative hypotheses on why the massacre took place. The Philippine government asserted that the commandos had mutinied because of poor pay and conditions. Others suggest that Marcos had used them to eliminate past political rivals and that they had become a political liability because they knew too much. In reality, though, they mutinied once they discovered that they were being trained to lead raids into Malaysia against fellow Muslims. "The Jabidah massacre provided both provocation and metaphor" for the Muslim community: Muslims in the service of the country were betrayed and murdered.[17]

The political leader of Sabah, Tun Mustapha, himself an ethnic Tausig with family in Jolo, was angered by the continued Philippine claim to the territory.[18] The Jabidah Massacre confirmed his worst fears of Philippine intentions and he began to arm small groups of Moro rebels to fight the Philippine government.

In 1972 Marcos imposed martial law, which threatened the local political elites. Marcos disbanded local armies and militias, integrating them into the national Philippine constabulary, which was subordinate to the military, confiscating some 500,000 weapons in the process. Marcos then awarded all "barter trade" to the army's Southern Command, taking away the lucrative smuggling rackets controlled by local politicians.[19] All of a sudden, local political elites who benefited from the political status quo with Manila had their source of wealth stripped from them, leading to a strident independence platform.

The MNLF Revolt

Nur Misuari, a professor at the University of the Philippines, formed the Moro National Liberation Front in 1968 and left the Philippines for Sabah in the early 1970s, where Tun Mustapha provided arms (in particular a conduit for Libyan weapons) and training. The MNLF began an armed insurgency in 1972 (the Bangsamoro People's Liberation Army); aided by funding from supporters in Malaysia and Libya between 1973 and 1975, it was able to field approximately 30,000 soldiers, tying down some 70 to 80 percent of the Philippine armed forces by 1975.[20] The military budget had increased fivefold to $325 million to finance the war. A high casualty rate of 100 per month led to mass desertions and low morale.

The MNLF rebellion suffered a number of difficulties. For one, there was a very robust Philippine military response. Despite a substantial flow of Libyan weapons, the MNLF forces were outgunned. By 1973, however, the MNLF was able to field a 15,000-man army.[21] Second, it began to lose popular support because of high civilian casualty rates (an estimated 50,000 by 1976). Third, it lost critical foreign support. In 1974, Malaysia passed Resolution No. 18, which changed official policy toward supporting Moro autonomy rather than independence; then in 1976, Tun Mustapha lost the state election. Fourth, the MNLF movement was woefully uncohesive, and there was little centralized control over all of the various different component groups. Misuari fled to Sabah and then to Libya. Most of the leaders, including Vice Chairman Salamat Hashim, were in Tripoli in 1974, removed from field command.

Marcos was under international pressure to negotiate, including from the OIC states that threatened to cut off sales of oil to the Philippines. He began a high-profile development scheme, the Southern Philippines Development Authority, headed by his wife, Imelda, to work on infrastructure and other social welfare programs. He also established a mosque in Manila and the Islamic Studies Center at the University of the Philippines.[22]Additionally, he entered into peace talks with the MNLF in Tripoli. In 1976 the first lady was dispatched to Libya to negotiate an end to Libyan aid to the MNLF with Muammar Khaddafy.[23] In December 1976 the Tripoli Agreement was reached; Mindanao was to receive its own assembly and Islamic courts, as well as a future referendum on autonomy for all thirteen provinces in the Moro region.

The peace lasted for nine months until the MNLF realized that Marcos had no real intention of granting the Regional Autonomous Government the autonomy that he had promised in the accord. As McKenna put it: "The governing bodies of the nominally autonomous regions were cosmetic creations with no real legislative authority and no independent operating budget. They were headed by martial law collaborators and rebel defectors, many of whom were *datus* and all of whom were absent from the province more often than not."[24] Fighting resumed in March 1977—following the massive influx of Christians into the region—but the insurgency never regained its fervor, as the MNLF became riddled with factionalism. By 1981, the MNLF had fewer than 10,000 fighters, and many were defecting as Marcos began to invest in the Cotabato-Agusan River Basin Development Program. The MNLF also maintained close ties with elected political leaders; thus, while it was fighting the government, the MNLF also had a stake in electoral politics. This tended to dissipate the revolutionary and independence fervor of the organization.[25] Divided over peace and autonomy, Nur Misuari's left-wing populist policies also alienated many within the organization who viewed his secularism with disdain.[26] Misuari was forced into exile in Saudi Arabia and Libya.

The Emergence of the MILF

Following a second round of peace talks held in Libya in 1977, aimed at restoring the 1976 Tripoli Agreement, a serious rift emerged in the leadership of the MNLF. At a meeting of the MNLF central committee in Mecca in 1977, Misuari was confronted with a leadership challenge, and he responded by attempting to purge his rivals from the MNLF central committee. While Misuari favored the creation of an independent Islamic state, Salamat Hashim founded a breakaway group of fifty-seven officers, known as the New Leadership, that supported autonomy. [27] But it was more than that. According to a senior MILF official, the split arose for two reasons: "questions of leadership and questions of Islam and ideology."[28] There were criticisms of Misuari's leftist beliefs, corruption, his dictatorial style and refusal to support collective leadership, and his favoritism toward ethnic Tausigs. As Zaccaria Candao, the former governor of Maguindinao and a close ally of the MILF explained:

> One, Misuari had dictatorial tendencies. Decisions [of the central committee] were not collective. Two, he mismanaged funds of the Front. Field commanders received reports that Libya and other sympathetic benefactors contributed huge amounts to be spent for the purchase of arms and the operations of field commanders. According to them, they received trickles only of these funds. Three, the Moro war is a *jihad,* or a holy war. Misuari

> aligned himself with the communists. Communism and the struggle of the Moros, of course, are not compatible.[29]

Misuari expelled Salamat in December 1977. Salamat then moved his new organization to Cairo, Egypt, and then to Lahore, Pakistan, in 1980 where it engaged in more diplomatic activities. The Moro Islamic Liberation Front was formally established in 1984.

The MILF grew in both military strength and popular support. The leadership of the MILF likes to attribute the latter to the fact that it has more nonsecular aims. According to Salamat, "The MILF adopts the Islamic ideology and way of life. Furthermore, the Islamic Front believes in the Islamic concept of state and government." As an early platform asserted: "All *Mujihideen* under the Moro Islamic Liberation Front adopt Islam as their way of life. Their ultimate objective in their *jihad* is to make supreme the word of Allah and establish Islam in the Bangsamoro homeland."[30]

The MILF grew at first not because of its Islamic fervor but because of the rapidly deteriorating economic condition of the country under martial law. Between 1980 and 1983, the economy shrunk by 15 percent and the country was $27 billion in debt, notwithstanding the estimated $5 billion to $10 billion plundered by Marcos. Rampant inflation, the collapse of commodity prices, and the massive devaluation of the peso and the oil stocks of the 1970s led to dire economic conditions for the average Filipino. The bottom 20 percent of the population possessed 5.5 percent of the national income while the top 2 percent held 53 percent.

The Ouster of Marcos and the Growth of the MILF

The ouster of Ferdinand Marcos in 1986 and the restoration of democracy under the Aquino regime had several important implications for the Moro movements. An attempt to reunify the two Moro groups failed in late 1986. Then, in January 1987, the MNLF formally relinquished its goal of independence for a Muslim homeland in favor of an autonomy agreement with the government, under pressure from Malaysia and the OIC. This gave the MILF the confidence to shift its stance and seek independence. Although no peace agreement or autonomy deal was reached at the time, there was movement on both sides. For instance, as a concession, the Aquino administration established the Autonomous Region of Muslim Mindanao (ARMM) in 1990;[31] arguably it was an autonomous government in name only, as no agreements had been reached with any of the Muslim rebel groups.

In January 1987, Cory Aquino met with Al Haj Murad, the MILF chief of staff, to arrange a cease-fire and to invite them into the peace process along with the MNLF. The MILF rejected the overture and thereafter established a shadow parallel government, utilized Islamic courts to dispense justice, and began to use overt political means to further its independence drive. The MILF elucidated a four-stage socioeconomic program: Islamization, strengthening the MILF organization, military build-up, and self-reliance. By the mid- to late 1980s, the MILF broadened its base of support from the ulamas, imams, and the rural poor, and it began to win the support of Muslim urbanites and professionals who campaigned for MILF goals openly through the political process. The MILF organized mass prayer rallies and supported political candidates and the founding of the Islamic Political Party. Pro-MILF leader Zaccaria Candao won an overwhelming majority of the popular vote in 1988. He evoked Islam in political rallies and advocated Islamic populism.

There is one incident that is indicative of the MILF's popular support. In 1986 Hadji Murad was driving from the Islamic stronghold of Marawi when his jeep broke down and he was arrested by the Philippine police. This was a huge coup for the police. But the police station was immediately surrounded by thousands of armed civilians who gave the police an ultimatum to release Murad. Governor Zaccaria Candao threatened to resign if the police did not immediately release the MILF leader. Murad was released that day.[32]

The Aquino administration was interested in negotiating a settlement in Mindanao, as the government was confronted with a very powerful communist insurgency. The New People's Army grew rapidly and was able to field some 10,000 to 12,000 soldiers during this period. One intelligence officer confided to me that during 1987 to 1989, there was an informal agreement between the New People's Army/Communist Party of the Philippines (CPP), the MILF, and the MNLF "in order to carry out an all-out offensive against the government." The officer said that the formal agreement pledged that the NPA/CPP would cede the entire island of Mindanao, Palawan, and the Sulu Archipelago to the Muslims if the alliance defeated the Philippine government.[33]

The ARMM

A battlefield stalemate led to a real desire on the part of the MNLF and the government to come to terms. In February 1992, while still on the presidential campaign trail, secretary of national defense Fidel Ramos made a secret trip to Libya where he met Khadaffy and tried to convince him to put pressure on his Moro clients to return to the negotiating table. Nur Misuari's MNLF faction did so, and talks began in October 1992. An autonomy agreement was reached in 1996. Former Moro National Liberation Front chief Nur Misuari became the head of the Southern Philippines Council for Peace and Development and the governor of the Autonomous Region of Muslim Mindanao.[34] The ARMM includes the four provinces of Sulo, Tawi-Tawi, Maguindanao, and Lanao del Sur, accounting for 12,000 square kilometers, roughly 4 percent of Philippine territory.

Misuari was under intense international pressure to sign. The OIC established the Group of 6 to monitor the accord, which in addition to Libya included Malaysia and Indonesia, close Association of Southeast Asian Nations allies of the Philippines. Libya, which was under international sanctions for the Lockerbie bombings, had its own reasons for appearing moderate and facilitating the autonomy deal.

To date the ARMM has had a very mixed record. On the one hand, it did bring peace between the MNLF and the government. On the other hand, because war continued with the MILF (as well as the communist New People's Army and Abu Sayyaf), there was still an extremely heavy military presence in the region, retaining the feel of life under martial law, one of the key grievances of the Muslims in the first place. Still, 5,070 MNLF combatants laid down their arms, and 2,200 were integrated into the Philippine armed forces and national police. Many MNLF fighters, however, refused and instead engaged in banditry or assisted the other two Muslim armies, the MILF and the Abu Sayyaf.

There really have not been any long-term economic benefits to the ARMM and the citizens. Again, this is partly because an insurgency is still being waged. But the fact of the matter is that since the autonomy agreement was signed in 1996, there has been little noticeable increase in the standard of living. The region is as impoverished and strife-torn as it was in 1996, and it remains the poorest region in the country. The Philippine government has allocated the ARMM some 27 billion pesos, in addition to millions of dollars in foreign assistance. Yet much of the money has been squandered, gone to large projects or to support Misuari's profligate lifestyle. As one political analyst put it: "He was obsessed with showcase projects like bullet trains and an international airport for Jolo. But he did little to encourage micro-enterprises, improve educational access and raise the quality of health services for a community with the highest degree of illiteracy, malnutrition, unemployment and infant mortality."[35] Public disappointment with his performance was palpable. Even former supporters, such as Malaysian prime minister Mahathir Mohammed, who had helped broker the 1996 accord, complained that not much had been done for the benefit of the people.

Little foreign investment has come into the region, though foreign aid has. The U.S. government provided some $4.5 million to train 15,000 of approximately 40,000 former MNLF fighters to plant corn, breed fish, or grow seaweed since 1998, with plans to spend $3 million more in the coming years.[36] A large portion of the Asian Development Bank's (ADB) $349 million in loans for the Philippines has been earmarked for Mindanao. One official from the ADB told me that the ADB's goal is to alleviate poverty, not necessarily assist the government's plans in Mindanao, though he acknowledged a strong and positive correlation between poverty and rebellion. The ADB earmarked $50 million for basic education in Mindanao, $40 million for forest resources, and pledged to support the "government's efforts to ensure sustained peace and development in the area."[37]

Not all of the blame should be heaped on Misuari. I was surprised to learn during the course of interviews in the ARMM how critical officials there are of the Philippine government, which many accuse of failing to live up to the agreement and truly grant autonomy to the region. Phrases such as "imperial Manila" were all too common, and there were bitter complaints over the revenue-sharing agreement. Despite "autonomy," the ARMM still remits 60 percent of its revenue to the central government and in turn gets only 10 percent back. However, Mindanao is the wealthiest region of the country in terms of natural resources. "We produce more, but enjoy less," said one ARMM official.[38] He complained that Makati, the country's financial center, "rapes Mindanao" to support the corruption in Manila.

The government experienced a real setback in its Muslim policy on November 19, 2001, when a faction of the MNLF, led by Nur Misuari, took up arms again. In nearly two weeks of fighting, some 147 people were killed. In April 2001, the MNLF fifteen-man executive council voted to oust Misuari for mismanagement, electing him honorary chairman of the ARMM. The body ruled collectively until November 26, when a gubernatorial election for the ARMM was held.[39] The executive committee nominated Parouk Hussin (Farouk Hussein), who also won the endorsement of the Gloria Macapagal Arroyo administration. Misuari did not stand for reelection, arguing that the polls were a "violation" of the September 1996 peace treaty, which he renounced.[40] He called for a boycott of the election, though few supported him. Angered at being neutralized, Misuari led 400 to 600 followers to attack a military outpost on Jolo on November 19, in a bid to stop the election, effectively ending the five-year peace treaty. One hundred and thirteen people were killed in a week of fighting. President Arroyo ordered "full force" to be deployed in the quelling of the Misuari rebellion and ordered that Misuari be placed under "preventative suspension."[41] Within days there was a court order for his arrest, and Misuari fled the country. He was arrested by Malaysian authorities and deported to the Philippines to stand trial. The revolt was a real blow to the government, which tried to use the success of the ARMM as an inducement to get the MILF to accept autonomy.

Despite Misuari's rebellion, the bulk of the MNLF seems committed to the peace agreement with Manila. Gubernatorial and legislative elections for the ARMM were held on November 26, 2001, as planned, with about 1.2 million voters taking part. The new ARMM government led by Parouk Hussin remains committed to the autonomy agreement and intends to work with the government to develop poverty-alleviation programs rather than the high-profile development projects favored by Misuari. "We can't stabilize [the ARMM region] if there is no development," he warned.[42] The Arroyo administration has fully backed the MNLF's new development program. The government quickly announced that it would allocate $20 million in aid that the Saudi Arabian government had offered in 2000 but with which Misuari never developed a project plan. The government also announced that half of a $55 million aid package from the United States would be disbursed in the ARMM. Arroyo promised Hussin additional aid for financial and fiscal reforms, education, housing subsidies, expanding the national health-care plan to the ARMM, and cleaning up the banking sector's bad loans. While in Washington, Arroyo secured $260 million in loans and loan guarantees from the World Bank for infrastructure development in Mindanao.[43]

The MILF at Arms

The MILF rejected both agreements between the MNLF and the government and, with an army of 11,000 to 12,000 troops, is still fighting for a Muslim homeland.[44] "The demand of the Moro Islamic Liberation Front is precisely no less than an independent (sovereign) Moro Islamic state," Hashim said. The MILF's long-term plan "is to continue this war until independence is granted."[45] The MILF had a visceral reaction to these agreements that recognized the Philippine Constitution and the government's sovereignty over the region. And the MILF began to engage in overt mass politics, throwing its support behind the Bangsamoro People's Consultative Assembly (BPCA), a political movement whose leaders and goals are closely affiliated with the MILF. The assembly is committed to the establishment of an Islamic state and rejected the MNLF's treaty. Roughly 200,000 people participated in the organization that was clandestinely arranged by the MILF, though the group denied it. It took place in their heartland, some forty kilometers from Camp Abu Bakar.[46] The chairman of the organizers was Abhoud Syed Mansur Lingga. He also denied that the MILF organized the meeting but admitted that it encouraged its troops and followers to attend. Jaafar Ghazali, the MILF vice president for political affairs said, "Our central committee this month will be meeting to consider the assembly's resolution, and it is likely that we will adopt it."[47]

The MILF organized the conference for several reasons: (1) as a rebuke to Misuari, who believed that he alone was the representative of the Muslim community; (2) as a "show of force in the negotiations" before the organization entered into talks with the government;[48] and (3) to increase popular support and awareness in the hopes that it could force the government to accept a referendum on creating an independent Islamic state.

At the same time, the MILF organized the ulamas, who have risen in legitimacy, at the expense of traditional aristocratic elites, the *datus*. The MILF was behind several conferences, ulama summits, the first held in 1998 in Sultan Kudarat. The ulamas were soundly behind the MILF, whose goal was to establish an Islamic state and who had imposed *sharia* law and Islamic courts, including a Taliban-style "morals police" in their base area of Camp Abu Bakar. Although the MILF itself debates what is an Islamic state, arguing that there are currently none to serve as a guide, the organization instead promotes religiosity. The ulamas who have encouraged the people to follow Islam have been able to tap into a growing Islamic consciousness. To this day, the MILF—through front organizations—promotes Islamic values, culture, religious teachings, and Arabic lessons; it is in this way that it has been able to increase its own popular support and legitimacy vis-à-vis the MNLF.

The MILF refuses to accept anything less than autonomy for the Muslim-dominated provinces of Mindanao, which include Maguindanao, Lanao Del Sur, as well as Basilan, Sulu, and the Jolo chains. By 1996, the MILF controlled roughly 10 percent of Mindanao, though it dominated two provinces.[49] "The only thing that we can compromise on," said Hashim, "is the extent of the territory of the Islamic state."[50] The MILF grew substantially in strength in the 1990s and was feeling more confident in talks with the government. A July 1997 cease-fire confirmed government recognition of "liberated zones." In December 1997, the MILF held its fifteenth general assembly and was so assured of its hold on the territory that the assembly was all but public knowledge. Salamat Hashim made his first public appearance in more than a decade and gave a press briefing. The MILF was far more assertive and confident than it ever was.

Getting the MILF to the Table

The Philippine government is acutely aware that the ARMM will have only limited success until it can negotiate peace with the MILF. And three weeks after the Ramos administration signed the autonomy agreement with the MNLF, it established a negotiating committee for the MILF. Under the Ramos administration, there was significant progress. In June 1997, Ramos ordered the army to stop attacking MILF bases, and on July 18, 1997, a cease-fire was signed that lasted for almost three years. Ramos then began a series of infrastructure projects to both woo the MILF leadership to the benefits of peace and undermine popular support for the rebels. In addition to several large development projects in the ARMM, the government began to implement projects in MILF-held territories. These projects include: Narcisso Ramos Highway linking Cotabato to Marawi, including a fifteen-kilometer road to the MILF headquarters at Camp Abubakar; a water system for 10,000 people; an irrigation system for 2,500 people; and the Malmar dam (not completed).

President Ramos asserted that these projects all came at the request of MILF commander Salamat Hashim and that the government allocated 100 million pesos ($2 million) for these projects as a sign of goodwill. The Ramos administration was convinced that acceptance of government funding for the projects signaled the MILF's desire to seek an autonomy agreement with the government, not full independence.[51] On February 6, 1998, the Ramos administration went beyond the cease-fire agreement by signing a confidence-building agreement with the MILF.

However, the peace process broke down in 2000, when the Joseph Estrada administration considered the development projects as "unnecessary" and that they were "simply coddling the MILF."[52] Estrada ordered renewed attacks on the MILF after the government claimed that, in violation of the cease-fire, MILF forces occupied regions that the military had withdrawn from. By July 2000, the government had retaken much of the lost territory.[53] Yet Estrada may have had a point. The Ramos administration was naïve to think that these projects were enough to get the MILF to abandon its independence drive. MILF leaders whom I interviewed admitted that they were simply using the government to fund development projects and that they had no intention of being seduced into a quid pro quo. The Narcisso Ramos Highway is a case in point. The MILF allowed the government to build a road through their heartland, only to seize it in the late 1990s. Only after protracted battles did the government retake control—and even that, as witnessed by this author, is very tenuous indeed.

As Eid Kabalu, the MILF spokesman, explained, "The government views the Moro problem in an economic light. The government wants [development] aid first. Hopefully it will get the MILF to change its position."[54] A senior political adviser to the MILF concurred: "What the government wants is to focus on development. They believe that it [the Moro problem] is an economic issue. . . . But Islam has a spiritual view. The government's way of looking into the problem is fixed—but it is wrong."[55]

The State of the MILF Revolution

With Estrada's ouster in May 2001, the Arroyo administration surprised the MILF by announcing a unilateral cease-fire and has renewed peace talks with the MILF.[56] A cease-fire was signed in Tripoli in July 2001.

The MILF seems quite confident of its current position. First, it has not been defeated on the battlefield. Although it has no air or naval forces, it is able to field between 12,000 and 15,000 fighters. The MILF has eight divisions in Mindanao and other smaller units in Basilan, Sulu, and Tawi-Tawi. That said, the organization knows that it cannot militarily defeat the AFP and is now refocusing its efforts on the political front.

Second, the MILF is taking advantage of the dissatisfaction expressed by many in the MNLF about the ARMM. The MILF believes that the other Muslim groups, including the MNLF, tacitly support its war effort and would be happy if the MILF were to win independence. In the MILF's eyes, the ARMM is a failure by every measure, pointing to popular support for the MILF's movement as proof. The organization also looks to the fact that the MNLF's executive committee and the MILF entered into unity talks in August 2001 in Kuala Lumpur. MILF officials assert that the MNLF is now seeking an alliance because they no longer trust the government's sincerity in implementing the autonomy agreement.

There is another way of looking at the unity talks. When asked if the unity talks meant that the MILF was softening its position, and now, like the MNLF, accepting autonomy rather than formal independence, Eid Kabalu said: "The negotiations from the Unity Alliance does not change the stance of the MILF to regain our lost independence. . . . The issue of unity is an internal issue of the Bangsamoro people. We must be united."[57]

Third, the MILF is actively working through the political system. Like the MNLF, the MILF influences local politics in the Sulu Archipelago through ties with local political leaders. MNLF and MILF activists and their allies have campaigned for and won elections in the region. But they are much more confident of their popular support. They have used mass rallies, such as the Bangsamoro People's Consultative Assembly, to mobilize popular support for the movement.[58] Now the MILF is using civil society forces to push for an independence referendum—an East Timor–style solution.[59] "A peaceful settlement is our goal," Kabalu said. "A referendum will settle the issue once and for all."[60] Abhoud Lingga stated that "A referendum is the only viable, civilized, peaceful, and democratic way of solving the problem."[61]

Fourth, the MILF is pleased by what it sees as an increasing trend toward a more Islamic society. When asked about the state of the revolution, Abhoud Lingga said that Islamic consciousness of the community was growing.[62] He gave many examples, including mosque attendance, especially by the urban middle class and professionals; open discussion of Islamic issues by people, not just ulamas; the airing of Islamic TV and radio programs; and the wearing of head scarves by women. Islamic education is now being undertaken and linked up to the secular education system, and many Islamic teachers are donating their time to teach at *madrasas*. But most of all, Lingga spoke about the growth of political consciousness of the people, specifically the consciousness of the Muslim community of being a separate nation—a Bangsamoro.

With such confidence, the MILF reentered peace talks with the government on October 15, 2001. Government sources see this as a highly positive development, and, despite a few skirmishes, the cease-fire has held up reasonably well.[63] Yet in the MILF's eyes, the cease-fire is purely tactical, giving the MILF a chance to regroup and rearm.

One of the real stumbling blocks has been the issue of economic rehabilitation in MILF zones, namely, the resumption of the development projects launched by the Ramos administration, which the MILF deems as a goodwill gesture.[64] The talks have broken down, however, because the Philippine government wants to "co-develop" the projects with the MILF. The MILF says that the government is trying to amend the Tripoli Agreement and demands that only they get to lead and manage all development projects in their zone.[65] So far, the government has not pledged any funds for development projects—and will not, until the MILF agrees to joint development.

Further talks were hampered by the introduction of U.S. military personnel to advise the Philippine military's war on the Abu Sayyaf.[66] Although there was a trilateral agreement signed in early 2002 between the United States, the Republic of the Philippines, and the MILF that U.S. forces would not enter MILF-held territory in Basilan and Jolo in pursuit of the Abu Sayyaf, some "hawks" in the Philippine and U.S. governments wanted to go after the MILF. Hardliners in the Philippine armed forces, buoyed by the support and training of the United States, disagreed with the Arroyo administration's accommodationist policy. Following the stalemate in the Malaysian-brokered peace talks, sporadic conflicts erupted in a resumption of war in February 2003, when 5,000 Philippine troops backed by air support overran an MILF base camp near the town of Pikit. Peace talks are currently suspended indefinitely. The dilemma is that there are clear ties between the MILF and Al-Qaida, yet the Philippine government knows that the MILF has considerable popular legitimacy and controls significant amounts of territory. The government has tried to keep the United States from fighting or even officially designating the MILF as terrorists because it needs to get the MILF to the negotiating table. The MILF remains suspicious of U.S. intentions but has been pleased that the Arroyo administration has been able to keep the MILF off of both the UN and U.S. lists of terrorist organizations for fear that such a designation would threaten future peace talks. Ironically, the Arroyo administration was able to persuade the United States to designate the communist New People's Army a terrorist organization, though it has no known ties to international terrorism.

Malaysia

Muslim grievances in Malaysia are of a very different nature from the secessionist aims of the Muslim groups in the southern Philippines. Sixty percent of the Malaysian population is Muslim, and the government has always reflected this. The Chinese and Indian communities accepted the political dominance of the ethnic Malays in return for citizenship, and government policies since 1971 have favored the Malay *bumiputras* (literally "sons of the soil"), while Islam is the state religion. Islam in Malaysia has always been synonymous with tolerance and pluralism. Yet more fundamental and uncompromising Islam has steadily gained in power since the 1970s.

The British Colonial Legacy

The British colonial authorities worked with the preexisting Malay aristocracy and ruled in the name of the sultans. To that end, the British tended to work alongside Islam and saw the religion as an important centripetal force that pulled the various colonies in the Malaysian region together. Religion, itself, was never at odds with the colonial power. However, although it was not a major force in the anticolonial struggle, it was an important component: "Islam was never seen as threatening nationalism and the *Ulama* aligned themselves with the nationalists."[67] As Mohammed Abu Bakar put it: "Malay nationality and religion were practically synonymous. They also shared the same short term objective as the nationalist, namely the political liberation of Malaya."[68]

Following World War II, the British returned to Malaya expecting to reassert their colonial authority but were unexpectedly confronted by a unified Malay opposition led by Onn bin Jaafar (1895–1962), the leading anticolonialist and the founder of the United Malays National Organization (UMNO). Jaafar, though a senior British colonial administrator, convened the All Malaya Congress in Kuala Lumpur, comprising 200 delegates representing forty-one Malay organizations, in March 1946. The congress supported the formation of a single Malay political association, and Jaafar founded UMNO in May 1946 and became its president. When the British acquiesced and decided to give Malaya independence, it was a foregone conclusion that power would be handed over to the Malays.

Jaafar, however, split with UMNO's leadership over the issue of race. Jaafar envisioned UMNO being a multiethnic party that included representatives from the country's Indian and Chinese communities, which made up more than a third of the population. In 1950, the UMNO membership rejected Jaafar's proposal opting for the continuation of communal-based parties. In 1951, Jaafar left UMNO and was succeeded by Tunku Abdul Rahman who negotiated independence and the establishment of the Federation of Malaya on August 31, 1957.[69] In 1963, the Federation of Malaysia was established incorporating the British territories of Sarawak, Sabah, and Singapore.

Since its founding in 1963, Malaysia's political system has had to deal with the realities of forging a nation out of peninsular Malaysia, Chinese-dominated Singapore, and Sabah and Sarawak on the island of Borneo. As in Indonesia, the majority of the Muslim population in Malaysia is very moderate and embracing of pluralism. The country is ruled by the National Front, a coalition of three main parties (UMNO, the Malaysian Chinese Association, and the Malaysian Indian Congress) that represent the three major ethnic groups in the country: Malays, Chinese, and Indians.

During the 1959 negotiations that led to the creation of Malaysia, the leaders of the three ethnic communities reached an understanding that, in return for citizenship and full legal and economic rights for the Chinese and Indians, the Malays would dominate the civil service and political leadership. Ostensibly barred from the public sector, the more urbanized ethnic Chinese community went on to dominate Malaysia's private sector, causing a widening socioeconomic gap among the ethnic communities. In 1970, Malays only held 2.4 percent of corporate wealth, while Chinese held 34.3 percent and foreign individuals and corporations (mainly British) 63.3 percent.

The New Economic Policy

Economic disparities were a cause for concern. In 1965 the Bumiputra Economic Congress was held, and for the first time economic aspirations were presented in racial terms. As a result, the Bumiputra Bank was established to channel capital to Malay-oriented projects and Malay-owned corporations. Nevertheless, communal tensions increased, culminating in the May 13, 1969, race riots in which 196 people were killed. The riots broke out when a mainly Chinese opposition party sharply eroded the majority of the Malay-dominated National Front coalition. After the riots, the government took great steps both to strengthen the Malay identity of the state and improve the socioeconomic position of the Malay community. From May 1969 to March 1971, democracy was suspended and the National Operations Council ruled by emergency powers. During this period, the government implemented the New Economic Policy, a radical affirmative action program that sought to improve the standard of living of the *bumiputras*. The New Economic Policy had two goals: to reduce and eradicate poverty regardless of race, and to eliminate the identification of race with economic function so that no ethnic group would be identified with a specific occupation.

To achieve the first goal, the government concentrated on developing the countryside where the majority of Malays lived. Poverty fell from 74 percent of Malays in 1970 to 6 percent for all Malaysians in 1994.[70] A rising tide raised all boats. The Malay share of national wealth increased from 1.5 percent in 1969 to 23 percent in 2003, though well below the envisioned 30 percent. At the same time, literacy increased to more than 80 percent, while infant mortality fell to 11 per 1,000 live births.[71]

To achieve the second goal, the government adopted a radical affirmative action program so that jobs and higher-education opportunities reflected the racial composition of the country. In addition to affirmative action, the replacement of English with Malay as the official language and language of instruction by 1982 greatly favored the Malays at the expense of the minority communities. As part of the affirmative action program, 64 percent of seats at public universities were saved for Malays. The government set goals for the share of corporate equity owned by Malays from 2.5 percent in 1970 to 30 percent by 1990. To achieve this, the government discriminated against ethnic Chinese and citizens of other countries in favor of *bumiputras* by giving Malay businesses special preferences, licenses, contracts, and credits, while putting pressure on Chinese and foreign-owned firms to take on Malay partners.

In June 1991, after the NEP expired, the government unveiled its National Development Policy that contained most of the NEP's policies and goals, though without specific equity targets and timetables, which in effect renewed the NEP for an additional ten years. As a Malay middle class and upper class emerged after three decades of affirmative action, there are now growing calls to end race-based programs and policies, yet they are supported by the majority of the rural-based *bumiputras,* whose standard of living still remains below the national average. The NEP remains the sacred cow of Malaysian politics. In April 2001, the government released a new plan, the National Vision 2020 Policy, which is committed to many of the NEP's original goals. Mahathir Mohammed and his deputy prime minister, Abdullah Badawi, remain critics of the preferential treatment they consider "mollycoddling" and have called on Malays to "throw away their crutches."

In addition to the NEP, there were other concrete steps to Islamicize Malaysia, beginning with the premiership of Mahathir Mohammed. In 1981, he established the Islamic Consultative Body (ICB) to ensure that no development plans or government policies were contrary to Islam. In the same year, Mahathir announced the Inculcation of Islamic Values Policy that articulated a model of corporate Islam.[72] In 1983, two other Islamic institutions, the Bank Islam Malaysia Berhad and the International Islamic University, were established. An Islamic insurance corporation was established in 1985. In 1990 Labuan was developed as an offshore financial center for Islamic banking, and in the mid-1990s Malaysia began issuing Islamic bonds. In the 1980s, society itself became more Islamicized with Islamic attire, and separation of the sexes more encouraged in public. The new capital of Malaysia, Putrajaya, has the largest mosque in all of Southeast Asia.

The National Front's Political Dominance

Because of these policies and years of rapid economic growth, the National Front held a monopoly of political power, with UMNO dominating the Malay population and the National Front (Table 2.1). The Malaysian Chinese Association (MCA) and the Malaysian Indian Congress (MIC) accepted this because the National Front was able to maintain societal harmony and prevent any further bloodletting. The National Front has ruled Malaysia continuously since independence in 1957.

Although Malaysia is a democracy, it is often portrayed as a quasi-authoritarian state. The National Front's political hold on the parliamentary system undermines the perception of democracy. The tyranny of repeated legislative majorities and the unlikelihood of losing them gives rise to antidemocratic

Table 2.1 UMNO's Percentage of Parliamentary Seats

Year	1969	1974	1978	1982	1986	1990	1995	1999
Percentage	45	61	57	61	68	53	65	37

behavior by the government. Moreover, the government manipulates the media and often uses the draconian Internal Security Act (ISA), which allows it to detain individuals for up to two years without trial, for political purposes.

The Emergence of PAS and the Islamization of Malay Politics

Despite UMNO's dominance, which led the anticolonial and independence movement, it was never able to win the support of all Malays because it was seen as "an organization representing largely the administrative elite, scions of the royal houses and others who were willing to accommodate multiracialism."[73] Moreover, in colonial Malaya, there was a vibrant tradition of private Muslim education in *pondoks* (elementary schools) and *madrasas*. The most famous of these schools was the Maahad Il-Ehya Assyarif Gunung Semanggul, which became very politicized in its teachings and was the precursor to the main Islamic party in the country, Parti Islam SeMalaysia (PAS). PAS was founded in 1951 and was dominated by Islamic teachers from *pondoks* or ulamas, the children of wealthy peasants who could build a broad base of support in the countryside.[74] In the first postindependence election, in 1959, PAS won control of two state governments, in Terengganu and Kelantan (where Malays made up more than 90 percent of the population). Although it lost Terengganu in 1961, it held onto Kelantan until 1977. It has large bases of support in those two states as well as in Perlis and Kedah.

Following the 1969 race riots, PAS grew into a nationally known party that claimed to be supported by 40 percent of Malays and an alternative to UMNO as a protector of Malay rights. Although PAS was explicitly a communal party, its support in the early years came from its attacks on the socioeconomic gaps between the Malays and Chinese and the declining position of the Malay peasantry. PAS has long called for the establishment of a theocratic state, and its long-term goal is to turn Malaysia into an Islamic state, though not through radical revolution but through the ballot box. To that end, they champion Malay and Islamic causes: the recognition of Bahasa Malay as the country's only official language and the restriction of non-Malay privileges, such as in dress, dietary provisions, and education.

Alongside the growth of political Islam was the steady growth in Islamic fundamentalism starting in the 1970s. Fundamentalism began to take hold for several reasons. First, although the NEP affirmative action program began in 1971, the socioeconomic gap between Malays and Chinese was enormous and unlikely to be overcome quickly; frustration abounded as disparities did not disappear. Second, the Malay community's "perceptions of inferiority generated high levels of anxiety, and the appeal of radical Islam was partly that it could resolve such anxieties by offering moral certainties and legitimating an unthinking rejection of new ideas."[75] Third, and more to the point, creating an Islamic society was a better guarantee than a simple government program in "establishing a protective barrier against economic competition from non-Muslims."[76]

Fourth, there was a real upsurge in the appeal of Islamic fundamentalism in Malaysian universities. Islamic study groups, known as *dakwahs,* emerged and spread rapidly, In the context of a fairly authoritarian political regime, they were one of the few channels through which students could air their views and protest government policies. The first and most prominent *dakwah* was the Muslim Youth Movement of Malaysia (ABIM), co-founded in 1972 by a young student activist, Anwar Ibrahim. Many others emerged during the 1980s. The largest, the Islamic Republic Group, has close institutional ties to PAS. It was estimated that by the 1980s, 60 to 70 percent of students had ties to a *dakwah.*[77]

To counter the rising political popularity of the Islamists, UMNO and the National Front co-opted PAS in the early 1970s, but the union was short-lived. PAS became more strident, beginning in 1972, about creating an Islamic state, not just advocating closing economic gaps or adopting Malaysian as the state language. UMNO responded by building up its own Muslim credentials, by supporting an Islamic university, and creating Islamic banks.

But UMNO also used the stick. Prime Minister Mahathir first made his name in 1974–1976 when he was education minister. In that role, he crushed political activism on campuses through the passage of the draconian Universities and University Colleges Act, which bans students from joining political parties and limits their rights to free speech and assembly.[78] Anwar Ibrahim was arrested in 1974 under the ISA and held for two years after leading a demonstration against the government's failure to cope with rural poverty. UMNO expelled PAS from the United Front in 1977 and then co-opted individuals such as Anwar Ibrahim. Anwar became a member of UMNO in 1981–1982 as a youth leader and quickly rose through the ranks, culminating in his positions of minister of finance and deputy prime minister. Ironically, when Anwar served as minister of education from 1986 to 1991, he did not lift the political restrictions on students.

The result of the growing Islamization of Malaysia was that UMNO had to adopt a more public Islamic stance to counter assertions that it was secular and not a true defender of Malay rights. Soon after he became prime minister, Mahathir announced several "Islamic policies" including the "inculcation of Islamic values" in government in 1984. Thereafter, religion became a required subject in school, while Islamic values were to become an important component of the country's economic and financial system.[79] Malaysian replaced English as the medium of instruction in universities. The government made overtures to the Islamicists: an Islamic bank, the Islamic university, and the grand mosque in the newly constructed capital, Putrajaya.

Likewise, in Malaysia's foreign policy, there was a discernible tilt toward the Organization of the Islamic Conference states, away from the Commonwealth and the Non-Aligned Movement.[80] Malaysia began to support a host of Muslim movements in the world, from Palestinians to the Arakanese in Myanmar to the Chechnyans and Bosnians.[81]

The Growth of PAS: The Kelantan Experience

During the 1980s and into the early 1990s, PAS was an important opposition party that had its base of support in the northeast, where poor rural Malays had benefited the least from the government's economic development program. In the 1978, 1982, and 1986 national elections, PAS won more than 50 percent of the seats in Kelantan and between 40 and 50 percent in Terengganu, Perlis, and Kedah. Yet in the other nine Malaysian states, it could only poll between 20 and 33 percent.[82] PAS grew in power in the 1990 election when it recaptured Kelantan State.

PAS also benefited from an intraparty leadership transition in 1982 that saw the rise to power of a leadership under Fadzil Noor, who wanted to promote Islamic issues and not just Malay communal issues. More fundamental, and under more radical leadership, PAS tried to implement *hukum hudad,* the Islamic criminal code. Though forbidden by the constitution and blocked by the federal government, PAS hoped to draw a clear distinction between itself and the secular UMNO.[83] The government played into PAS's hands when it had to intervene in PAS-controlled states to protect the rights of non-Muslims. As Fadzil Noor stated, "Malaysia will become an Islamic state when it places *Sharia* law 'above anything else.'" Sharia is the cornerstone of the PAS agenda. As Hadi Awang, the current PAS leader said, "An Islamic state must be guided by the Koran and the Hadith. If we do not have *hudud*, what kind of Islamic state are we?"[84]

The first attempts to implement *sharia* at a local level came in 1990, with PAS's electoral victory in Kelantan State. The PAS provincial leader, Nik Aziz Nik Mat, tried to fulfill his campaign promise of implementing "Islam as a way of life." He immediately banned gambling, closed nightclubs, and restricted the sale of alcohol. In 1991 the Kelantan State Assembly passed a bill prescribing Islamic law, but the federal government blocked its implementation in 1993.[85] PAS benefited from other factors as well, most important, public disgust with official corruption. Nik Aziz always had a clean image in contrast to the corruption and cronyism associated with UMNO politicians. "The perception of people toward the PAS government is that we're very clean," he said. "We succeeded in reducing corruption in government and in the private sector. We've implemented a policy of transparency."[86]

Yet the economy of the overwhelmingly agrarian Kelantan always lagged behind the national average, consistently Malaysia's poorest state. In 1998, per capita income was only 4,067 ringgit, one-fourth of the national average. Foreign investment also lagged. From 1994 to 1999, it was only 60 million ringgit, less than one-tenth of the level of the next lowest state, Perlis. By 2000, its per capita income was 4,293 ringgit ($1,130), or one-third of the national average.[87] What explains the closing of the gap is that the overwhelmingly agrarian economy was not as affected by the Asian economic crisis; thus, it was the decline of other states' per capita income and not a net increase in Kelantan's. Kelantan in some ways is a poor advertisement for the party's credentials to govern at the national level. But Nik Aziz is not concerned: "When I first campaigned in 1990 I never promised that Kelantan would be an advanced economic state free of poverty. The importance was to teach the masses basic Islamic principles. I have struggled to create a system free of usury and Western capitalist practices."[88] However, relative to Malaysia's growth in the 1990s, Kelantan's moribund rates were disconcerting. Clearly the federal government neglected Kelantan, withholding funds to punish the electorate who voted PAS into power. But Kelantan is also to blame, as its laws make it difficult for noncitizens to purchase land: Ninety-four percent of the state's 1.4 million people are Malay, so Chinese have no incentive to come and invest.[89] But PAS has not mismanaged the economy, and basic public services are administered as effectively as elsewhere in the country.

The Arrest of Anwar Ibrahim

PAS gained considerable strength in Malaysia after 1998, when Prime Minister Mahathir sacked his popular deputy prime minister and heir apparent, Anwar Ibrahim, who was arrested and convicted on two different charges, corruption and sodomy. Anwar is currently serving a fifteen-year sentence (not concurrent prison terms, which is a legal norm in Malaysia). The government's heavy-handed tactics against Anwar—his sacking, arrest, and beating while incarcerated—caused a considerable popular backlash, especially from Muslim Malays, formerly the backbone of the ruling coalition, who were already suffering under the Asian economic crisis. According to one Malaysian academic, Farish Noor, "Anwar was crucial because he was the only UMNO leader perceived by the public to have Islamic credentials."[90] Anwar's trial, moreover, showed the degree to which Mahathir had emasculated a once strong and independent judiciary for political purposes. Anwar, who was popular among Malay youth and Muslims, kept many in UMNO's ranks. Following his ouster, large numbers of students and Muslims defected to the ranks of the Alternative Front (Berisan Alternatif), a loose coalition of opposition parties led by PAS. The arrest of Anwar Ibrahim and the political backlash that ensued transformed PAS into the country's largest opposition party.

Since Anwar's arrest, PAS has grown from a small fringe party to become the single largest opposition party that now represents nearly 30 percent of the Malay community. Between 1978 and 1995, UMNO held 53 to 56 percent of the total parliamentary seats.[91] Suddenly this dominance was challenged. At the time of Anwar's sacking, the National Front held 163 of 192 seats, or 85 percent; and the opposition had to win 65 seats to deny the National Front a two-thirds majority. PAS failed to do so, but in the 1999 elections the National Front lost eighteen seats, dropping to an uncomfortable 56.6 percent of Parliament. The majority of those lost seats were in the Malay heartland of the northeast. In the 1999 election, over half of Malay voters in peninsular Malaysia sided with the opposition. Previously UMNO accounted for 70 to 80 percent of that constituency. Thus, UMNO has had to rely on their Indian and Chinese coalition partners even more, further alienating their core Muslim constituency and creating fodder for PAS's propaganda. This implied that UMNO no longer represented the majority of bumiputras. PAS now controls two of the thirteen federal governments, in Kelantan and Terengganu. At the national level, PAS controls 14 percent (27 of 193) of parliamentary seats (and 64 percent of all the opposition's 42 seats).

It is true that many voters in 1999 turned to PAS simply as a protest vote against the government. One academic who surveyed PAS supporters found that the majority "did not vote for PAS primarily because they wished to live in an Islamic state, although some added that the reason that PAS had credibility was because its leaders had the moral authority of Islam."[92] We cannot read too much into PAS's electoral success or infer that there is a radical shift to more Islamic values in society. But interestingly, one person noted that "Islam is slowly taking over Reformasi," the opposition movement, known as the Alternative Front.[93] This fragile coalition with Parti Kedalin Nasional—founded by Anwar Ibrahim's wife (Wan Azizah Wan Ismail) in June 1998—and the ethnic Chinese opposition party, the Democratic Action Party (DAP), was held together on the "strong emotions surrounding the harsh treatment of the former deputy prime minister."[94] The Alternative Front broke down by September 2001, after a surprising twenty-two-month alliance, when PAS refused to drop its long-standing goal of establishing an Islamic state.[95] Many people in Malaysia's large ethnic Chinese minority, which dominates the DAP, fear they would lose freedoms under an Islamic state. PAS feels no need to compromise on this issue, as its strength is increasing and the party is making strong inroads into government territory in other states, though it suffered an electoral defeat in Sarawak in September 2001. It believes that the goal of establishing an Islamic state is what makes it different from the ruling UMNO party and expects support to continue to grow.

The more PAS was able to attract middle-class voters, women, and young professionals, the more it looked like a mainstream political party. It really reached out and tried to broaden its appeal. PAS membership jumped 20 percent to roughly 120,000 members in the ten months following Anwar's ouster and now claims to have 800,000 members.[96] Keidalan, another opposition party, registered between 100,000 and 200,000 members. This is all the more staggering, especially when one considers the real political machine UMNO has in the countryside. UMNO has 2.7 million members and has branches in almost every village—a true grassroots presence. One party official is assigned to ten households in every village.[97]

PAS has also benefited from the growing Islamicism of the country's youth. PAS runs a network of Islamic schools that are an attractive alternative to secular public schools, especially in the countryside. Some 700,000 students attend *madrasas* in Malaysia. Moreover, PAS has supported a growing number of students studying in Islamic universities and *madrasas* abroad. Currently, between 700 and 1,500 Malaysian students are studying in Pakistani *madrasas*, up from 100 a decade ago, though the government has no official number because the students are privately funded. Estimates are that some 300 students return annually.[98] PAS acknowledges that it arranges studies for many of the students who go there on their own, though it insists that it does not finance them or send them there. Farish Noor, who studies the growth of Islamicism in Malaysia, notes that most students return radicalized and that there is a shift among young Malays toward a jihad mentality. Says Noor: "The vocabulary of political debates is already all about *jihad* and martyrdom and heaven and hell. That kind of rhetoric is dangerously inflammatory."[99] Within the universities, PAS is likewise very strong.

PAS claims that sales of its newspaper *Harakah* quadrupled to 300,000 from 75,000, even though the government forced it to publish biweekly, rather than twice a week, and vendors have to put the newspaper in a rack for "PAS party members only."[100]

Terengganu

PAS won a landslide victory in Terengganu State in the 1999 election. It was not a surprise. Terengganu is 95 percent Muslim, and many turned to the party as a protest vote against UMNO and Mahathir. PAS dropped many of its aging candidates for Parliament, replacing them with a new slate of younger candidates. UMNO, by contrast, ran veteran politicians, making them look like the party of the corrupt status quo.

PAS had to prove to the nation's electorate that it could run the entire country on moderate Islamic lines and accommodate the Chinese and Indian communities. Maintaining high rates of economic growth in Terengganu is essential because it has to differentiate itself from Kelantan, the other PAS-controlled state, whose economy is stagnant, in part due to PAS's control over it since 1990. Terengganu leaders have been more pragmatic economically and have tried to create a level playing field for small- and medium-sized firms. Terengganu leaders have also tried to downplay fears of unisex salons and separate checkout lines while encouraging women to stay gainfully employed.

There were also important economic implications of PAS's victory. Terengganu is one of the three states that produces oil and natural gas. In 1998–1999 it earned between 500 million and 600 million ringgit ($130 million to $160 million) annually from oil royalties—5 percent of the country's gross revenue. PAS demanded an increased percentage. In 2000, the federal government punished Terengganu by cutting off the royalties that it used to receive from off-shore oil drilling. The funds now are remitted directly to Kuala Lumpur and then reallocated to schools, hospitals, and other services in the states, bypassing the state government. The oil revenue made up almost 80 percent of Terengganu's budget. "We were robbed," said Mustafa Ali, the economic chief for Terengganu and a senior PAS leader. "They did this just for political mileage, to put us in a difficult position."[101]

The experience of ruling in Kelantan and Terengganu has improved PAS's standing. It is no longer a fringe opposition party; it has proven that it can govern effectively. This has improved PAS's own confidence about its chances of victory in future elections and has led to a sense of defeatism amongst UMNO politicians in the Malay heartland. This has also ameliorated concerns of the electorate, especially the non-Malays. PAS is poised to not only retain control of Kelantan and Terengganu in the 2003 elections, but to make substantial inroads and possibly gain control of the BN-controlled states of Perlis, Perak, and Kedah. Tellingly, in a by-election in July 2002 in Prime Minister Mahathir's home state of Kedah, UMNO only won by 283 votes.

The Politics of Sharia

Islam has always been under state control in Malaysia, and the ulamas have always chafed at having *sharia* law be superseded by secular law. Islamic morality and *fiqh,* or jurisprudence, was not vigorously enforced in Malaysia in the 1960s and 1970s. But with the Islamic revival in the 1970s and 1980s, religious leaders pushed for a greater role for *fiqh* in governing society. *Sharia* courts deal with inheritances, divorces, and issues of morality, but not criminal law. All Muslims are subject to Islamic law, and since all Malays are officially regarded as Muslims, that means two-thirds of Malaysia's 23 million people are subject to *sharia*. Interpretation of *sharia* is made by the ulama of each of the country's thirteen states. These ulamas have some enforcement power. Still, the Islamic criminal code, *hukum hudud,* in Malaysia is very moderate compared to Saudi Arabia or Iran.

Mahathir has always been very critical of *fiqh*, which he considers to be dogmatic and unfair to women. In a 1996 speech to Islamic jurists, Mahathir condemned the imposition of *hukum hudud*. At the 1997 UMNO conference, he condemned the ulamas as being too dogmatic and specifically spoke out against the pressure on women to cover their heads and for men to grow beards. That year he attempted to put *sharia* under federal control so that the ulamas in the states dominated by PAS could not interpret and enforce Islamic law in ways that contravened public policy.[102] For example, in 1991, the Kelantan State Assembly passed a law legalizing *hukum hudud*, which the government later found unconstitutional and barred its implementation in 1993. Likewise, in March 2002, the Terengganu State government announced that it would amend its constitution to incorporate *sharia* and the *hudud,* despite challenges from the federal government and assertions from the police that they would not enforce it.[103]

Shaping public policy is now quite high on the ulamas' agenda. In September 1999, the imams in several mosques abandoned their state-prepared sermons and entered into antigovernment tirades. Most mosques are state supported to a degree, and each sermon is prepared or vetted by each state's religious authorities.[104] Since Anwar's sacking, the ulamas have increased their criticisms of the government. Several preachers were sacked. PAS proposed a bill in Parliament in 1998 that mandated the death penalty for apostasy. Although the bill was easily defeated by the National Front, it scared the general public.[105]

There is also justifiable concern regarding how much control the state has over the ulamas. Although they are state appointed, they are often at odds with state policy over religion and social issues. Moreover, many have close ties with and share the goals of the PAS leadership whom they attended school with. For example, in 2000, the ulamas readdressed the apostasy bill, supporting a mandatory one-year sentence in a "faith rehabilitation center," rather than death. Again the law was not passed, but it did win considerable support from both PAS and UMNO, demonstrating the ulamas' independence from the state and tacit support for PAS's agenda. No matter whether the ulamas were appointed in UMNO- or PAS-controlled states, it is important to understand that they are cut of the same cloth; they studied together at Al-Azhar or other Islamic universities in the Middle East and share the same worldview and goals. Although short of the apostasy law, the Berisan Nasional–led government urged in April 2000 that "state laws be amended to stop Muslims from deviating from Islam."[106]

And this leads to an even greater concern for UMNO: the vast division in its own ranks between the urban-based leadership who are focused on development and eschew fundamentalism and its majority rural-based membership who are far more pious and conservative. To date there has not been a clash between these two competing interests. Yet if there is another major economic downturn, or another important vote such as with the apostasy bill, considerable infighting could result and cause mass defections to PAS. Many UMNO party members remain in the ranks for patronage reasons, not ideological reasons, and it is not uncommon for UMNO politicians from the conservative Malay heartland to identify more with PAS.

PAS, for its part, has faced its own factional divisions between the ulamas and individuals with a more modernist outlook. These divisions were exacerbated by the September 11 attacks. On the one hand, PAS hoped to distance itself institutionally from extremism, that is, it supports Islamicism, not jihadism. PAS legislator Syed Azman admitted, "Yes, there are Malaysian students who are a bit radical or a bit extreme, and the government is trying to connect this small group with us, but PAS members who believe in anything except the rule by the ballot box have to leave the party."[107] Yet the conservative clerics have been much more vociferous in their calls for jihad against the United States. Nik Aziz declared a jihad against the United States and threatened to send his followers to Afghanistan while the late PAS president, Fadzil Noor, requested that the government send and equip Malaysian volunteers to fight in Afghanistan. Noor stated that although PAS would not "direct" its members to go to Afghanistan, "those who feel that they are up to it and have the means to take on the *jihad* path in whatever way they can, can go ahead."[108]

Prime Minister Mahathir, an outspoken critic of the Islamic movement, has explicitly linked PAS to the Malaysian extremists currently in Afghanistan and Pakistan: "They are all from PAS," he said, "but it seems they were acting independently because they feel that the democratic way could never bring power to the party. So the manner which can bring power to PAS is through militancy."[109] Whether Malaysians actively participate in the jihad in support of bin Laden, Al-Qaida, and the Taliban, it is clear that Malaysia will increasingly become, as Deputy Prime Minister Abdullah Ahmad Badawi warns, a new international center for Islamic terrorism.

In sum, Malaysia has become more Islamic since the early 1990s. It has been the case of the tail wagging the dog. Although Prime Minister Mahathir Mohammed asserts that the country is already an Islamic state, the vocal and politically assertive PAS has forced UMNO into a defensive position. UMNO has had two options: to reinforce its secular policies to distance itself from PAS or to become more Islamic itself in an attempt to woo PAS supporters or prevent UMNO members from defecting to PAS. Until September 11, the UMNO leadership was clearly choosing the latter course of action. As Patricia Martinez noted:

> Likewise, while it is widely known that PAS has enacted the *shari'a's hudud* in Kelantan and *ta'azir* [disgracing the criminal, a punishment for lesser crimes] in Terengganu, many are less cognizant of the slew of Islamization policies and Islamic law enactments in BN [Berisan Nasional]-controlled states. As a result of the tenth general election when most interpretations were that Islam, more than race, defined the outcome, UMNO has embarked on a *da'wa* (mission) to Islamicize itself, the government and the nation.[110]

Under UMNO, Malaysia has become more Islamic, and unlike Indonesia, where there are moderate mass-based Muslim organizations such as the Nahdlatul Ulama or the Muhammadiyah that speak out against the radical Islamists, there is no Islamic alternative to PAS in Malaysia.

Indonesia

Unlike other countries where Islam was a fundamental impediment to democracy and secularism, in Indonesia, Islam was a source of civil society and democratization.[111] As the U.S. deputy secretary of defense and former ambassador to Indonesia Paul Wolfowitz said, "Indonesia stands for a country with a Muslim majority that practices religious tolerance and democracy, and which treats women properly and believes that Islam is a religion of peace. Indonesia ought to be a model of what Islam can be."[112] However, in the past few years, economic turmoil and political instability have led to a surge in Islamic political parties and militant organizations, all committed to turning Indonesia, the world's largest Muslim country, into a pure Islamic state.

Islam and Nation Building

Being the world's largest Muslim state, Islam comes in many political and social forms in Indonesia. There is incredible diversity. Yemeni traders brought Islam to Indonesia approximately 700 years ago. Islamic culture did not replace Javanese culture but became thoroughly synthesized with it. Thus, Indonesian Islam developed autonomously from that in the Middle East and had to coexist with preexisting social structures and authority systems. The pilgrimage to Mecca never became a common practice in Indonesia until the nineteenth century.

Dutch colonial policies strove to prevent Islam from becoming a focus of nationalism. The Dutch tried to emasculate religious leaders by working with the *priyayi,* the traditional Javanese aristocracy that ruled during the precolonial era, whom the Dutch co-opted and turned into senior-level colonial administrators. *Penghulu,* mosque officials, were always kept subordinate to the comprador *priyayi* who maintained a stake in continued Dutch colonial rule. In 1912, two Islamic organizations were founded, the Muhammadiyah and the Sarekat Islam (the Islamic League), which was more militant and suppressed by the Dutch. In 1926 the Nahdlatul Ulama (NU), the Revival of Religious Scholars, was founded in reaction to the more modernist Islamic organizations that challenged the traditional authority of the *kiai,* the local Islamic leaders. For the most part—although there were clearly exceptions—these organizations concentrated in welfare, social work, education, business, and health issues and avoided explicit participation in politics.

The Japanese, who occupied Indonesia from 1941 to 1945, began to use Islam to build up anti-Western sentiments and established the Office of Religious Affairs, which was given authority over Islamic issues at the local level. In 1943, the Japanese required all Muslim organizations to be folded into a single organization, the Masjumi, which was committed to making Islam the official state religion. The Masjumi became the leading Indonesian political party in the war of independence against the Dutch, building a base of support on its Islamic credentials. The idea of Islamic statehood spread rapidly throughout the archipelago in the 1940s and 1950s, and many were upset at General Sukarno's ideology of Pancasila, which falls short of either making Islam the state religion or turning Indonesia into an Islamic state. Sukarno wanted to establish a secular state and assuage the ethnic minorities who dominated the outer islands, and he dropped the demands enshrined in the draft constitution, known as the Jakarta Charter, that called for the new state to be governed by *sharia*. Thus, Pancasila speaks only of one god, rather than Islam by name.

Muslims were very important in fighting the Dutch, and in 1947 the Darul Islam (DI), a movement now associated with terrorist Osama bin Laden, founded the Indonesian Islamic Army. The following year, the Darul Islam attempted to establish a secessionist Islamic state in West Java, arguing that Sukarno's guerrillas were as much an enemy as the Dutch: "By rejecting Islam as the sole foundation of the state, [the government] had made itself as evil an enemy as the Dutch."[113] This period became known as the "triangular war" between the Darul Islam secessionists, led by Sekar Madri Kartosuniryo,[114] Sukarno's nationalist forces, and the Dutch. On August 7, 1949, Kartosuniryo declared the founding of Negara Islam Indonesia, an Islamic state in West Java. Unlike other Muslim groups, Darul Islam never compromised with the secular government regarding Pancasila and the constitution. When Kartosuniryo refused to submit his rebel army to the command of Sukarno's republican army, his forces were attacked on Sukarno's orders. On December 20, 1948, Kartosuniryo called for a jihad against the Dutch, but the republicans were his primary target. Support spread to central Java, Aceh, and south Sulawesi. In 1953, Acehnese revolted and declared their districts to be loosely aligned with the Darul Islam. The Darul Islam rebellion lasted until 1962, when its leader was captured and executed and the movement was driven underground. The Darul Islam organization exists to this day, and in many ways it operates much the way the Muslim Brotherhood operated in Anwar Sadat's Egypt. Although it is still an illegal organization, it is more or less tolerated, and members run for political office on the tickets of other parties. There are some fourteen factions of the DI movement, each one claiming to be the true heirs of Kartosuniryo.

Sukarno's secular government, with Pancasila as the official ideology, denied Muslim radicals the place in government that they demanded as well as *sharia* as the foundation of the legal order. Sukarno believed that with Islam as the basis, Indonesia could never be a "unitary" state. To that end, in 1952 the NU quit the Masjumi and established its own political party. But the

NU was very progressive, and it supported the creation of a secular, non-Islamic state that promoted Pancasila.[115] From 1952 to 1973, the NU acted as an independent political party.

Islamic groups suffered several setbacks, including the 1955 elections when the majority voted for secular parties or parties not principally defined as Islamic. The secular NU, for example, won 18 percent of the vote, far more than any Islamic political party. Yet, Sukarno's populist economic policies and dalliance with the Communist Party (PKI) alarmed the conservative Muslims in the countryside who were alarmed at the PKI's calls for land reform, violent social revolution, and a secular state. The religious leaders, the *kiai,* felt extremely threatened by PKI calls for the radical redistribution of land, and in the end they threw their lot in with the anticommunist generals.

Islam in the New Order

In 1965, the Muslim parties and social organizations threw their support behind the military coup led by Major General Suharto. And the *kiai* led the witch hunt against the communists, which saw the liquidation of almost half a million PKI members. Once he consolidated power, Suharto put Muslims under wraps and denied them a seat at the political table. Like Sukarno, Suharto rejected the Jakarta Charter and continued to pursue a secular course. Both the pursuit and avowal of an Islamic state were illegal acts under the New Order regime. Suharto's regime tried to steer a middle course between the far left, the PKI, and the far right, the Islamicists.

Although two large Muslim social organizations were allowed to remain functional, their activities were circumscribed and political activities banned. In 1973 the government forced all political parties, except for the ruling party, Golkar, to merge into two amalgam parties. The secular parties merged into the Democratic Party of Indonesia (PDI). The four Islamic parties merged into the Partai Persatuan Pembangunan—the United Development Party, or PPP. The NU, which was very moderate and tended to support the status quo under the New Order, was the largest component of the PPP. Under the corporatist political system, the Muslim elite were given a seat at the table, and the compliance of their constituencies was more or less assured. To ensure loyalty and compliance, all funding for the PDI and PPP came from the state in annual allocations from the state secretariat. Unable to raise their own funds to engage in political activities, the PDI and PPP were completely dependent on the state.[116] Any challenge to Suharto resulted in their economic ruin. The charade of Suharto's democracy continued.

There were several instances where the Muslim parties tried to flex their muscles and push for the establishment of *sharia*. The first and most important instance was in 1973 with the passage of the nonsecular marriage law, the first successful attempt to codify *sharia*. Although the laws were defeated, there were many instances when Suharto was forced to make concessions to the Muslims. For example, in 1966, to pay back the Islamic community for their support, Suharto passed a law mandating religious education in schools, with state-certified teachers and texts, which was vigorously enforced.[117]

Yet, as Adam Schwarz notes, thereafter Suharto set out to emasculate Islam politically.[118] During the New Order era (1965–1998), he ruthlessly manipulated the Muslim community, controlling them and ensuring that they were serving his political purposes. Suharto cracked down on all their political activities, and the Muslim community remained relatively quiescent for several decades. The official state ideology, Pancasila, did not make Islam the state religion but guaranteed religious freedom in general. All religious organizations had to support Pancasila, namely, secular rule, in their charters, or they would be banned; Islam was not an exception.

Although Suharto was successful in politically defanging Islam, as a social force it grew tremendously. As Schwarz notes, in the political straitjacket of the New Order regime, "Islam is seen as a safe alternative to the heavily circumscribed political structure."[119] Islamic schools, mosques, and Muslim publications were the only fora for public policy debate—all the more so because the state was increasingly unwilling to crack down on them. Thus, Muslim social organizations were always more capable than the two legal opposition parties, the PDI and PPP, in pushing for policy changes.

A telling example of this was that in 1984, the NU abandoned all political activities, quitting the PPP, to refocus itself on its mandate of religious, cultural, and social activities. Under the leadership of Abdurrahman Wahid, the NU adopted "Kembali Ke Khittah 1926"—the spirit of 1926—urging the NU to reject overt politics, arguing that it was better able to advocate social change outside of politics. Wahid argued that as the New Order did not allow political discourse, membership in the PPP and participating in the charade of politics was actually destructive and distracted the NU from accomplishing its goals.[120] Organizations like the NU became very powerful and were able to chip away at the authoritarian New Order.

By the mid-1980s, Suharto was again concerned about the growing power of the Muslim community, and he set out to co-opt them. At that same time, the economy was slowing, mired in the Suharto clan's corruption, and the New Order began to reach out to Islamic movements to help legitimize the regime. This sounds contradictory, and indeed it was, but it was Suharto's modus operandi. He appealed to hard-line Islamicists for they, too, were against democratic reforms that were being demanded by a growing portion of the population. Between 1988 and 1993, Suharto made a number of concessions to the Muslim community:

- The founding of an Islamic bank.
- Enhancing the authority of Islamic courts.
- Lifting the ban on the veil worn by women in schools.

- The founding of an Islamic newspaper, *Republika,* in 1992.
- Increased Islamic TV programming, including educational programs to teach Arabic.
- More funding for Islamic schools and Muslim schools.
- The promotion of more Islamic generals.[121]

Suharto also created a new state-controlled Muslim organization in 1990, the Association of Muslim Intellectuals (ICMI), to co-opt Muslim intellectuals. Led by Suharto loyalists, especially B. J. Habibie, who would later become his vice president and succeed him in 1998, the organization set out to discredit the NU and Wahid, whom Suharto was unable to oust from the organization's leadership in December 1994.[122]

An Islamic, or "green," faction in the military also wanted to manipulate religious tensions to weaken democratic opposition to the New Order regime. Moderate Muslims were targeted and discredited. A leader of this green faction was Suharto's son-in-law, Prabowo, who was linked to suspicious anti-Christian and anti-Chinese riots that got blamed on NU activists.[123] Prabowo became closely aligned with a conservative Islamic leader, Ahmad Soemargono, the head of the Indonesian Committee for Solidarity with the Islamic World (KISDI) and a real anti-Western firebrand.[124] Soemargono was the first outspoken Islamic leader at the tail end of the New Order regime and has, in many ways, dominated the debate in the post-Suharto era. A military think tank, the Center for Policy and Development Studies, became the green faction's headquarters.

Most ICMI members were disgusted with these acts, as well as the Suharto family's (and their cronies') rampant corruption, and they began to defect. *Republika* became an outspoken critic of the New Order regime, and many ICMI members joined the pro-democracy forces—a loose coalition of Wahid's NU, Amien Rais's Muhammidya, and Megawati Sukarnoputri's PDI.[125] In the end, Islamic leaders, including those in ICMI, turned on Suharto because they believed, correctly, that he was simply using them and Islam for his own political ends. They have made their presence felt ever since.

Since the collapse of the New Order regime in May 1998, there has been an enormous proliferation of Islamic political parties and a surge in radical groups, but there is no political consensus or single leader. As in Malaysia, a number of such groups have acknowledged or are suspected of having ties to Osama bin Laden and Al-Qaida. According to one Islamic academic, 30,000 Indonesians studied in Middle Eastern and especially Pakistani *madrasas.*

Aceh

Radical Islam's spread in Indonesia cannot be completely separated from the secessionist movement in Aceh that was waged from 1976 to 1979 and then again since 1989. Acehnese have a history of violent secessionism that dates back to the colonial era when it was the last region conquered by the Dutch, and with considerable loss of life. The Darul Islam rebellion in the late 1950s, won Aceh "special region" status in 1959, which gave it greater freedom for applying Islamic law at the local level.[126]

The government responded to the 1976 rebellion by the Free Aceh Movement (Gerakan Aceh Mederka, or GAM) with brutality and systematic human rights atrocities. By 1979, the government believed that the rebels had been crushed. Aceh was gradually brought into the Indonesian mainstream, and the ruling party of the New Order regime, Golkar, made strong inroads. By 1987, Golkar won more than 51 percent of the vote, its first majority in the province. But systematic human rights abuses by the military and the diversion of Aceh's vast natural resource wealth (mainly from Mobil gas fields) to Jakarta led to a resumption of the rebellion. GAM has renewed its insurgency with the avowed goal of creating an independent Islamic state governed by *sharia*. Its leader, Hasan di Tiro, won considerable support from Libya, which armed the movement and provided training for some 600 Acehnese.[127]

The Acehnese do have legitimate grievances, especially regarding revenue sharing. For example, in the 1990s only 7 percent of Aceh's revenues stayed in the province,[128] and all revenue from Indonesia's oil and gas production went directly to the central government. Aceh's gas exports in 1998 were worth $1.3 billion, though it got almost none of that revenue.

The growth of militant Islam in Aceh also is a result of the military's handling of the insurgency. In 1991, the military put Aceh under "operational military status," and for more than a decade the TNI, the Indonesian armed forces, fought a brutal counterinsurgency campaign and committed egregious violations of human rights in the process. Almost 3,000 deaths are believed to have been caused by security forces, and roughly 2,000 people are missing. The military's approach drove more people into GAM's arms, as some 90,000 people lived in sixty-one refugee camps, a fertile ground for recruitment. GAM for its part was quite brutal as well. GAM pressured village leaders and clerics to lead mass exoduses to refugee camps in order to help win international sympathy.[129] Brutality in Aceh is also a result of the fact that the central government gives the TNI only 25 percent of its operating costs, forcing the military to make up the rest. Local riot police are paid sixty cents per day, less than the cost of a pack of cigarettes. Thus, they extort local businessmen, kidnap, kill, and engage in marijuana trafficking.

Under the Wahid administration (1999–2001), there was some progress in reaching a political settlement. Many of the 20,000 troops and 11,000 police were withdrawn. On April 23, 1999, the government passed the Law on Intergovernmental Fiscal Relations that allowed provinces to keep more of their wealth earned from natural resource extraction. The law also devolved administrative power to the nation's 306 *kabupaten,* or districts.[130] The central government offered the provinces 15 percent of government's share of net oil revenue, 30 percent of gas revenue, and 80 percent of income derived from forestry, mining, and fisheries. Before the law was implemented, the central government collected 85 percent of gross oil revenue and 70 percent of gross gas revenue. In 1997–1998, oil and gas production amounted to 35.4 trillion rupiah—$4.1 billion, or 32.7 percent of government revenue. Eighty-nine percent of national wealth flowed into Jakarta.[131] Already the Acehnese provincial government had the right to implement *sharia*. Wahid also gave them autonomy over education, political, and economic management.

Although the TNI withdrew on August 7, 1999, and the armed forces chief, General Wiranto, apologized for "excesses," the August 30, 1999, independence referendum in East Timor emboldened the Acehnese to continue their struggle. Peace talks broke down in 2000, though resumed half-heartedly under President Megawati Sukarnoputri in 2001. Like the military, Megawati is a fervent nationalist who is determined to prevent any additional secessionism. As the International Crisis Group (ICG) wrote in a 2000 report, neither Megawati nor the military is "prepared to countenance the possibility of either Aceh or Irian Jaya winning independence from Indonesia and both continue to regret the 'loss' of East Timor."[132] And while she has expressed regret and apologized for human rights abuses, she offered only limited autonomy. As fighting resumed in 2001, in October, Megawati extended a government order to allow the military to continue its operations in the province, where some 1,200 people had been killed in 2001 alone. By July 2002, the TNI requested an additional 8,000 troops, in addition to the 21,000 soldiers and 15,000 police already in the province to counter GAM's 1,800 lightly armed guerrillas. The military has also lobbied the government to impose an "emergency." The government demanded that GAM drop its demand for independence and accept the Special Autonomy Act, which gave Aceh a greater share of revenues from natural resource extraction and greater political autonomy as the basis for negotiations. A peace accord between GAM and the Indonesian government was signed on December 9, 2002, giving the Acehnese greater autonomy. Elections were scheduled for 2004, but the peace process broke down again in April 2003, when it was apparent that GAM leaders only saw autonomy as the first stage in their bid for independence. By May, the TNI had launched a brutal offensive against GAM involving more than 50,000 troops.

Many devout Muslims in the rest of the country have decried the violence targeted at their fellow Muslims. Since peace talks began in Geneva in the late 1990s, the military has reintervened, angering the growing number of radical Islamists in the rest of the country who share GAM's vision of creating an Islamic state. Under the New Order regime, there was no wide criticism of Aceh, and since Suharto's fall in 1998, Islamic politicians have been speaking out. Many Islamicists in the country decry secessionist movements, and many do not support Aceh's bid for independence. But they do share GAM's hatred of the secular and overly centralized regime in Jakarta, and they are certainly able to empathize with Islamic groups who have suffered under the regime's systematic repression.

Illiberal Democracy

The single greatest explanation of the surge in Islamic politics has been Indonesia's democratic transition and the Parliament's emergence as the dominant political institution. Under the New Order regime, the Parliament (DPR) had "very little input in either the formulation or implementation of state policy. Nor did the DPR exercise vigorous oversight of the executive branch."[133]

With the collapse of the New Order in May 1998, political constraints were lifted for the first time in decades, and Islamic organizations were quick to capitalize on the liberal political conditions and newfound freedoms of the press and organizations. Indeed, it was Islamic organizations that provided the bulk of the demonstrations that brought Suharto down. As Robert Heffner argues, Islam, rather than being a conservative antidemocratic force, was the single most important force for political change and democracy.

> Since the late-1980s, the largest audience for democratic and pluralist ideas in Indonesia has been, not secular nationalist, but reform minded Muslim democrats. Nowhere in the Muslim world have Muslim intellectuals engaged the ideas of democracy, civil society, pluralism, and the rule of law with a vigor and confidence equal to that of Indonesian Muslims.[134]

At the same time, the military has withdrawn from politics, rejecting its policy of *dwifungsi,* or dual function. The TNI's withdrawal from its once dominant role in politics has created more "political space." The military is still supportive of secular rule, but "by comparison with the military of the early-1980s, they are also willing to accept a greater Islamic presence in society."[135]

The Islamic resurgence was also brought on by economic factors. The Indonesian economy was near collapse in the midst of the Asian economic crisis, which only brought to light the enormous socioeconomic disparities between the *pribumis,* or the native Muslims, and ethnic Chinese, not to mention Suharto's secular cronies. Corruption was so endemic that Islamic leaders were able to present themselves as the only clean politicians in the country, and the number of Islamic-based parties proliferated. In 1999, the Muslim leader Abdurrahman Wahid, better known as Gus Dur, was elected president, but only after a coalition of Islamic parties known as the Central Axis threw their support behind him to bar the secular leader and woman, Megawati Sukarnoputri, whose new PDI-P party won the most number of seats.[136]

Wahid had considerable popular support at the start of his administration. The head of the country's largest Muslim organization, the 35-million-strong

NU, he was a longtime critic of Suharto and the New Order regime. He also preached a very moderate brand of Islam that appealed to the majority of the population and embraced political, ethnic, and religious pluralism. Wahid built his credibility on tolerance and pluralism. Yet he squandered his support through incompetence, poor administration, and the mishandling of the economy. And he lost the support of the military by forcing them out of politics and ceding East Timor.

The Emergence of the Laskar Jihad

In the midst of this political crisis emerged a new crisis: sectarian violence in the Malukus, or Spice Islands, which have a large Christian community. The ethnic balance was already upset by Suharto's transmigration policies that led to large numbers of Javanese and Madurese being forced to move to the outer islands in the 1970s to 1980s. A modest group of Christian militants fearful of becoming outnumbered by the Muslim community sought to become an independent state. In 1999, a small fight exploded into large-scale communal warfare. Christian paramilitaries, some of whom were remnants of the secessionist group from the 1950s Republic of the South Malukus, killed more than 500 Muslims in one massacre in December 1999, sparking Muslim retaliation. The fighting, however violent, was fairly contained, until the introduction of external forces, the largest of which was the Laskar Jihad.

Jafar Umar Thalib established the Laskar Jihad in January 2000.[137] Born in Malang, East Java, in 1962, the grandson of a Yemeni trader and son of a *pesentren* imam, Thalib left Java in 1986 at the age of twenty-four to study Islam at the Al-Maududi Institute in Lahore, Pakistan. He was drawn to the jihad and entered a mujahidin training camp where he was influenced by the "Caller" Ahlus Sunah Wal Jama'ah ulama of Yemen, who fought in Afghanistan with the mujahidin. Ahlus was a preacher of *khwarji,* a school of teaching that seeks to establish an Islamic state by means of revolution. Thalib dropped out and spent the next two years fighting with the mujahidin.

Thalib served with the Mujahidin Afghanistan between 1987 and 1989, fighting with the As Sayaf faction near the Khyber Pass, and in 1987 he met bin Laden in Peshawar. According to the lore, he shot down five Soviet helicopters. In 1989, he returned to Java. Like so many of the other Southeast Asian returnees from Afghanistan, he became a preacher and established a *pesentren,* a Muslim boarding school, north of Yogyakarta. Thalib was a member of the influential Group of 272, which signified the number of Indonesian mujahidin who returned to the country. He became a critic of the New Order regime and chaffed under secular rule: "We don't like *Pancasila* because it means that Islam is the same as other religions. This is not so. We believe that Islam is the highest religion and the best."[138] Thalib and other hard-line Muslim leaders established the Forum Kommunikasi Ahlus Sunna

Wal Jamaah to propagate the puritan *salafi,* the Wahhabi school of Islam. He advocated *khwarij* and the establishment of an Islamic state. "There is no way for Muslims to get respect from non-Muslims except through *jihad,*" he asserted.[139]

In late 1999, the Forum Kommunikasi sent a fact-finding team to the Malukus to investigate the allegations that Christians were killing Muslims while government forces stood by. The team declared the Christians to be *kafir harbi,* belligerent infidels, and demanded a jihad to be waged to kill them and protect the victimized Muslim community.[140] In January 2000, he organized the first gathering of Laskar Jihad in a Yogyakarta football stadium. Posters and word of mouth announced the event. In March, Thalib established a military-style training camp near Bogor in West Java. Arguing that there was an international campaign to create a "Christian republic" in the heart of Indonesia, by May he sent some 3,000 fighters to the Malukus armed with machetes and crude weapons "so that they could feel safe in their own country."[141] Thalib announced that anyone who died fighting the *kafir harbi* would become a martyr:

> We founded this movement in order to support Muslims in eastern Indonesia. They were slaughtered by the thousands in Molucca. The government did nothing to defend the Muslims. Subsequent governments did not defend them from Christian attacks. In light of this situation, we had no choice but to found the Laskar Jihad organization, to protect our Muslim brothers in eastern Indonesia.[142]

Thalib went on to say that the Abdurrahman Wahid government was anti-Islamic: "It is positioned to oppress Muslim interests and protect those of the infidels."[143] This has to be seen in the context of what was happening in East Timor—the former Portuguese and predominantly Christian enclave that won independence after years of armed struggle and a UN-sponsored referendum in August 1999. Thalib spoke of a Christian conspiracy for Christian-majority regions to secede, thereby weakening Muslim Indonesia. To that end, he found considerable political support from politicians and many military leaders who were angered by East Timor's independence and the threat of further secessionism.

The influx of the Laskar Jihad paramilitary tipped the balance in favor of the Muslims, despite government pledges that they would not be allowed to leave Java.[144] Christians were ethnically cleansed from Ternate, the North Maluku capital. At the height of the conflict there were up to 4,000 Laskar Jihad troops in the Maluku region. In June 2000, they overran a police (Mobile Brigade, or Brimob) station and seized 832 firearms and more than 8,000 rounds of ammunition, appropriating police trucks and other equipment.

There has also been question of external support for the Laskar Jihad, especially from Al-Qaida. According to *Tempo,* bin Laden, who met Thalib in

1987, offered funding for Laskar Jihad, but Thalib turned it down, though the JI's Laskar Mujahidin did not.[145] Thalib explains that he turned it down because he questioned bin Laden's piety, asserting that bin Laden is "very empty about the knowledge of religion."[146] Thalib went to great pains to distance himself from bin Laden and the Al-Qaida network, though he had never previously done so. "Laskar Jihad does not have ties with Al-Qaida or any other organizations that are associated with Osama bin Laden or any form or part of his network. Laskar Jihad distances itself from Osama bin Laden and his followers."[147] The organization, however, is unclear about its funding. I have witnessed fund-raisers shaking people down in the streets of central and east Java. The Laskar Jihad's Web page provides account details for an account at the Bank of Central Asia, Indonesia's largest bank, to which wire transfers can be made from anywhere in the world. One Laskar Jihad fund-raiser stated in an interview that the average donation is about RP70,000 ($6.60), about half of the cost of sending a fighter to the Malukus. Most alarming have been recent reports about an audit of the Indonesian armed forces indicating that of $20 million that was missing, up to several million of which had been funneled directly to Thalib and the Laskar Jihad. Increasingly there is more evidence that Thalib's assertion that the Laskar Jihad is a home-grown, locally funded movement is a sheer lie and that his organization exists because of covert aid from Islamists within the Indonesian military and from the Al-Qaida network.

According to Thalib, jihad "does not just mean war. In the Quran there are 13 types of *jihad*. Sometimes it means peaceful struggle. Sometimes it means doing good works. Sometimes it means a fight against Satan, and sometimes it means against infidels." When asked which type of jihad it was in the Malukus, he answered, "All 13 at once."[148] In March 2001, Thalib declared the establishment of Islamic law in the Malukus. In all, around 9,000 people died in the Maluku strife.

During all of this, the military sat by condoning the violence. Although President Wahid explicitly forbade them from going to the Malukus, they were not so much as stopped once, and they even used state-owned ferries to go there. Thalib flew on commercial flights to Ambon, and there was no attempt to stop or detain him. In April 2000, the military training camp was closed down, and Wahid gave orders in mid-July 2000 to forcibly expel the Laskar Jihad from Ambon. But when they threatened mass reprisals against "Christian posts," the government backed down. Wahid left the Laskar Jihad alone so they would let up on their rhetorical attacks against the already embattled president who was staving off possible impeachment hearings. For short-term political gain, Wahid sacrificed his principles of tolerance and pluralism. Thalib dispatched an additional 1,300 troops.

There is evidence that the military allowed this to happen to discredit the civilian government that had tried to politically emasculate the military. But what it really points to is a breakdown in law and order, a condition that only benefits the extremists who are prone to violence. In June 2002, Laskar Jihad troops were still in the Malukus. Clearly the Laskar Jihad benefited from the domestic political situation and the contest of wills between President Wahid and the military. The military was angry at President Wahid for stripping them of their political role and were certainly looking for ways to discredit his administration. That in itself is alarming. The fact that a growing green faction in the military might also have played a role is another reason for concern.

And it was not just the military that appeared indifferent or complicit: Many mainstream politicians not only failed to stop Thalib's forces but endorsed them.[149] Antisecessionist and nationalist sentiments were very heartfelt by the political leaders, and Thalib was viewed as a hero by both co-religionists and nationalists alike. Thus, Thalib has enjoyed considerable protection and impunity. Although Thalib was briefly detained for ordering the stoning of an adulterer in mid-2001, he was released immediately. Following the March 2002 truce, there were a number of attacks and bombings attributed to the Laskar Jihad, who tried to sabotage the agreement. In April 2002 Thalib was again arrested, this time for his allegation that the Megawati Sukarnoputri regime was cooperating with the Republic of the South Maluku's secessionist group. Even then, the country's Islamist vice president, Hamzah Haz, visited him in jail in an apparent display of solidarity. The Laskar Jihad's second in command, Ayip Syafruddin, continued to live and operate freely, and the Laskar Jihad expanded its operations into Sulawesi, Irian Jaya, and briefly (and unsuccessfully) Aceh. It has more than seventy offices around the country. If anything, because of its jihad in the Malukus, the Laskar Jihad grew in popularity and claimed to have roughly 10,000 members. In January 2003, Thalib was acquitted of all charges that he incited violence in the Malukus.

On October 16, 2002, days after the terrorist bomb attack in Bali left 202 people killed, the Laskar Jihad announced that it was disbanding and that Thalib would focus on his students and writing.[150] This announcement should be met with considerable suspicion as the Laskar Jihad knows when to lay low. Following 9/11, they were one of the most reticent Islamic groups in the country. Now they understand the political liability of being Islamic fundamentalists. The Laskar Jihad made a show of withdrawing some 300 troops from Ambon, though a fraction of the total number there, and their paramilitaries in Sulawesi and Irian Jaya remain in place. Moreover, the parent organization, the Forum Komunikasi wal Sunnah wal Jamaah, still operates with offices in seventy cities around the country, and it runs businesses and several *madrasas*.

Politically it remains an important organization, though Thalib is against democracy, which he considers "incompatible with Islam," and he does not endorse any political party.[151] Thalib argues that any state should be governed by *sharia,* God's law, rather than the law of individuals, and that democracy should be replaced by a council of Islamic scholars. This council would have the power to appoint the president and have control over government policy.

The Laskar Jihad is only one of many radical Islamic groups whose goal is to establish an Islamic state governed by *sharia*. The Darul Islam, one of the older political movements in Indonesia, remains active. Other Islamic groups include the Islamic Youth Movement, the Defenders of Islam, the Indonesian Committee for Solidarity with the Islamic World, the Anti-Zionist Movement, the Indonesian Muslim Students Action Front, and the Muhammadiyah Students Association. The Defenders of Islam, formed in 1998, is now the largest radical Muslim group in the country and was able to organize demonstrations of more than 10,000 people in Jakarta in October 2001.

Democratic Islam and the Jakarta Charter Redux

Islam was already a sensitive issue in Indonesia. The continuously dismal state of the economy has driven many to religion for solace. Antipluralist Muslims are a distinct minority in Indonesia. However, their numbers are growing, and many commentators note that now it is politically incorrect to challenge Islamic militancy. As Paul Wolfowitz complained about the lack of outspokenness by secular politicians, "There clearly aren't enough Indonesians who are saying clearly and publicly that this terrorism is a terrible problem that has to be dealt with."[152]

The sheer number of Islamic parties in Parliament is staggering, though they do not always get along and are often divided owing to their leaders' personal rivalries. By 1998, there were eighty political parties, twenty of whom were Islamic-oriented. Yet they were powerful enough in 1999 to prevent Megawati Sukarnoputri from becoming president, despite the fact that her party won the largest number of seats in the Parliament and instead supported Gus Dur. When he squandered his support through incompetence, poor administration, and the mishandling of the economy, the Parliament felt it had no choice but to act, especially after the military withdrew their support for him. The July 2001 impeachment/replacement of Gus Dur angered some Islamicists in Indonesia. And the once tolerant Gus Dur threatened that if he were ousted there would be a social revolution in the country. In the end, there was little upheaval, and the majority of Indonesians greeted his replacement by his vice president and rival, Megawati Sukarnoputri, with a palpable sense of relief.

Politically, there are three large Islamic political parties with nationwide followings, but they frequently have trouble cooperating, and the rivalries among their leaders is legendary. The three parties are the Crescent and Star Party (led by Yusril Ihza Mahendra, minister of human rights); the Justice Party (led by M. Hidayat Nur Wahid); and the United Development Party (led by Hamzah Haz, vice president). They are in no way a monolithic bloc that could impose their agenda. Together these three parties controlled 15 percent of the votes in the 1999 general election.[153] By comparison, Megawati's party, the PDI-P, held 30.6 percent of the seats in the DPR and 26.6 percent in the upper-house of Parliament (MPR). However, their ability to form working alliances with more moderate Muslim parties, such as Gus Dur's National Awakening Party or Amien Rais's National Mandate Party, gives them even more clout. This was evident in 1999 when the Central Axis, which together controlled just over 20 percent of the seats in the DPR, was able to block Megawati's election as president and elect a compromise candidate of their own.

Indonesia's political system is a hybrid whereby the president and the vice president are elected separately. Although it is not a parliamentary system whereby the president requires a parliamentary majority and shifting coalitions can quickly bring down a presidency through votes of no confidence, the president is elected by the DPR and Megawati does have to be concerned about a growing coalition of forces against her within the Parliament.[154] The vice president has no real reason to work with the president or be supportive of the administration's policies.

Hamzah Haz was very critical of the United States after the September 11 attacks, and his rhetoric was inflammatory. He blamed the attacks on the United States and stated that the attacks might "cleanse U.S. sins." There is considerable public support for his view. Indonesia's top Islamic authority, the Council of Indonesian Ulamas, called for "all Muslims to unite in a *jihad* against the United States and its allies if Afghanistan is attacked" on September 25. "We ask for all the Muslims of the world to unite and gather all their forces to fight in the name of Allah in a *jihad* if an aggression by America and its allies occurs against Afghanistan and the Islamic world."[155] Immediately following the attacks on the United States, there were five straight days of mass demonstrations to protest the U.S. use of force and potential invasion of Afghanistan. The U.S. Embassy was closed September 11–12, and it sent home all nonessential staff and dependents; the U.S. private sector followed suit.

Hamzah Haz has also been at odds with the president over the issue of decentralization. Whereas Megawati supports a strong central government and has resisted ceding fiscal and political power to the provinces, Hamzah Haz and many other Islamic parties have used the decentralization policies, implemented in 1999, to endorse provinces to impose their own *sharia* laws. The vice president also led the movement to enshrine the position of *sharia* in the constitution, arguing that "Muslims must be obliged by the *sharia*."[156] In the fall of 2001, Haz led a coalition of Islamic parties to force a vote over a constitutional amendment to include those ten words (seven in Indonesian) of the Jakarta Charter: "with obligation to follow Islamic *sharia* law for its adherents."

The vote was decidedly against the inclusion of the Jakarta Charter. But that it took place at all is significant for three reasons. First, debate over the

Jakarta Charter was stifled for fifty-five years, as neither Sukarno nor Suharto would countenance its inclusion. Second, although only two parties at first supported its inclusion—Yusril Ihza Mahendra's Crescent and Star Party and the vice president's own United Development Party—when the vote took place, many other parties jumped on the bandwagon to score political mileage. The most egregious example of this was Amien Rais' National Mandate Party. Ironically, in 1998–1999, Amien Rais contended that the Jakarta Charter's inclusion in the constitution was not likely or even desired:

> The Islamic state has been put behind them by 95 percent of Muslim leaders and also the rank and file. I have not seen any significant pockets within the Islamic community in this country who are still aspiring to see the application of syariah Islam in Indonesia. The concept of an Islamic state in Indonesia has not been an issue at all since Soeharto's downfall.[157]

Third, there is considerable popular support for the implementation of *sharia*. In a late 2002 survey published in the respected weekly *Tempo*, the Hidayatullah State Islamic University found that the number of people who supported *sharia* had grown by 10 percent over the previous year and that 71 percent of all respondents supported the limited application of *sharia* for Muslims. The pollsters estimated that the number of supporters for *sharia* now total more than 130 million people. To be sure, there were some caveats: Only 46 percent of respondents felt that legislators should be Islamists, and only 33 percent wanted the harsh Islamic criminal code, *hukum hudud*, implemented; 36 percent of the respondents favored women wearing head scarves, and 51 percent supported the idea that women should only travel outside the home with a male relative. Even allowing for polling errors, the survey concluded that there was a growing Islamist constituency.[158]

A 2003 survey by the Pew Center for People and the Press demonstrated increased religiosity in Indonesia, both socially and politically: 86 percent of respondents agree that currently Islam plays a large role in Indonesian politics, and 82 percent agreed that Islam *should* play a role in politics. One of the most surprising results, showing a growing degree of Islamic conservatism was the figure that only 22 percent of Indonesians felt that women should be permitted to work outside the home; a sentiment that was shared closely by both men (20 percent) and women (24 percent). There is a sense that religion should be a personal issue, rather than a state imposed one: 86 percent of Indonesians believed that the decision to wear head scarves should be made by women themselves; only 14 percent believed that it should be a legal policy. And 99 percent of the respondents believed that it was necessary to believe in God in order to be moral. There is also a growing sense of Islamic identity. The poll found that the number of Muslims who believed that their religion was under siege in Indonesia almost doubled: from 33 percent in

2002 to 59 percent in 2003. Moreover, 80 percent of the respondents feel more solidarity with the Islamic world than they did in the past.[159]

The Islamic parties remain a minority in the country and will likely remain so in the near future, unless the secular leadership fails to resuscitate the economy and create opportunities for the country's 40 million unemployed. Today they make up 15 percent of parliamentary seats, but they are poised to gain more in the 2004 elections. The best estimates are that radical Muslims make up only 5 percent of the population, but 5 percent of the country's 210 million population is a significant number. Importantly, Indonesia's two mass Muslim organizations, the NU and the Muhammadiyah, are outspoken in their defense of the secular state. They remain influential checks on the Islamists, yet often their leaders' political ambitions get in the way, and they either form alliances with the Islamists or adopt their positions on popular issues. This is not to say that these organizations themselves are not changing. For example, the man expected to take over the Muhammadiyah in 2005, M. Din Syamsuddin, has actively defended Muslim radicals and militants such as Jafar Umar Thalib and Abu Bakar Ba'asyir and supports the debate over *sharia*.[160] The fact is that under Suharto, Islam could not be used for political purposes. In the post-Suharto era, Islam is now not just a political force, but it is moving to the political center. The Islamists have effectively linked Islam to nationalism to broaden their appeal. As they grow and gain in popularity, we should expect to see a similar phenomenon as in Malaysia, where the secular parties adopt Islamist policies to either win back the electorate or prevent their own members from defecting.

Thailand

Like the Philippines, Thailand seems to be an incongruent loci of a militant Islam, but the roots are firmly planted. Thailand is a devoutly Buddhist country. Ninety-five percent of the population is Theravada Buddhist, and religion is one of the defining factors of Thai nationalism. Although there is a Muslim population in the southern part of the country, it constitutes 3.2 million people, or less than 5 percent of the population. However, Muslims dominate the three southern provinces, Yala, Pattani, and Narathiwat, accounting for 1.3 million of the 1.7 million people, and giving them more of a Malay character than a Thai one. As in the Philippines, religious distinction coupled with geographical remoteness gave rise to a small-scale secessionist movement. For a variety of reasons, unlike the Philippines, it never developed into a mass-based movement, but it has remained a source of concern for the Thai government.

Thailand's history is punctuated with wars against Muslims. Beginning with the Ayuddahya kingdom in the fifteenth century, Thailand began to exert strong influence over the Malay Peninsula, interrupted only with Thailand's frequent wars with Burma. The founding of the Chakri Dynasty in 1782 led to the forcible imposition of a tributary system over the northern Malay states of Kedah, Pattani, Kelantan, and Terengganu. Every three years, the leaders of these states were forced to travel to Bangkok to make obeisance, but Thai rule was fairly benign as long as the Malay rulers accepted Thai suzerainty.[161] For the most part, they did.

British colonization of Malaysia, on the one hand, saved Malaysia from further domination by the Thai. On the other hand, the British accepted a degree of Thai suzerainty over the region, and the British East Indies Company went so far as to lease Penang from the Thai court.[162] With King Chulalongkorn's government reforms in the 1890s, Thailand developed a strong centralized bureaucracy and central control over the provinces. The Malay *prathesaraj* (local Muslim aristocrats) were put under the direct control of the Ministry of Interior. And unlike the Philippines the central government was strong enough that it did not have to cut autonomy deals with the local Muslim kings.[163] Local elites who controlled revenues and patronage never emerged, as governors and other administrators were sent from Bangkok. So, unlike the Philippines—where local-level government officials tacitly supported the Muslim separatists—in Thailand, separatists were never able to create alliances with local politicians who resisted efforts to centralize political control.

Yet in many ways, the Thai are responsible for the rise of Islamic fundamentalism in northern Malaysia. Whereas the British established a secular legal system parallel to the Islamic courts, the Thai also had no division between the secular and the nonsecular; thus, they allowed the Islamic political and legal systems to dominate in the northern provinces. In 1897 the British and Thai signed a secret agreement that recognized Thai suzerainty over Kelantan and Terengganu, as long as the Thai denied commercial access to the region to third parties, that is, European competitors of Britain. Following a series of commercial deals between British businessmen and the Kelantan government, Thailand became increasingly concerned about losing control. Angered at increasingly independent Malay governors, in February 1902 Thailand had to put down a rebellion. Thereafter, the Malay governor requested "British protection and a British Resident."[164] In October 1902, there was another Anglo-Thai agreement, but this one saw the departure of the Thai garrison from Malaysia. Under duress, in 1909, the Thai turned over all Malay states to the British. The current border between the two states, delineated in the 1909 treaty, however, left three provinces within Thailand with a majority Muslim/Malay population. During World War II, the Thais, who were aligned with the Japanese, retook the northern Malay provinces but were forced to return them at war's end.

Muslim Secessionism

Political power in Thailand in most of the post–World War II era was dominated by anticommunist and development-oriented military officers who were determined to maintain centralized control over the country. The military never countenanced autonomy for anyone, much less the Malay Muslims, and the military had near total political control. Only when Thailand experienced brief democratic interludes, namely, from 1945 to 1947 or 1973 to 1976, were demands for autonomy or independence "voiced with any vigor."[165]

The Thai military not only had political power, it had a lot of experience in countering rebellion and insurgency. Surrounded by countries in the midst of civil wars—Myanmar, Laos, Cambodia, Malaysia—not to mention their own communist insurgency that at one point had 12,000 guerrillas, the Thai military had ample experience in counterinsurgency warfare. It also had ample support from the United States, both in financial and technical terms, to deal with its security issues.

There were two Muslim separatist groups in Thailand, the Pattani United Liberation Organization (PULO), and the smaller Barisan Nasional Pembebasan Pattani (Pattani National Liberation Front, BNPP).[166] PULO was founded in the early 1970s with the goal to establish an independent Muslim state. At their peak there were no more than 3,000 Muslim separatist fighters (mainly in PULO, but also in other groups) and they have waged a sporadic secessionist campaign since the 1970s, but with almost no results to show for it for a number of reasons.

First, there was considerable cooperation between Thailand and Malaysia in dealing with joint security issues along their common border. There were many Malaysian Communist Party (MCP) members who had been driven out of Malaysia by the British in the 1950s who had sought sanctuary in Thailand. The Thais, fearful of the MCP cadres linking up with Thai Communist Party (TCP) members, denied MCP rebels sanctuary in Thailand. In a 1964 agreement, the Thais reluctantly allowed 400 to 500 Malaysian police to cross the border in hot pursuit of communist rebels, a right that the Thais only relinquished in 1976.[167] By 1981, the MCP's strength had declined by one-third to only 2,000 men. In December 1989, a formal peace treaty was signed by the MCP and the Malaysian government.

Malaysia had its own reason to limit its support for the Thai Muslims. Malaysia is a predominantly Muslim country, but it was concerned about Islamic radicals in Thailand linking up with radicals in Malaysia. In short, bilateral cooperation led to the virtual annihilation of both states' security concerns along the border: the MCP, TCP, PULO, and the BNPP. By the late 1980s, there were only some 300 to 500 Muslim guerrillas. In 1993, the Thai government offered a general amnesty and nearly half of the remaining force laid down their arms. Today Muslim militants number between 150 and 200.

Second, there has never been any large-scale repression of Muslims that would create a broader anti-Thai movement in society. The guerrillas were never able to capitalize on wide-scale public discontent. In part, the Thai army was careful. One thing that is telling is that in 1987, Prime Minister Prem Tinsulanonda, himself a former general, shifted the Internal Security Operating Command from the military's Supreme Command to the prime minister's office, signaling a shift from a military solution to a political-economic solution to the insurgency. Muslims were not discriminated against. Indeed, Thailand's former foreign minister in the late 1990s, Surrin Pittsuwan, is a Muslim.

The third reason that the insurgency has been kept under control is that Thailand's rapid economic development tended to help raise the standard of living, including for most of the Muslims in the south.

Fourth, though the insurgency received some financial and military sponsorship from Libya and Syria in the 1970s, state sponsorship was very limited. Some PULO officials were trained by the Palestine Liberation Organization in Syria, and the Libyans also provided training for a small number of officers. Most weapons were purchased from illegal brokers within Thailand.

The final reason that the insurgency was never able to develop a mass following is that since the promulgation of the 1997 constitution, Thai politics have been greatly decentralized and there is now an unprecedented degree of local autonomy.

Muslim Grievances

Thai Muslims do have legitimate grievances, in addition to feeling left out of the Buddhist Thai nation. The economy of the south has always lagged far behind the rest of the country that enjoyed some of the fastest growth rates in the world during the 1980s into the 1990s. According to the government's National Economic and Social Development Board, Muslim communities dominate two of the four poorest provinces. Narathiwat Province, the poorest in the country, has a poverty rate of 45.6 percent, while Yala, another Muslim-dominated province, has a poverty rate is 37.9.[168] The government provision of health care, education, and welfare has clearly been inadequate, and since 1980, the government has sought to remedy this disparity.

The Thai government has not been completely to blame. In one high-profile case, the Muslim community has held up a major development project that the Thai government believes would be a boon to their economy. The project in question is a $500 million trans–Thai-Malay gas pipeline. With an overlapping claim to an offshore natural gas field, the Thai and Malaysian governments agreed to jointly develop the field. The pipeline has been in the planning stages since 1979; it would be part of a regional gas network that was conceived in 1990 and a boon for both Thailand and Malaysia, as Southeast Asian states now use natural gas to generate approximately 40 percent of their electric needs, more than any other fuel.[169] The Malaysians agreed to route the pipeline through southern Thailand in order to help the Thai government cope with its restive Muslim community by improving their economy. Yet the Thai Muslims rallied against the pipeline, arguing that it benefits Thailand, not themselves, while endangering their traditional way of life. There has been both a fear of the negative effects of globalization and a fear that leaks will destroy the local fishing industry. Malaysia has been so frustrated that it considered scrapping the Thai pipeline altogether and searching for alternative routes.

In addition to the economy, the Muslim community has complained that they have few domestic religious educational facilities and that the Thai Ministry of Education gives academic recognition to only a handful of Islamic universities abroad, making it hard for returning graduates to find work. It has also demanded the establishment of Islamic courts and Islamic banks, to little avail.[170]

The Thai government does have some reason to be concerned about Islamic schools. Ismail Lufti, the rector of Yala Islamic College, and a firebrand Wahhabist, has amassed a large following and incited the Muslim community to pressure the government to abandon its support of the United States and has called for boycotts.

But the Thai government has not completely ignored the needs of the Muslim community; if it had, the insurgency would still be going strong. For example, Islam is not at all repressed, and Thai Muslims have considerable religious freedom. There are some 2,000 mosques around the country, including 434 in Narthiwat Province alone. The government has an advisory board for Muslim issues, the National Council for Muslims, that advises the Ministry of Education and Ministry of Interior.[171] The government has financed Islamic educational institutions, pilgrimages to Mecca, and has supported several hundred Islamic primary and secondary schools.

For these reasons, the Muslim insurgency has never proved to be a serious security threat for the Thai government. Nonetheless, the insurgency has not been eliminated. In 1995, PULO had a soul-searching congress whose members acknowledged that their movement suffered serious setbacks between 1988 and 1994 and that it had lost popular support. The congress elected new leadership who launched a series of military attacks to renew attention to their cause.[172] By the end of 1997, PULO claimed to have killed 146 Thai soldiers and wounded at least 80 more. In April 2001, Muslim separatists bombed the Hat Yai train station and a hotel in Yala. Although blamed by Prime Minister Thaksin Shinawatra, PULO denied the attacks. In a late April 2001 visit to Malaysia, Thaksin reportedly gave his counterpart, Mahathir Mohammed, a list of fifteen PULO members who were inside Malaysia. The Thai insurgency under PULO was in its death throes, but several smaller, more radical groups emerged in the 1990s.

Cambodia

Like Thailand, Cambodia is a devoutly Buddhist society, though it too has a small and aggrieved Muslim population. Under the rule of the Khmer Rouge, from 1975–1979, the Cham Muslims were the most persecuted minority, and their population fell by more than 75 percent, from over 300,000 people to 70,000. Although the Cham population has recovered slightly, and now numbers approximately 120,000, they remain poor and neglected by their government. The community's needs are acute. To support this aggrieved community, there has been a steady inflow of Gulf money and outflow of students to study in foreign *madrasas*. Middle East charities funded the construction of more than 120 mosques; there are now 150 up from 20. Annually, 80 students study in Middle Eastern and Pakistani *madrasas* where they are taught in the doctrinaire Wahhabism. In neighboring Malaysia 400 students study on scholarships funded from Gulf charities. Cambodia's own Ulama's Council contends that between 10 and 15 percent of the Cham Muslims now espouse Wahhabism, rather than the indigenous moderate Suffism.

In addition to its small but increasingly radical population, Cambodia is attractive to militant groups for other reasons. It has always been a center of illegal arms trading, as the former Khmer Rouge and other rebel groups, not to mention corrupt elements in the military, sell their weapons. Cambodia is also a leading center of money laundering, especially for illegal drug proceeds from Burma and Laos. Cambodia has no financial oversight capacity and a completely corrupt bureaucracy. Its borders are porous and it has almost no computerized immigration system in place. In short, Cambodia is one of the most attractive "countries of convenience."

The Legacy

Southeast Asian countries were fertile ground for groups such as Al-Qaida since the 1990s. They each had vast socioeconomic disparities, historical animosities, lingering insurgencies, bouts of sectarian conflict, and political disenfranchisement. Thousands of Southeast Asians who had studied in Middle Eastern *madrasas* or had joined the mujahidin returned to the region in the 1990s determined to right historical, political, and socioeconomic wrongs and injustices.

Al-Qaida did not simply arrive in the region and establish a network from scratch, but rather they found groups who had already been established and had legitimate grievances that they had been fighting for a prolonged period. The historical roots of militant Islam are not new in the region, but their links to international terrorist groups are. Al-Qaida was able to graft onto existing movements as well as establish independent cells. More important, it was able to link the organizations to create a complex network throughout the region.

Notes

1. I will refer to this territory as the Moro islands.

2. Thomas M. McKenna, *Muslim Rulers and Rebels: Everyday Politics and Armed Separatism in the Southern Philippines* (Berkeley: University of California Press, 1998).

3. Bernardo M. Villegas, *A Filipino Vision for Recovery* (Manila: University of Asia and the Pacific, 1997), 23.

4. The Sultanate of Maguindanao included current-day Cotabato, Lanao, Davao, Bukidnon, and Zamboanga.

5. In the 1920s, again the British favored the establishment of an independent "Federated Sulu States Union." For more on this early history, see Nicholas Tarling, "The Establishment of the Colonial Regimes," in Nicholas Tarling, ed., *The Cambridge History of Southeast Asia, Vol. 2, Part 1, From c. 1800 to the 1930s* (New York: Cambridge University Press, 1999), 21–24.

6. The Kiram-Bates Treaty was signed on August 2, 1899. A similar agreement was signed with the sultan on Maguindanao.

7. The Department of Mindanao and Sulu, the civil administration, existed between 1914 and 1920. From 1920 to 1937, as the Americans began to transfer authority to Filipinos, it became known as the Bureau of Non-Christian Tribes.

8. McKenna, *Muslim Rulers and Rebels,* 132.

9. James Hamilton-Paterson, *America's Boy: A Century of Colonialism in the Philippines* (New York: Henry Holt, 1998), 342.

10. "A History of the Bangsmoro People," MoroJihad.com.

11. Eva-Lotta E. Hedman and John T. Sidel, *Philippine Politics and Society in the Twentieth Century* (New York: Routledge, 2000), 170; McKenna, *Muslim Rulers and Rebels*, 122–123.

12. McKenna, *Muslim Rulers and Rebels,* 140.

13. Ibid., 143. The Islamic scholars who returned were given a new title, *ustadz.*

14. Ibid., 201.

15. Ibid., 205.

16. *Konfrontasi* ended following the coup that saw the ouster of Achmed Sukarno from power. In August 1966 his successor, General Suharto, signed a peace treaty with Malaysia and accorded Malaysia full diplomatic relations.

17. McKenna, *Muslim Rulers and Rebels,* 143.

18. The Philippines formally continued to claim the territory until Corazon Aquino's administration withdrew the claim. The 1987 constitution does not mention Sabah or assert a territorial claim to it. In November 1987, Aquino submitted a bill to Congress to formally renounce Sabah, though Congress never acted on it.

19. MNLF and MILF guerrillas "drew sustenance from the density of remaining cultural, economic and political linkages across the Sulu zone. Smuggling and the government-sanctioned 'barter trade' between southern Philippine ports and Labuan provided a regular 'predatory income' for rebel commanders through protection rents, piracy and shareholder profits, and the thousands of Muslim Filipinos working (illegally) in Malaysian Sabah or on fishing boats in the tuna-rich waters off North Sulawesi served as a network for arms, training, and recruitment." Hedman and Sidel, *Philippine Politics and Society in the Twentieth Century*, 170.

20. General Fortunato U. Abat, *The Day We Nearly Lost Mindanao: The CEMCON Story*, 3rd ed. (Manila: FCA Publishers, 1999), 165–166.

21. On October 7, 1971, the Libyan leader Colonel Muammar Khaddafy stated that if "the genocide still went on against the Muslims in the Philippines," he would

assume responsibility" for protecting them. That year he established the Islamic Call Society (ICS) to support Islamic revolutions around the world. The ICS became a major force in Libyan foreign policymaking and had offices not just in Africa but also in Thailand, Malaysia, the Philippines, and Indonesia. Khaddafy, through the ICS, became the major patron of the MNLF. In 1982, Khadaffy established Libya's Anti-Imperialism Center to aid revolutionaries and Islamic causes around the world.

22. McKenna, *Muslim Rulers and Rebels,* 166.

23. Imelda Marcos's account of the meeting can be found in Hamilton-Paterson, *America's Boy*, 343.

24. McKenna, *Muslim Rulers and Rebels,* 168.

25. Hedman and Sidel, *Philippine Politics and Society in the Twentieth Century,* 171.

26. "In the end, the MNLF could not overcome the semi-feudal and communal structure of the Muslim community." See Yong Mun Cheong, "The Political Structures of the Independent States," in Nicholas Tarling, ed., *The Cambridge History of Southeast Asia, Vol. 2, Part 2, From World War II to the Present* (New York: Cambridge University Press, 1999), 98.

27. Hashim Salamat was born on July 7, 1942, in Pagalungan, Maguindanao. He left for Mecca in 1958, where he remained for further study. In 1959 he went to Cairo and enrolled in Al-Azhar University, where he graduated in 1967 and received a master's degree in 1969. In Egypt he claimed to be an active leader of the students in 1962 who would form the core of the MNLF military wing, which he claims that he founded. In 1972, he left Egypt for Libya, Saudi Arabia, and Pakistan. In 1975 Hashim led the MNLF delegation to the Tripoli Peace Talks. See "Interview with Salamat Hashim: The Muslim Separatist Rebel Leader Wants the 'East Timor Formula,'" *Asiaweek,* March 31, 2000.

28. Interview with Eid Kabalu, MILF spokesman, Cotabato, January 9, 2002.

29. Marguirita Cojuanco, "The Role of the MILF in the Mindanao Problem," National Defense College of the Philippines, 1988.

30. Cited in McKenna, *Muslim Rulers and Rebels*, 208.

31. The ARMM was established on November 6, 1990, by Republic Act 6734. It was legally possible because of the promulgation of a new constitution in 1987 that allowed for the establishment of autonomous regions.

32. McKenna, *Muslim Rulers and Rebels,* 282.

33. Interview with Philippine National Police official, Manila, January 17, 2001.

34. The SPCDC was a transitory administration under the direct supervision of the Philippine president to promote peace and implement and monitor development projects in Mindanao.

35. Luz Baguioro, "Misuari's Downfall," *Straits Times (ST),* November 27, 2001.

36. Deidre Sheehan, "Swords into Ploughshares," *Far Eastern Economic Review (FEER),* September 20, 2001, 30–31. This program of the United States Agency for Economic Development is known as the Livelihood Enhancement and Peace Project. For more on this project, see Dan Murphy, "Filipinos Swap Guns for Rakes," *Christian Science Monitor (CSM),* March 5, 2002.

37. "ADB Readies $349M in Loans for RP," *Philippine Daily Inquirer (PDI),* January 3, 2001.

38. Interview with ARMM media affairs officer, Cotabato, January 9, 2002.

39. Luz Baguioro, "Moro Front and Abu Sayyaf Link Up to Halt Polls," *ST*, November 20, 2001.

40. One report stated that Misuari's term of office actually expired in March 1999, when new elections were scheduled, but he complained and threatened to dis-

rupt the peace process. The administration of Joseph Estrada gave in to his demands to postpone the elections. Luz Baguioro, "Misuari's Downfall."

41. AFP, "Macapagal Orders Full Force vs. Attacking Misuari Faction," *PDI*, November 19, 2001. The presidential adviser on the peace process is Eduardo Ermita.

42. Raissa Robles, "New Mindanao Chief Sworn In," *South China Morning Post (SCMP)*, December 5, 2001.

43. Blanche S. Rivera and Edwin O. Fernandez, "ARMM Poll Winners Set To Be Proclaimed," *PDI*, December 2, 2001; Robles, "New Mindanao Chief Sworn In"; "Arroyo to Inject $50 Million into Mindanao," *SCMP*, December 11, 2001; "Arroyo Confronts Muslim Revolt After Securing US Aid," *SCMP*, November 24, 2001.

44. Deidre Sheehan, "Swords into Ploughshares," 30–31.

45. "Perhaps the Moro struggle for freedom and self-determination is the longest and bloodiest in the entire history of mankind," interview with Salamat Hashim, *Nida'ul Islam* magazine (April–May 1998).

46. Rigoberto Tiglao, "Moro Reprise," *FEER*, December 26, 1996, to January 2, 1997, 22.

47. Ibid.

48. Ibid.

49. Rigoberto Tiglao, "Southern Discomfort," *FEER*, February 19, 1998, 26–27.

50. Ibid., 27.

51. Interview with President Fidel V. Ramos, Manila, January 15, 2001.

52. Ibid.

53. Department of National Defense, *The Philippine Campaign Against Terrorism*, (2001), 5.

54. Interview with Eid Kabalu, MILF spokesman, Cotabato, January 9, 2002.

55. Interview with Abhoud Sayed M. Lingga, chairman of the Bangsamoro People's Consultative Assembly, Cotabato, January 9, 2002.

56. Jesus Dureza is the presidential assistant for Mindanao and the lead negotiator for the government. In February 2001, President Arroyo ordered the Department of Justice to lift all charges against Salamat Hashim and five other MILF leaders for the December 30, 2000, terrorist bombings in Manila.

57. Interview with Eid Kabalu, MILF spokesman, Cotabato, January 9, 2002.

58. Interview with Abhoud Lingga, chairman of the Bangsamoro People's Consultative Assembly, Cotabato, January 9, 2002. Lingga asserts that at the first BPCA, held in 1996, there were 1 million attendees and 2 million attendees at the second BPCA in 2001.

59. "Interview with Salamat Hashim: The Muslim Separatist Rebel Leader Wants the 'East Timor Formula,'" *Asiaweek*, March 31, 2000.

60. Interview with Eid Kabalu, MILF spokesman, Cotabato, January 9, 2002; interview with Abhoud Sayed M. Lingga, chairman of the Bangsamoro People's Consultative Assembly, Cotabato, January 9, 2002.

61. Interview with Abhoud Sayed M. Lingga, chairman of the Bangsamoro People's Consultative Assembly, Cotabato, January 9, 2002.

62. Ibid.

63. Although the talks broke down after six days, a "manual" on how the cease-fire would be implemented was agreed to, and local-level military commanders would meet to review the implementation guidelines. AFP, "GRP-MILF Peace Talks Advance with Cease-Fire Operating Pact," *PDI*, October 18, 2001; AFP, "Peace Talks with MILF Still on Track After Hitting a Snag," *PDI*, October 22, 2001.

64. AFP, "New Round of Talks with MILF Begins in Malaysia," *PDI*, October 15, 2001.

65. Interview with Eid Kabalu, MILF spokesman, Cotabato, January 9, 2002.

66. The MILF stated that it is against the United States interfering in the fight against the Abu Sayyaf, arguing that it would "complicate the peace talks with the government." Clearly the Abu Sayyaf is an embarrassment to the MILF. The leader of the MILF delegation to the peace talks, Murad Ibrahim, stated that the Abu Sayyaf's "link with the Osama Bin Laden group is doubtful" and that there is "no clear link." But even if they are linked, "they are a small group" that did "not justify US military action." Cited in BBC, *East Asia Today*, October 18, 2001.

67. Mona Abaza, "Islamic Fundamentalism in the Middle East and Southeast Asia," *Sojourn* 6, no. 2 (1991): 227.

68. Mohammed Abu Bakar, "Islam and Nationalism in Contemporary Malay Society," in Taufik Abdullah and Sharon Siddique, eds., *Islam and Society in Southeast Asia* (Singapore: Institute of Southeast Asian Studies, 1986), 156.

69. Onn founded the multiethnic Independence of Malaya Party (IMP). The IMP never won a large base of popular support or was able to challenge the UMNO-led coalition's monopoly of power.

70. Murray Hiebert and S. Jayasankaran, "May 13, 1969: Formative Fury," *FEER*, May 20, 1999, 46.

71. S. Jayasankaran and Murray Hiebert, "Malaysian Dilemmas," *FEER*, September 4, 1997, 18.

72. For more, see Mohamed A. Haneef, "Islam and Economic Development in Malaysia: A Reappraisal," *Journal of Islamic Studies* 13, no. 3 (2001): 278–281.

73. Cheong, "Political Structures of the Independent States," 83.

74. David Brown, *The State and Ethnic Politics in Southeast Asia* (New York: Routledge, 1994), 223–224.

75. Ibid., 250.

76. Ibid.

77. Ibid., 250–251. Also see Chandra Muzaffar, *Islamic Resurgence in Malaysia* (Selangor: Penerbit Fajar Bakti, 1987), 24, 56.

78. Simon Elegant, "Ferment on Campus," *FEER*, November 4, 1999, 22.

79. Barbara Watson Andaya and Leonard Y. Andaya, *A History of Malaysia*, 2nd ed. (Honolulu: University of Hawaii Press, 2001), 332.

80. Shanti Nair, *Islam in Malaysian Foreign Policy* (New York: Routledge, 1997).

81. Andaya, *A History of Malaysia,* 333.

82. Harold Crouch, *Government and Society in Malaysia* (Ithaca, N.Y.: Cornell University Press, 1996), 65.

83. Ibid., 67.

84 Christopher Lockwood, "The Greening of Malaysia, the Changing of the Guard: A Survey of Malaysia," *The Economist*, April 5, 2003, 6.

85. S. Jayasankaran and Murray Hiebert, "PAS Time," *FEER*, March 18, 1999, 11.

86. Murray Hiebert, "Man of Faith," *FEER*, July 1, 1999, 18.

87. Ibid., 19.

88. Vatikiotis, "Trusting in God, Not Riches," 27.

89. Ibid.

90. S. Jayasankaran, "Politics of the Pulpit," *FEER*, September 16, 1999, 22.

91. Between 1978 and 1995, UMNO accounted for between 64 and 74 percent of National Front seats in the peninsula. The National Front has been able to dominate national politics and has always maintained a two-thirds majority in Parliament: 1974 (88%), 1978 (85%), 1982 (86%), 1986 (84%), 1989 (71%), 1995 (84%), 1999 (76%). UMNO has been able to maintain this domination of politics for three reasons: the

growing Malay population; favorable constituency boundaries (in 1995 Malays formed a majority in 101 of 144 constituencies); and UMNO's patronage system and machine politics organization. Following the 1989 election debacle, UMNO split after Tengku Razaleigh lost his leadership contest with Mahathir. Razaleigh and his supporters founded Semangat '46 and entered a coalition with PAS and the Democratic Action Party. In 1996 Razaleigh disbanded his party and rejoined UMNO.

92. Patricia Martinez, "The Islamic State or the State of Islam in Malaysia," *Contemporary Southeast Asia* 23, no. 3 (December 2001): 480.

93. Murray Hiebert and S. Jayasankaran, "Wake-up Call," *FEER*, March 18, 1999, 11.

94. Andaya, *A History of Malaysia*, 330.

95. Sulaiman Jaafar and Johannes Ridu, "Nik Aziz: We Are Not Worried About the DAP Pullout," *New Straits Times* (*NST*), September 29, 2001.

96. Simon Elegant, "The Will to Win," *FEER*, June 24, 1999, 11; Murray Hiebert, "Signs of the Times," *FEER*, July 1, 1999, 17.

97. Elegant, "The Will to Win," 11.

98. The Malaysian government admitted that it sent religious students to study Islam in "West Asian countries and Egypt" on official scholarships but never to Pakistan. See Nelson Fernandez, "Students Who Underwent Afghan Military Training Weren't Government Scholars," *NST*, September 30, 2001; and Lorien Holland, "Schools Cast a Wide Net," *FEER*, September 27, 2001.

99. Elegant, "Getting Radical."

100. Murray Hiebert, "Call of the Imams," *FEER*, December 10, 1998, 19.

101. Lorien Holland, "Party of Islam? Well, Sort Of," *FEER*, June 28, 2001, 26.

102. S. Jayasankaran, "Whose Religion?" *FEER*, September 11, 1997.

103. The federal government asserts that the *hudud* is unconstitutional because the federal government has jurisdiction over criminal law.

104. S. Jayasankaran, "Politics of the Pulpit," 22.

105. S. Jayasankaran and Murray Hiebert, "PAS Time," 10.

106. Martinez, "The Islamic State or the State of Islam in Malaysia," 482.

107. Lorrien Holland, "Schools Cast a Wide Net."

108. "PAS Will Not Order Its Members to Fight in Afghanistan," *ST*, October 14, 2001.

109. Ramlan Said and Abdul Razak Ahmad, "PM: Military Action Not the Way," *NST*, September 29, 2001.

110. Martinez, "The Islamic State or the State of Islam in Malaysia," 481.

111. Robert W. Heffner, *Civil Islam* (Princeton: Princeton University Press, 2000).

112. "Indonesia Ought to Be a Model of What Islam Can Be, Says Wolfowitz," *ST*, November 28, 2001.

113. Cited in Adam Schwarz, *A Nation in Waiting: Indonesia in the 1990s* (Boulder, Colo.: Westview Press, 1994), 169.

114. Born on February 7, 1905, in East/Central Java, Kartosuniryo was an excellent organizer and very charismatic, with some experience in national politics. He was virulently anti-Dutch and was a leader of an anticolonial paramilitary force. He enhanced his credentials by withdrawing from politics during the Japanese occupation and did not participate in the Masjumi.

115. Douglas E. Ramage, "Social Organizations: Nahdlatul Ulama and Pembangunan," in Richard W. Baker, M. Hadi Soesastro, et al., eds., *Indonesia: The Challenge of Change* (Singapore: Institute of Southeast Asian Studies, 1999), 204.

116. M. Djadijono, "Economic Growth and the Performance of Political Parties," in Baker and Soesastro, et al., *Indonesia: The Challenge of Change*, 126–128.

117. Robert W. Heffner, "Islam and the Nation in the Post-Suharto Era," in Adam Schwarz and Johnathan Paris, eds., *The Politics of Post-Suharto Indonesia* (New York: Council on Foreign Relations Press, 1999), 42.

118. Schwarz, *A Nation in Waiting*, 173–175.

119. Ibid., 164.

120. Ramage, "Social Organizations," 205.

121. ABRI always had a disproportionate number of Christian generals as a way to check the Muslim community. Yet when Benny Murdani became an outspoken critic of corruption within the Suharto family, Suharto purged many Christian generals associated with Murdani, as well as Murdani himself.

122. Hefner, "Islam and the Nation in the Post-Suharto Era," 55.

123. Ibid., 57–58.

124. Prabowo was implicated for the May 13–15, 1998, riots in Glodok (Chinatown) and the murder of several students at Trisakti University. It was thought that Prabowo wanted to instigate mass political unrest to justify martial law and prevent the ouster of Suharto.

125. In 1996, Suharto orchestrated the ouster Megawati from the PDI leadership, replacing her with a loyalist. The purge caused massive demonstrations against the regime that did not abate until Suharto's ouster in May 1998.

126. In Aceh, the imposition of *sharia* law includes the following provisions: Muslim women must wear chadors, or head scarves; men must join Friday prayers; bars, discos, massage parlors, and pool halls are banned; alcohol is forbidden; extramarital sex is forbidden; pornography and gambling are forbidden.

127. "Deadly Suspicion," *FEER*, July 25, 1991, 18.

128. John McBeth and Margot Cohen, "Loosening the Bonds," *FEER*, January 21, 1999, 10.

129. Margot Cohen, "Captives of the Cause," *FEER*, September 2, 1999, 16–17.

130. John McBeth, "Too Little, Too Late," *FEER*, May 12, 1999, 28.

131. Ibid., 29.

132. ICG, *The Megawati Presidency,* Asia Report No. 9 (September 10, 2000).

133. Ramli Surbakti, "Formal Political Institutions," in Richard W. Baker and Hadi M. Soesastro, et al., eds., *Indonesia: The Challenge of Change* (Singapore: Institute of Southeast Asian Studies, 1999), 68.

134. Heffner, "Islam and the Nation in the Post-Suharto Era," 49.

135. Ibid., 66.

136. After being ousted as head of the PDI, Megawati formed the PDI-P, the Democratic Party of Indonesia for Struggle.

137. Online at www.laskerjihad.or.id.

138. Sadanand Dhume, "Islam's Holy Warriors," *FEER*, April 26, 2001.

139. Ibid.

140. As Sydney Jones noted, the people who were most concerned with "defending the interests" of Muslims in the Malukus were not the local Muslims themselves. Sydney Jones, Asia director, Human Rights Watch, testimony to the U.S. Commission on International Religious Freedom Hearings, Washington, D.C., February 13, 2001.

141. Dan Murphy, "Indonesia's Far-Flung 'Holy War,'" *CSM*, August 23, 2000.

142. Interview—Amir of Lashkar Jihad of Indonesia," Islamic News and Information Network, March 25, 2002.

143. Ibid.

144. ICG, *Indonesia: Overcoming Murder and Chaos in Maluku,* Asia Report No. 10 (December 2000).

145. "Waiting for Osama's Blessing," *Tempo*, September 18–24, 2001.

146. Warren Caragata, "Radical Blasts," *Asiaweek,* October 5, 2001.

147. Online at www.laskarjihad.org.

148. Murphy, "Indonesia's Far-Flung 'Holy War.'"

149. Michael Davis, "Laskar Jihad and the Position of Conservative Islam in Indonesia," *Contemporary Southeast Asia* 24, no. 1 (April 2002): 12–32, esp. 15–19.

150. Interview with Jafarr Umar Thalib, Jakarta, January 10, 2003.

151. Ibid.

152. "Indonesia Ought to Be a Model of What Islam Can Be, Says Wolfowitz."

153. ICG, *The Megawati Presidency* (September 10, 2001), 3.

154. Ibid., 13.

155. When asked if a jihad meant an armed conflict against the West, council spokesman Dien Syamsuddin reportedly said: "No, fighting in the name of Allah can mean many things." But there is plenty of room for misinterpretation, and the weight of the council's views is strong as they are read in the more than 60,000 mosques around the country.

156. Devi Asmarani, "Syaria Law? Jakarta Offers New Criminal Code Instead," *ST*, October 19, 2001.

157. Amien Rais, "Islam and Politics in Contemporary Indonesia," in Geoff Forrester, ed., *Post-Soeharto Indonesia: Renewal or Chaos?* (Singapore Institute of Southeast Asian Studies, 1999), 198–202.

158. "Dreams from Villages of God," *Tempo*, December 30, 2002, 32–35.

159. Pew Global Attitudes Project, *Views of a Changing World* (Washington, DC: Pew Research Center, June 2003): 34–35, 42–45.

160. Sadan and Dhume, "The New Mainstream," *FEER*, January 9, 2003, 46–48.

161. Andaya, *A History of Malaysia,* 110–112.

162. Ibid., 111.

163. Ibid., 194–196.

164. Ibid., 199.

165. Hedman and Sidel, *Philippine Politics and Society in the Twentieth Century,* 176.

166. See W. K. Che Man, *Muslim Separatism: The Moros of the Southern Philippines and the Malays of Southern Thailand* (Quezon City: Attaeneo de Manila University Press, 1990); and Syed Serajul Islam, "The Islamic Independence Movements in Patani in Thailand and Mindanao of the Philippines," *Asian Survey* 38, no. 5 (May 1998): 441–456.

167. The Thais were angered by a Malaysian military plane that entered Thai airspace. Previously, Malaysian police were allowed to pursue MCP rebels eight kilometers into Thailand for up to seventy-two hours. Border security cooperation resumed in late 1976 following a military coup in Thailand that brought an anticommunist government to power. In January 1977, joint and coordinated attacks began, lasting into the 1980s. At the time, the MCP was estimated to be 1,800 to 2,300 men strong. In 1981 the Thais drove several hundred PULO members into Malaysia, though the Malaysian government failed to provide the same degree of assistance to the Thai government.

168. Supara Janchitfah, "Southern Muslims Plead for Understanding," *Bangkok Post,* September 30, 2001.

169. Wayne Arnold, "A Gas Pipeline to World Outside," *NYT*, October 26, 2001, C1, C6.

170. Supara Janchitfah, "Southern Muslims Plead for Understanding."

171. The five members are appointed by the king. The head of the National Council runs a division in the Department of Religious Affairs in the Ministry of Education.

172. PULO, "The Year of National Reorganization (1998–1989)," www.pulo.org.

CHAPTER 3

From Parochial Jihadis to International Terrorists: Exploiting the Philippines

THIS CHAPTER WILL EXPLAIN HOW THE AL-QAIDA NETWORK OF OSAMA BIN LADEN was able to first extend its tentacles into Southeast Asia, by aligning with several Philippine militant groups and by establishing independent cells to conduct terrorist operations against U.S. targets. The Philippines was thoroughly penetrated and was used not just for recruiting terrorists but for safe houses, training centers, domiciles of shell corporations and Islamic charities, places of investment and money laundering, as well as locations for planning and executing attacks.

It may seem strange to think of Islamic-based terrorism having ties to the devoutly Catholic Philippines. Yet according to U.S. officials, "The Philippines have become a major operational hub [of Al-Qaida], and it's a serious concern."[1] Some of the worst terrorist plots in recent memory were planned in the Philippines, including Ramzi Yousef's plot to down eleven U.S. jetliners in "48 hours of terror," and every major terrorist plot by Al-Qaida against the United States has had some ties to the Philippines.

Ramzi Yousef's plot, known as Oplan Bojinka, has been covered in some detail in both the press and books.[2] The goal here is not to revisit the terrorist plot in excessive detail but to explain how it affected the course of development of terrorist and militant groups in the region. One thing that is absolutely clear is that in 1995, when the Ramzi Yousef cell was broken up and he and his two co-conspirators were arrested, no intelligence or law enforcement agencies looked beyond that case. Ramzi Yousef was treated as a lone wolf there in the Philippines—to conduct a single operation. No one examined the links to regional militant groups, nor did they examine the terrorist infrastructure that was established. In all, there were only three arrests, and the entire network of individuals and Islamic charities was left in place.

The Philippines has long been a base of operations for terrorist groups aside from Al-Qaida. As mentioned in the previous chapter, although Libya was a key sponsor of the Moro Islamic Liberation Front and the Moro National Liberation Front and provided the bulk of their monetary assistance and military equipment, these groups, along with the communist New People's Army, also received weapons funneled from the Palestine Liberation Organization. In December 1987, the Philippine National Police broke up a large cell of the Abu Nidal terrorist group, arresting five Palestinians carrying Jordanian passports. In May 1995, a large LTTE (Tamil Tiger) cell was also broken up and nine LTTE members were arrested, including one of their top political leaders, Selvarjah Balasingam. Hamas has also used the Philippines as a small base of operations or to attack U.S. targets, but not to link up with domestic insurgent groups as Al-Qaida has done.

The Philippines has also been the victim of state-sponsored terrorism. On January 19, 1991, an Iraqi terrorist operation to blow up the Thomas Jefferson Cultural Center was uncovered when an Iraqi agent was killed as a bomb he was trying to arm outside a U.S. Information Agency library in Manila detonated. At the same time, a bomb left outside the U.S. ambassador's residence in Jakarta was defused. Investigators believed that the two bombs were delivered via a diplomatic pouch and were in retaliation for the government's support of the U.S.-led Operation Desert Storm in Iraq. The Iraqi consul general, Al Ani, was subsequently declared persona non grata. A similar situation occurred in February 2003, when Iraqi diplomats were accused of supporting the rebel Abu Sayyaf Group as part of Iraq's plan of creating a global Muslim backlash to the U.S.-led war against Iraq. However, no terrorist group or state sponsor has had the effect of Al-Qaida, which effectively united with other groups, backed them, found common cause, and linked them into a global network in support of their operations.

The MILF's Afghan Connection

The Moro Islamic Liberation Front is currently the leading Muslim rebel movement fighting the Philippine government. The MILF fields between 12,000 and 15,000 combatants. In many cases, the movement has legitimate grievances. The Philippine government acknowledges this and thus continues to enter into political negotiations with the front. Nonetheless, whereas the MILF may have legitimate national-liberation aspirations, to that end the MILF has forged links with international terrorist groups, notably Al-Qaida, for financial support, especially in 1995–1996 when funding from Libya substantially waned.

The roots of MILF contact with Al-Qaida date back to the period of the Soviet invasion of Afghanistan, when the MILF sent an estimated 500 to 700 Filipino Muslims to undergo military training and join the mujahidin. According to a classified Philippine intelligence report, the MILF dispatched the trainees in three waves.[3] The first group of 600 was sent to Pakistan in January 1980. Most traveled under travel documents and visas acquired after receiving false employment with a Middle East firm. This has remained the MILF's modus operandi, as the Philippines sends an estimated 7 million people overseas annually as overseas foreign workers (OFW), 1 million to the Middle East alone. The rest traveled as either Islamic scholars or pilgrims to Mecca. The first group was met in Pakistan by Salamat Hashim, the MILF's founder, before being transferred to camps in Afghanistan. Of the 600, only 360 underwent the yearlong military training; 180 of these actually joined the mujahidin.[4] A second but smaller batch was dispatched. The third batch of trainees was sent in groups of five, using student visas or OFW contracts as cover.

The MILF saw the training in Afghanistan as very important in the development of the movement. A Philippine intelligence report notes that "usually those selected were on field commander status, with leadership potential, with armed followers and had money to finance the trip." The MILF saw the mujahidin as an essential program to train and indoctrinate a new generation of leaders. "We needed more mujahidin who would understand Islam completely," said one veteran who returned after three years of training and then ran the MILF's own military school. They were exposed to intense warfare against a highly armed adversary; they were trained in explosives, bomb-making, and both guerrilla and urban warfare. As Hashim Salamat concluded: "The MILF derived a lot of experience because the camp was subjected to air and artillery attack. Our fighters were exposed to a more serious war and advanced weapons including missiles and armored vehicles. They met revolutionaries from all over the world."[5]

Although the MILF paid for its fighters to go to Afghanistan, it was a costly endeavor. Throughout the Soviet period, there is little indication that the MILF was receiving large amounts of external funding to support its volunteers and training in Afghanistan. The steady flow of external funding began in the early 1990s. A wealthy Saudi, Osama bin Laden, a scion of the largest construction magnate in the kingdom who had joined the mujahidin, established Al-Qaida in 1988 to facilitate Muslims worldwide to join the jihad in Afghanistan and to forge an international network. Al-Qaida understood that to better support the MILF, it needed a permanent presence in the Philippines, which could also serve as a base of operations for the region.

Mohammed Jamal Khalifa Establishes a Network

Osama bin Laden already had some ties to the Philippines. In 1988 he dispatched his brother-in-law, Mohammed Jamal Khalifa, to the Philippines to recruit fighters for the war in Afghanistan.[6] Khalifa was already engaged in radical Muslim politics and was a senior member of the Muslim Brotherhood in his native Lebanon. From late 1985 to 1987, Khalifa ran the Peshawar office of the Saudi Muslim World League, where he was active in sending recruits to join the mujahidin. He had close ties to two of bin Laden's top financiers, Wael Jalaidin and Yasin al Qadi, the latter of whom was the head of the Muwafaq Foundation that was designated by both the Saudi and U.S. governments as a terrorist front.[7]

Bin Laden clearly saw the potential of a jihad in the southern Philippines, and he was alarmed at the secular MNLF's ongoing peace negotiations with the Philippine government. In his eyes, the MNLF was selling out and abandoning the goal of establishing an Islamic state. Already, bin Laden believed that the Afghan experience had to be replicated around the world, with local Muslim groups taking on their oppressive secular governments.

Khalifa traveled throughout the Moro region to recruit and facilitate the jihadis' travels to Pakistan. He left the Philippines in either 1989 or 1990 but returned in 1991 to establish a permanent Al-Qaida network.[8]

Khalifa married a local woman, Alice "Jameela" Yabo, the sister of a young Islamic student at Mindanao State University, Ahmed A. Hamwi (Abu Omar), who had close ties to the MILF and other Muslim radicals.[9] Omar and Khalifa met at a conference in 1988 sponsored by the Islamic International Relief Organization.[10] This marriage helped Khalifa get established and accepted into the local Muslim community; it was a strategy that Al-Qaida employed frequently in Southeast Asia. Khalifa established a rattan furniture import-export company as a front, Khalifa Trading Industries, and purchased products specifically from the Muslim region of Mindanao. This company was not profitable, but it was sustaining. More important, though, it was a good cover for Khalifa to transfer funds into the country and broaden his network in Mindanao. Other Khalifa-owned or -affiliated firms included Daw'l Immam Al Shafee, Inc., ET Dizon Travel, Pyramid Trading and Manpower Services, and a realty firm. It was through the latter firm that he was able to get visas for people traveling to Pakistan and Afghanistan.

Khalifa's most important contribution to Al-Qaida's regional network was the establishment of several Islamic charities that were used to channel funding to Muslim insurgents and terrorist cells. At the time, Khalifa was officially the regional director for the Saudi-based charity, the Islamic International Relief Organization, responsible not just for projects in the Philippines but also in Indonesia, Thailand, and Taiwan.[11] The IIRO was actually established in 1978 but co-opted in 1979 by Saudi Arabian intelligence in order to serve as a financial conduit for Saudi, U.S., and Gulf-state funding to the mujahidin in Afghanistan.[12] In the early 1990s, the IIRO decided to have separate directors for each of the countries, and Khalifa became the IIRO director for the Philippines. The IIRO claims to have begun charitable work in the Philippines in 1988,[13] but according to documents registered at the Philippine

Securities Exchange Commission, the IIRO was legally incorporated in the Philippines on September 20, 1991, with offices in Makati and in several cities in Mindanao, including Cotabato and Zamboanga. Khalifa was listed as the IIRO's president and chairman of the board of trustees.[14]

As with most of the Islamic charities that have been implicated in terrorist financing, Khalifa's charities did do some good work, albeit for politically motivated purposes. According to the Philippine national security adviser, Roilo Golez, Khalifa "built up the good will of the community through charity and then turned segments of the population into agents."[15] The IIRO's charitable activities included the construction of an orphanage and dispensary in Cotabato and dispensaries and pharmacies in Zamboanga. The IIRO funded a floating clinic to serve Muslims in remote villages in western Mindanao. It provided food and clothing to internally displaced people who fled war zones. In addition, IIRO funding went to schools and scholarships. Khalifa established Al-Maktum University in Zamboanga using funds from the IIRO. The IIRO asserted that it always did this if not in cooperation with the government then with at least official approval.[16]

The IIRO quickly caught the interest of the Philippine police and military intelligence, which saw it as a front organization for insurgent activities. "The IIRO which claims to be a relief institution is being utilized by foreign extremists as a pipeline through which funding for the local extremists are being coursed through," a Philippine intelligence report noted.[17] An Abu Sayyaf defector acknowledged that "the IIRO was behind the construction of mosques, school buildings and other livelihood projects" but only "in areas penetrated, highly influenced and controlled by the rebel group Abu Sayyaf."[18] For example, in Tawi Tawi, the director of the IIRO branch office was Abdul Asmad, thought to be the Abu Sayyaf's intelligence chief before being killed on June 10, 1994. Many IIRO projects were located in Campo Muslim, a poor Muslim community in Cotabato, a majority Christian city in a Muslim region. This was seen as part of an attempt to help the MILF broaden its base of support from the countryside into urban areas. Scholarships, likewise, were given to students to become Islamic scholars. The Abu Sayyaf defector said the IIRO was used by bin Laden and Khalifa to distribute funds for the purchase of arms and other logistical requirements of the Abu Sayyaf and MILF: "Only 10 to 30 percent of the foreign funding goes to the legitimate relief and livelihood projects and the rest go to terrorist operations."[19]

Anzar, the Abu Sayyaf Group defector, said bin Laden and Khalifa financed the urban warfare and terrorism training in both Libya and in the Philippines of recruits to the Abu Sayyaf, including Edwin Angeles, the founding Abu Sayyaf vice commander and intelligence chief. During this time, Khalifa served as an adviser to the Abu Sayyaf but was primarily a conduit for money. "In the case of bin Laden and Khalifa, they are not combatants, so they give material support. Money. Lots of money."[20] The more they engaged in terrorism, the more financial support poured in from bin Laden and Khalifa. The earliest financial dealings between the ASG and Khalifa date to 1991, when the group was founded.

Khalifa established several other charities and Islamic organizations in the Philippines, ostensibly for charity and religious work but that channeled money to extremist groups, including a branch office of the Saudi charity MERC International and two local nongovernmental organizations, the Islamic Wisdom Worldwide Mission (IWWM), and the Daw'l Immam Al Shafee Center.

Perhaps the most important NGO was the little-known International Relations and Information Center (IRIC). Abu Omar, Khalifa's brother-in-law, started working at the IRIC in 1993, first as a volunteer, and became its director in 1994. The chair of the IRIC was Zubair, described by Philippine intelligence as Khalifa's "business partner."[21] The IRIC engaged in numerous activities, for the most part philanthropic: livelihood projects, job training (carpentry, fish farming, and farming), orphanages, Islamic schools, and other social work.[22] The IRIC would later be revealed as the primary financial conduit to Ramzi Yousef and his terrorist cell.

Khalifa also used the Philippines as a base for Al-Qaida's other international operations. The *South China Morning Post* reported that "in 1994 a Jordanian religious teacher, Adbullah Hashakie, told Jordanian police . . . he received $50,000 from Khalifa to finance bombings and assassinations in Jordan."[23]

In addition to Khalifa was another important Al-Qaida operative, Mohammed Sadiq Odeh, who lived in Davao where he participated in terrorist activities and was an important financial officer for Al-Qaida.[24] Following his 1990 recruitment into Al-Qaida and his subsequent training, in Khost, Afghanistan, he was sent first to Somalia, before coming to the Philippines where he had acquired a degree in architecture from a Philippine university in 1990. He was a suspect in a 1993 bombing of a cathedral in Davao. In 1994 he was sent to Kenya, but in 1995 he returned to the Philippines where he was arrested for possession of explosive devices. In the Philippines he helped plan the August 7, 1998, attack on the U.S. Embassies in Tanzania and Kenya.[25]

Osama bin Laden, himself, may have traveled to the Philippines in the winter of 1993 to expand his network.[26] There is some evidence that he came posing as a potential investor, meeting with government officials to facilitate his purchase of properties and to establish accounts. Even if this is unfounded, Khalifa was doing the job for him.

According to interviews with Philippine intelligence officials, Khalifa developed his network very slowly and carefully. In their eyes he did a meticulous and professional job. One counterintelligence official said that it would have taken him at least that long to develop a similar network that was able to elude government suspicion. Although Philippine authorities had some concerns about Khalifa, the fact is they had no idea of the extent of his operation.[27] He was well respected in the community and included members of the Philippine elite to sit on his boards of directors, and he was able to get the Saudi Arabian Embassy to assist with his charities.

Forging the MILF–Al-Qaida Connection

Once established in the Philippines, Khalifa began to provide considerable amounts of covert assistance to the MILF in two ways: financially and through training. In addition, he provided overt funding development projects in zones under MILF control or to areas that constituted core constituencies of supporters, such as the dispensary in Campo Muslim in Cotabato. In a 1998 interview, Al Haj Murad, the MILF vice chairman for military affairs, admitted that bin Laden and Khalifa provided "help and assistance" to MILF cadres who volunteered in the 1980s to help the Taliban struggle against the Soviet-backed Afghanistan government.[28] On February 7, 1999, Salamat Hashim, the MILF leader, admitted in a BBC interview to receiving aid from bin Laden, though again qualifying that it was humanitarian aid for mosque construction and social welfare. In addition to the MILF's own statements, the MILF's links to the Al-Qaida network have been revealed by Wali Khan Amin Shah, Mohammed Sadiq Odeh, and Wadih el Hage, three Al-Qaida operatives currently arrested.[29]

One must understand how important Al-Qaida funding was becoming for the MILF because its traditional supporter, Libya, was reducing military assistance to both the MILF and the MNLF. The Libyan government at the time was trying to improve its international standing and get the sanctions that were imposed after the Lockerbie bombing lifted. To that end, Muammar Khaddafy resumed his leading role as a broker in the Mindanao peace process. Libya reduced funding and materiel support to both groups, its main source of leverage. And it eventually succeeded, in part, as Nur Misuari's MNLF signed an autonomy agreement with the government in September 1996. The MILF, however, refused to sign the agreement, opting for continued war and eventual independence. The Libyans were in a bind. They could not be seen as a supporter and a key negotiator in the conflict with one faction while still arming the other faction. Yet the Libyans were loath to lose their influence over the MILF. There is ample evidence that the Libyans are still "in the game." A military intelligence officer stated that many of the MILF weapons they still capture are of Libyan origin, but the massive support that was provided in the 1980s has waned considerably, forcing the MILF to find alternative sources of funding and support.[30]

The MILF, which had a more diversified revenue stream than the MNLF, was able to continue fighting. Clearly much of MILF resources came from within. General Fortunato Abat, the former military commander in the region, stated in his memoir that the MILF tended to go on the offensive when its local economic interests were being threatened. Indeed, in the 1990s, the MILF began to engage in more car-jackings, kidnappings, drug trafficking, and extorting money from legitimate businesses.[31] The MILF denies this and says that such acts are "un-Islamic."[32] The MILF also runs legitimate businesses, including several manpower agencies, such as Pyramid Trading and Manpower Services, that are active in the dispatching of the 1 million Philippine OFWs to the Middle East each year. In addition to revenue from these companies, the MILF also receives kickbacks from other Moro OFWs to the Middle East. The MILF has a vast network of financial holdings and front companies, including many in Manila. The MILF also relies on covert funding from legitimate Islamic charities, especially the World Assembly of Muslim Youth, Islamic Wisdom Worldwide, and the Islamic Da'wah Council of the Philippines.

In 2003 the MILF also denies all links to Osama bin Laden and Al-Qaida. Although it admits having a relationship with Khalifa, it argues that Khalifa was simply a philanthropist and that he only engaged in social work. The MILF spokesman asserted that "Khalifa was cleared by the U.S. government. They found he had no links to bin Laden."[33] When asked to respond to the 1998 quote of Al Haj Murad, that the MILF did indeed receive aid and funding from bin Laden's Al-Qaida network, the MILF spokesman said that statement "was taken out of context."[34]

The second type of assistance that the MILF has received from Al-Qaida has been in the form of training, both in Mindanao and abroad. For example, Al Haj Murad of the MILF admitted to receiving "substantial help and assistance from bin Laden including the training of his fighters in bin Laden's camps in Afghanistan." In September 2001, a Philippine senator asserted that bin Laden had attempted to recruit some sixty-nine MILF fighters who applied for employment in a Saudi company allegedly owned by bin Laden.[35] This fits the past way in which the MILF has exfiltrated its fighters out of the Philippines and into Pakistani and Afghan training camps.

More common, however, was the infiltration of Middle Eastern trainers into MILF camps. Beginning in the mid-1990s, Pakistan began to clamp down on foreign jihadis entering the country. Instead, a steady flow of trainers began to arrive in the Philippines to train MILF and Abu Sayyaf guerrillas in country. Perhaps the most important Al-Qaida trainer was al-Mughiri al-Gaza'iri, a commander of an Al-Qaida camp in Afghanistan and a close associate of Abu Zubaydah. Al-Gaza'iri came to the Philippines in 1995 and taught in the MILF's Camp Abu Bakar. Another important Al-Qaida trainer was Omar al-Faruq.

The MILF denies that there have ever been foreign trainers and asserts that this is government propaganda to tarnish its legitimate freedom-fighting force as a terrorist organization.[36] Yet this denial belies considerable evidence to the contrary. Several military intelligence personnel have told me that they have found individuals wearing turbans in MILF camps they have overrun, and men with very heavy beards, uncharacteristic for Filipinos. In mid-2000, the Philippine army found the bodies of several Middle Eastern and Pakistani trainers at an MILF base they captured. An Arab mujahidin fighter was monitored visiting the MILF's camp in Abu Bakar in May to June 2000.[37] At that time, the Philippine government deported two French Algerians with ti es to the GIA (the Algerian terrorist organization) and the MILF to France where they were arrested.[38] In addition to the bodies of foreign trainers, the Islamic armed forces personnel have recovered considerable amounts of documentation, such as visas and passports. Following the Philippine government's capture of the main MILF base, Camp Abu Bakar, in 2001, intelligence personnel discovered a camp within the base specifically for foreign trainers and trainees, Camp Hudaibie. More recently the MILF established a camp near Cotabato for foreign trainers, and it also has a large training center on Tawi Tawi. Philippine military intelligence believes that in total the MILF has played host to several hundred trainers from the Middle East.[39]

Al-Qaida placed a large number of instructors in MILF camps not just to assist the MILF but also for other jihadis in the region, such as the Malaysian Kampulan Mujahidin, Jemaah Islamiya, and Laskar Jundullah. With their secure base areas, geographic proximity, and porous borders, it was far easier and more cost-effective for Al-Qaida to bring its trainers to the region than bringing hundreds of Southeast Asian militants to Pakistan and Afghanistan. A senior MILF cadre, Sulaiman, who himself had trained in Afghanistan, has become an important trainer in MILF camps and is a key liaison between the MILF and foreign militants and Al-Qaida operatives in Southeast Asia who train in MILF camps. Jemaah Islamiya members not only trained at MILF camps but were also active fund-raisers for the MILF. Of the thirty-six people detained in Singapore, four were not found to be JI members but active supporters and fund-raisers for the MILF. For example, Husin Abdul Aziz, a fifty-two-year-old Singaporean who had trained at an MILF camp, donated $20,000 of his own money to the movement and raised in Singapore an additional $20,000 for the MILF.[40] Habibullah Hameed, another detainee, raised an additional $40,000 over many years for the MILF. Eid Kabalu, the MILF spokesman, refused to answer any questions regarding his group's links to the JI or other Indonesian extremist groups. All he said was that "the conflict in Indonesia is very hot" and that "nothing has been proven."[41]

Nevertheless, the links are considerable. On August 1, 2000, there was a bomb attack on the residence of the Philippine ambassador to Indonesia carried out by Jemaah Islamiya operatives. As will be discussed in Chapter 4, the bombing cum assassination attempt of the Philippine ambassador was interpreted as a "thank-you note" to the MILF for its assistance in training. The bombing was conducted by an Indonesian Al-Qaida and JI operative, Fathur Rohman al-Ghozi, who trained JI personnel in bomb-making at MILF camps.

Fathur Rohman al-Ghozi and Al-Qaida played a significant role in establishing the terrorist wing of the MILF, which has hitherto been engaged almost solely in conventional guerrilla warfare. The MILF's Special Operations Group was established in 1999 by Muklis Yunos,[42] who had trained in Al-Qaida camps in Afghanistan in the early to mid-1990s with Fathur Rohman al-Ghozi. The group was designed to carry out urban terrorist warfare and engaged in its first bombings in metro Manila in December 2000. The group, which has several hundred members divided into fourteen divisions, has been implicated in bombings throughout the Philippines since then, especially at times when government forces are on the offensive.

The role of foreign trainers was manifested in another way: a suicide attack on October 14, 1997. At the time, morale in the MILF was quite low. The MNLF had just signed an autonomy agreement with the government, and the MILF had suffered a series of battlefield losses. To raise morale and demonstrate how committed to the Islamic cause the MILF soldiers should be, two foreign trainers—an Egyptian, Mohammed Gharib Ibrahimi Sayed Ahmed, and a Saudi Arabian, al-Maki Ragab—carried out a suicide attack on the headquarters of the VI Infantry near Cotabato, killing six.[43] The MILF denied its involvement, and the MILF has never been known to resort to suicide attacks. Many thought that it was a symbol of the group's support by Muslim radicals from around the world.[44] Philippine military officials who spoke to me admitted that the suicide attack did have the desired effect and that afterward the morale of the MILF went up dramatically.

The links between the MILF and the Al-Qaida network are well established. There is ample evidence that during the 1990s the MILF received funding and training from Al-Qaida operatives. For the most part this money came through the Al-Qaida network established by Mohammed Jamal Khalifa, in particular the IIRO and the IRIC. The connections were both ideological and personal. On the one hand, MILF chairman Salamat Hashim spent a lot of time in Pakistan and knew many of the leaders of the Arab brigades of the mujahidin that were led by bin Laden. The MILF, wary of being too dependent on Malaysian and Libyan arms and money, which dropped off dramatically after 1995–1997, convinced them of the importance of seeking alternative sources of funding and armaments. Ideologically, bin Laden saw the MILF as being committed to establishing an Islamic state, unlike Nur Misuari who eventually sold out to the government in September 1996 and became the governor of the Autonomous Region of Muslim Mindanao. The MILF, in bin Laden's eyes, was worthy of funding. The relationship between the MILF and Al-Qaida was significant. Philippine intelligence intercepted regular telephone calls between Abu Zubaydah, a senior Al-Qaida operations officer, now in U.S. custody, and Salamat Hashim, Yusof Alongon (the head of the MILF Finance Committee), and Abdu Nasser Nooh (the MILF's liaison officer in Manila).[45]

Following the September 11 attacks on the United States, the MILF has come to realize that its past public acknowledgment of links is a liability, and it is struggling to do damage control. In an interview Eid Kabalu called such allegations "part of a grand design to have us labeled as terrorists." They now claim ties were simply humanitarian or social and educational projects run through Khalifa's charities. They have also gone out of their way to distance themselves from the Al-Qaida attacks on the United States. It was probably heartening for the Gloria Macapagal Arroyo administration to hear the MILF leadership reject bin Laden's October 8, 2001, call for a jihad against the United States and its allies and announce that it was respecting the cease-fire in preparation for the October 2001 peace talks. According to the MILF spokesman: "The MILF is far from the fighting and our efforts are directed towards the peace process in Mindanao."[46] In the eyes of MILF members, they are a legitimate Islamic group that has legitimate grievances. As mentioned in the preceding chapter, the MILF has been focusing on an overt political movement to gain support for an East Timor–style independence referendum. For its part, the Arroyo administration has formally blocked attempts by the United States to formally designate the MILF as a terrorist organization, something that many in the administration of George W. Bush have pressed for. It is not that the Philippine president disbelieves that links exist between the MILF and Al-Qaida; rather, the government knows that the MILF has legitimate grievances and considerable popular support and legitimacy. A political negotiation is necessary that would be politically impossible if the MILF was designated a terrorist organization by either the United States or the United Nations.

The Abu Sayyaf Group and the Afghan Connection

Of greater public interest than the MILF is another splinter group, the small but very violent Abu Sayyaf Group, formally Al Harakat Al Islamiya. The ASG was named on the list of twenty-seven individuals and organizations whose assets were frozen by the United States on September 24, 2001, and is one of twenty-eight terrorist organizations designated by the U.S. Department of State.

The origins of the Abu Sayyaf can also be traced to Afghanistan. In the early 1980s between 300 and 500 Moro fundamentalists arrived in Peshawar, Pakistan, to serve with the mujahidin. One of them, Ustadz Abdurajak Janjalani, emerged as their leader.[47] Janjalani was the son of a local ulama and became a fiery Islamic orator himself. He attended Islamic universities in

Libya and Saudi Arabia before joining the mujahidin and fighting the Soviets for several years. Police intelligence documents indicate that Janjalani's studies in Syria and Libya were financed by Khalifa.[48]

In Peshawar, Janjalani befriended a wealthy Saudi supporter of the mujahidin, Osama bin Laden. Janjalani and his younger brother, Khaddafy Janjalani, received training in the late 1980s to 1990s at a training camp near Khost, Afghanistan, that was run by a professor of Islam, Abdur Rab Rasul Sayyaf, whose belief in the strict Wahhabi interpretation of Islam found him favor with many wealthy Saudis, including Osama bin Laden.

Janjalani was committed to waging a jihad back in his native Philippines to create a pure Islamic state (based on Salafi Wahhabism) in the Moro islands. Following the Soviet withdrawal from Afghanistan, Janjalani began making frequent trips between his home in Basilan and the Peshawar-Afghan border region, recruiting supporters. Ten leading MNLF officials who felt sidelined or disagreed with Nur Misuari joined Janjalani, including Ustadz Wahab Akbar and Abdul Ashmad. When Osama bin Laden wanted to expand his Al-Qaida network, he turned to Janjalani to establish a cell in Southeast Asia. This cell would also be an important base of support for terrorist operations. Despite ties between Al-Qaida and the MILF, they were just developing in the 1990s and had not reached their full potential. Moreover, the MILF indicated no interest in conducting or assisting terrorist operations. It was not until 1999 when the MILF founded its Special Operations Group that it began to be engaged in terrorism; beforehand, it remained focused on waging conventional guerrilla war.

For Simon Reeve, bin Laden was looking to expand his global network and was looking for new cells to support; Janjalani was looking for money to grow his movement; and Yousef was looking for a new mission. "It all came together" in Peshawar in 1991, said Reeve.[49] Philippine National Police (PNI) intelligence documents suggest that Ramzi Yousef strongly encouraged the formation of the Abu Sayyaf Group to serve as his contact and support group in the Philippines. At the time, Ramzi Yousef, the mastermind of the 1993 World Trade Center bombing, was teaching bomb-making at the Khost camp. Ramzi Yousef and Janjalani struck up a close friendship, according to Reeve, in early 1991.[50] Yousef traveled with Janjalani to the Philippines from December 1991 to May 1992 at bin Laden's request, where he trained ASG members in bomb-making in their camp on Basilan Island. When Yousef was introduced to Janjalani's assistant and a leader of the Abu Sayyaf, Edwin Angeles,[51] he was introduced as an "emissary from bin Laden" and referred to as "the chemist," owing to his proficiency in bomb-making. He spent a short period of time in the southern island of Basilan where he trained approximately twenty Abu Sayyaf militants in the art of bomb-making.

In addition to providing funding to Janjalani, bin Laden also provided expertise to the new organization. Wali Khan Amin Shah, who fought alongside bin Laden in Afghanistan and who was a close personal friend, was dispatched to recruit, organize, and assist the Abu Sayyaf.

In 1991, the ASG received some P12 million ($6 million) from foreign sources—mainly from Al-Qaida but also from Libya, among others.[52] On January 29, 1992, the ASG received some P160,000 from Khalifa. The ASG began to receive large deliveries of weapons—mainly Libyan models—from Victor Blout, the Tajik arms dealer who was later linked to both the Taliban regime and Al-Qaida.[53]

Very quickly, the organization—seen as small but lethal—made its mark. Abu Sayyaf began its terrorist attacks in the Philippines in 1991 when it killed two U.S. evangelists in a grenade blast in the city of Zamboanga. ASG operatives attacked Ipil in April 1995 and in February 1997 assassinated a Catholic bishop. Between 1991 and 1996, the Abu Sayyaf Group was responsible for sixty-seven terrorist attacks, more than half of which were indiscriminant bombings. All led to the death of fifty-eight people and 398 injuries.

Through Janjalani's sermons and notoriety following a series of kidnappings and massacres, other gangs of Moro brigands in the Sulu islands began to accept him as their chief. Abu Sayyaf grew in strength when it began receiving more Al-Qaida funding.

Ramzi Yousef and Oplan Bojinka

Although the Abu Sayyaf's scope primarily focused on its domestic grievance, the group had links to the broader Al-Qaida network. As mentioned above, while in Khost, Janjalani came into contact with Ramzi Yousef, who moved to the Philippines via Pakistan in mid-1994 following the February 26, 1993, bombing of the World Trade Center. Using the Philippines as his base of operations, Yousef planned a series of spectacular terrorist plots. The Bojinka plots included the bombings of eleven U.S. jetliners and the assassination of the pope, who visited the Philippines in early 1995.

Philippine police believed that Yousef relied on Abu Sayyaf contacts and intended to recruit Abu Sayyaf operatives to help carry out his plan. Although there is no direct evidence linking Abu Sayyaf to these failed terrorist attacks, the Abu Sayyaf claimed credit for the December 1995 bombing of a Tokyo-bound Philippine Airlines flight, which police believe was a rehearsal for Yousef's plan to down U.S. aircraft.

Even at this point, the Philippine authorities had no idea that one of the U.S. most-wanted terrorists on the list was in their territory. Intelligence officials had increased surveillance of the ASG on June 10, 1994, after a series of bombs went off in Zamboanga, attributed to the ASG, killing more than seventy-one people. The first tip-off that there were connections to international terrorist group is that a leading suspect was carrying a letter claiming responsibility for the bombings, signed by the Al Harakat Al Islamiya, the same group that claimed responsibility for the 1993 attacks on the World Trade Center. The one suspect detained, Abdul Asmad, was believed to be the international liaison officer of the ASG.[54] Yet officials still were unaware of Yousef's presence in the country. The police began to increase surveillance of foreign nationals from the Middle East and began scrutinizing phone records. In September 1994 six ASG members were arrested and a cache of weapons was seized in Zamboanga. Interrogation of the suspects directed the police to Manila, where they began to increase surveillance on the IIRO and especially Abu Omar's IRIC. What struck the police was that many of the names that kept on turning up in their investigations were somehow linked to Khalifa's IIRO or the IRIC.

One person who came under their close attention was Tareq Kaved Rana, a Pakistani, whom Philippine police believed to be closely associated with international terrorists. In December 1994, a suspicious fire razed Rana's house in Paranaque.[55] By the time investigators got there, the place was cleaned out, but forensic tests indicated that the fire was caused by combustible chemicals, the same chemicals that were later discovered to be the hallmark of Ramzi Yousef's bombs.

Philippine intelligence officials were already on heightened alert because of an upcoming visit of the pope, and they dramatically increased surveillance of suspected Muslims. On January 3, 1995, a report came in that twenty young Muslim men had been engaged in some sort of "highly regimented training," indoctrination exercises, and Quranic study at a beach resort south of Manila in Batangas, from December 31 to January 2.[56] On January 3, the twenty were arrested—fifteen were foreign nationals (Egyptians, Palestinians, and Pakistanis), and five were Muslim Filipinos. Police officials became convinced that a major terrorist act targeting the pope was in the works. However, despite the arrest of the twenty Muslim radicals in Batangas, the police were still unaware of the greater plot against the pope. The twenty were seen as foot soldiers, not leaders.

At this point Ramzi Yousef was already in Manila. He moved there sometime in September 1994 to begin planning a second round of attacks on U.S. targets and acted with the utmost secrecy. While in the Philippines he used seven different aliases and leased room 603 of the Dona Josefa Apartment in the name of a Turkish student.

The terrorist cell in Manila centered around Mohammed Jamal Khalifa, Ramzi Yousef, and three other key individuals, and there were approximately fifteen others with limited knowledge of the operation. Everyone in the cell had very specific functions, and in many cases, once those functions were completed, they left the country.[57]

Perhaps the most important person in the cell was Khalid Shaikh Mohammed (Salem Ali). Mohammed would become one of the most important Al-Qaida leaders and a key planner of their deadliest attacks against U.S.

targets. Shaikh Mohammed was thought to be a major operational planner for the 1993 World Trade Center Bombing as well as Oplan Bojinka, the 1998 East African Embassy bombings, and the USS *Cole* attack in October 2000. The U.S. Federal Bureau of Investigation (FBI) also named him a key planner of the September 11 attacks. Within Al-Qaida, he is known as the "Brain," owing to his operational knowledge and key role in the planning of Al-Qaida attacks. He was on the FBI's most wanted list since 1995. He is a fascinating and almost romantic figure; for years he stayed a step ahead of the law, escaping from the Philippines, Qatar, and Pakistan. Educated in the United States at a North Carolina college, he then went to Pakistan and Afghanistan in 1986 at the urging of his brother, a member of the mujahidin. There he met Osama bin Laden and became a member of Al-Qaida. He arrived in the Philippines in early 1994 following his nephew, Ramzi Yousef, and posed as a Qatari plywood exporter. Mohammed lived a luxurious and a bizarrely conspicuous lifestyle for a terrorist in the Philippines, and he often visited diving resorts. He courted a dentist, renting a helicopter to fly over her office to impress her. He was captured in 2003.

The second most important individual was Wali Khan Amin Shah, a close associate of Osama bin Laden and Ramzi Yousef. Bin Laden spoke highly of Shah, referring to him as the "Lion" but had "no comment" as to whether Shah worked for him.[58] He was born on the Pakistani-Afghan border, which explains why conflicting reports say he holds one or the other nationality. Wali Khan was very important in establishing the financial network and serving as a logistician for the operation; he was not a bomb-maker but played a key role. He previously worked for the IIRO in Peshawar, Pakistan, and was carrying an IIRO identification card when arrested.[59] Wali Khan traveled extensively between the Philippines, Malaysia, Hong Kong, and Thailand. Abu Omar admitted to knowing Wali Khan in the Philippines as early as 1993. Wali Khan was associated with a Khalifa-run company in Malaysia. Intelligence reports make clear that they believed he was in charge of financial logistics for the Yousef cell. He carried an ATM card in the name of Carol Santiago. He also had a Hong Kong Bank letter and other information linking him to a Malaysian firm, Konsojaya SDN, BHD, which he founded in 1994 to provide logistical support for the operation. On December 15, 1994, he was issued a three-month visa for Malaysia from the Malaysian Embassy in Pakistan, indicating that he may have intended to seek haven in Malaysia after the pope's assassination.

Another important cell member was Abdul Hakim Ali Hasmid Murad, a Pakistani born in Kuwait on April 1, 1968, and a close associate of Ramzi Yousef. He had first come to the Philippines between November 1990 and February 1991 and then returned from 1992 to 1994. He was trained in bomb-making in Lahore, Pakistan, in August 1994 by Ramzi Yousef. When Yousef ordered him to the Philippines, in December 1994, he apparently came very reluctantly, as Yousef confiscated his passport. Murad was a trained commercial pilot and later revealed to authorities that it was his plan to hijack a commercial airliner and crash it into CIA headquarters, foreshadowing the September 11 attacks.

Other cell members included:

- Abu Omar, the brother-in-law of Khalifa and the director of the IRIC, who was an important money man for the cell.
- Munir Ibrahim, described as a wealthy Saudi Arabian from Jeddah, thirty to thirty-five years of age, who first met Wali Khan Amin Shah in 1992 in Karachi, Pakistan. He was an important financial conduit for the cell who fled the Philippines on January 9, 1995.
- Amein Mohammed, a Pakistani who, with Wali Khan, established the firm Konsojaya in Malaysia.
- Adel Annon and Mustafa Al-Zainab, who had been living for years in Manila, establishing legitimate businesses to serve as a front for radical activities. Anon ran a *halal* ("kosher") butcher, the Mindanao Meat Shop on L.H. del Pilar Street in Ermita. Al-Zainab purchased the Al-Tanor Restaurant (see Figure 3.1).

The cell also relied on several bar girls and girlfriends, Carol Santiago, Rose Mosquera, and Amanda Custodia. These women for the most part were not aware of the scope of the operations, though they had some suspicions. They were important in opening accounts in their own names as well as registering cell phones and beepers in their own names. All of the bills for the various cell phones and beepers went to a single post office box that was leased at the SM Megamall in Manila.

Yousef and Wali Khan Amin Shah established a shell company, the Bermuda Trading Company, as a cover to purchase chemicals. Most of the chemicals were imported, probably from Singapore. The second front company used in the operation was Konsojaya SDN, BHD. Incorporated on June 2, 1994, Konsojaya was ostensibly a general trading company engaged in palm oil trading with Pakistan and Afghanistan and honey imports from Sudan and Yemen. Konsojaya's original board of directors included:

Wali Khan Amin Shah
Medhat Abdul Salam Shabana
Riduan bin Isumuddin (Hambali)
Hemeid H. Alghamdi
Noralwizah Lee Binti Abdullah (Hambali's wife)
Amein Mohammed
Amein Alsanani (managing director)
Annamalai A/L Sundrasan (secretary)

Figure 3.1 Mohammed Jamal Khalifa and the Ramzi Yousef Cell, 1994–1995

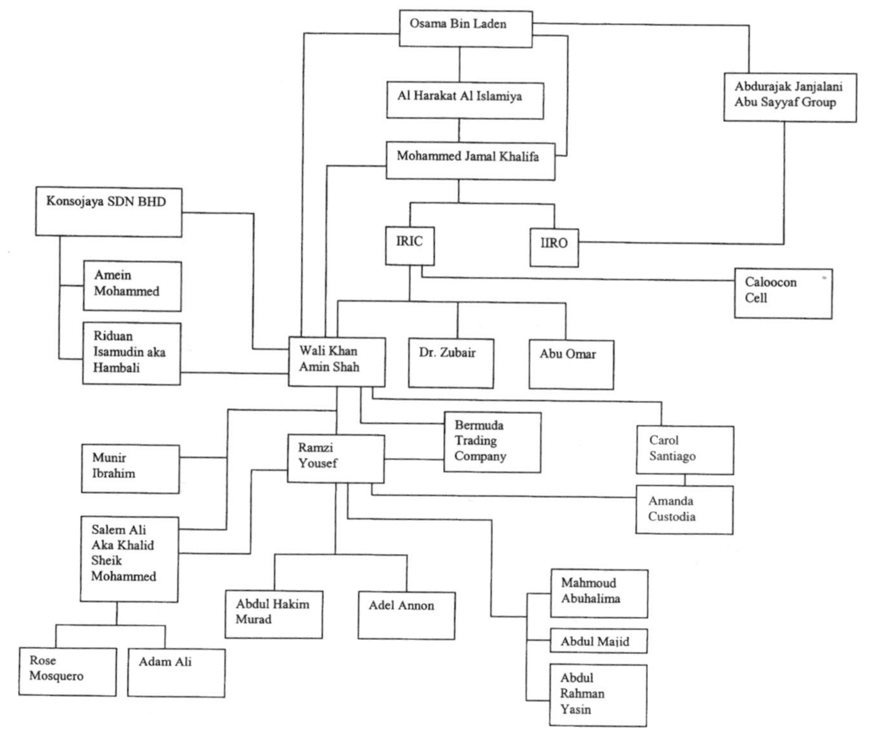

The firm was capitalized with RM100,000, and all but two of the 6,000 shares were controlled by Wali Khan and Shabana. At a later date, a new five-member board was elected and did not include Hambali, a senior Al-Qaida member and the head of operations for the Jemaah Islamiya, his wife, or Amein Mohammed.

Bojinka Revealed

On December 10, 1994, a Philippines Airlines 747-200 Flight 434, carrying 273 passengers and twenty crew en route from Cebu to Tokyo, was forced to make an emergency landing after a bomb went off in the cabin, killing a Japanese businessman. This bombing, though claimed to be the work of the Abu Sayyaf Group, was a dry run to test Yousef's plan to bomb eleven U.S. jetliners.[60] Yousef planted the bomb during the trip's first leg from Manila to Cebu where he disembarked. This bomb was Yousef's trademark: a small nitroglycerine bomb set off by a Casio watch. The full operation entailed five individuals, including Yousef, Wali Khan Amin Shah, Abdul Hakim Murad, Adel Anon, and Khalid Shaikh Mohammed who were to all depart different Asian cities, placing timed bombs on planes during their first leg of a trans-Pacific flight; they would then transfer to another flight and arm a second bomb. It was a meticulously planned operation. The bombs were to detonate simultaneously over the Pacific. If successful, roughly 4,000 people would have been killed.[61]

By mid-December Yousef had returned from Cebu to the Dona Josefa Apartment on Quirino Avenue in Malate using the name Jary Asweta Hadid, the passport of a Turkish student. He was later joined by Abdul Hakim Murad who very reluctantly flew in from Pakistan to help Yousef make the bombs for the eleven flights. On the evening of January 6, 1995, a fire broke out in Ramzi Yousef's apartment as he and Murad were mixing chemicals. As the air filled with poisonous gas, they had to flee the premises. The firemen found an entire apartment full of volatile chemicals, four large timing devices, a pipe bomb, as well as books and manuals on the manufacture of bombs. They also found a laptop computer that had the plans for the terrorist attacks, twelve fake passports, and a business card belonging to bin Laden's brother-in-law, Mohammed Jamal Khalifa.

In the aftermath of the fire, Yousef immediately fled the scene. Security surveillance cameras spotted his red Toyota Corolla at a Manila hotel, but the police were unable to attain a search warrant that night. By the next morning, he left for Cebu, then to Zamboanga, where he eventually made it to Kuala Lumpur through Sabah. Yousef did not stay in the region long. He traveled to Thailand and then to Pakistan where he was arrested in February 1997 on a tip-off to U.S. intelligence. He was extradited to the United States where he was convicted twice in two separate trials: first for the Bojinka plot and then for plotting to destroy the World Trade Center in a 1993 bomb attack. He is serving a life sentence in a federal prison.

Abdul Hakim Murad was arrested when he returned to the Dona Josefa Apartment on Yousef's orders to dispose of the incriminating evidence and collect Yousef's laptop. Following his arrest, he was taken to police headquarters at Camp Crame where he was held and interrogated for six weeks before being rendered to the United States in April 1995. His "interrogations" were brutal affairs, and in court testimony he claimed he was beaten to within half an inch of his life. Although he admitted to the plot to assassinate the pope via a radio-frequency detonated pipe bomb, Philippine officials were still not sure of who they had or what his links to international terrorists were. While detained, he also admitted that he planned to attack the CIA headquarters in an act that foreshadowed the September 11 attacks. Murad, a trained pilot, intended to hijack a commercial jetliner and, following the takeover of controls, crash it into the CIA headquarters.[62] Murad also spoke of plots to use crop dusting planes to spray biological and chemical weapons over U.S. cities. Murad was convicted for the Bojinka plot along with Yousef in September 1996. Murad was also suspected for a supporting role in the 1993 World Trade Center bombings. On May 16, 1998, he was sentenced to life in prison.

The laptop computer found in the apartment led the police to the girlfriends, Amanda Custodia, Rose Mosquera, and Carol Santiago. On January 11, 1995, the police followed Carol Santiago to an apartment on Singalong Street, Makate, the home of Wali Khan Amin Shah. The police arrested Shah that day as he was leaving the building apparently in flight and with a considerable amount of incriminating evidence, including several passports, a handgun, bomb-making implements, timers, bomb-making manuals and documents, and a map with the pope's intended route marked on it.

Under interrogation Wali Khan admitted his links with Mohammed Jamal Khalifa and Ramzi Yousef. He also admitted that he had conducted training in bomb-making for the Abu Sayyaf Group in Zamboanga. This course taught urban commando skills, bomb-making, and jihad indoctrination for nineteen members of the ASG. Yet in a most peculiar circumstance, Wali Khan escaped from prison on January 13. When I asked a senior intelligence official who was responsible for breaking up the Ramzi Yousef cell, he admitted that it was "very strange to me,"[63] but he also suggested that Wali Khan may have been released intentionally in the hope that he would lead investigators to Ramzi Yousef.[64] The police knew that Yousef was already in Kuala Lumpur because of intercepted cell phone calls to his girlfriend, though they had no cooperation from their Malaysian counterparts in tracking Yousef down. One official complained to me, off the record, that the Malaysians gave Yousef "sanctuary." Indeed, Wali Khan did go immediately to Malaysia. By then, however, Yousef apparently had fled to Thailand. Wali Khan was arrested in February

1995 on Langkawi Island (discovered because he is missing two fingers, the legacy of a land mine in Afghanistan) and rendered to the United States on December 2, 1995. Since August 1998, Shah has cooperated with the U.S. government and to date has still not been sentenced, yet he was convicted along with Murad and Yousef in September 1996.

Prior to the operation going awry, Mohammed Jamal Khalifa was arrested December 26, 1994, in California when he was discovered to be on a Jordanian terrorist watch list. He was held without bail for several months by immigration authorities and charged with visa fraud and providing false information. When he was arrested, the FBI seized documents that link him to terrorist training, including lessons on security measures and jihad. But the United States was never able to convict him on a more serious charge. He was deported to Lebanon where he was already tried, convicted, and sentenced to death in absentia for conspiracy to carry out terrorist acts. He was retried and acquitted of terrorism charges and allowed to move to Saudi Arabia. Though Khalifa has denied involvement in bin Laden's recent activities, he had admitted very close ties in the past. Yet during a post–September 11 crackdown by the Saudi Arabian government on known bin Laden associates, Khalifa was arrested but later released.[65] Currently a businessman in Saudi Arabia, he is believed to still manage bin Laden's investments in Southeast Asia.

Lone Wolves

Despite these arrests, the entire terrorist infrastructure that Khalifa, Wali Khan, Khalid Shaikh Mohammed, and Ramzi Yousef established was left operational. There were only three arrests, and many got away or were released for lack of evidence. U.S. authorities seemed pleased that they had captured the ringleaders of the 1993 World Trade Center bombing and washed their hands of the Philippines. As mentioned previously, at first Ramzi Yousef was treated as a lone wolf, not part of a broader network. Even later when he was firmly linked to Al-Qaida, there was no thorough analysis of Al-Qaida's Southeast Asian operations. No one asked why Al- Qaida came to the Philippines in the first place, other than to conduct a one-time terrorist operation. No one analyzed the network that was established and the deep links between it and home-grown Muslim insurgencies or to individuals and organizations across Southeast Asia. No one questioned what of the network was left in place.

Without U.S. support, there was little political incentive for the governments of the region to confront the issue. The Philippine government asserted that all of the charities run by Khalifa in the Philippines that were used to funnel money to the Abu Sayyaf Group and the MILF were shut down.[66] The links between Khalifa and Yousef and the fact that Wali Khan Amin Shah was supposedly an employee of the IIRO were too much for the Philippine authorities to countenance, and Khalifa was denied reentry. However, one senior intelligence official complained, "We could not touch the IIRO" due to Saudi Arabia's political clout.[67] It took the Philippine government almost six years to shut down the IIRO office in the Philippines. Since 2000, the IIRO still has funded projects in the country through its representative offices in Malaysia and Indonesia. The IRIC's operations, office, and staff were taken over by another Islamic charity, the Islamic Wisdom Worldwide Mission, headed by a close Khalifa associate, Mohammed Amin al-Ghafari, in 1995.[68] The IWWM also has a long history of providing money to the MILF. Other charities and NGOs established by Khalifa and his associates, including Islamic Studies Call and Guidance (ISCAG),[69] the Islamic Information Center led by Nedal Al-Dhalain, and the Daw'l Immam Al Shafee Center, likewise, remain operating.[70]

The extent of the Ramzi Yousef cell terrified Philippine security officials who began to understand the degree to which their country was penetrated by terrorist groups. At first they were nearly paralyzed by this realization. As General Jose Almonte, at the time the national security adviser to President Fidel Ramos, told me, they were in complete and utter shock over the scope of Oplan Bojinka. They could not believe it because it was "too fantastical. So out of, you know, so anti-God. You do not think that even a man with a diabolical mind could do that."[71]

The Ramzi Yousef Al-Qaida cell was broken up by accident and then by good police work, but not through penetration by an intelligence agency. Thus, if there was one positive outcome, it was a growing consciousness that the Philippines was thoroughly penetrated by terrorist cells. Philippine authorities increased their monitoring and intelligence capabilities, which led to a few results. Following further investigations into the plot to assassinate the pope, police broke up another Al-Qaida cell in Caloocon, a suburb of Manila, in late March 1995. Those arrested had served in Afghanistan with the mujahidin and were all thought to be followers of the radical Egyptian cleric, the blind Shaikh Abdurrahman Omar. The cell was plotting ways to avenge and win the release of Abdurrahman who was arrested and convicted for his role in the 1993 bombing of the World Trade Center. However, all fourteen individuals were later released due to a lack of evidence. Some fled the Philippines while others stayed—but all jumped bail. Several members of this cell were put under heightened surveillance. The arrests did lead authorities to uncover another plot, the assassination of President Ramos and other high-ranking officials and foreign ambassadors in retaliation for Murad's arrest. This was to be followed by a chain of bombings of commercial centers, the U.S. Embassy, the International School, government buildings, department stores, and Catholic churches. In December 1995 police arrested Adel Annon, a member of the Ramzi Yousef cell still at large. During the raid, police discovered grenades, dynamite, rockets, bomb-making components, and travel documents in his possession.[72] Increased surveillance of radical groups also led the police to break up a nine-man cell of the Tamil Tigers in May 1995.

General Almonte asserted that the Philippines raised the alarm to the international community and in 1996 even hosted a major international conference on counterterrorism but was unhappy to find that states were not taking the issue seriously. The United States, in particular, thought the matter was resolved with Yousef's arrest. No one, as a senior Philippine military intelligence official said to me, thought that Oplan Bojinka was simply part of a greater plot.[73] Almonte believed that the United States did not take the international scope of the Al-Qaida network seriously. When the cell was discovered, it was in the final stages of a number of spectacular attacks. The planning and scope of the Yousef cell was staggering. Bin Laden proved that he could establish an autonomous cell impervious to detection.

Focus on bin Laden was directed elsewhere, away from Southeast Asia. At this point, bin Laden seemed to have lessened his interest in the Philippines and was determined to take his jihad to the Holy Land, from where he would drive out both U.S. forces and their secular puppet regimes. Bin Laden's operation had moved to Khartoum, Sudan, and after 1996 to Afghanistan, where he became truly intent on creating an international network and a business empire to fund it. It was at this time that his attacks on the House of Saud led to his being stripped of his Saudi citizenship. Cells continued to be developed in the Philippines and elsewhere in the region, but the region became secondary to Al-Qaida.

The Decline of Abu Sayyaf

The breakup of the Ramzi Yousef cell in Manila also had far-reaching consequences for the Abu Sayyaf Group. Abu Sayyaf members played important supporting roles, though not leadership roles in the cell. Yousef really did not trust them or think them capable enough to carry out serious terrorist acts. He used his own men, all flown in from the Middle East. Yousef and Wali Khan were willing to train members of the ASG, but they did not rely on them to the degree that observers have indicated. At most, members of the ASG provided logistical services and assisted Yousef and Wali Khan in exfiltrating the country.

Most important, the Yousef–bin Laden connection was the major source of their funding. Without a steady supply of Al-Qaida funding, the group atrophied. Omar al-Faruq, a key Al-Qaida operative who was dispatched to the region in 1995 and who was a trainer at the MILF camps, was responsible for forming a union between the small ASG and the MILF to create a stronger jihad force. But al-Faruq was spurned by the ASG who did not consider the MILF a reliable jihad partner. The reality is that they were angered that the MILF was not sharing Al-Qaida funding with them. ASG leaders even accused the MILF of skimming Al-Qaida funding meant for them.[74] The MILF and the ASG entered into several rounds of negotiations about joining forces, but such an alliance never occurred.

The ASG fell into further decline following the death of Janjalani in a shoot-out with police on December 18, 1998. His lieutenant, Edwin Angeles, was arrested in January 1999 and became a government informer. Since then, the Abu Sayyaf has split into two or three factions and their commitment to establishing an Islamic state now seems secondary at best. The Abu Sayyaf fell into decline, riddled with factionalism; in recent years it has become more of a criminal nuisance with no apparent links to international terrorist organizations. According to the Philippine presidential spokesman, Rigoberto Tiglao, since the death of Janjalani, "the band has degenerated into a criminal kidnap for ransom group using Islamic militancy as a ruse to gain the support of a few Muslim villages in Basilan island where they take refuge. The Abu Sayyaf Group has split into two groups because of their squabbles over ransom money."[75] As one U.S. diplomat said to me, "They're wannabes."

Janjalani's younger brother Khadaffy, who seems more engrossed with kidnapping and hostage taking, heads one faction. He is based on the island of Basilan. Another brother, Hector, was captured by the Philippine government and arrested for masterminding a string of bombings in Manila in December 2000.[76] He was arraigned on December 6, 2001. Another, but small faction on Jolo Island is headed by Galib Andang, known as "Commander Robot," who broke away from the Moro National Liberation Front. Robot was a former Nur Misuari bodyguard who has been running a kidnapping racket for years.

Abu Sabaya, the nom de guerre of Aldam Tilao (also called Ahmad Salayudi), who headed the largest faction of the ASG, continued to fight the Philippine army with considerable success until he was killed in June 2002 in a joint U.S.-Philippine operation. Abu Sabaya studied criminology in Saudi Arabia but was drawn by the jihad to Afghanistan after being trained in Libya and Pakistan. He was reportedly banished from a training camp for troublemaking. Abu Sabaya's forces also engaged in kidnapping, and he has reportedly collected $25 million in ransom that he uses to arm his troops, though this is clearly a high estimate.

One only has to look at a chronology of ASG operations to chart the loss of international funding. From 1996 to 2000, the ASG engaged in some 266 terrorist activities. During this time, estimates of the ASG's manpower and firepower by Philippine intelligence grew by 14 percent annually. In 2000, the ASG had completely degenerated into a bunch of kidnapping gangs. There were three major incidents that renewed attention to this organization.

1. March 2000: The ASG kidnapped fifty-five people—schoolchildren, teachers, and a priest in Basilan.

2. April 2000: The ASG kidnapped twenty foreigners and a Filipino from a diving resort on the Malaysian island of Sipidan.
3. May 2001: The ASG kidnapped thirty tourists from the Don Palmas diving resort on Palawan.

Rather than serving as evidence of international terrorism, these incidents are seen as part of a plan for the ASG to get wider international attention, to divert Philippine military pressure, and to distance itself from the larger but less radical MILF, which seems embarrassed by the Abu Sayyaf.[77] The MILF spokesman condemned these attacks as being completely un-Islamic. "Most of their activities are against Islam. We do not sanction most of their activities."[78] One Abu Sayyaf defector said that he quit the movement "because the group lost its original reason for being. The activities were not for Islam but for personal gratification. We abducted people not any more for the cause of Islam but for money."[79]

Terrorist analyst Rohan Gunaratna has written that there is little evidence that the group receives voluntary contributions from individuals, NGOs, or commercial companies.[80] In addition to kidnapping, the ASG engages in extortion, and collects taxes from peasants, fishermen, coconut growers, and businessmen. The ASG also engages in marijuana cultivation, and on July 24, 1999, PNP forces destroyed approximately 70,000 marijuana plants worth P20 million ($10 million).[81]

According to a Basilan politician, "It was easier to deal with them when they had a single leader—and an ideology. Now, these guys are in it for the money, and there's no stopping them."[82] The demands for $1 million ransoms per hostage have led many to consider the Abu Sayyaf as nothing more than a criminal menace rather than a secessionist insurgency with legitimate grievances. By September 2002, the ASG only had between 200 and 400 fighters and recruited through high salaries rather than religion or ideology. As the Philippine national security adviser Roilo Golez said, "We have no evidence that Abu Sayyaf has gotten financing from bin Laden recently. Otherwise they would not have to resort to kidnapping."[83] Thus, the Bush administration's assertion that the ASG is linked to Al-Qaida is tenuous, at best.

Although they have continually demanded the freedom of Ramzi Yousef and Abdurrahman Omar, links to Al-Qaida and international terrorism are dormant if not severed. As a Filipino Muslim journalist who had spent a week with the ASG told me, the links had been cut: "Before they were tied to bin Laden, but now no. They are independent. They get money from kidnappings. They are an independent cell."[84] He continued: "How they are linked to Osama bin Laden now is a spiritual link" because of a "shared interpretation of jihad." Yet on September 24, 2001, the Abu Sayyaf Group was named on the first list of twenty-seven individuals and organizations whose assets were frozen by the United States because of their links to the Al-Qaida network.

The Philippine government has played this for all it's worth, receiving more than $100 million in military assistance in 2002 alone. From January to July 2002, some 1,300 U.S. troops, including 160 special operations forces, were in the Philippines engaged in a joint training, Operation Balikatan. Although, most U.S. troops withdrew in July 2002, a second training mission planned for early 2003 was put on hold because of a dispute over the role that U.S. troops would play, under the Philippine Constitution.

There are three reasons to still be concerned about the ASG. The first is that the group is a dangerous criminal gang that threatens law and order and impedes development. For that reason alone it should be eliminated.

The second reason is that international networks may still want to maintain the relationship with the ASG. Presidential spokesman Rigoberto Tiglao stated that Philippine intelligence officials had monitored any suspected terrorist from the Middle East who had recently gotten into contact with Abu Sayyaf leaders but "found the new leaders as bandits with no interest in global terrorism."[85] They are devoid of ideology—even a radical interpretation of Islam. But Al-Qaida is on the run and will turn to any group that will help them get reestablished. Whereas there is not a lot of evidence to suggest continued financial flows, through 2000 there were personnel flows. In October 2000, hostages who escaped from their Abu Sayyaf captors asserted that two Yemenis were in the camp advising the Abu Sayyaf in September and October.[86] One ASG defector stated that there were four foreign instructors (three Afghans and a Syrian) in the ASG camp in Tugas, on Sulu Island.[87] On October 2, 2002, the ASG conducted a bombing in Zamboanga, which killed three people, including a U.S. Special Forces soldier; this operation was held in conjunction with two Indonesian members of the Jemaah Islamiya and supported by a Jordanian resident of the Philippines who is linked to the Palestinian terrorist group Hamas. On October 18, a bomb ripped through a bus in metro Manila. Philippine intelligence documents and sources point to a strong degree of collusion between the MILF's Special Operations Group, its urban terrorism unit, and the ASG. There is also evidence that Iraq had tried to form links with the group in early 2003 as part of its international effort to stir up Muslim resistance to the United States and its allies.

Finally there is the question that the ASG is a financial conduit to other Al-Qaida cells in the region. The Libyan government interceded and negotiated the release of the Sipidan hostages in August 2000. In return $15–20 million was paid to the ASG as a grant for development and social welfare from the Khaddafy Foundation. President Khaddafy's son, the former Libyan ambassador to the Philippines, Rajab Azzarouq, has remained involved in Mindanao affairs. The fact is, no one knows what happened to the roughly $15–20 million in ransom money that was paid to the ASG. It has not gone into weaponry. As one senior intelligence official said to me, "If we sum up the assets and firearms that they [the ASG] bought for the money, $2 million is enough to buy all the weapons they have." Nor has it been invested in the community; such a staggering sum in one of the poorest regions of the country would be readily noticeable. Granted some may have gone to bribes and kickbacks, but the bulk of the money is missing. It also raises the question of whether Libya, while condemning terrorism and serving as sponsors of the peace program, is still funding terrorist groups. Was the payment to the ASG a convenient way to launder money and transfer it to other terrorist cells in the region? When I put this hypothesis to a U.S. diplomat, he did not discount it and stated that the United States was still watching the Libyans very carefully. The Philippine president's office has disowned this assertion posed by its own intelligence agencies.[88]

Conclusion: Al-Qaida's Lingering Presence in the Philippines

The greatest threat to the Philippines, in terms of international terrorism, does not come from the Abu Sayyaf or the MILF but in the continued presence of independent cells of Al-Qaida operatives who are networking with counterparts throughout the region. That is why there is something woefully disturbing about the U.S. government's obsession with a military defeat of the ASG. Even if the group was eliminated, Al-Qaida will remain active in the Philippines. Philippine intelligence and Department of Defense officials have conveyed the same sentiment. They understand, though, that it is a political decision, and in return for massive amounts of aid from the United States, they have to dance to Washington's tune.

The Philippines remains a "country of convenience" and is attractive to terrorist groups for a myriad of reasons, none of which can be remedied in the near future. And they are not problems that a military alone can address. There are fundamental institution-building needs that can only be addressed over the long term.

Until then, Al-Qaida can be expected to continue to avail themselves of the Philippines. For example, two Palestinians and a Jordanian were arrested in December 2001 in a suburb of Manila. All three were classmates in Kuwait, and all have connections to Mohammed Jamal Khalifa. Mohammed Sabri Selamah, a Palestinian, arrived in the Philippines in 1986 and ran a local branch of Khalifa's IIRO and was thought by Philippine intelligence to be the point man in the southern Philippines for Al-Qaida. Hasan Ali, a Jordanian, came to the Philippines in 1985. Masrie Ahma Abed, a Palestinian, lived with Ramzi Yousef when he first came to the Philippines in 1990. On December 27, 2001, a Jordanian man, Hadi Yousef al-Ghoul, was arrested in his home west of Manila. Police seized 281 sticks of dynamite, three cell phones (thought to be detonators for the explosives), dry cell batteries and wires, and Islamic poems in Arabic, as well as anti-U.S. documents.[89] Al-Ghoul lived in the Philippines for almost two decades, though he had no documentation. He married a Filipina and established a small women's clothing stall. According to a senior police officer, "Al-Ghoul is a member of one of the terrorist cells in the Philippines assigned to carry out a string of bombings in metro Manila." More important, he was seen as a mid-level Al-Qaida money man who provided cash to locally based Jemaah Islamiya operatives to whom he was believed to be financially supporting. Every Thursday, al-Ghoul "withdrew a huge amount of money from a local bank," yet police investigations would not reveal the source of the funding.[90]

No one appreciated the degree to which Al-Qaida's Philippine cells were linked to other regional militant and terrorist groups. When Oplan Bojinka was broken up, Al-Qaida shifted its regional base of operations to Malaysia and began to develop its own regional arm, a complex transnational network, the Jemaah Islamiya, the subject of the following chapter.

Notes

1. Tim Weiner, "American Action Is Held Likely in the Philippines and in Indonesia," *New York Times* (*NYT*), October 10, 2001, A1.

2. Simon Reeve, *The New Jackals: Ramzi Yousef, Osama bin Laden, and the Future of Terrorism* (Boston: Northeastern University Press, 1999).

3. Department of the Interior and Local Government, "Country Report of Republic of the Philippines" (paper presented to the International Conference on Counter Terrorism, Baguio City, Philippines, February 18–32, 1996, 5). Technically speaking the MILF was not formed until 1984, but Salamat Hashim had already split with the MNLF in December 1977, moved his headquarters to Lahore, Pakistan, and led the "New Leadership" wing of the MNLF until the MILF was formally established. For the sake of simplicity, I will refer to the New Leadership faction of the MNLF as the MILF.

4. Ibid., 6.

5. Interview with Hashim Salamat, *Nida'ul Islam* magazine (April–May 1998).

6. The second of Khalifa's four wives is the older sister of bin Laden.

7. Matthew Levitt, "Saudi Financial Counter-Terrorism Measures (Part II): Smokescreen or Substance," Washington Institute for Near East Policy, Policy Watch #687, December 10, 2002.

8. Department of National Defense, *The Philippine Campaign Against Terrorism*, Camp Aguinaldo, Quezon City (2001).

9. Yabo is a convert to Islam hailing from Zamboanga del Sur. Abu Omar was a student in Turkey in the mid-1980s and engaged in radical Islamic activities. He was one of four foreign students banned by the Turkish government for his suspected role in a 1986 bombing. Afterward he attended Mindanao State University, a hotbed of Islamic activism in Marawi, Mindanao. Marawi is adjacent to the MILF "liberated zone" and is a very important MILF trading and smuggling center. He received a master's in public administration in 1988.

10. Philippine National Police (PNP), *After Intelligence Operations Report*, Camp Crame, Quezon City, February 27, 1995.

11. The Philippine National Police intelligence report surprisingly does not mention Malaysia, which may be an oversight. See Ibid., appendix.

12. The IIRO has legitimized itself and grown. It has more than thirty offices, and its activities cover more than seventy-five countries in different parts of the world.

13. Adnan Khalil Basha, "Largest Islamic Relief Organization Maligned," Letter to the Editor, *Philippine Daily Inquirer* (*PDI*), August 18, 2000.

14. Christine Herrera, "Gemma Linked to Bin Laden Group Funding Sayyaf, MILF," *PDI*, August 10, 2000. Based on IIRO documents at the Securities and Exchange Commission, Khalifa was one of five incorporators who signed the documents of registration; another was Khalifa's wife.

15. Mark Lander, "US Advisors May Aid Philippine Anti-Terror Effort," *NYT*, October 11, 2001, B4.

16. Basha, "Largest Islamic Relief Organization Maligned."

17. Christine Herrera, "Bin Laden Funds Abu Sayyaf Through Muslim Relief Group," *PDI*, August 9, 2000.

18. Ibid.

19. Ibid.

20. Ibid.

21. Zubair immigrated to the Philippines in 1985 and married a local convert to Islam, Shedha Enriquez.

22. PNP, *After Intelligence Operations Report.*

23. Khalifa was later extradited to Jordan from the United States to face charges for bombings, but he was acquitted.

24. Interview with a major of the Intelligence Service, Armed Forces of the Philippines (IS-AFP), Camp Aguinaldo, January 24, 2002.

25. Odeh was arrested entering Pakistan on the day of the embassy bombings using a fake Yemeni passport. He quickly confessed his role in the bombings and was handed over to Kenyan authorities and later the Americans. On March 31, 2001, he and Wadih el Hage were found guilty of conspiring to kill Americans for their role in the U.S. Embassy bombings in Kenya and Tanzania. Mamdouh Mahmud Salim, who was also convicted in the bombings, lived in the Philippines between 1996 and 1998 and was believed to have been a cell member of Odeh. Raymond Burgos, "FBI Seeks Philippine Help in Hunting Down Terrorists," *PDI*, September 30, 2001. Also see Department of National Defense, *The Philippine Campaign Against Terrorism.*

26. Carlos H. Conde, "Muslim Cleric Confirms bin Laden Visit to Mindanao," *PDI*, November 13, 2001.

27. Interview with a counterintelligence official, Quezon City, January 16, 2002.

28. Herrera, "Bin Laden Funds Abu Sayyaf Through Muslim Relief Group."

29. Wadih el Hage was a Lebanese Christian convert to Islam, born on July 25, 1960, who later emigrated to the United States. He became bin Laden's secretary while he was based in the Sudan. El Hage was responsible for establishing a network of charities in East Africa to launder and funnel money to Al-Qaida. He and Odeh were convicted on May 31, 2001, for conspiring to kill Americans in the bombing of the two U.S. embassies in Kenya and Tanzania.

30. Interview with a captain of AFP intelligence, Marawi, Philippines, January 11, 2002.

31. The city of Marawi, the major conduit to the MILF base area of Camp Abu Bakar, has been identified as not just a major smuggling route via the MILF base in Butig but a major drug trafficking route into the Philippines. General Fortunato Abat, *The Day We Almost Lost Mindanao: The CEMCOM Story II* (Manila: FCA, 1999), 163–165. See also, interview with a captain of AFP intelligence, Marawi, Philippines, January 11, 2002, and interview with a counterintelligence official, Quezon City, January 16, 2002.

32. The MILF asserts that these acts—such as by the Pentagon Group—are either loose cannons or criminal gangs that the government tries to label as MILF splinter groups for propaganda purposes. Eid Kabalu said that the MILF leadership refuses to get involved anymore in negotiating releases of kidnapped victims, because the government, rather than thanking the MILF, accuses the MILF of having control over the rogue groups. Interview with Eid Kabalu, MILF spokesman, Cotabato, January 9, 2002.

33. Ibid.

34. Ibid.

35. Lira Lalangin, "Bin Laden Seen Recruiting Ex-MILF," *PDI*, October 24, 2001.

36. Interview with Eid Kabalu, MILF spokesman, Cotabato, January 9, 2002. Asked to comment on government reports that foreigners were found in camps that the government had overtaken, Eid Kabalu stated that it was actually a mistake by President Estrada. Estrada, according to Kabalu, was trying to denigrate the MILF and said that its members were "not even Filipinos." This actually pleased the MILF at the time, because it thought that Estrada had actually publicly acknowledged that the Bangsamoro people were their own nation.

37. Raymond Burgos, "FBI Seeks Philippine Help in Hunting Down Terrorists," *PDI*, September 30, 2001.

38. Donald G. McNeil, Jr., "French Hold Suspected Terrorist Tied to bin Laden," *NYT*, June 28, 2000, A4.

39. Luz Baguioro, "JI Militants May Have Links with Separatist Group," *Straits Times* (*ST*), September 18, 2002.

40. Singapore-based fund-raisers and supporters of the MILF under detention include Husin Abdul Aziz, Sakahan Abdul Rahman, Habibullah Hameed, Faizal Khan Gulam Sarwar, and Mohamed Agus Ahmad Selani. The latter two were arrested in December 2001 but released and served with restriction orders. "Jemaah Islamiya Forged Links with Regional Groups," *ST*, September 20, 2001.

41. Interview with Eid Kabalu, MILF spokesman, Cotabato, January 9, 2002.

42. Formally the Special Operations Group is the 303rd Brigade, 3rd Field Division of the MILF.

43. Interview with a counterintelligence official, Quezon City, January 16, 2002. This official stated that the one was a Jordanian, the other a Palestinian.

44. Rigoberto Tiglao, "Southern Discomfort," *Far Eastern Economic Review* (*FEER*), February 19, 1998, 27.

45. Interview with a colonel in PNP Intelligence, Manila, June 27, 2002.

46. Agence France Presse (AFP), "MILF Ignores bin Laden Call for Holy War," *PDI*, October 8, 2001.

47. Janjalani was born on Basilan Island and was encouraged to study Islamic law in Saudi Arabia. He emerged in Afghanistan.

48. Department of the Interior and Local Government, "Country Report of Republic of the Philippines," 6.

49. Reeve, *The New Jackals*, 156.

50. Ibid., 136.

51. Edwin Angeles (Yusuf Ibrahim) fought the Soviets in Afghanistan. Following his return to the Philippines in 1991, he was captured by PNP/AFP forces, and recruited to serve as a double agent for the government. He was released and rejoined the ASG but was soon after killed (most likely by the ASG).

52. Rohan Gunaratna, "The Evolution and Tactics of the Abu Sayyaf Group," *Jane's Intelligence Review* (July 2001).

53. Donald G. McNeil, Jr., "Belgium Seeks Arms Deals with Suspected Qaeda Ties," *NYT*, February 27, 2002.

54. PNP, *After Intelligence Operations Report.*

55. Ibid.

56. Ibid.

57. Interview with a colonel in the PNP-PSG, Makati, January 15, 2002; PNP, *After Intelligence Operations Report*, Camp Crame, Quezon City, Philippines, February 27, 1995.

58. In the Miller interview, bin Laden stated, "As to what you say about him working for me, I have nothing to say."

59. When arrested he was found with seven passports, most bearing the same picture of him, but only the Afghan passport had his real name; the others had aliases. In the Philippines he used the name Osama (Ausama) Asmorai.

60. On December 1, 1994, Wali Khan Amin Shah also tested one of the bombs in the Greenbelt Theater in Manila. No one was killed in the blast, though several people were injured.

61. For detail, see Reeve, *The New Jackals*, 90–91.

62. Murad was a licensed commercial pilot who studied at the Continental Flying School in Pasay City from November 1990 to January 1991; in November 1991 he enrolled in a pilot training school in Dubai and later enrolled at Coastal Aviation in Newburn, North Carolina. There was an alternative plan to fly a small aircraft filled with explosives into the CIA headquarters, rather than a commercial jetliner. Said Akhman, a Ramzi Yousef associate in the Philippines, was thought to be the intended pilot for this operation. Akhman was extradited to the United States from the Philippines. See Raymond C. Burgos et al., "Plots to Use Planes in US Attack Uncovered in RP," *PDI*, September 12, 2001.

63. He said that the resources of the PNP and other intelligence agencies were stretched to the absolute limit; now that the cell had been broken up, his unit was completely inundated with arranging new security arrangements for the pope's visit, which had not been canceled. Interview with a colonel of the PNP-PSG, Makati, January 15, 2002.

64. Ibid.

65. Neil MacFarquhar, "Saudi Dilemma: A Native Son, a Heinous Act," *NYT*, October 5, 2001.

66. "Full Text of Palace Letter to the *New York Times*," *PDI*, October 12, 2001.

67. Interview with a major in the IS-AFP, Camp Aguinaldao, Quezon City, January 24, 2002.

68. Interview with a colonel in the PNP-IS, Malate, June 25, 2002.

69. ISCAG is led by Humoud Mohammad Abdulaziz Al-Lahem and has very close ties to the MILF. Yusop Alongan and Abdul Nasser Nooh established construction companies that received contracts to build mosques for the ISCAG, which passed on money to the MILF. ISCAG also pays for the education of the children of many MILF leaders.

70. These charities were all linked to a cell of militant students and *madrasa* teachers in Luzon, known as the Rajah Solima Movement (RSM) that was broken up in early 2002. Although the group was rather amateurish, it bothers Philippine police and intelligence officials for two reasons. First, the group had clear ties to the MILF and the ASG. As it was based in Luzon, a Christian stronghold, it seems that the Muslim rebels wanted to expand the battlefield to relieve some of the pressure the government was putting on them. The leaders of the RSM received direct support, both money and weapons, from Salamat Hashim. Ahmed Muslim Santos and his two broth-

ers traveled to Abu Bakar in August 1999 to meet with MILF leaders, and in December 2001 Santos underwent military and explosives training at Camp Bushra at Lanao del Sur. The RSM has received funding from the Darul Hijra Foundation, which was founded by several MILF members including Abbas Kansi, Abdul Nasser Nooh (MILF liaison officer in Manila), Khairoden Macarya, Abdulla Akmad, and Bashir Hasan, and is under the unofficial leadership of Yusop Alongan, the MILF Financial Committee chairman. Shaikh Omar Lavilla, another RSM leader, received support from Khaddafy Janjalani, the head of the ASG. Khaddafy promised the RSM P10 million in late 2000. Omar and Janjalani were classmates at Mindanao State University. Second, it had clear ties to Khalifa's financial network. Interview with a PNP-IS official, Makate, June 27, 2002.

71. Interview with General Jose Almonte, Manila, January 23, 2001.

72. Glenn Schloss, "Seeds of Terror in Asia," *South China Morning Post* (*SCMP*), November 1, 2001.

73. Interview with a major in the IS-AFP, Camp Aguinaldo, Quezon City, January 24, 2002.

74. "An Update of the Recent Bombing in Mindanao and Metro Manila," November 25, 2002.

75. "Full Text of Palace Letter to the *New York Times*."

76. "Government Junks Abu Demand to Free Bandit Leader for Americans," *PDI*, October 24, 2001.

77. Deidre Sheehan, "Estrada's Mindanao Troubles Grow Worse," *FEER*, May 11, 2000.

78. Interview with Eid Kabalu, MILF spokesman, Cotabato, January 9, 2002.

79. Cited in Jose Torres, Jr., *Into the Mountain: Hostaged by the Abu Sayyaf* (Quezon City: Claretian Publications, 2001), 41.

80. Gunaratna, "The Evolution and Tactics of the Abu Sayyaf Group."

81. Ibid.

82. McGirk, "Perpetually Perilous," *Time* (Asia), June 15, 2001.

83. Conde, "Muslim Cleric Confirms bin Laden Visit to Mindanao."

84. Interview with Philippine Information Agency journalist, Cotabato, January 9, 2002.

85. "Full Text of Palace Letter to the *New York Times*."

86. "Separatist Rebels Met Arab Pair, Say Former Captives," *SCMP*, October 15, 2001.

87. Torres, *Into the Mountain*, 34.

88. "Palace Disowns Info vs. Libya," *PDI*, April 3, 2002.

89. Hadi Yousef al-Ghoul was arrested by Philippine police in March 1995 for his links to other Al-Qaida operatives arrested in the Bojinka plot. Al-Ghoul was later released for lack of evidence but kept under surveillance. Tonette Orejas, "Cops Nab Jordanian; Al Qaida Links Eyed," *PDI*, December 28, 2001.

90. Al-Ghoul was released from prison after posting bail on January 12, 2002, but within hours he was taken into custody by immigration agents. He claims that he was framed by the police. Investigators believe that there was a link between al-Ghoul and Fathur Rohman al-Ghozi, the former being a pay master for the Jemaah Islamiya network. Tonette Orejas, "Terror Suspect Arrested After Posting Bail," *PDI*, January 13, 2002; Orejas, "Cops Nab Jordanian; Al Qaida Links Eyed"; interview with a major in the IS-AFP, Camp Aguinaldo, Quezon City, January 24, 2002.

CHAPTER 4

Jemaah Islamiya and Al-Qaida's Expanding Network

THE RAMZI YOUSEF CASE WAS ALWAYS PORTRAYED AS A PHILIPPINE PROBLEM, BUT this is a dangerously naive proposition. In 1995 when the Ramzi Yousef cell was broken up and he and his two co-conspirators were arrested, no intelligence or law enforcement agencies questioned why Al-Qaida came to the Philippines and whether the organization was linking up to regional groups. There were only three arrests, and the entire infrastructure was left in place. Al-Qaida suffered a setback, but it simply shifted its area of operations to elsewhere in the region, especially Malaysia.

Southeast Asia was appealing to the Al-Qaida leadership in the first place because of the network of Islamic charities, the spread of poorly regulated Islamic banks, business-friendly environments, and economies that already had records of extensive money laundering. Al-Qaida saw the region, first and foremost, as a back office for its activities (especially to set up front companies, fund-raise, recruit, forge documents, and purchase weapons) and only later became a theater of operations in its own right.

In addition to using Southeast Asia as a back office for its operations, Al-Qaida set out to accomplish three major goals. First, it sought to graft onto or co-opt preexisting radicals, radical movements, and groups. This raises some large and disturbing questions: At what point did parochial radicals, who had otherwise been concerned with a localized political grievance, become internationalists? And at what point did they take their struggle to the next higher level, and how did that process occur?

The second goal was to link these groups into a truly transnational network, the hallmark of Al-Qaida activities. In most instances the existing radical groups focused primarily on their domestic grievances and objectives and tended to have little contact with one another. The introduction of Al-Qaida into the region in the early 1990s changed that completely. Suddenly, networks between once unconnected groups were established, as Al-Qaida understood the benefits in eluding law enforcement when working across borders. When one tries to understand the scope and the complexity of the Al-Qaida network in Southeast Asia—with all of the independent cells and existing groups that are linked to Al-Qaida and Osama bin Laden's lieutenants—it is alarming.

The third goal was for Al-Qaida to establish a regional arm of its own that would be able to become financially independent and technically proficient enough to plan and execute terrorist attacks. The organization became known as Jemaah Islamiya.

The Malaysian Stage

The loss of Al-Qaida operative Mohammed Jamal Khalifa and the Philippines' cell was a blow to Al-Qaida in the region. Yet Al-Qaida was too important to abandon altogether so the focus shifted at first to Malaysia. Malaysia was attractive to Al-Qaida for a number of reasons. Most fundamentally, as Chapter 2 discussed, Malaysian society was becoming increasingly Islamic, and Malaysian foreign policy in the 1990s reflected this. Although ASEAN (the Association of Southeast Asian Nations) remained at the core of the country's foreign policy, Malaysia began to focus more of its diplomatic efforts and concerns on Islamic issues and become a more active member of the Organization of the Islamic Conference.

Second, Malaysia accorded radical groups with a great infrastructure upon which to build their networks. As an Islamic banking and financial center, not to mention one of the world's hottest economies in the 1980s–1990s, it was an unassuming place to establish front companies from the Middle East. Between 1993 and 1996, at least one Al-Qaida front company that we know about was established in Malaysia. Al-Qaida members have testified that the country's Islamic banking network was essential to Osama bin Laden's operations in the 1990s.

Third, there were huge flows of people between the Middle East and Malaysia, and there were no visa requirements for citizens of OIC states. This was obviously very important, but even more so was that, since the 1990s, Malaysia allowed the use of and penetration of their country by international terrorist networks; as long as they did not plot against Malaysia, their presence was tolerated. For example, many Acehnese GAM (Free Aceh Movement) operatives and leaders availed themselves of Malaysia, angering Indonesia. Even with the case of Ramzi Yousef and Wali Khan Amin Shah, both fled to Malaysia because they hoped to rely on an existing Al-Qaida network to protect them and facilitate their further travels. However, when I spoke to Philippine intelligence and police officials, they unanimously conveyed utter frustration with their Malaysian counterparts until after the September 11, 2001, attacks. In another example, in 1998–1999, top aides to two of the most senior Algerian terrorists, Antar Zouabri, a GIA (Algerian Armed Islamic Group) leader, and Hassan Hattab, the head of a GIA faction, both moved to Malaysia. By this point, most intelligence analysts believe that Al-Qaida had already co-opted the GIA network in Europe and Hattab was a known associate of bin Laden.[1]

Most alarming was that starting on January 5, 2000, there was a major meeting of key bin Laden lieutenants, who, for four days, planned both the attack on the USS *Cole* in October 2000 and the September 11 hijackings as well as reviewed the failed millennium bombing attacks. The attendees of the meeting included

- two of the September 11 hijackers, Khalid al-Mindhar and Nawaq al-Hazmi;[2]
- Tawfiq bin Atash (Khallad), who the Federal Bureau of Investigation described as "the intermediary between bin Laden himself and the [USS *Cole*] attack planners" and "a key operative in Osama bin Laden's Terrorist Network";
- Khalid Shaikh Mohammed;
- Ramzi bin al-Shibh, a close associate of September 11 leader Mohammed Atta and named as the missing twentieth hijacker;[3]
- Fahad al-Quso, who was responsible for the U.S. Embassy attacks in East Africa;
- Ahmad Hikmat Shakir, an Iraqi Al-Qaida operative; and
- Riduan Isamuddin, a senior Al-Qaida leader in Southeast Asia and the operational chief of Jemaah Islamiya.

Because Malaysia is a predominantly Muslim country, it is easier for radicals and terrorists to fit in. The FBI described Malaysia in January 2002 as a key springboard state for Al-Qaida operations, including the September 11 attacks on the United States, though it later retracted the statement. Nonetheless, it's very clear that in the mid-1990s, Al-Qaida and other groups looked upon Malaysia as an important back office for operations in the region.

For many years Malaysian authorities publicly downplayed the threat posed by radical Islamists. Much of the reason for this is that Prime Minister Mahathir Mohammed's insecurity about being a Muslim Malay has manifested itself in so many of his government's policies. Whereas he had done so much to create a progressive, modern, and tolerant Muslim state, he saw any talk of Islamic terrorism as an attempt to brand Malaysia (and all Muslims) as extremists—a way for the West to hold Malaysia back. Over time, Mahathir became vulnerable to the adverse sentiment from his own Muslim Malay constituency, which has only compounded the problem.

The community of Islamic radicals that Al-Qaida has grafted onto includes not just Malaysians but also foreigners. In the late 1980s to early

1990s, Malaysia became one of the most important transit points for Southeast Asians traveling to Pakistan and Afghanistan to join the mujahidin. Most of the Indonesian students who went to Afghanistan in the 1980s, according to Abdullah Hehamahuwa, the former head of Indonesia's Muslim Student Association—who himself joined the mujahidin, "were people who were forced to leave their country to Malaysia where they signed up for *jihad* in Afghanistan."[4] These veterans would form the core of the militant network in Southeast Asia. Additionally, Malaysia became a refuge for radical Indonesian Muslims who had fled the Suharto regime.

Home-Grown Militants

Kampulan Mujahidin Malaysia

Malaysia's main opposition party, PAS (the Parti Islam seMalaysia), had many supporters who grew disenchanted with Malaysian politics and the democratic process that they felt would continue to maintain the National Front's monopoly of power. A small number of PAS members began to advocate a violent jihad and established a covert group, the Kampulan Mujahidin Malaysia (KMM). This extremist group within PAS advocates jihad, and it has passed edicts that U.S. soldiers must be killed because they have repeatedly oppressed Islamic countries.[5]

The Kampulan Mujahidin (sometimes called the Malaysian Mujahidin Group) was founded on October 12, 1995, by a veteran of the Afghan Mujahidin, Zainon Ismail.[6] There was not a large number of Malaysians in the mujahidin, but between 1979 and 1989, two groups underwent military training with the mujahidin; most of the trainees were religious students studying in Pakistan who "heard the call" to jihad.[7] Afghanistan was the core of the KMM. Some forty-five members of the group, nearly half of the membership, had either fought against the Soviets or had trained in Al-Qaida camps there in the 1990s.

One of the most important veterans was Nik Adli Nik Aziz, who has led the KMM since 1999. Many believe, however, that this is a politically motivated allegation as Nik Adli Nik Aziz is the son of PAS's spiritual leader, Nik Aziz Nik Mat. Critics charged the government with a politically motivated arrest in order to discredit Nik Aziz and PAS. Yet if the arrest was politically motivated, it was also politically very courageous, especially before September 11, when Prime Minister Mahathir Mohammed looked quite weak and vulnerable in the polls as PAS was surging. The evidence against Nik Adli, however, was strong, and it is interesting that Nik Aziz, himself, has never really come out to defend his son.

Nik Adli fits into a pattern that we see around Southeast Asia. Upon returning to Malaysia in 1996 from Afghanistan, he became an Arabic teacher in the Sekolah Menengah Arab Darul Anuar, a PAS-run school, outside of the PAS stronghold of Kota Baru, Kelantan's capital. The school, which was founded by his father, is a bastion of Malaysian Islamic fundamentalism and Wahhabism. Nik Adli used the school as a base of operations and recruitment. Upon graduation, a majority of the school's 1,400 students will go on to further study in Egypt, Saudi Arabia, Jordan, or Pakistan before returning to become religious teachers and expanding the network.[8]

By 1999, Nik Adli had become committed to waging a violent jihad against the Malaysian state, which he considered to be secular and oppressive. In 1999 he purchased a large cache of weapons in Thailand, including twenty-four pounds of explosives. That same year he studied bomb-making with the Moro Islamic Liberation Front in the southern Philippines. He also began to link up with exiled Indonesian radicals, such as Abu Bakar Ba'asyir, Abdullah Sungkar, Riduan Isamuddin (Hambali), and Mohammed Iqbal Rahman (Abu Jibril) Abdurrahman. The KMM dispatched its members to train in MILF camps as well as fight against Christians in the Maluku Islands in Indonesia starting in 1999.

Al-Ma'unah

The small and shadowy Al-Ma'unah Islamic sect in Malaysia that suddenly emerged in mid-2000 is another example of a home-grown militant group that claimed to be fighting on behalf of suppressed Muslims and to establish a "pure" Islamic state. Mohammed Amin Razali, the sect's leader, was a student of the West Java–based Negara Islam Indonesia, an extreme and cult-like movement that grew out of the Darul Islam movement in the 1950s and 1960s. Amin served in Afghanistan in the 1980s, returning to Malaysia to become a preacher. In July 2000, the group made headlines after it seized more than 100 weapons from two military stockpiles in northern Perak State. Two government officials were killed before the group surrendered after a four-day standoff. On December 27, 2001, nineteen members of the sect were convicted for plotting the violent overthrow of the Malaysian government. Mohammed Amin Razali and three others were sentenced to death. Al-Ma'unah is effectively neutralized and never posed a serious threat. Unlike the KMM, Al-Ma'unah never linked up with a mainstream political group.

The Roots of Jemaah Islamiya

In addition to home-grown militants, Malaysia was also home to a large number of Islamic radicals from Indonesia, including up to 800 Indonesians who fought with the mujahidin in Afghanistan between 1983 and 1989 and then returned to Malaysia, fearing persecution at home from the Suharto regime.[9] These individuals coalesced around a pair of radical clerics who had fled Indonesia, Abdullah Sungkar and Abu Bakar Ba'asyir.

The origins of the Jemaah Islamiya network are found in Indonesia, dating back to the 1960s. In the 1960s, the radical clerics Abdullah Sungkar and Abu Bakar Ba'asyir, both of Yemeni descent, established a pirate radio station that advocated the imposition of *sharia*, which got them into trouble with the Suharto regime.[10] The two considered themselves the ideological heirs of Sekarmadji Maridjan Kartosuwirjo—the founder of the Darul Islam. The two met when they were both leaders of the Geragan Pemuda Islam Indonesia, an Islamic youth movement. In 1972, Abu Bakar Ba'asyir and Abdullah Sungkar established an Islamic boarding school in Solo, Al-Mukmin. The school, which opened with thirty students, grew rapidly, and in 1976 it moved to a four-hectare compound outside of the city; it now has 1,900 students with plans to expand.[11] The school continued to attract more pupils, many of whom went on to study in Egypt's Al-Azhar University or Pakistani or Saudi Arabian *madrasas*.[12] The school taught a hard-line and literal interpretation of Islam based on Salafi Wahhabism and the philosophies of the nineteenth-century Islamic cleric Mohammed Abdu Rahid Rida. The school's alumni reads like a who's who of Southeast Asian terrorism.

On November 19, 1978, Ba'asyir and Sungkar were arrested by the Suharto regime and were sentenced to nine years for violating a 1963 subversion law. A second court upheld the conviction but lessened the sentence to four years; the two were released in 1982. Ba'asyir saw the September 1984 massacre of Muslim protestors by the army in Tanjong Priok as a declaration of war and stepped up his vitriolic attacks of the New Order regime; a series of bombings in 1984–1985 were allegedly encouraged by Ba'asyir. In 1985, the supreme court overturned the appeals court's conviction and reimposed the original nine-year sentence; Ba'asyir and Sungkar immediately fled to Malaysia. Sydney Jones noted that "the government's case against the two men rests far more on the content of statements urging disobedience to secular authority than on any evidence of an underground organization."[13] Government authorities remained suspect. Although the school was allowed to reopen, one of its masters, Abdul Qadir Baraja, was arrested for writing the *Jihad Guide Book* for his students, which urged jihad against all opponents of *sharia* law.[14]

Abu Bakar Ba'asyir and Abdullah Sungkar found a safe haven in Malaysia where they lived and preached openly for several decades and built up a large following of radical Indonesians who had fled the Suharto regime and radical Malays. Their escape and resettlement was arranged by Abdul Wahid Kadungga, a radical Muslim who had fled to Europe in 1971 and formed the Muslim Youth Association of Europe—which put Kadungga into close contact with Muslim leaders from around the world, and especially the Muslim Brotherhood.[15] The preachers lived in a small town on the Malacca Strait, which had ferry service to Indonesia. They served as a way station for Indonesians and Malaysians who were on their way to Afghanistan and Pakistan to study and fight the Soviets or train in one of the forty Al-Qaida camps that were established in the 1990s. Sungkar traveled to Pakistan and the Afghan border region in the early 1990s where he met bin Laden and other senior Al-Qaida members and where he pledged *bayat*, a form of allegiance to bin Laden.

Sungkar and Ba'asyir were revered figures. Their speeches attacking the New Order regime and demanding the implementation of *sharia* won them a large and devoted following. As Sungkar stated in a 1997 interview:

> Suharto, using force, makes it compulsory for the Islamic community to accept Pancasila as the only foundation for the nation, political parties and organizations. . . . His regime still applies the system "detect, defect and destroy" when applied towards the Islamic movement which it distrusts and regards as subversive.[16]

To that end, Sungkar espoused violent jihad to create Dawlah Islamiya (Islamic state). Sungkar contended that the Islamic community had to build up three strengths: Quwwatul Aqidah (faith's strength); Quwwatul Ukhuwwah (brotherhood's strength); and Quwwatul Musallah (military strength).[17] In the process he made explicitly clear that the Islamic community worldwide would be important contributors in the process of building up these three faiths.[18] For Ba'asyir and Sungkar, the world was rigidly divided in two:

> Allah has divided humanity into two segments, namely the followers of Allah and those who follow Satan. The party of God, and the party of Satan. God's group, and Satan's group. And God's group are those who follow Islam, those who are prepared to follow his laws and struggle for the implementation of Sharia, that is [Hisbullah]. Meanwhile what is meant by Satan's group is humanity which opposes Allah's law, humanity which wishes to bring pressure to bear upon Allah's law, and wishes to throw obstacles in the path of the implementation of Allah's law. . . .
>
> Because the character of followers of Satan is always opposing Allah . . . there is no non-believer who allows the development of Islam, who will allow Islam to be free; non-believers must work hard to threaten Islam and the laws thereof. This is the character of non-believers. Non-believers will always expend their wealth to impede the way of God, to impede the law of Islam. Non-believers will expend not insignificant sums to destroy Islam. This is the character of non-believers.[19]

Preaching this vitriolic and literal interpretation of Islam, one that presented Muslims as being under attack, Ba'asyir and Sungkar built up a loyal following of supporters and disciples. One of their disciples was Riduan Isamuddin, known commonly as Hambali, a young Indonesian from West

Java, born in 1966, the second of thirteen children born to a local imam. A devout Muslim, Hambali turned to people like Ba'asyir and Sungkar as his role models. His home in Pamokolan, West Java, was the heartland of the DI movement. Unable to gain entrance into a Malaysian Islamic school, in 1985 he went to Malaysia anyway where he worked as a common laborer. In 1987, he traveled to Afghanistan and became a member of the Kommando Jihad. He was trained in the camp of Abdul Rasul Sayyaf, leader of Ittihad-I-Islami, the Islamic Union for the Liberation of Afghanistan, one of the seven mujahidin forces fighting the Soviets. He was trained in bomb-making and combat, but Hambali's real skills were in organization and management. Hambali became an important figure in the mujahidin's back offices, responsible for bringing in foreign jihadis from Southeast Asia and managing logistics; it was in this capacity that he came into close contact with Osama bin Laden. Unable to return to Indonesia, he moved back to Malaysia, which had no visa requirements for citizens from OIC states. He married Noral Wizah Lee, a Malaysian-Chinese woman from Sabah who converted to Islam, and supported himself through preaching and selling medicine. He worked closely with Sungkar and Ba'asyir, teaching and recruiting young Muslim males.

Ba'asyir and Sungkar also linked up with another radical Indonesian cleric, Mohammed Iqbal Rahman (Abu Jibril). Abu Jibril, the son of a man imprisoned by the Suharto regime for his commitment to establishing an Islamic state, was himself imprisoned in the early 1980s for his radical Islamic activities. Upon his release, he went into self-exile in Malaysia. There he was recruited into the ranks of the mujahidin and fought in Afghanistan. Jibril was not only a capable fighter but a charismatic leader and became a trainer in Afghan camps. He returned to Malaysia and worked closely with Sungkar and Ba'asyir developing the Jemaah Islamiya and became the head of training for Al-Qaida in all of Southeast Asia. Abu Jibril, like Hambali, had lived in the town of Sunggai Manggis since 1993, fifty miles south of Kuala Lumpur, which was home to a large immigrant community from Indonesia.

All four of the individuals were itinerant preachers, unaffiliated with any mosque (whose imams are employees and regulated by the Malaysian government). Instead, they preached jihad in private settings before groups of devoted followers whom they slowly cultivated across Malaysia and also in Singapore. For their efforts, they were paid MR200–300 ($50–80) for a two-hour sermon. They began to espouse the doctrine of *Nusantara Raya*, the establishment of a pan-Islamic republic, incorporating Malaysia, Indonesia, southern Thailand, and the southern Philippines.

Establishing the Network, 1993–2000

Following Sungkar's meeting with Osama bin Laden sometime in 1993–1994, Ba'asyir and Sungkar charged their deputies Hambali and Abu

Jibril with establishing a network of militant cells throughout the region. Ba'asyir and Sungkar were steadfastly committed to their faith, but at some point they were willing to cross the line. In their eyes, doing so was the only way to effect change in Indonesia. Al-Qaida taught the importance of international links and the utility of working across borders for a greater good.

One point that deserves particular attention is that although Jemaah Islamiya was founded in 1993–1994, it did not conduct its first terrorist acts until 2000. The leaders spent those first six or seven years patiently building up their network—recruiting, training, and strengthening technical proficiency. They were not impatient, nor did they try to conduct operations that they were unprepared for or which would put their organization in jeopardy. The leaders thoughtfully put into place a network of supporters and organizations that would sustain the JI over time.

As mentioned previously, Hambali was an associate of Wali Khan Amin Shah and Khalid Shaikh Mohammed. On June 2, 1994, he and Wali Khan established Konsojaya SDN, BHD, a front company that provided logistical services—especially the procurement of bomb-making materials—for Ramzi Yousef's Oplan Bojinka. Hambali was one of eight directors of the firm, along with Wali Khan. Hambali's wife, Noral Wizah Lee, was also on the Konsojaya board of directors. When Wali Khan Amin Shah fled the Philippines in 1995, it was to Hambali that he turned to get him a new identity.[20]

Hambali was the key link between Al-Qaida and Jemaah Islamiya. He was a member of both, and in the late 1990s Hambali became a member of Al-Qaida's Regional Advisory Council (*shura*), one of the only non-Arabs to do so. According to one regional intelligence official, he was "operationally more important than Abu Bakar Ba'asyir."[21] According to Khalid Shaikh Mohammed's interrogation report, by 1996 Hambali was an important member of Al-Qaida's media committee. The committee, which was led by Mohammed, was responsible for publicizing Al-Qaida's exploits; running websites; disseminating propaganda, recruiting videos, and DVDs; and issuing press releases. We must be clear that Jemaah Islamiya is not the same as Al-Qaida but an important regional component of the group. Individual JI members do not pledge *bayat* to Osama bin Laden, though several top JI leaders are concurrently Al-Qaida members. JI was at Al-Qaida's disposal, serving as a back office and assisting Al-Qaida in its operations, and later conducting joint attacks. In the mid-1990s, following the failure of Oplan Bojinka and the dislodgement of a large number of Al-Qaida members from the region, Hambali focused more of his efforts on developing Jemaah Islamiya.

The most important goal of the JI's leaders was recruitment at all levels. Yet membership into Jemaah Islamiya is highly selective, comprising three phases over many years. "We are not a mass organization," said one senior Jemaah Islamiya official. "We want people who will be loyal to the aims of the group."[22] Abdullah Sungkar, Abu Bakar Ba'asyir, Hambali, and Abu

Jibril launched an active recruiting campaign through their sermons in Malaysia and Singapore. "He [Abu Jibril] was a great preacher," Abu Bakar Ba'asyir said in an interview. He could "really inspire people to jihad,"[23] and he built up a large following among Islamic hard-liners. Likewise, Khalid Shaikh Mohammed, who came to Southeast Asia in 1996 on an inspection tour, told his U.S. interrogators that Hambali was "charismatic and popular among his recruits." Many of the adults targeted were from the Indonesian community. Unlike its affiliate, the KMM, which recruited anyone, the Jemaah Islamiya network tended to recruit more middle-class individuals, and even the poorer members were not desperately dispossessed. Mohammed Sobri, for example, was a private in the Malaysian army who began attending sermons by Sungkar, Ba'asyir, Abu Jibril, and Hambali, recruiting more members. "We stopped believing in the democratic process," Sobri said. "So we felt that *jihad* was the only way to change the government."[24]

In Singapore, recruitment focused on lower-middle-class Malaysians and Indonesians, who made up only 15 percent of the republic's population. However, they were educated in state schools, had served in the military, and been socialized into the society, which is what has been so hard for Singapore authorities to grapple with. These were moderately educated individuals with steady jobs and with no apparent leanings to radical Islam. The JI members who were arrested between December 2001 and September 2002 ranged in age from thirty to fifty-four and were seemingly average citizens. They were not seen in the local mosques, instead preferring to congregate together—as the local mosques did not espouse Wahhabism. As a Ministry of Home Affairs spokesman said, "I wouldn't call them a marginalized group. These are people with jobs, with homes and families."[25] They were slowly indoctrinated into the group through a mixture of peer pressure, group thinking, and religious indoctrination.

In addition to the Indonesian migrants and exiles, JI leaders focused on recruiting alienated intellectuals and technical students. The center of their recruitment efforts was among Universiti Tecknologi Malaysia (UTM) lecturers and students. UTM, located across from Singapore in Johor, has traditionally been a hotbed of Islamic radicalism.

Finally, they tried to recruit young people. Hambali, for example, ran Quranic summer camps established to "covertly talent-spot and recruit future JI members from among the participants and their families," according to a regional intelligence agency. In the early 1990s, Abdullah Sungkar purchased a plot of land and established an Islamic boarding school outside of the southern Malaysian city of Johor, near UTM. The Al-Tarbiyah Luqmanul Hakiem School became the center of JI's recruiting efforts. Its master, Ali Ghufron, who took the name Mukhlas, would later become the head of the JI's Malaysian cell and in 2002 the head of operations for the JI.[26] Students of this school included another Indonesian, Abdul Aziz (Imam Samudra), who went on to train in Afghanistan and would become the mastermind behind the October 2002 bombing of a Bali nightclub.

At its peak, the Al-Tarbiyah school had approximately 500 students in the late 1990s. There remained very close ties between the Al-Mukmin and Al-Taribiyah schools, as activists and teachers regularly shuttled between the two. In 1997 Mukhlas stopped teaching at the school, and moved to Lamongan, Indonesia, to concentrate on the development of another Islamic boarding school.

One aspect that is striking about the JI is what a family affair the organization is. When one begins to uncover the network, it is apparent that there are dozens of familial nodes and an Arabic penchant for forming alliances through marriages. Indeed, marriages to locals are how outsiders such as Mohammed Jamal Khalifa and Omar al-Faruq were able to penetrate and gain the acceptance of the local communities so well and quickly. The familial relations tend to transcend generations; many of the JI figures discussed below are the children of Darul Islam leaders. Here are two examples of how these nodes work:

1. Abdullah Sungkar, the founder of JI, is the older brother of Said Sungkar, who was arrested in December 2002 in Solo for his role in the Bali bombing. His son-in-law, Ustadz Yassin (Syawal), became the head of the Laskar Jundullah, a JI paramilitary in 2002.
2. Ali Ghufron (a.k.a. Mukhlas), an Islamic preacher and close affiliate of Ba'asyir and Sungkar, became the master of the Al-Tarbiyah Luqmanul Hakiem School in Johor (where several of the Bali bombers were trained). He was the older brother of Amrozi, who was arrested for his role in the Bali attack, and also of Ali Imron, who set up his own *madrasa* in East Java that was linked to Ba'asyir and Omar al-Faruq. Mukhlas's brother-in-law, Hashin bin Abbas, was arrested in Singapore in January 2002.

The recruitment process occurred in phases. The first phase involved screening individuals, including their family background and knowledge of Islam. Once a student was selected, Hambali enrolled them at *pesentrens* (boarding schools) and *madrasas* for further Islamic studies. Many young radicals were sent to Pakistan and Afghanistan. The third phase of the training/recruitment regimen was physical and military training in either Al-Qaida camps in Afghanistan or in MILF camps in the Philippines.

In addition to recruiting, the JI leaders were engaged in three other activities: establishing a network of cells in each country in the region, training their recruits, and establishing front organizations. Rather than detailing each of these, I will describe the roles of each of the cells, as every JI cell seems to have had a particular responsibility in the pursuance of the organization's overall mission: the creation of a pan-Islamic state in Southeast Asia.

Organizational Structure

Jemaah Islamiya has a formal structure, with Abdullah Sungkar and Abu Bakar Ba'asyir serving as the group's *amirs*, or spiritual leaders. Hambali became the chairman of the five-member Regional Advisory Council. Other members included Abu Jibril, Agus Dwikarna, Abu Hanifah, and Faiz bin Abu Bakar Bafana. Bafana, a Malaysian businessman and former Singaporean, was a key aide to Hambali. He ran Marebina, a large construction firm in Malaysia, and was an important financial backer of the JI. In addition to the five-member Regional Advisory Council were the JI secretaries and Fikri Sugondo, the elementary school master at Ba'asyir's Al-Mukmin *pesentren* and a close personal aide of Abu Bakar Ba'asyir and Zulkifli Marzuki, a senior accountant in charge of JI's front companies. Other top lieutenants include Aris Munadar, Abu Fatih, and Irfan S. Awwas.

Beneath the *shura*, Hambali appointed several lieutenants to establish *mantiqi,* or cells, in their respective countries.

- Mantiqi 1 covered peninsular Malaysia, Singapore, and southern Thailand.
- Mantiqi 2 covered Indonesia.
- Mantiqi 3 covered the Philippines, Brunei, eastern Malaysia, Kalimantan, and Sulawesi, Indonesia.
- Mantiqi 4 was being developed to establish cells in Australia and Papua (Irian Jaya).

Each *mantiqi*, in turn, had several subcells, or *fiah*. The JI has between 500 and 1,000 members—though the former is a more likely estimate—spread throughout the region. The JI cells in each of the four states, Malaysia, Singapore, Indonesia, and the Philippines, were fairly independent from each other and had very specific functions. Each took advantage of a certain aspect of their host state for their operations (Figure 4.1).

The Malaysian Cell

With an estimated 200 members, the Malaysian cell is perhaps the largest cell in the JI. It is led by Abu Hanifah and Faiz bin Abu Bakar Bafana. At least thirteen members were trained in Afghanistan, and many others were trained at MILF camps in Mindanao. The Malaysian JI cell recruited actively among both Indonesian exiles and educated Malays. At least five senior JI members and recruiters were lecturers at UTM. Many of the JI members are well edu-

Figure 4.1 Jemaah Islamiya

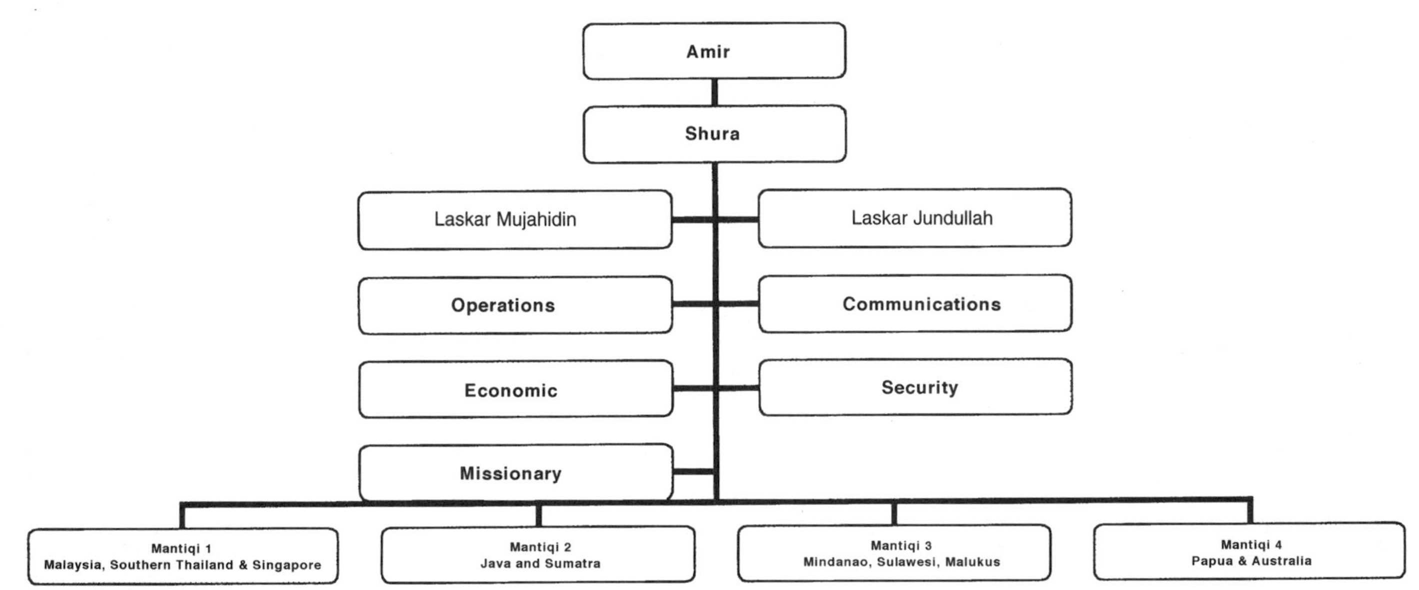

cated, and twelve who were arrested had university degrees—five from institutions in the United States, Great Britain, and Indonesia, the remainder from Malaysian universities.

The Malaysian cell had five discernable functions. First, it worked very closely with the KMM in Malaysia, with whom there is considerable overlap in membership. Abu Jibril was a spiritual leader of the KMM. The KMM sent fighters to Ambon beside JI paramilitaries, and two KMM members were convicted of the August 2001 Atrium Mall bombing in Jakarta: Taufik Abdul Halim and Sahari Bin Mohammad Irsayad, both of whom received training in Pakistan and Afghanistan.

Second, the Malaysian cell was the primary conduit between the JI and Osama bin Laden and Al-Qaida in Afghanistan. The Malaysian cell was the logistical hub for dispatching JI operatives to Afghanistan for training. Hambali secured JI members with visas by getting them "enrolled" in Pakistani *madrasas*. Up to 100 JI operatives from the region were sent to Afghanistan for training in Al-Qaida camps. This cell also ran its own camp in Negri Sembilan, in southern Malaysia, that was used by both the Malaysian cell and the Singapore cell to train new recruits.

Third, the cell was responsible for recruiting and education. Much of the recruiting was done through the Al-Tarbiyah Luqmanul Hakiem School, which also played a central role in JI's overall structure. Funding for the school and most of its bills were paid by a mid-level JI figure, Wan Min Wan Mat, a lecturer at nearby UTM.[27] An important JI treasurer, Wan Min allocated some $33,000 for the Bali nightclub bombing to Mukhlas, the master of Al-Tarbiyah and the organizer of the Bali attack.

Fourth, the Malaysian cell was responsible for establishing several front companies that could be used to channel Al-Qaida funds and procure weapons and bomb-making material. In addition to Konsojaya, other Malaysian front companies run by Al-Qaida have been discovered, including: (1) Green Laboratory Medicine SDN, BHD, established October 6, 1993; (2) Infocus Technology SDN, BHD, established July 13, 1995; and (3) Secure Valley SDN, BHD, established October 4, 1996.

Green Laboratory Medicine, a medical testing facility, was established by JI operative Yazid Sufaat, a former Malaysian army captain and U.S.-trained biochemist. Sufaat, who had studied at California State University in the 1980s, returned to Malaysia in 1987 to become a biochemist. He was reproached by his family for his loss of Islamic values while abroad and began attending prayer sessions when he came into contact with a radical preacher, Hambali. Once Sufaat was recruited into Jemaah Islamiya, Hambali instructed him to establish several front companies. Green Laboratory Medicine was established primarily to purchase large quantities of ammonium nitrate, a chemical fertilizer used in making bombs.[28] By October 2000 he had already procured and transferred four of the twenty-one tons of ammonium nitrate that he was instructed to purchase. Sufaat also established Infocus Technology, a Malaysian Internet firm that was used to get Zaccarias Moussaoui into the United States. The federal indictment against Moussaoui asserts that he received a letter from Infocus Technology in October 2000 that appointed him their marketing consultant for the United States, Europe, and the United Kingdom, and it was signed by Yazid Sufaat. Through this letter, he is thought to have been able to secure a visa to the United States. He was paid a retainer of $2,000 per month.[29] Infocus Technology denied having any contact with Moussaoui, much less hiring him as their marketing consultant, and asserted that the letter was a forgery. Yazid Sufaat told Malaysian investigators that the money was actually never paid. Additionally, it was at Yazid Sufaat's apartment that the key meeting between the eleven bin Laden lieutenants was held in January 2000. In June 2001 Sufaat traveled to Afghanistan where he was trained by Al-Qaida.

There are also cases in which JI members established businesses, received contracts and businesses from JI supporters, and then plowed the proceeds back into the organization. According to the Singapore government's *White Paper*, "All JI-run businesses had to contribute 10% of their total earnings to the group." This money was to be channeled into the JI's special fund for Islamic causes, called Infaq Fisabilillah, or the jihad fund.[30] The Infaq Fisabilillah fund was controlled by the JI chief of operations, Hambali, and used to support the cost of travel and training of members to Al-Qaida camps in Afghanistan and MILF camps, to purchase arms and explosives, and subsidize JI-run *madrasas*.

The Al-Risalah Trading Company of Malaysia is one such example. The Al-Risalah Trading Company was established by the son-in-law of Abdullah Sungkar, Feri Muchlis bin Abdul Halim, with some RM25,000 in start-up capital. Hami, a forty-six-year-old, was an Indonesian with permanent residency in Malaysia. His firm obtained a coveted license that allowed it to contend for government contracts. To that end, it had been awarded contracts to install water pipes in Selangor, to provide stationery for a school, and had just received a contract to build two schools in Selangor. In the first two cases, the person who accepted the tender was a suspected member of Jemaah Islamiya, and both Sungkar and Halim have been detained under the draconian Internal Security Act. Halim was arrested April 17, 2002, for suspected involvement in JI and the KMM.

Another JI firm was uncovered in February 2003, with the arrest of Abdul Manaf Kasmuri, a former Malaysian army colonel, who headed a UN peacekeeping operation in Bosnia in the mid-1990s. Kasmuri led the Bosnian peacekeeping operation with distinction until he became disenchanted with the UN's failure to protect the Bosnian Muslim community, especially after the massacres following the Serb invasions of the six UN-designated "safe havens." Kasmuri began to support the Bosnia army's Seventh and Ninth Battalions, which were comprised of foreign jihadis, many of whom were Al-Qaida members and veterans of the mujahidin in Afghanistan. When he became too close to them, he was forced to take early retirement in 1995. He returned to Bosnia and became involved in aid work, when he was recruited into Al-Qaida. He spent time in Afghanistan, posing as a Filipino. He returned to Malaysia, and though he was wanted by Malaysian police, he became the human resources manager for an Islamic financial institution Koperasi Belia Islam,[31] based in Kuala Lumpur, that has close ties with the Islamic Youth Movement founded by jailed former deputy prime minister Anwar Ibrahim. Kasmuri was also significantly involved in a JI-linked company called Excelsetia, as a shareholder and director.

Excelsetia was a privately owned general trading company that was run out of the offshore haven of Labuan. Two of the other four directors/shareholders were senior JI officials, Zulkifli Marzuki and Faiz bin Abu Bakar Bafana, both of whom are now under detention, one in Malaysia and one in Singapore.[32] Zulkifli Marzuki, an accountant, was the auditor for most of the JI-related companies including those set up by Yazid Sufaat, Infocus Technology and Green Laboratories Medicine.

In addition, there are ongoing investigations of between three to six general trading companies in Bangkok, Thailand, that have been linked to firms on the UN list of designated terrorist-supporting organizations. These include three Middle Eastern general trading companies that have had offices in Thailand since 1997, including Al Jallil Trading Ltr. Co. Ltd., Al Amanah Enterprise Co. Ltd., and Sidco Co. Ltd. These three firms were raided by Thai intelligence officials following joint investigations with U.S. and Israeli intelligence officials.[33] There are also investigations of many Al-Qaida-linked firms in Malaysia. In June 2003, the U.S. Department of the Treasury designated eighteen individuals and nine Malaysian companies as terrorist funders, the first designations in Asia. All of these firms were controlled by JI members and all donated 10 percent of their proceeds into the Infaq Fisabilillah, controlled by Hambali. These firms included Excelsetia, Marebina, Twin Two Trading Co., Gulf Shores, Shafatex Niaga, Min Hwa Envelope, and Mawashi Corporation.

Finally, the Malaysian cell was responsible for establishing a cell in Australia. Abu Bakar Ba'asyir and Abdullah Sungkar made eleven visits to Australia in the 1990s. Other JI members also traveled there and recruited and fund-raised from among the large Indonesian exile community.[34] One, Kusmir Nesirwan Nesirwan, a Sydney taxi driver, was a JI operative in the Malukus.

The Philippine Cell

The Philippine cell was the smallest of all the JI cells, but it was very important in terms of being a major logistics cell for the network responsible for acquiring explosives, guns, and other equipment.

The cell leader was an Indonesian, Fathur Rohman al-Ghozi (Mike). Born on February 17, 1971, in Central Java, al-Ghozi, had studied at Abu Bakar Ba'asyir's *pesentren*, Al-Mukmin, from 1984 to 1990, before going on to study at a Pakistani *madrasa* starting 1990. In Pakistan, he was recruited into Jemaah Islamiya by a Malaysian businessman and a member of the JI *shura*, Faiz bin Abu Bakar Bafana. He was trained by Al-Qaida in Afghanistan in 1993–1994, where he was introduced to several MILF personnel and was dispatched to the Philippines in late 1995 to early 1996 to make contacts and set up a JI cell. Al-Ghozi carefully established the cell, opening bank accounts, networking, and recruiting. He also learned the local language well enough that a Philippine police official said "he could pass himself off completely as a Filipino."

Al-Ghozi was the JI's liaison with the MILF, which was a very important position, as so many members of the JI were trained in MILF camps. In December 1996 al-Ghozi traveled to the MILF headquarters, Camp Abu Bakar, to train both MILF personnel and JI personnel in bomb-making. His key contact was Sulaiman, an MILF cadre with whom he had trained in Afghanistan. Sulaiman was responsible for international operations and covert liaisons for the MILF. Over the next three years, al-Ghozi was in and out of the Philippines. He was sent back to the Philippines in March 1998 for six months, where he conducted another bomb-making course for MILF and JI personnel.[35] He returned to Indonesia, after applying for a Philippine passport in the name of Randy Andam Alib.

Omar al-Faruq, a Kuwaiti in his early thirties, was another important Al-Qaida trainer in the MILF camps in the mid- to late 1990s. After being recruited into Al-Qaida, al-Faruq was trained at the Khyaldan training camp in Afghanistan for three years beginning in 1992. In 1995 he, along with al-Mughira al-Gaza'iri, an Al-Qaida camp commander, was dispatched by Abu Zubaydah to the Philippines.[36] The top JI trainer at the camp was Omar al-Hadrani.

The liaison with the MILF was important for another reason. As discussed in the previous chapter, al-Ghozi and the other JI and Al-Qaida trainers in the MILF camps played a formative role in establishing the MILF's own terrorist arm in 1999–2000, the Special Operations Group. In return, Muklis Yunos, the commander of the Special Operations Group, who trained with al-Ghozi in Afghanistan, put al-Ghozi in touch with Hussain Ramos, a supplier of explosives to the MILF. This was essential, as in the fall of 2000, al-Ghozi was ordered to procure a significant quantity of explosives for JI operations. In one meeting in Kuta Kinbalo, Malaysia, Faiz bin Abu Bakar Bafana ordered him to purchase "five to seven tons of explosives which would be brought to Singapore for use there" and wired him $18,000 for a down payment from a Singapore bank to al-Ghozi's three accounts at the Philippines National Bank.[37] Al-Ghozi withdrew 250,000 pesos ($4,850) from a bank in November 2000 and began purchasing explosives in Cebu; later al-Ghozi admitted to purchasing more than 1,100 kilograms of TNT.[38] To support the MILF, al-Ghozi was recruited to assist and finance Muklis in a series of bombings in metro Manila on December 30, 2000, that killed twenty-two people. In November 2000 he transferred seventy kilograms of explosives to the MILF for use in terrorist attacks, "in retaliation for the 'all-out war'" launched by the Joseph Ejercito Estrada administration against the MILF in 2000.[39]

The importance of training in the MILF camps to the development of the Jemaah Islamiya cannot be overstated. Although most policymakers and journalists emphasize the number of individuals who trained in Al-Qaida camps in Afghanistan, the number is only about fifty individuals from the MILF and nineteen who were arrested in Malaysia and at least eight Singaporeans. To be sure, these individuals were often in leadership positions, but far more individuals trained at two MILF bases in Mindanao, Camp Abu Bakar and Camp Obaida. There they learned bomb-making, weapons training, surveillance, sabotage, communications, and cell formation.

In addition to purchasing explosives, al-Ghozi was responsible for the purchase of light arms and assault rifles that were used by the JI's two paramilitary arms that were engaged in sectarian conflict in Indonesia starting in 1999. The arms were shipped to Poso for Agus Dwikarna's Laskar Jundullah and for Abu Jibril's Laskar Mujahidin Ambon. The Malaysian Coast Guard in mid-2001 intercepted a huge cache of mainly M-16s en route from Zamboanga to Ambon. And when al-Ghozi was arrested in March 2002, he had seventeen M-16s buried in his yard.

The Singapore Cell

The Singapore cell was not large, with perhaps sixty to eighty members. But in 2001, the JI leadership made the decision to attack U.S. and Western targets there. Thus, Singapore became the operational locus of the network, and the Singapore cell was responsible for planning and coordinating the attacks. As Singapore's Internal Security Department put it in the White Paper, each of the *fiah* saw "their role as mainly providing logistical and other support to foreign terrorist elements who would determine when and what to attack." Once the truck bombs were assembled, suicide bombers from the Middle East were to be infiltrated into the city-state to carry out the attacks.

The Singapore cell was headed by Ibrahim bin Maidin, a fifty-one-year-old superintendent of an apartment building. He had no formal religious training but was trained by Ba'asyir, Hambali, Sungkar, and Abu Jibril, who frequently visited Singapore to preach in private sessions. He had trained in Afghanistan in 1993. Maidin recruited almost all the JI members through a religious class that he taught in private residences. Many Singaporeans were also recruited into the JI Malaysia cell through their studies in some of the JI-run *madrasas* including the Al-Tarbiyah Luqmanul Hakiem School in Johor. Maidin was the *amir* of the group, while operations were led by Mas Salamat Kastari.

The Singapore JI cell had five functional units: operations, security, missionary work, fund-raising, and communications. Beneath the operations unit there were three subcells, each tasked with surveilling different targets: Fiah Ayub, Fiah Musa, and Fiah Ismail.

Fiah Ayub was led by Mohammed Khalim Jaffar, a thirty-nine-year-old printer, who met Maidin in 1989–1990 and was trained by Al-Qaida in Afghanistan from September 1999 to April 2000. He was a local JI trainer. Fiah Ayub was developing two separate attacks: (1) a bombing of the Yishun MRT station where a shuttle bus picked up U.S. naval personnel and brought them to the Sembawang wharf and (2) a USS *Cole*–styled suicide attack of a U.S. naval vessel in the narrow channel between Changi and Pulau Tekong. Jaffar also had a listing of more than 200 U.S. firms operating in Singapore and had marked three as potential targets. A videotape (narrated by Hashim bin Abas, an electrical engineer and the cell's treasurer) of the Yishun surveillance was found in the rubble of Mohammed Atef's house in Kabul. The attack on this soft target was planned back in 1997 but never executed.

Fiah Musa was led by Mohammed Ellias, a twenty-nine-year-old manager, and Mohammed Nazir Mohammed, a twenty-seven-year-old ship traffic assistant. This *fiah* was responsible for the bombing of the U.S. Embassy, as well as the British and Australian High Commissions and the Israeli Embassy. Fiah Musa was instructed to procure twenty-one tons of ammonium nitrate and secure warehouse space that could be used to make truck bombs. Ellias and Mohammed were instructed by Fathur Rohman Al-Ghozi in bomb construction. Six Al-Qaida suicide bombers were to arrive from the Middle East to carry out the truck bombings. This *fiah* had also instructed member Andrew Gerard, a thirty-four-year-old aerospace technician at Singapore Technologies, to photograph and find suitable targets at Paya Lebar airbase, which is used by the U.S. Air Force. In addition to Fathur Rohman al-Ghozi, this *fiah* was assisted by a Canadian-Kuwaiti, Mohammed Mansur Jabarah, who surveilled different targets in Singapore in October.[40]

Fiah Ismail was the smallest and newest cell, formed after September 11, and was instructed to identify suitable U.S. commercial targets in Singapore.

One of the most important functions of the Singapore cell was fund-raising. Members of the cell donated 2 percent of their salaries to the JI in the early 1990s and 5 percent by the end of the decade. Singaporean investigators believed that 25 percent of the funds raised were given to the Malaysian JI cell and 25 percent to the Indonesian cell. The transfers were conducted by individuals. The remaining funds were used by the Singaporean *fiah* for equipment, operations, and overseas training. The Singaporean JI cell was also very involved in fund-raising for the MILF. Of the thirty-six people detained in Singapore between December 2001 and August 2002, four were not found to be JI members but active supporters and fund-raisers for the MILF. For example, Husin Abdul Aziz, a fifty-two-year-old Singaporean who had trained at an MILF camp, not only donated $20,000 of his own money to the movement but raised in Singapore an additional $20,000 for the MILF.[41] Another person detained in August 2002, Habibullah Hameed, also raised $40,000 over many years for the MILF.

The Indonesian Cell

The least is known about the Indonesian cell. In the mid-1990s, there appears to have been very little JI activity in the authoritarian state. Yet following the fall of Suharto in May 1998, there was a surge in JI activity as hundreds of radical Indonesians returned to the archipelago. The Indonesian cell would provide the bulk of the membership, and it was in Indonesia that the JI developed its two paramilitary arms: the Laskar Mujahidin and the Laskar Jundullah in 1999 to 2000.

The Indonesia cell is thoroughly connected to Abu Bakar Ba'asyir's overt political organization, the Mujahidin Council of Indonesia (MMI), a large umbrella grouping for approximately 100 small radical and militant groups from across the archipelago. In Indonesia, the JI operated at a much more overt level then JI cells in neighboring states. To that end, the Indonesian cell has emerged as the center of JI operations, taking advantage of the government's unwillingness to crack down on them. This culminated in the October 2002 bombing in Bali, in which 202 people were killed. Many Indonesians who were recruited by and part of the Malaysian JI cell returned to Indonesia after 1998, including Mukhlas and Imam Samudra.

In addition to recruitment and running a network of radical *madrasas*, the Indonesian cell was responsible for running a network of training camps, including seven in Sulawesi and a training camp at the Pesentren Hidyatullah on Balikpapan, Kalimantan, in January 2002. This camp was run by three fundamentalists, Abdul Hadi, Syawal, and Rida. Abdul Hadi was later implicated in a September 2002 grenade attack on U.S. diplomatic facilities in Jakarta, while Syawal, the son-in-law of Abdullah Sungkar, became the head of the Laskar Jundullah in April 2002. The Indonesian cell was also very important in liaising with Al-Qaida linked Islamic charities and became an important conduit for foreign funding.

The Fall of Suharto

The fall of Indonesian president Suharto in May 1998 created a radically changed political environment in the archipelago. The strongman's resignation left a weak democracy in which there was intense political competition between the new president and a parliament that had a newfound and intense sense of empowerment. Strong central government control also broke down as the provinces clamored to redress the historical legacy of overcentralization and demanded more autonomy and revenue sharing.

Suharto's fall had another important impact: Hundreds of radical Muslim exiles returned to Indonesia and demanded political space. They were encouraged by statements of political leaders that it was no longer tenable that the position and aspirations of all people and interests could be ignored.

The most important exiles who returned at this time were Abdullah Sungkar and Abu Bakar Ba'asyir, who set up their operations at their Al-Mukmin *pesentren* in Solo. Abu Jibril and Hambali were left in charge of developing the JI network in Malaysia. Sungkar and Ba'asyir threw themselves into the new political environment, feverishly working to build up a constituency of individuals committed to turning the post–New Order government into a true Islamic state. Although Sungkar died in 1999, soon after his return, Ba'asyir entered into the realm of politics and tried to make order of the groups and parties that had proliferated since 1998.

The most important of the groups was the Darul Islam movement that had somehow survived underground during the Suharto era. Although it is technically an illegal organization, many of its members operate quite openly, similar to the Muslim Brotherhood in Anwar Sadat's Egypt. Although they are officially banned, many members run for parliamentary seats on the tickets of other parties, and most of the electorate is aware of their Brotherhood membership. Darul Islam is not a unified force, however, and there are some fourteen factions. Their leadership structure and coordination is not known. I see them as a disparate group, with no central leadership, each of the factions believing that it alone is the sole heir to the legacy of the DI movement of the 1950s–1960s.

Other groups that have a degree of popular support or notoriety include the Islamic Youth Movement, the Defenders of Islam, Indonesian Committee for Solidarity of the Islamic World, the Anti-Zionist Movement, the Indonesian Muslim Students Action Front, Negara Islam Indonesia,[42] and the Muhammadiyah Students Association. The Defenders of Islam, formed in 1998 and led by Habib Rizaq, is now the largest radical Muslim group in the country and was able to organize demonstrations of over 10,000 people in Jakarta in October 2001.

In mid-2000, Ba'asyir established the Mujahidin Council of Indonesia. The group ostensibly is a civil society organization that tries to implement *sharia* peacefully and through the democratic process. It is an overt organization headquartered in Yogyakarta that serves as an umbrella organization and coordinating body for many militant and hard-line Islamic organizations and groups who are committed to the establishment of an Islamic state. As Ba'asyir put it,

> The MMI is an institution where a lot of people from a lot of Muslim groups including the NU [Nahdlatul Ulama] and Muhammadiyah gather at one table to discuss how to get our vision of *sharia* implemented into national laws. . . . The long-term strategy is to get Indonesia 100 percent based on *sharia*. As long as Muslims are the majority, the country should be ruled by *sharia*.[43]

Another member of the MMI put it this way: "I think that the MMI is no less, no more, an NGO whose goal is the empowerment of those who have experienced oppression." I believe that Ba'asyir considers himself as the ideological heir of Sekarmaji Marijan Kartoswiryo, the founder of Darul Islam, and that the MMI is the organizational heir of the movement. Although he would not come out and say this, as Darul Islam is still an illegal organization, Ba'asyir clearly respects Sekarmaji and believes that he has a personal and religious responsibility to continue the work of the Darul Islam.[44]

Ba'asyir completely denied any militant or subversive role of the MMI, saying that such assertions came from conspiracy-minded and anti-Muslim foreign governments. He likewise denied the existence of the JI, saying it is the creation of Malaysian and Singaporean intelligence. To be sure, until the October 12 Bali attack, Indonesian police intelligence officials acknowledged JI's presence elsewhere in the region but denied its existence in Indonesia or any links to the MMI.[45]

Yet there is substantial evidence that the MMI is a front for Abu Bakar Ba'asyir's militant and terrorist activities. The MMI is clearly part of a regional Jemaah Islamiya network. One only has to look at the MMI's leadership to see that it is simply a who's who of Southeast Asian terrorism. For example, the MMI's board includes Abu Jibril and Agus Dwikarna; both headed JI's two paramilitary arms and both were members of the JI *shura*. The head of the Fatwah Council is Abdul Qadir Baraja. The MMI's director of daily operations is Irfan Suryahardy Awwas, the younger brother of Abu Jibril, who was arrested in 1983 for his role as a leading Muslim student activist and sentenced in February 1986 to thirteen years on subversion charges, though released in 1993. Irfan S. Awwas is also the chairman of Hiddyatullah Press and Wihdah Press, two MMI-owned publishing houses that produce radical Islamic texts and anti-U.S. and -Zionist tracts. Beneath Ba'asyir, the group's *amir*, is Fikri Sugundo, the JI secretary, a close personnel lieutenant, and a master of the elementary school of the Al-Mukmin *pesentren*.

The MMI held its first and only congress in 2000 and currently has branches in thirty cities throughout Indonesia. The MMI does not keep membership lists and thus it is impossible to accurately guess the size of its membership (Figure 4.2).

The MMI also serves as an important financial conduit, especially getting foreign money to the very small radical groups, which otherwise would be unable to network abroad. Much of Al-Qaida's funding is thought to come

Figure 4.2 MMI Organization Structure

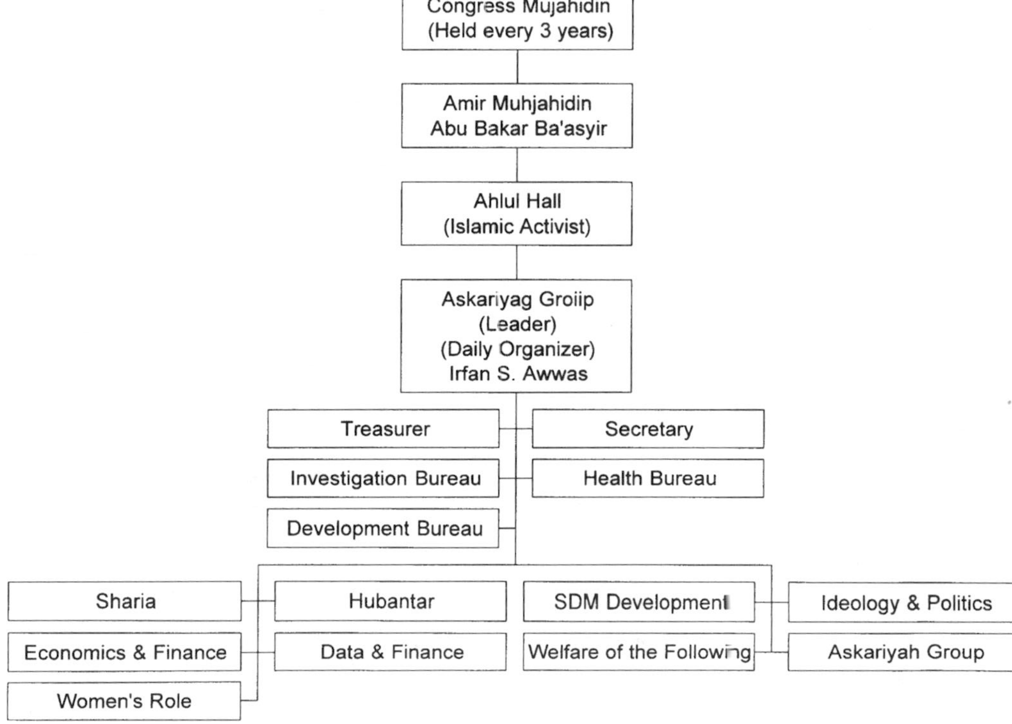

from charities, either unwittingly or intentionally siphoned off. This is possible because Al-Qaida inserted top operatives in Southeast Asia into leadership positions in several charities. Indonesian intelligence officials estimated that 15 to 20 percent of Islamic charity funds are diverted to politically motivated groups and terrorists. JI and Al-Qaida leaders assumed leadership positions, often becoming regional branch chiefs, or formed alliances with several important Saudi-backed charities, including the Medical Emergency Relief Charity (MER-C), the Islamic International Relief Organization, and Al-Haramain, as well as an Indonesian charity that served as their counterpart or executing agency, KOMPAK. The leadership of these charities in Indonesia is overlapping. For example, Agus Dwikarna, the fourth in command of the MMI, was the local representative of the Saudi charity Al-Haramain in Makassar in South Sulawesi. One Al-Qaida official admitted that Agus Dwikarna was the largest single source of Al-Qaida funds into Indonesia and also a branch officer of KOMPAK.[46]

Finally, the MMI is an important recruitment channel for the JI: Fathur Rohman al-Ghozi and three of those arrested in Malaysia were Indonesian members of the MMI. The MMI runs a number of Islamic boarding schools throughout the archipelago, which are important recruiting mechanisms. Other MMI *pesentren* include Pesentren Hidayatullah in Balikpapan, Kalimantan, and Pesentren Darul Aman, in Gombara, Ujung Pandang.

Al-Qaida looked upon the new political environment in Indonesia with great interest. and was heartened by the lack of political will to challenge the increasingly active and vociferous radicals. Like Malaysia, the Indonesian government repeatedly denied that international terrorist groups such as Al-Qaida operated in their country. Although evidence kept surfacing that Indonesia had become an important Al-Qaida base of operations and source or recruits, it was not until the terrorist attack in Bali did the government start to admit that there was an Al-Qaida presence in the region. Both the United States and neighboring states were frustrated with Jakarta's intransigence and unwillingness to arrest suspected militants or even freeze their assets.

Al-Qaida has taken advantage of the political instability and has looked upon Indonesia as a new frontier. In June 2000, two top bin Laden lieutenants, Ayman al-Zawahiri and the late Mohammed Atef, were dispatched to Indonesia and traveled to the secessionist state of Aceh and the strife-torn Maluku islands.[47] According to a leaked Indonesian intelligence report, "Both of them were impressed by the lack of security, the support and extent of the Muslim population" and clearly saw Indonesia as an important new base of operations. The intelligence report concluded that "this visit was part of a wider strategy of shifting the base of Osama bin Laden's terrorist operations from the subcontinent to Southeast Asia."[48]

There was considerable skepticism that Al-Qaida was penetrating the archipelago. Harold Crouch argued that the concern over Al-Qaida's penetration in Indonesia was overstated. While he acknowledged that many of the radical groups in Indonesia probably had received money from Al-Qaida, he did not believe that the money "decisively influenced their behavior." He qualified this even more by stating that "it is hard to believe that Indonesian radical Islamic organizations needed such outside assistance."[49] Likewise, Sydney Jones of the International Crisis Group contended that the Jemaah Islamiya leader Abu Bakar Ba'asyir was simply a former political prisoner with little evidence to support the assertion that he was a terrorist.[50] These viewpoints reflected the general consensus but proved to be woefully inaccurate in the wake of the Bali attack.

The emergence, or reemergence, of these groups is significant for another reason: They began to receive support from outside forces, committed to supporting an Islamic state in Indonesia. Darul Islam factions have admitted to having ties to Al-Qaida for some time, including "military collaboration." These links were formed in the 1980s, when Darul Islam members volunteered to fight in Afghanistan. Al-Chaidar, one of the faction heads, has admitted to receiving RP1.2 billion ($243,000) from Al-Qaida: "Yes, we've gotten funding and assistance from the bin Laden group since we went helping Afghanistan in the 1980s."[51] "The relationship between Darul Islam and Osama bin Laden is just undeniable," he continued, though qualifying his statement that only some factions had a "special relationship."

Jihad in the Malukus

The sudden collapse of the Suharto regime led to a change in strategy for the JI. Clearly, much of the JI leadership moved back to Indonesia where they engaged in politics, networking, and recruiting. But the real turning point in the JI's operations came in 1999 with the outbreak of sectarian conflict in the Malukus. If we closely analyze where the JI was focusing its efforts, it was not in terrorism. In the late 1990s, Hambali and Abu Jibril were fund-raising furiously and putting together the JI's paramilitary arms, the Laskar Mujahidin and the Laskar Jundullah.

It cannot be emphasized enough what an important event the jihad in the Malukus and Poso was to the JI. The influx of some jihadis escalated the conflict to a new level. More important, the jihads in the Malukus and Poso were a formative experience for the participants—every bit as important as the jihad against the Soviets was in the 1980s, albeit to a smaller number of people. The Maluku conflict gave the members of the Laskar Jundullah, Laskar Mujahidin, and the Laskar Jihad their taste of jihad. It whetted their appetites for more. Thousands of people were members of these groups and have now returned home, much the way the members of the G272 returned to Indonesia from Afghanistan in the late 1980s to early 1990s, ready to lead their own jihads to implement *sharia*.

The conflict was manipulated and used by Al-Qaida to a much greater degree than anyone imagined at the time. There is a reason for this: Afghanistan provided Al-Qaida with its inspiration, the first generation of Al-Qaida members, and symbolism. For the organization to rejuvenate itself, it was necessary to wage Afghan-like jihads around the world, to come to the defense of Muslims pitted against aggressive secular states. Thus, Al-Qaida ruthlessly manipulated conflicts in Chechnya, Bosnia, and Indonesia, as well as many other spots. Al-Qaida dispatched fighters, trainers, and material assistance. In return they were able to recruit, gain the support of new groups in new regions, and use the jihads as an effective propaganda tool for fund-raising and recruitment. While all of these conflicts had indigenous roots and causes, Al-Qaida certainly got involved, to a degree that was not appreciated by scholars, journalists, and intelligence officials. Al-Qaida's role in these conflicts needs to be reevaluated.

The Laskar Mujahidin was established in 1999 by Abu Jibril, who recruited among Indonesian exiles living in Malaysia who were inspired to return home to fight a holy war. According to Abu Bakar Ba'asyir, Abu Jibril "could really motivate people to *jihad*."[52] Ba'asyir noted that Abu Jibril was primarily involved in fund-raising for the jihad in the Malukus, though he sometimes went there himself. "He gave them spirit to fight for their right to defend themselves." Jibril first traveled to the Malukus in January 2000, leading several hundred jihadis, and "introduced a centralized command structure" and led attacks on Christian communities by high-speed boats. In one massacre, on July 19, 2000, 250 Christians in the town of Galela were killed.[53]

Although there were only some 500 Laskar Mujahidin fighters in the Malukus, they were far better armed and disciplined than the largest group, the Laskar Jihad, until they raided a police armory. The Laskar Mujahidin was equipped with not only high-speed boats but automatic weapons. The group had close links with the JI cell in the Philippines that had supplied them with small arms and automatic weapons. Abu Jibril's forces also liaised closely with Al-Qaida operatives who were funding and filming the Malukus crisis for propaganda and recruiting purposes.

The second JI paramilitary group, the Laskar Jundullah, a small militant organization that conducted sweeps of foreigners in Solo and was at the forefront of sectarian conflict in Poso, Sulawesi, was founded by M. Kolono and Agus Dwikarna in October 2000. It was the armed wing of Dwikarna's civil society organization, the Committee for Upholding Islamic Law in South Sulawesi, that was committed to implementing *sharia*.[54] Dwikarna stated that the Laskar Jundullah was for the group's "internal security" only.[55] Laskar Jundullah was funded by Al-Qaida through Omar al-Faruq and funds skimmed from the Saudi Al-Haramain Foundation, which Dwikarna headed. It also received funding from the charity KOMPAK, a branch office of which

Dwikarna also headed. KOMPAK, the largest Islamic charity in Indonesia, was established in 1999 due to the "humanitarian crisis" in the Malukus.[56] Dwikarna was also the regional head of KOMPAK's founding organization, Dewan Dakwah Islamiah Indonesia, and the number four official in Abu Bakar Ba'asyir's MMI. Al-Faruq also worked closely with Ahmed al-Moudi, the head of the Al-Haramain Foundation office in Jakarta. Al-Haramain, as well as the IIRO, worked closely with KOMPAK. Following Dwikarna's arrest in the Philippines in early 2002, the Laskar Jundullah was taken over by Abdullah Sungkar's son-in-law, Ustadz Yassin Syawal, who had been trained in Afghanistan in the late 1980s or early 1990s.

Chapter 2 detailed the January 2000 founding and the activities of the Laskar Jihad in the Malukus. The group's hard-line Muslim leader, Jafar Umar Thalib, raised a paramilitary group that was much larger than Jibril's Laskar Mujahidin forces. In all, the Laskar Jihad fielded some 3,000 individuals, including locals. For the most part they were poorly armed and disciplined. Yet the influx of the Laskar Jihad paramilitary tipped the balance in favor of the Muslims,[57] and shortly thereafter Christians were ethnically cleansed from Ternate, the North Maluku capital. In all, an estimated 9,000 people died in the Maluku strife.

With the ongoing debate over whether the Laskar Jihad is linked to Osama bin Laden's Al-Qaida organization, it is important to raise a few points. The first is that Abu Jibril did not coordinate his activities with Jafar Umar Thalib and that there were often conflicts and street fighting between the two groups over control of turf. Although conflicts broke out on the ground, Thalib has coordinated his operations in Indonesia with Abu Bakar Ba'asyir. Indeed, the Laskar Jihad attends and is a member of Ba'asyir's umbrella organization, the Mujahidin Council of Indonesia.

The second point to be raised about the Laskar Jihad is that its links to Al-Qaida are unclear. Despite vehement assertions by Thalib that Laskar Jihad does not have ties with Al-Qaida or any other organization associated with Osama bin Laden's network, and that "Laskar Jihad distances itself from Osama bin Laden and his followers,"[58] there is little evidence that there are not ties. Thalib, who met bin Laden in 1987, says that the Saudi offered funding for Laskar Jihad but that Thalib turned it down, though the Laskar Mujahidin did not.[59] Thalib explains that he questioned bin Laden's piety and asserted that bin Laden is "very empty about the knowledge of religion."[60] Yet they share the same worldview, the same sense of Muslim persecution, and the same goals of establishing an Islamic state. Rather than being a part of the Al-Qaida organization, Thalib simply ascribes to its ideology and worldview.

These holy wars gave the JI the network what they needed, a core of members and supporters. It gave them a taste of jihad, and the fact that the government did not curtail their activities served to embolden them.

Al-Qaida Comes to Indonesia

Al-Qaida's role in the conflicts in the Malukus and Sulawesi was significant. For one thing, Al-Qaida provided significant funding for the paramilitaries. According to the Darul Islam's Al-Chaidar, Indonesian militant radicals "maintain contact with the international Mujiheddin network, including Osama bin Laden's group. . . . Wherever a *jihad* is in force, this network provides money and weapons and all tools needed for the *jihad*, and they mobilize fighters to go to the *jihad* area," Al-Chaidar said. "This is exactly what is happening in the Malukus. Osama bin Laden is one of those who have sent money and weapons to *jihad* fighters in the Malukus."

Additionally, the Maluku conflict served to attract radical Islamicists from around the Muslim world. For example, seven Afghans arrived in Ambon on July 7, 2000, and were spirited away by Laskar Mujahidin forces. They joined some 200 other Afghan, Pakistani, and Malays. Abu Abdul Aziz and one other bin Laden lieutenant were dispatched to Ambon in the height of the crisis, and Mohammed Atef visited the Malukus in June 2000.

The Maluku crisis convinced Al-Qaida's leaders that the emphasis of their jihad in Southeast Asia should be shifted to Indonesia. To that end, there was a flow of top Al-Qaida operatives in the region between 1999 and 2001. They trained, funded, armed JI militants, and established the financial infrastructure to make these groups sustaining. The most important operatives were Omar al-Faruq, Seyam Reda, and Parlindigan Siregar, whose stories and roles were complex and overlapping.

Mahmoud bin Ahmad Assegaf (Omar al-Faruq), a Kuwaiti, was recruited into Al-Qaida in the early 1990s and trained in Afghanistan between 1992 and 1995. In 1995, he was sent by Abu Zubaydah to the Philippines, where he conducted bomb-making courses for both MILF and JI operatives.[61] He also served as a liaison to the Abu Sayyaf Group. Sometime in 1998–1999, al-Faruq was dispatched to Indonesia to take advantage of the power vacuum and breakdown of central government authority to establish Al-Qaida cells. By this time, he was one of Al-Qaida's most senior-ranking officials in Indonesia. Labeled an Al-Qaida "financier," he ran a small Islamic charity office in Jakarta where he was an active fund-raiser.

Al-Faruq became a close associate of a senior Indonesian JI operative and MMI leader, Agus Dwikarna, whom he lived near in Makassar (Ujung Pandang) in South Sulawesi, but his real entree into the radical community came through marriage. Al-Faruq married a local woman, Mira Augustina, the twenty-four-year-old daughter of a Jemaah Islamiya operative named Haris Fadillah (Abu Dazar). Haris Fadillah, a veteran of the Afghan Mujiheddin, was the head of Abu Jibril's Laskar Mujahidin forces. He was killed in the Malukus on October 26, 2000.

Al-Faruq and Dwikarna served as the guides and escorts for Mohammed Atef and perhaps Ayman al-Zawahiri, the third and second in command, respectively, of Al-Qaida, when they visited Indonesia in June 2000. They were escorted to Aceh and then the Malukus, searching for new locations to establish terrorist training facilities.

In addition to supplying financial support to the group, al-Faruq networked furiously in 2000–2002 with militant leaders around the archipelago. In late 2001 to early 2002 he established a number of small training camps, including one in Kalimantan and a number in Sulawesi that were used by MMI and JI recruits.[62]

One of the camps in Sulawesi ties in another important Al-Qaida operative, Parlidigan Siregar, whose story came to light half a world away when Spanish police broke up a major Al-Qaida cell. Imad Eddin Barakat Yarkas, a.k.a. Abu Dada, a Syrian and the ringleader of a large Al-Qaida cell in Spain and one of Osama bin Laden's top lieutenants in Europe, had made several trips to Indonesia and Malaysia, as well as the United Kingdom, Turkey, and Afghanistan. According to Spanish court documents, in Malaysia and Indonesia, Yarkas operated openly, with the support of the governments, as he sought to recruit fighters for the wars in Bosnia and Chechnya. He was connected to the ringleader of the September 11 attacks on the United States, Mohammed Atta, and hijacker Ramzi bin al-Shibh.[63]

The investigation led to the arrest of Louis Jose Galan Gonzalez, a Spanish convert to Islam, who had received his training in Indonesia in July 2001. Further investigation and wiretaps used by Spanish police revealed that Yarkas and Indonesian Al-Qaida operative Parlindungan Siregar, an aeronautical engineer who lived in Spain, had established a terrorist training camp in central Sulawesi, unbeknownst to Indonesian authorities. According to a European intelligence official, Dada was a key recruiter. He did with Siregar what he did with Mohammed Atta and others: "He spotted a Muslim boy, away from home, a student in a technical branch and recruited him."[64] Siregar probably spent a year in Afghanistan where he was trained and eventually became an instructor. According to a European intelligence official, Siregar also spent time in Italy where he worked with an Italian Al-Qaida cell in Milan. He was sent to Poso on Dada's orders.

Siregar, who was said to be the right-hand man of Yarkas, was already under twenty-four-hour surveillance by Indonesian intelligence since returning from Spain in late 2000, though police intelligence officials claim to have lost track of him as soon as Yarkas was arrested.[65] The camp was run by Omar Bandon, an Indonesian who fought in Afghanistan against the Soviets. It is unknown how many people were actually trained in the camp, located ten miles outside of Poso, which was established to bring in Al-Qaida operatives from the Middle East to train JI recruits—all the more important after the

MILF lost their main base, Camp Abu Bakar, in fighting in 2001. Some have questioned why the Poso camp would have been under Dada's control, as he was a top Al-Qaida official in Europe. However, it reinforces our understanding of the autonomous cell-like nature of Al-Qaida. There can be many autonomous Al-Qaida cells working side by side.

Both Siregar and al-Faruq were seen in video footage taken by Al-Qaida in training camps, in which another Al-Qaida operative was seen turning over new weapons and leading the group in prayer. That footage was in the possession of a third Al-Qaida operative in Indonesia, Reda Seyam. Reda, a German of Egyptian descent, was arrested in Indonesia on September 17, 2002. He was one of six people who al-Faruq named in his interrogation, though through the alias Abu Daud. Reda came to Indonesia in August or September 2001 after a several years' stint in Bosnia using a false German passport with the name Hans Walter Kreis. In Bosnia, he directed a branch of the German charity Menschen Helfen Menschen (People Helping People) and fought with other foreign jihadis in the Ninth Battalion against the Serbs. He received two awards from the Bosnian president for his valor and charitable works. In Bosnia, he also established an office of the Saudi firm Twaik. Before Bosnia, Reda was described as an ordinary guy who was well integrated into German society. He drank, married a German woman, had a regular job. He was recruited into Al-Qaida by a mujahidin and became increasingly radicalized.

In Bosnia, Reda was involved in "documentary" film productions—graphic videos of Muslims being massacred or of Muslims bravely fighting back Serb aggression, as well as a host of other dubious business ventures. Reda used these videos to fund-raise back in Saudi Arabia and solicit Gulf funding for his charity in Bosnia. Reda was also known to have been in contact with Ramzi bin al-Shibh in Bosnia.

Before coming to Indonesia, Reda briefly lived in Saudi Arabia, where a significant amount of intelligence suggests that he hosted several very important Al-Qaida meetings. He traveled to Qatar where he applied to be a cameraman for the Al-Jezeera TV network but was rejected. In Indonesia, Reda again applied to be a correspondent for the Al-Jezeera TV network, though he was not hired there either. It would have been perfect cover for the trained cameraman and video editor. Reda lived in a comfortable South Jakarta house, which he leased for two years. He had no visible signs of income, though he had founded a charity, Yayasan Aman (Peace Foundation). He had traveled on several occasions to MILF-held territory in the southern Philippines. Reda was engaged in similar work in Indonesia as he was in Bosnia. When he was arrested, police cataloged an entire house full of video-making equipment, editing machines, video cameras, and a sophisticated laptop computer. Reda produced propaganda videos of the jihads in the Malukus and Poso, which were marketed under the name of both Agus Dwikarna's Committee to

Uphold the Implementation of Sharia Law in South Sulawesi and the Indonesian charity KOMPAK. Eighteen tapes were found in his home, of which three were already edited and produced works. The documentaries' focus was on two Jemaah Islamiya paramilitaries, Abu Jibril's Laskar Mujahidin and Agus Dwikarna's Laskar Jundullah. Several of the videos were produced by Aris Munandar, a senior JI operative and senior aide of Abu Bakar Ba'asyir. Featured in several of the documentaries was Omar al-Faruq. Reda acknowledged his relationship with al-Faruq but stated that his time with Faruq was limited. Reda was also linked to another senior Al-Qaida operative in the region, Rashid. Also seen in the videos were Al-Qaida member Parlindigan Siregar and several other senior Al-Qaida operatives from Bosnia, including a Middle Easterner known to be his best friend and one of the only people allowed in his editing studio. One witness has testified that it was Reda's voice heard on one of the videos produced for KOMPAK. Likewise, upon being shown the video, the witness instantly recognized his camera work, asserting that his Bosnian films were shot in the same manner. German investigators have compared film footage on his laptop with other videos produced. Reda is also believed to have edited and produced a video put out by KOMPAK of Fadillah Haris's funeral, a polished and moving film. Haris, the father of Mira Augustina, Omar al-Faruq's wife, was killed in the Malukus on October 26, 2000. Haris was the commander of Abu Jibril's Laskar Mujahidin forces in the Malukus and a senior JI leader.

German and Indonesian intelligence officials suspect that Reda was also the head of finances for Al-Qaida in Southeast Asia, and there is some evidence that he transferred roughly $74,000 in cash from Osama bin Laden to Omar al-Faruq. In addition to his links with Al-Haramain and KOMPAK, he was linked to another charity, the Komite Zakat Infaq Dan Shadaqah ISNET, which solicited funds from Indonesians living abroad for use in the Malukus and Poso. Although there was considerable incriminating evidence in his apartment and computer (including photos of potential targets), much of it was circumstantial. Reda revealed nothing in his interrogations to Indonesian or German investigators. Terrorism charges were dropped; he was tried on an immigration charge and sentenced to ten months in January 2003 for working as a cameraman on a tourist visa. German investigators remain suspicions and intend to prosecute Reda when he is released and deported from Indonesia. U.S. intelligence officials have taken possession of two of his computer hard drives. The U.S. government tried to arrange his rendition in November 2002, but there was a political backlash against the Indonesian government for rendering Omar al-Faruq and Hafiz Mohammed Saad Iqbal.

Despite evidence of substantial Al-Qaida activity within its borders, the Indonesian government was divided over what to do. While the police denied Al-Qaida's presence in Indonesia, A. M. Hendropriyono, the head of the State

Intelligence Agency (BIN) has tried to force the government's hand in declaring a war on terrorism. For example, despite Spanish evidence of a training camp, the Indonesian authorities did little to investigate or cease its operations until communal violence broke out in mid-December in the central Sulawesi town of Poso. Muslim paramilitaries, armed with machine guns and rocket-propelled grenades, forced thousands of Christians to flee.[66] Among those seen fighting were foreign and Arab troops from the Poso terrorist camp. Although the press failed to report it, the elite Kopassus forces, under the command of General Hendropriyono's son-in-law, attacked the camps. Six foreigners (two Afghans, two Pakistanis, and two Arabs) were detained. The six were thought to be Al-Qaida operatives who conducted training of Laskar Jundullah and other Al-Qaida operatives in the Poso camp. The police initially refuted the report, calling the six men "tourists."[67] Hendropriyono acknowledged that it was not just a Laskar Jihad or Laskar Jundullah base: "The training site was not used by Indonesians, but by foreigners . . . while those who are involved in the conflict in Poso are Indonesians against fellow Indonesians, Muslims against Christians."[68] Hendropriyono stated that "Poso has been used by international terrorist groups to support activities they plan from outside the country." A BIN report, *Al Qaida's Infrastructure in Indonesia*, stated clearly that:

> The training camp led by Omar Bandon consisted of 8–10 small villages located side by side on the beach, equipped with light weapons, explosives, and firing range. Participants of the training are not only from local people but also from overseas. The instructor of physical training in the camp is Parlindungan Siregar, a member of Al Qaida's network in Spain.[69]

Other officials were more cautious. Bambang Susilo Yudhono, the coordinating minister for political and security affairs, stated, "We will not conclude straight away that we have found a terrorist camp," and "currently we have yet to determine which organization had used the site and for what."[70] The national police chief, Da'i Bachtiar, said that authorities were still investigating Al-Qaida's role in the Poso fighting. Later, under intense political pressure, Hendropriyono retracted his statement.

Evolving into a Terrorist Organization: The JI from 2000 to 2001

Such equivocation by the Indonesian government emboldened both the JI and Al-Qaida to escalate their operations to a new level. Although the JI was founded in 1993–1994, it did not commit any known terrorist acts until 2000, after years of planning, training, and gaining confidence in the Malukus and

Poso. The JI carried out operations according to their limited capabilities, against soft targets with a limited loss of human life.

Beginning in 2000, there was a spate of terrorist attacks around the region, though neither regional security services nor journalists nor academics ever linked the attacks. The first attack was in April 2000, in Yala, Thailand, in which a train station and hotel were bombed. In July 2000 a Jakarta mall was bombed by a Malaysian man. In August 2000, the Philippine ambassador to Indonesia was the target of a bombing. The attack was conducted by Indonesian JI operatives and was seen by many as a "thank you" note to the MILF, which had provided training and assistance to the group. Hambali returned to Indonesia in October 2000 and planned a series of bombings against thirty churches whose pastors were vocal in their support of Christian paramilitaries in the Malukus and Sulawesi. The bombings were planned with Omar al-Faruq, a senior Al-Qaida representative in Indonesia, on Abu Bakar Ba'asyir's orders. Funding for the bombing, R180,000, was provided by Faiz bin Abu Bakar Bafana, a senior JI leader. Ba'asyir's goal was to "spark a religious civil war in Indonesia."[71] Hambali then returned to Malaysia, now wanted by Indonesian authorities. As mentioned above, the JI and the MILF engaged in joint operations also in December 2000, when the light rail in metro Manila was bombed.

For the most part, these attacks were not overly successful. For example, in the case of the church bombings in Indonesia, JI operatives set thirty bombs, though only eighteen went off, killing a total of fifteen people. This was a far cry from their intended goal of killing thousands. These bombs were small and directed against soft targets. But these bombings gave JI members confidence, and they had to be seen as training runs. The JI knew that they could make bombs, they knew that they could carry out attacks, and regional security forces seemed to have no knowledge of who was behind them. The JI, like its parent organization, Al-Qaida, always placed a high premium on education and training. As more JI operatives were recruited and trained in Al-Qaida camps in Afghanistan and the southern Philippines, their technical proficiency increased, the network became more developed, and Al-Qaida and the JI plotted larger-scale operations against harder targets.

JI operatives were very important support personnel in Al-Qaida operations in Southeast Asia. The first case was in mid-2000, when JI members assisted a six-man Yemeni team plan the truck bombing of the U.S. Embassy in Jakarta, though the attack was thwarted.[72] Following the September 11, 2001, attacks on the United States, Al-Qaida was planning a series of spectacular attacks against U.S. interests across the region. In August 2001, a young Canadian-Kuwaiti Al-Qaida recruit, Mohammed Mansour Jabarah, was trained by Khalid Shaikh Mohammed and Hambali, who was in Karachi, Pakistan, at the time. According to a Canadian Secret Intelligence Service report, Khalid Shaikh Mohammed

> told Jabarah that Jabarah's job would be to provide money for a suicide operation in the Philippines. Jabarah would be the go-between for the local SE Asian operatives and AQ. Jabarah was not asked to be a driver or a suicide bomber for an operation as there were hundreds of others in Afghanistan eagerly ready to fill that role. He was considered a more valuable entity given his abilities, language capability and his clean Canadian passport.

In Kuala Lumpur, Jabarah met with Hambali and Faiz bin Abu Bakar Bafana before being sent to Manila, where he met with the JI cell leader Fathur Rohman al-Ghozi. In Manila, the two surveilled the U.S. and Israeli embassies. Al-Ghozi said that he already had one ton of explosives and needed additional time and money to purchase three more tons. Jabarah, however, was under pressure from the Al-Qaida leadership to carry out an attack in the region quickly. He and al-Ghozi traveled back to Malaysia in October 2001 and met with Hambali, Bafana, and a few other operatives. Al-Ghozi explained that the U.S. and Israeli embassies were poor targets, as the U.S. Embassy was sufficiently far from the road that a truck bomb would not damage it, whereas the Israeli Embassy was in an office tower. The decision was made that al-Ghozi would eventually return to the Philippines to purchase more explosives. Before that, he and Jabarah were sent to identify targets in Singapore.

The group, which included several Singapore JI members, surveilled their potential targets by car: the U.S. Embassy, Israeli Embassy, British Embassy, Caltex Oil Company, the American Naval Shipyard and docks, the Yishun MRT station, and the American Club. Video footage was taken and reviewed by Hambali in Kuala Lumpur and then later found in the wreckage of Mohammed Atef's house in Kabul, Afghanistan. In all, seven targets were chosen. These included the U.S. Embassy, the British Embassy, the Israeli Embassy, and several office towers owned or occupied by U.S. firms: the Bank of America office building (GCL Tower), American International Assurance (AIA), the American Club, and Caltex Oil Company. Al-Ghozi, who estimated that seventeen tons of explosives—at a cost of $160,000—were needed to conduct all those operations, returned to the Philippines to procure them in November 2001. With four tons, the U.S. and Israeli embassies would be targeted; with an additional two tons the AIA building could also be attacked. The Philippine explosives would be shipped to Batam, Indonesia, from where they could be smuggled into Singapore in small quantities. However, this was found to be too expensive, too hard to procure, and too hard to smuggle into the country. The Singapore JI cell had already procured four tons of ammonium nitrate and was trying to purchase seventeen more, as it was much cheaper and easier to procure than TNT. Instead, the cell decided to use six truck bombs, each with three-ton ammonium nitrate bombs. (By comparison, Timothy McVeigh's truck bomb used in the 1995 bombing of the Federal Building in Oklahoma City was between two and three tons.)

Jabarah returned to Kuala Lumpur and eventually was able to make contact with Khalid Shaikh Mohammed to whom he would need to send $50,000 to purchase the explosives. Soon after, Jabarah received $30,000 from an Al-Qaida financier in Malaysia and transferred it to another JI operative. He arranged for a secure warehouse in Singapore to be rented in order to construct the bombs. According to the Singaporean *White Paper*, Jabarah

> would bring his people down to Singapore to rig the bombs at the secured warehouse. The trucks would then be driven and parked at designated points near the targets. The local cell members would then leave the country as unknown suicide bombers arrived. These suicide bombers [believed to be Arabs] would be brought down to Singapore just a day before the planned attack.[73]

By December 2001, the JI was planning to conduct major suicide truck bombs with three tons of ammonium nitrate against hardened targets in Singapore. This is a far cry from the small bombs set in front of Indonesian churches just over a year previously.

JI Uncovered: December 2001 to January 2002

In early December 2001, Jabarah received an e-mail from Hambali entitled "Problem"; Faiz bin Abu Bakar Bafana, one of JI's leaders, had been arrested. Jabarah was instructed to go to Thailand and await Hambali.

The first break in the investigation into the JI came months before as the unexpected outcome of a bank robbery investigation in Malaysia. On May 18, 2001, KMM members botched a robbery of the Southern Bank in Petaling Jaya, outside of Kuala Lumpur. Although two KMM members were killed, one survived and his interrogation led to the arrest of nine others. The interrogation also brought up the name Hambali.

The Malaysians had been aware of Hambali and his links to international terrorists since January 2000 when the Central Intelligence Agency asked them to monitor the meeting of Al-Qaida lieutenants. They monitored Hambali's activities as he fund-raised in Malaysia for holy war in the Malukus, but Hambali committed no crime in Malaysia. With the investigation of the robbery, however, this alleged international terrorist was linked to a group of domestic militants who were trying to overthrow the government by force. Hambali was forced underground.

The Malaysians began to study Hambali's associates and became terribly alarmed. Abu Jibril was detained in May 2001 under the draconian Internal Security Act. That same month the Malaysian government shut down the Al-Tarbiyah Luqmanul Hakiem School and arrested twelve of its teachers for militant activity. But Malaysian authorities were still unaware of the central role these individuals played in the regional terrorist organization; they simply saw them as being linked to the focus of their investigation: the KMM.

PAS suffered a serious blow to its reputation when Zainon Ismail, Nik Adli, and eight other members of the Kampulan Mujahidin (seven of whom were also PAS members) were detained on August 4, 2001, for attempting to violently overthrow the Malaysian government and establish an Islamic state.[74] The police reported finding stockpiled assault rifles and grenades and linked the Kampulan Mujahidin to several recent crimes including the botched bank robbery, the assassination of state assemblyman Joe Fernandez, and several bombings of Christian churches and Hindu temples.[75] The Malaysian government believed that the KMM was planning to attack a U.S. naval vessel in Port Klang when the cell was broken up. The Malaysian government was on heightened alert, but there is no evidence that officials saw these individuals as linked to Al-Qaida or as being part of a regional terrorist organization. To that end, the government did not fully share the scope of the investigation with its neighbors.

Following the September 11 attacks, the Southeast Asian governments were on heightened alert. The first clue of this came in early October 2001, when a member of the Singapore cell, Mohammed Aslam bin Yar Ali Khan, told an acquaintance that he was going to Afghanistan, as he knew Osama bin Laden. This individual tipped off the police who began to monitor Ali Khan and his acquaintances, one of whom was seen with foreigners between October 14 and 16; they, of course, were Mohammed Mansour Jabarah and Fathur Rohman al-Ghozi, who were looking for targets in Singapore. Ali Khan suddenly left Singapore on October 4 for Pakistan. In November, Ali Khan was captured by Northern Alliance forces.

Ali Khan's interrogation confirmed the existence of the JI. In the course of the surveillance, Singaporean authorities were aghast to discover what an extensive bombing campaign was being planned against U.S. commercial, military, and diplomatic assets, as well as the British High Commission, the Australian High Commission, and the Israeli Embassy. They were also aghast to discover that JI's plot to build truck bombs was nearing completion and that significant amounts of explosives had already been smuggled into the country.

The investigation was coordinated with the Malaysians, who had a few breaks of their own. After the August 1 bombing of a Jakarta mall by a Malaysian, Taufik Abdul Halim, "Danny"—the brother-in-law of Zulkifli Hir, one of the KMM members who fled after the Southern Bank robbery[76]—the Malaysian government came to believe there was a second KMM cell and began to increase surveillance of suspected members. The Malaysian government arrested Yazid Sufaat as he returned from Afghanistan in October 2001. He had left Malaysia to "study theology" in June 2001 but was already under police surveillance, having come to their attention at the January 2000 lieutenants' meeting with Hambali and other Al-Qaida operatives, which was held in his apartment. The interrogation of Yazid Sufaat seemed to confirm the presence of a second cell. It was not until January 2002, however, that the Malaysian authorities finally concluded that it was not the KMM but the Jemaah Islamiya.

On December 3, the media announced Ali Khan's arrest by the Northern Alliance. Fearful that the news that Aslam bin Yar Ali Khan was arrested by the Northern Alliance would send his cell members into hiding, the Singaporean Internal Security Department decided to arrest cell members on December 8. On December 9, the first six people were detained in Singapore and fifteen were detained in Malaysia. By the end of the month, fifteen were detained in Singapore though two were later released. Several suspects were also found with two tampered Singaporean passports and fifteen forged Philippine and Malaysian immigration stamps. Also found were night vision goggles, literature on bomb-making, and maps and photos of the Paya Lebar airbase used by U.S. forces. An additional surveillance videotape was found in the office of Faiz bin Abu Bakar Bafana. One of the ringleaders was found with a Canadian passport in the name of Mohammed Mansour Jabarah. The suspects were also engaged in fund-raising for other radical Islamic groups, including the MILF.

On December 14, Singapore intelligence officials learned of the surveillance videotape taken by a JI member of potential U.S. military, commercial, and diplomatic targets in Singapore, which was found in the rubble of Mohammed Atef's house in Kabul, Afghanistan, by U.S. intelligence agents. They did not receive a copy of the video from the United States until December 28. "The tapes offered useful corroboration," said a minister of home affairs spokesman. "But by then we had wrapped it up."[77] Indeed, the individual who took and narrated the video, Hashim Abas, admitted his role to the Internal Security Department on December 26. Also turned over by U.S. intelligence were digital photographs and maps of the naval facility that was frequently used by U.S. naval warships.

Around that time, Singaporean officials received a report from Indonesian officials of a September 28 meeting of JI leaders who were planning a synchronized attack on U.S. embassies in the region. The scope of the cell was much larger than anyone had imagined. Captured were Faiz bin Abu Bakar Bafana and Ibrihim Maidin, the spiritual leader and recruiter for the Singapore cell, but security officials realized that most of the individuals they had arrested were merely "foot soldiers." Mas Salamat Kastari, the Singapore cell's leader, and four others fled to Indonesia.[78] In addition to them, seven to eight others were believed to have escaped; less than half the cell was broken up.

The Bangkok Meeting: A Change of Strategy

News of the arrest of Faiz bin Abu Bakar Bafana was devastating to Hambali and the Al-Qaida leadership, as Hambali was instrumental in the planning of the attacks and had a thorough knowledge of the regional network. There is some evidence that in early December Hambali ordered his cell to abandon the Singapore plot and to carry out the original plan: the bombing of the U.S. and Israeli embassies in Manila because explosives were much more readily available. According to an FBI memorandum:

> During December 2001, Hambali advises Jabarah that they should cancel the Singapore operation and move the target back to the US and Israeli Embassies in the Philippines. Hambali believed that operations in the Philippines could be accomplished sooner since the explosives would not have to be shipped.[79]

Al-Qaida was under attack. Mohammed Atef had been killed in U.S. raids, and the attack on Tora Bora convinced Hambali that he needed to conduct a major bombing to take the heat off Al-Qaida. Hambali urgently needed Jabarah to get more money to Fathur Rohman al-Ghozi so he could purchase the explosives.

With Bafana's arrest, Hambali ordered Mohammed Mansour Jabarah to leave Malaysia and go to Thailand. In early January, Hambali hosted a major meeting in Bangkok to reevaluate the group's situation and to plan a new series of attacks. At the meeting the decision was made that the JI should focus on soft economic targets. There were five individuals who attended this meeting in addition to Hambali: Noordin Mohammed Mop Top, Dr. Azahari, Wan Min Wan Mat, Ali Gofri, and Mohammed Mansour Jabarah. Three were responsible for the October 2002 bombing of the Sari Nightclub in Bali in which 202 people were killed.

The meeting also represented another setback. On January 15, 2002, acting on a tip from Singapore intelligence (and in conjunction with three of their officers), Philippine National Police agents arrested the Indonesian national who had been in Singapore in October as he was about to leave for Bangkok. Fathur Rohman al-Ghozi was to be the seventh attendee of Hambali's conference. After several days of interrogation, Fathur Rohman al-Ghozi tipped off police to a cache of weapons, and the PNP raided a house in General Santos City on January 18, 2002. The police recovered fifty-four boxes, or one ton of TNT manufactured in Cebu, Philippines, which was to be shipped to Singapore. In addition, they recovered seventeen M-16 rifles, 300 detonators, six roles of detonating cords, and other bomb-making materials.[80] His interrogation led to the breakup of his cell: Police arrested three Filipinos—two brothers, Almuctar Malagat and Mualidin Malagat, and Mohammad Malagad—in raids on two other houses in General Santos City, and Mohammed Kiram, on January 21 in Marawi.[81]

The arrest of Fathur Rohman al-Ghozi tied together some loose ends. Al-Ghozi's admission that he participated in the December 30, 2000, bombings in Manila that killed twenty-two people gave the Philippine authorities the smoking gun they needed to link the MILF to Al-Qaida, which put them in a stronger position in the peace talks.[82] Authorities were also able to conclude that al-Ghozi was responsible for the August 2000 bombing cum assassination of the Philippine ambassador to Indonesia, again tying in the MILF with the Jemaah Islamiya. These revelations had a major impact in getting the MILF to the negotiating table and agreeing to accept a cease-fire in the first quarter of 2002.

Investigations continued throughout the spring in Singapore, Malaysia, and the Philippines, leading investigators to a much greater sense of the dense network that they were up against. On January 19, 2002, an additional seven Malaysians were arrested,[83] and nine more members of the Jemaah Islamiya cell were arrested in Singapore, yet two were later released.

On March 15, 2002, three Indonesian nationals believed to be affiliated with al-Ghozi—Agus Dwikarna, Tamsil Linrung, and Abdul Jamal Belfas—were arrested in Manila as they attempted to leave the country, based on intelligence from Singapore and Malaysia that they were JI operatives.[84] Although the three were found with two pieces of C4 explosives and a role of detonating cable, they all denied any connection to al-Ghozi and claimed that they were set up by Indonesian intelligence.[85]

The arrests caused a huge scandal in Indonesia because Linrung and Dwikarna were fairly prominent politicians. Tamsil Linrung was the treasurer of the National Mandate Party (PAN), the second largest Muslim political party; and Linrung and Dwikarna were both very senior officials in the national charity KOMPAK, an arm of the religious organization Dewan Dakwah Islam Indonesia, which has considerable political clout. Dwikarna was a powerful figure in Sulawesi and in the MMI. PAN officials, for their part, believe that Indonesia's National Intelligence Agency set up Linrung for political purposes.[86] Agus Dwikarna stated: "We strongly assume the existence of direct intelligence involvement. . . . In this case BIN was involved in our arrest."[87] Even the respected news weekly *Tempo* asserted that the three were set up simply because they were all members of Islamic groups and that Indonesian and Philippine intelligence services were simply trying to pressure Indonesian political leaders to get serious about terrorism.[88] Although considerable evidence emerged later about Tamsil Linrung's association with the JI,[89] he and Abdul Jamal Belfas were released under intense diplomatic pressure from Indonesian president Megawati Sukarnoputri.

Philippine officials and their counterparts in Malaysia and Singapore were much more troubled by Agus Dwikarna because he tied together many loose ends.[90] Dwikarna was on the Indonesian intelligence service's terrorist watch list and had already been under surveillance, as he was one of two escorts for Ayman al-Zawahari and Mohammed Atef during the visit to Indonesia in June 2000. He was the leader of the Laskar Jundullah, a member of the MMI's Organizing Committee, and a member of the Preparation Committee for the Application of Islamic Law in South Sulawesi, also part of the MMI. Although Dwikarna acknowledged that he aided groups in the Malukus and Poso Sulawesi, he claims he simply provided relief assistance through his charity, the Committee to Overcome Crisis (KOMPAK). Dwikarna was tried in a Philippine court and sentenced to seventeen years, despite the intervention of senior Indonesian officials.[91]

On April 18, 2002, Malaysian authorities conducted another sweep of suspected militants, detaining fourteen JI/KMM suspects, including Yazid Sufaat's wife, Sejahratul Dursina.[92] In their possession was a map of Port Klang, the Malaysian naval facility where U.S. warships make frequent port calls. On July 9, 2002, Philippine authorities arrested Hussain Ramos, a thirty-five-year-old native of Marawi who had procured more than one ton of explosives for al-Ghozi and was also affiliated with the MILF.

In August 2002, Singapore authorities arrested twenty-one more individuals, nineteen of whom were JI members. The remaining two were supporters and financial conduits for the MILF. Several of the twenty-one were trained in either Al-Qaida camps in Afghanistan or in MILF camps in Mindanao. This group, too, was very much focused on soft targets, including a pub where U.S. armed forces personnel frequented, chemical plants on Jurong Island, Changi Airport, as well as the Ministry of Defense headquarters. Most alarming were the planned attacks on the water pipelines that supply most of Singapore's water from Malaysia. The ulterior goal was to commit sabotage that would be portrayed as acts of aggression by Malaysian authorities. The attack on the pipeline was planned with the support of JI leader Mukhlas, the head of Mantiqi 1.[93] The goal of the pipeline attacks was to create heightened tensions between Malaysia and Singapore and spark racial unrest:

> Hambali aimed to stir up ethnic strife by playing up a "Chinese Singapore" threatening Malay/Muslims in Malaysia; he hoped that this would create a situation which would make Muslims respond to calls for militant *jihad*, and turn Malaysia and Singapore into another Ambon, where religious clashes have broken out between Christians and Muslims since January 1999, resulting in many deaths and injuries.[94]

As a result of the August arrests in Singapore, on September 26, 2002, Malaysian authorities arrested Wan Min Wan Mat, a forty-two-year-old university lecturer at UTM who was identified as a senior-level JI leader and treasurer based in Johor (across from Singapore) and identified eight other members of his cell.[95] Wan Min Wan Mat had also been responsible for paying the bills for the Al-Tarbiyah Luqmanul Hakiem School.

Regrouping in Indonesia

After the January Bangkok meeting, Mohammed Mansour Jabarah was sent out of the region. As Hambali said to him, "It will be a very big hit for us if you are arrested." Jabarah traveled from Thailand to the United Arab Emirates and then Oman where he was instructed by Khalid Shaikh Mohammed to escort senior-level Al-Qaida members to Yemen. He was arrested in Oman in March 2002 and later turned over to U.S. authorities by the Canadian government. But many of the other attendees of the meeting traveled to Indonesia, where they began planning for the Bali operation and other attacks. While officials in Singapore and Malaysia were confident that they had eradicated much of the senior Jemaah Islamiya leadership in their own countries, both expressed tremendous frustration about the lack of cooperation that they received from Indonesian authorities. Most JI fugitives were known to have left for Indonesia, but little assistance was provided.

Although Abu Bakar Ba'asyir was named by both Malaysia and Singapore as a prime suspect and a leader of the Jemaah Islamiya network, he continued to live and preach openly until October 2002. Although Ba'asyir was brought in for questioning on January 24, 2002, he was released the next day. A high-level Indonesian police delegation to Singapore and Malaysia was likewise not convinced of the evidence against Ba'asyir and refused to arrest him. He acknowledged teaching thirteen of those detained in Malaysia, Singapore, and the Philippines. In an interview with me, Ba'asyir denied being a member of Al-Qaida: "I am not a member of Al-Qaida, but I really respect the struggle of Osama bin Laden, who has bravely represented the world's Muslims in their fight against the arrogant United States of America and their allies." In April 2002, the Indonesian Supreme Court announced that it might arrest Ba'asyir on the grounds that he never finished serving the second half of his nine-year sentence, but it later threw the case out.[96]

One got the feeling throughout 2002 that no matter what evidence the Singaporeans and Malaysians offered the Indonesian police, it would never satisfy their evidentiary standards leading to Ba'asyir's arrest. Even the confessions of Omar al-Faruq did not move the Indonesians to reopen the investigation. It was only after the October 2002 Bali nightclub attack that the Indonesian government had the conviction to arrest Ba'asyir. He was linked to the 2000 church bombings but as of early 2003 has not been officially linked to the Bali attack. His detention was extended through April 2003 when he was put on trial for treason and his role in the December 2000 church bombing. I believe that he was willing to take some of the criticism simply to protect the real operatives of the JI cell in Indonesia, laughingly calling himself "the big terrorist of Southeast Asia."[97] As a senior JI leader, Mohammed Nasir bin Abbas, who was arrested in April 2003 in Indonesia, recounted in his interrogation, Ba'asyir told his subordinates that he was willing to become a "martyr" for the organization, and encouraged them to find a new amir, or spiritual leader, for the group. To that end, a 43-year-old militant Indonesian cleric and the son of a senior DI leader, Abu Rusdan, was elected the JI's amir in the fall of 2002. He, in turn, was arrested on April 21, 2003.

The four tons of ammonium nitrate purchased by Yazid Sufaat were found in March 2003 in southern Malaysia, hidden at a palm-oil plantation. Some explosives that al-Ghozi purchased were never recovered. Upon further investigation of the firm that sold explosives to Mukhlas and al-Ghozi, an inventory audit revealed that some 3,600 kilograms (four tons) of explosives are missing. It is unclear if al-Ghozi had previously shipped the explosives and simply has not revealed that to the police. As one investigator complained:

> It's clear that al-Ghozi's role in the Philippines was the large scale export, transportation and delivery of explosives to end users. In this case it was Singapore, and the plans were already hatched to bomb US embassies there. But we don't know who all the end users are.[98]

It became more clear who the end users were in early September 2002, and all the more evident that Indonesia remains the focal point of JI activity in Southeast Asia. Omar al-Faruq has admitted that he was ordered by Abu Zubaydah, before his arrest in early April 2002, and another senior Al-Qaida official, Ibn al-Shaikh al-Libi, to plan a series of attacks on U.S. targets in the region. To that end, al-Faruq admitted that he worked closely with Abu Bakar Ba'asyir, who gave him logistical support and offered JI operatives for the attacks.[99]

Al-Faruq planned a seaborne suicide attack on U.S. naval vessels that were in Surabaya in May 2002 for joint training operations with the Indonesian navy. He recruited a Somali Al-Qaida operative, Gharib, to lead the attack but was unable to recruit enough personnel.[100] This raises an interesting point. Like the Singapore JI cell, which was also planning a suicide attack on U.S. naval vessels, the actual attack was to be carried out by Middle Easterners flown in for the operation. Al-Faruq and Al-Qaida operatives in Southeast Asia may dream big, but they are unable to carry out major attacks themselves. That said, they are more than capable and clearly have the means to carry out a series of truck bomb operations against U.S. targets.

According to the CIA, al-Faruq received orders from Ibn al-Shaikh al Libi and Abu Zubaydah to "prepare a plan to conduct simultaneous car/truck bomb attacks against US Embassies in the region to take place on or about 11 September 2002."[101] Al-Faruq dispatched an Indonesian operative, Abu al-Furkan (a senior member of the MMI), to Malaysia to lead the bombing attack of the U.S. Embassy, while Ba'asyir supplied al-Furkan with one ton of explosives for the operation. These explosives were purchased by Ba'asyir's top lieutenant, Aris Munandar, from corrupt elements in Indonesia's armed forces.

On the basis of al-Faruq's confession and the confession of Mohammed Mansour Jabarah, both in U.S. custody, U.S. embassies in Malaysia, Indonesia, Cambodia, and Vietnam were shut down for the first anniversary of the September 11 attacks.[102] The U.S. Embassy in Jakarta was targeted with a two-truck-bomb attack to get through the perimeter gate. U.S. officials were furious with the response of Indonesian officials. In September 2002, a hand grenade was tossed into a U.S. Embassy residence compound, an attack attributed to JI. The U.S. Department of State withdrew its nonessential staff and families, and indicated that it planned to put Abu Bakar Ba'asyir and JI on its list of terrorist organizations in an attempt to pressure the Indonesian government.

In response to the widely reported confessions of al-Faruq and a widely circulated CIA memo obviously intended to pressure the Indonesian government to arrest Ba'asyir, the cleric has denied any relationship with al-Faruq. "He is lying," Ba'asyir said. "I never met him. He never knew me. I don't have any connection to media. . . . The US is launching a grand strategy to hinder the Islamic struggle. I am a Muslim. They are infidels. I have never known those two Arabs [Omar al-Faruq and Reda Seyem]." His lawyer, though, clarified his statement and said: "If they met, it was only as good Muslims and to share and exchange ideas about Islam. The CIA reports are fairy tales."[103] The Indonesian government, under pressure from the Americans and its neighbors, announced that it would "carry out an investigation" of Ba'asyir but went on to say that it would "not arrest Abu Bakar just because foreign governments have their suspicions of him."[104] The Indonesians distrusted the CIA report and resented U.S. pressure, and there was considerable popular and political pressure to withstand the United States.

The Indonesian government, for its part, was not completely intransigent and provided assistance to the United States with regards to foreign Al-Qaida operatives. For example, on January 11, 2002, Indonesian authorities rendered without a trial a Pakistani and Egyptian national, Hafiz Mohammed Saad Iqbal, to Egypt at the insistence of the United States, where he was wanted in connection with the Richard Reid shoe-bombing incident.[105] It is unknown why this suspected Al-Qaida operative came to Indonesia, whether escaping a Pakistani police dragnet or to lay the foundation for other escaping Al-Qaida operatives. He was later reported to have died in Egyptian custody during a "rigorous interrogation."

Then on June 5, 2002, before he could carry out the attacks on U.S. targets, Omar al-Faruq, a permanent resident in Indonesia, was arrested by Indonesian police.[106] Al-Faruq had come to the attention of U.S. and Indonesian intelligence officials earlier in the year with the arrest of Abu Zubaydah.

He had applied for but was denied an Indonesian passport in mid-2001. About to be deported, al-Faruq fled to the small village of Cijeruk outside Bogor, West Java. He was arrested and rendered to the United States and is currently detained in Bagram Air Force Base in Afghanistan, where he admitted to planning the September 11 anniversary attacks.

Bali

At the January 2002 meeting in Bangkok, Hambali expressed anger that so many of his colleagues and so much of his network was uprooted. He thus switched the potential targets, from symbolic targets, such as the U.S. and other Western embassies, to soft targets "to conduct small bombings in bars, cafes or nightclubs frequented by westerners in Thailand, Singapore, the Philippines and Indonesia."[107] This planning culminated in the tragic attack on the nightclub in Bali on October 12. Only with the Bali attack, which had a devastating impact on the Indonesian economy and reputation, did the Indonesian government begin to crack down and take the threat posed by terrorists seriously. On October 18, 2002, Abu Bakar Ba'asyir was detained for questioning, though only for his role in the December 2000 church bombings and not for the Bali attack, which he blamed on the Americans.[108]

Ninety-six of the victims of the Bali attack were Australians, provoking an immediate and firm response from the Australian government, which dispatched a large team of Australian Federal Police investigators. In addition, investigators from Japan, the United Kingdom, and the FBI provided much-needed technical assistance and intense pressure on the Indonesians.

At first, Indonesian authorities attributed the attack to Al-Qaida, not Jemaah Islamiya, hoping to place the blame on foreigners, not Indonesians themselves. In the immediate aftermath of the attack, Vice President Hamzah Haz came out and demanded that there not be any hasty link made between the attack and his friend, Abu Bakar Ba'asyir. The investigation, however, pointed in only that direction.

By April 2003, over thirty suspects in the bombing were arrested, many of whom had very strong links to Ba'asyir. The most important of those arrested was Ali Ghufron, "Mukhlas." Mukhlas moved to Malaysia in the early 1990s and fell under the sway of Abu Bakar Ba'asyir and Abdullah Sungkar. Like Abu Jibril and Hambali, he became a preacher, recruiting for JI. Mukhlas eventually established the Al-Tarbiyah Luqmanul Hakiem School *madrasa* in Ulu Tiram, Johor, that was purchased by Sungkar and Ba'asyir. The school was near the University of Technology of Malaysia, which was a hotbed of JI activism, and supported by Wan Min Wan Mat, who provided Mukhlas with the $33,000 from Hambali for use in the attack. Mukhlas traveled frequently to Singapore where he preached, recruited, and fund-raised, and he eventually became a senior leader of Jemaah Islamiya, the head of

Mantiqi 1. Mukhlas returned to Indonesia in 1999, and in May 2001 Malaysian authorities shut down the *madrasa* and arrested twelve of its teachers. He was implicated by the Singaporean government in the plot to blow up the water pipelines to Singapore in August 2002 but was never caught. Singapore and Malaysian intelligence believed that Hambali fled the region and left Mukhlas in charge of all JI operations.

The first person arrested was Mukhlas's younger brother, Amrozi, who confessed to the bombing. Although he denied being a member of JI, the East Java auto mechanic became close to Abu Bakar Ba'asyir in the mid-1990s when both were living in Malaysia. Amrozi attended religious sermons by Ba'asyir and other Jemaah Islamiya leaders and was recruited into the group. Amrozi also admitted to participating in the 2000 bombing of the Jakarta Stock Exchange and in the bombing cum assassination of the Philippine ambassador to Indonesia. According to Indonesian investigators, Ba'asyir visited Amrozi's auto-repair shop a week before the attack where Amrozi was attempting to file off the vehicle identification number on the engine block of the Mitsubishi minivan he purchased in June for the attack. Amrozi also admitted to purchasing the ammonium nitrate used to build the 110-kilogram bomb. He was married to Khoiriyanah Khususiyati, a neighbor of Fathur Rohman al-Ghozi.

Another brother of Mukhlas, Ali Imran, also had ties to Ba'asyir. Ali Imran ran a small *madrasa,* the Al-Islam boarding school, in their East Java village of Tenggulun. The *madrasa* was established in the late 1990s with money from Omar al-Faruq, and Abu Bakar Ba'asyir was a frequent guest at the school. Interestingly, several automatic weapons were recovered on his property that had the same serial numbers as those looted from police stockpiles in the Malukus in 2000, further linking the JI to the sectarian conflicts.

On November 21, 2002, the mastermind of the Bali attack, Imam Samudra, was arrested. Imam Samudra was already wanted by Indonesian authorities for the Christmas bombings in 2000, though when interviewed in June 2002, police officials denied that he was a member of the JI. Imam Samudra had left his home in Benten, Sumatra, in 1990 for the Al-Tarbiyah Luqmanul Hakiem School *madrasa* in Malaysia. Soon after, he left for Afghanistan where he spent two years in weapons and explosives training. He returned to Malaysia in 1993 and was recruited into the JI by Abdullah Sungkar. He traveled extensively to Malaysia and Singapore before returning to Indonesia in 1999.[109]

There were some twenty other arrests, yet for the most part they were foot soldiers and support personnel who had very little knowledge and understanding of the scope of the operation. Several of the lead bomb-makers escaped. Most important, the degree of deniability for Abu Bakar Ba'asyir is now quite tenuous.

We have to ask the question, "Why Bali?" Why would the JI leadership conduct an attack in the country that had not cracked down on their operations? There are three answers to this question. The first is that the perpetrators believed they would get away with it. They equated police inaction in the previous year with police incompetence. They did not understand the degree of political will that the police needed to conduct counterterrorist operations. Second, they wanted to cripple the Indonesian economy. Ba'asyir understood that in times of economic downturns, people turned to the mosque and were susceptible to recruitment into radical groups. Tourism is a $5 billion a year lifeblood for Indonesia, the only industry that has grown since the Asian economic crisis began in 1997. Third, radicals hope to cause a heavy-handed government reaction. As they expected to get away with the crime, they anticipated that government repression against the Muslim community would grow. That, in turn, would build up a larger constituency of loyalists and fuel membership. As Abu Bakar Ba'asyir said in an October 2002 sermon:

> If non-believers have the weapons capacity, the funding, then they will go to war against Islam. In the Koran Allah has said they will always wage war against you, they will always attack you as long as they have the capacity. Brothers and sisters Muslims, we now can feel the efforts of non-believers to threaten Islam. Jews and America are waging a war on Muslims in order that there are many participants, and those who do not wish to participate are attacked and those who wish to are given funding. Then in the process of waging war against Islam they use that which is mentioned in the Koran as values, they create a war wherein it is not clearly stated it is a war against Islam but they use a smokescreen which is currently being described as "terrorists." The non-believers of America and the non-believers of Israel are currently developing the issue of terrorism, however what they mean by terrorism according to the definition of America, are all of the followers of Islam. All followers of Islam in this world are terrorists.[110]

But what about the bombers themselves? Why Bali? What motivated them to perpetrate this act? Clearly many were young and naïve, susceptible to their leaders. The interrogation of Imam Samudra is telling. When asked about the motivations of his jihad, he answered: "I carry out jihad based on the following background and motives":

> a) To fight against the savage American Crusade Armed Forces and their allies (England, Australia, Germany, France, Japan, Orthodox Russia, and others),
> b) As the duty of a Muslim to avenge the heartbreak of the death of 200,000 innocent women, elderly men, and children because of the tons of bombs dropped in Afghanistan on September 2001, Ramadan 1422 H,
> c) Because Australia intervened in the effort to segregate Timor Timur [East Timor] from Indonesia, all of which is an International Crusade conspiracy,
> d) The intervention of the Crusade Armed Forces in collaboration with the Hindu heathen troops in India in the massacre of the Muslims in Kashmir,
> e) As an answer to the savage intervention of the Crusade Armed Forces in the Muslim cleansing scheme at Ambon, Poso, Halmahera, etc.,

f) In defense of the Bosnian Muslims who were slaughtered by the Crusade Armed Forces,
g) Carrying out the *Fardlu'ain* duty for Global Jihad towards Jews and Christians all over the world (in Muslim countries),
h) As *Ukhuwah Islamiyah* between one Muslim to another, regardless of geographical boundaries,
i) Executing the will of Allah in *An Nisa* verse 74–76 on the duty to defend weak men, women, and innocent babies who are always the target of the atrocities of the American terrorists and their allies,
j) As a "harsh reprimand" to Jews and Christians led by American heathens in oppressing and tainting the Islamic holy land, where the Revelation of the Prophets descended,
k) So the American terrorists and their allies understand that the blood of the Muslim Community is not shed for nothing, and it must not be treated disrespectfully and made the target of American atrocities,
l) So American terrorists understand the pain and suffering of losing a mother, husband, child, or wife whom they have treated with disregard in the Muslim communities in the world,
m) To prove to Allah that we have done all we can to protect the weak Muslims and fought against the oppressors and the American terrorists and their allies (may Allah curse and destroy them, amen).[111]

Imam Samudra concluded by stating that everyone in his cell was infused with similar teachings and beliefs and was willing to engage in the bombing. As Ba'asyir asserted in an October 2002 sermon:

> The government of Indonesia right now is being directed by America to service its needs and the primary need of America is to bury Islam particularly in Indonesia. Therefore following on from this, America will be able to direct political and economic affairs in accordance with its own desires. Because of this, let us defend our religion, let us begin to defend our religion. . . . Hence our religion Islam, our nation and our country is currently being threatened by foreign races with all manner of libels, with the bombings in Bali, with explosions everywhere, all of those are the plots of nonbelievers whose aims are to weaken and profane the believers of Islam. Therefore, accordingly they can exert power over this country in order that it may be taken advantage of. Brothers and sisters let us hope for and be conscious of the defence of Islam, let us embark upon Jihad for Allah, let us struggle to implement the law of Allah and let us apply a unity within ourselves between all Muslims.[112]

The Current State of JI

Regional security services have done a very good job of countering the terrorist threat in recent times and have arrested several of JI's senior leaders and thwarted their largest operations. Between December 9, 2001, and June 2003, a number of people have been arrested: roughly eighty in Malaysia, thirty-one in Singapore, nearly fifty in Indonesia, and a dozen in the Philippines. The

March 2003 arrest of Khalid Shaikh Mohammed, Al-Qaida's operations chief, who had close ties and operational experience in Southeast Asia, was a further blow to the organization. That the JI is now focusing on soft targets such as tourist venues rather than hardened, though symbolic, targets indicates decreased capabilities. They are less able to plan and execute terrorist attacks than they were in 2001. Since Bali, Indonesian officials have had the political will to take on the Al-Qaida and Jemaah Islamiya networks. Several important operatives were arrested in early 2003, including Mas Salamat Kastari, and Indonesia can no longer be a relatively safe haven for JI operatives on the run from Singapore and Malaysia.

That said, one would be foolish to underestimate JI's capabilities or goals. First, there was a concerted effort to rebuild their organization and reorganize. According to the interrogation report of Mohammed Nasir bin Abbas, who was arrested in April 2003, new leaders were quickly elected to replace those arrested. Following Abu Bakar Ba'asyir's arrest in October 2002, many of the surviving JI operatives elected a new amir, Abu Rusdan, a very hardline and militant cleric. Abu Dujana was elected as the secretary with two assistants, Ustad Mustofa and Oni. No replacement for Mukhlas, the head of Mantiqi 1, was elected. The head of Mantiqi 2 is Abu Fatih. Mohammed Nasir bin Abbas was the head of Mantiqi 3 until his arrest and Abdul Rahim is head of Mantiqi 4.

Second, although senior organizers and foot soldiers have been arrested, there are still at least twelve important operatives at large and an endless pool of foot soldiers and recruits. JI leaders who remain at large include Hambali and Abu Hanifiah from Malaysia; Husain bin Ismail, Mohammed Rashid Bin Zainal Abidan, Ushak Mohammed Noohu, and Mohammed Hassan Bin Saynudin, and at least six others from Singapore who are in Indonesia; Irfan S. Awwas and Fikri Sugundo who live openly in Indonesia; and Omar Bandon and Parlindigan Siregar who are on the run in Indonesia. Philippine authorities believe that one other Indonesian cell member in the country escaped. Malaysian authorities believe that several lecturers from the Universiti Tecknologi Malaysia were senior JI members and recruiters who fled to Indonesia. These include Dr. Azahari bin Husin, Zulkefli bin Marzuki, Noordin Mohammed Mop Top, Shamsul Bahri bin Hussein, Abdul Razak, Amran, Zulkifli, and Mohammed Rafi bin Udin. In terms of the Bali bombers, Dr. Azahari, Dul Matin, and Joni Indrawan (Idris) all remain at large. The five-man Singapore cell—led by Mas Salamat Kastari, though he was arrested—remains at large. Syawal, Abdullah Sungkar's son-in-law and the head of the Laskar Jundullah, is also at large. Zubair, a Malaysian from Negri Sembilan with close links to PAS and the Kampulan Mujahidin Malaysia and a former mujahidin during the Afghanistan war, is also missing. The arrest of Muklis Yunos, the head of the MILF's Special Operations Group (SOG) on

May 26, 2003, was a real blow to the organization; yet the Philippine intelligence agency still believes the SOG has around 20–30 operatives.

Third, Al-Qaida and Jemaah Islamiya are working hard to rebuild their network and capabilities, and when they do so, they will refocus their efforts on larger-scale operations against hard targets or in more defended places, such as Singapore. Until then, we should expect to see more attacks, smaller, but no less lethal as with the December 5, 2002, bombing of a McDonald's in Makassar, Sulawesi, an attack attributed to the Laskar Jundullah. On April 27, 2003, at the start of Abu Bakar Ba'asyir's treason trial, a bomb exploded at Jakarta's airport, killing eleven. There is evidence that JI members are currently lying low and training in Bangladesh. The CIA believes that some 50 JI members have undergone training in MILF camps since the Bali nightclub attack; and until the MILF can be convinced that it is no longer in their political interest to cooperate with the JI and give them safe haven, the JI will be a threat to regional stability.

Fourth, the most striking failure in counterterror operations in Southeast Asia has been the inability of all states to shut down the financial pipeline of Al-Qaida in Southeast Asia. As of April 2003, no terrorist assets or funds have been seized in the region. The assets of two of the leading members of Jemaah Islamiya, Hambali and Abu Jibril, were blocked by the United States under Executive Order 13244 on January 24, 2003, eighteen months after Abu Jibril was arrested. Indeed, this is a problem around the world, not just a Southeast Asian problem. As of January 2003, only $113 million in Al-Qaida-linked assets were frozen, though none in Southeast Asia.

In late 2002, the U.S. Department of the Treasury's Office of Foreign Asset Control drew up a list of 300 individuals, charities, and corporations in Southeast Asia believed to be Al-Qaida and Jemaah Islamiya funders. Due to interagency politics, the list was winnowed down to eighteen individuals and ten companies. As one U.S. official said: "Most of the really sensitive names have been dropped, so it won't have the kind of impact that the full 300 would have, though there'll still be a few surprises."[113] But even in early June 2003, the list was still unannounced due to diplomatic and bureaucratic pressure. Yet Southeast Asia seems to have gained in importance to Al-Qaida's money men, according to U.S. law enforcement officials. Denis Lormel, the head of the terrorist financing tracking unit at the FBI, asserts that with the crackdown on Middle Eastern funding mechanisms, especially the financial centers in Abu Dhabi and other parts of the United Arab Emirates, Al-Qaida has increasingly relied on Southeast Asia to move its money and hide its assets.[114]

One of the most unlikely sources of Al-Qaida funding coming into the region was through the Om Al Qura Foundation in Phnom Penh, Cambodia. The foundation, which has offices in Bosnia, Somalia, and southern Thailand, was ostensibly established to address the needs of Cambodia's small Muslim population, which had been decimated under the Khmer Rouge from 1975 to 1978. Al-Qaida, always searching for states with poor regulatory frameworks as well as places no one suspects them, used the Om Al Qura Foundation for "significant money transfers" for both itself and Jemaah Islamiya—perhaps in the millions of dollars. On May 28, 2003, three foreign employees of the foundation were arrested, an Egyptian and two Thai Muslims, for plotting to carry out terrorist attacks in Cambodia. The arrest operation, which was conducted with a tip from and support of U.S. intelligence officials, led to the deportation of 28 teachers from the Al Mukara Islamic School and 22 dependents.[115] Already the threat of terrorism in the predominantly Buddhist nation was high: on the basis of the confessions of Omar Al-Faruq and Mohammed Mansour Jabarah, both in U.S. custody, U.S. embassies in Malaysia, Indonesia, Cambodia, and Vietnam were shut down in 2002 for the anniversary of the September 11 attacks. There was also concern that the ASEAN Foreign Ministers' Meeting, to be held in Phnom Penh in June 2003, would be targeted.[116] The Cambodian arrests demonstrate that Al-Qaida is far from defeated and is increasingly creative.

Fifth, the trials of the JI leader Abu Bakar Ba'asyir and the Bali bombers are likely to provoke a strong reaction on the part of Muslims. Abu Bakar Ba'asyir, for one, is being charged for treason under a post–September 11 counter-terrorism law. The controversial law angered many who saw it as a return to the nebulous subversion laws of the Suharto era. Several JI members who were called on to testify in Ba'asyir's trial, including Imam Samudra and Ali Gufron (Mukhlas), have refused to name Ba'asyir as the group's head, and most have recanted their earlier confessions. Mukhlas stated that "there's no way he would agree to bomb attacks," while Samudra dismissed the cleric as being old and moderate: "It's the age of the Internet, but he still talks about mysticism while Muslims are being slaughtered."[117] Those, such as Ali Imron, who have stated that Ba'asyir was the JI amir, have equivocated, and Ba'asyir, in turn, has denied knowing them.[118] Moreover, Ba'asyir's legal team has stymied the government's incompetent prosecution; and at the time of writing there is a very strong possibility that he will be acquitted. This would only vindicate Muslims in Southeast Asia who believe that the trial is politically motivated and being conducted on U.S. orders. The trials of the three main figures in the Bali bombing, Amrozi bin Nurhasyim, Imam Samudra, and Ali Gufron (Mukhlas) are likely to fare differently: Although Imam Samudra challenged the retroactive application of the anti-terror laws that he is charged under, the court ruled against him and the other bombers; all three have admitted their roles in the attack; none have shown any remorse, indeed all have shown a stoic defiance in the face of the death penalty. For the most part, Indonesians remain skeptical that the three are guilty, despite their confessions, and most at least sympathize with Imam Samudra's statement that he was "at war with the United States."

Finally, even if the JI is eliminated, the political, economic, and social conditions in Southeast Asia will simply give rise to new groups with similar ideological proclivities and goals.

The Rabitatul Mujahidin: Al-Qaida's Forays into Thailand, Myanmar, and Aceh

Omar al-Faruq, one of the senior-most Al-Qaida leaders in Southeast Asia, admitted that the Jemaah Islamiya had tried to establish links with Muslim militants elsewhere in the region, including Thailand and Myanmar.[119] In 1999 Abu Bakar Ba'asyir established a coordinating body known as the Rabitatul Mujahidin (RM). The RM was erroneously described at first as the armed wing of the Jemaah Islamiya, yet in reality it was simply a group of JI/MMI officials, including Tamsil Linrung, Agus Dwikarna, Al-Chaidar, Omar al-Faruq, and representatives from Aceh, Thailand, Myanmar, and Bangladesh. The Rabitatul Mujahidin only met three times, according to Faruq: the first time in late 1999, the second time in August 2000, and the last time in November 2000.[120] All meetings took place in Malaysia.

Al-Qaida in Thailand

There have never been strong ties between the Muslim insurgency in Thailand and international terrorist groups. Although militants in southern Thailand have long been a fact of life, for the most part they have given up their campaign to create an independent homeland. Most have worked as logistics operatives for the Acehnese rebels, GAM, and the MILF of the Philippines, serving as an important financial and arms conduit. It is clear that Al-Qaida operatives have used Thailand as a base of operations since the mid-1990s. Thailand has been the target of international terrorism before. In March 1994, a plot by bin Laden operatives to blow up the Israeli Embassy in Bangkok went awry by chance.[121] Ramzi Yousef and many other Al-Qaida operatives have passed through Thailand. After the September 11 attacks, the Thai supreme commander, General Surayud Chulanont, admitted that military intelligence was monitoring a "small number" of bin Laden operatives operating in Thailand, and that the government was cognizant that "countries in the Middle East provide training, education and financial support for fundamentalist groups in the south [of Thailand]."[122] Likewise, the secretary general of the Thai NSC, General Vinai Pattiyakul, acknowledged that some southern Muslim radicals had been trained in Afghanistan and Libya.[123]

There are two very small groups, the Wae Ka Raeh (WKR) and the Guragan Mujahidin Islam Pattani, that are thought to have some ties to Jemaah Islamiya and Al-Qaida; and the head of the WKR fought with the mujahidin in Afghanistan. For the most part, though, they are criminal gangs. The WKR is thought to earn 10 million Thai baht a year in contract killings and "enforcement."[124] It is evident from the confessions of Omar al-Faruq that the JI was rapidly trying to expand its contacts with the Guragan Mujahidin. Yet the Guragan Mujahidin remains a small and poorly funded organization, with only a hundred or so members. Moreover, one of its leaders was recently arrested in Malaysia for cross-border criminal activity. Another Thai-Muslim militant group, Pattani United Liberation Organization (PULO), is suspected of having ties to the Abu Sayyaf.

The arrests of two Thai nationals in Cambodia, on May 28, 2003, who were affiliated with the Al-Qaida front Om Al Qura Foundation, was a wakeup call to the Thai government. For the first time Prime Minister Thaksin Shinawatra publicly admitted that there were JI and Al-Qaida members in Thailand.[125] Soon afterward, on June 10, 2003, Thai police arrested three JI members in Narathiwat province in southern Thailand.[126] The arrests were a joint operation between Thai and Singaporean authorities, following the May 16, 2003, arrest of a senior JI Singapore cell member in Bangkok, Arifin bin Ali, who had also served as a JI trainer in MILF camps and assisted Mas Selamat Kastari. Arifin bin Ali (John Wong Ah Hung), who was rendered to Singapore, and the three others were planning to execute terrorist attacks against Western embassies and tourist venues in Pattaya and Phuket. Southern Thailand remains a hotbed of JI activity and sympathy. It was to there that most of the fugitives from Malaysia and Singapore fled in early 2002. They clearly had a support network there. Dr. Ismail Lufti, the rector of Yala Islamic College, and a firebrand Wahhabist, has amassed a large following and incited the Muslim community to pressure the government to abandon its support of the United States and has called for boycotts of U.S. products. Although there are suspicions about his involvement in the JI, it is clear that he and many others share the same goal and world view of Jemaah Islamiya.

However, Thailand is an important base of terrorist operations for much the same reasons as the Philippines: It is a nation of convenience and it is easy to get business taken care of there. First, Thailand is surrounded by countries that have been mired in war and ongoing insurgencies. And Thailand has always been awash in weapons, with the military itself deeply involved in the black market for arms, and it has played a key role in transporting surplus Chinese weapons for the Khmer Rouge to various armed ethnic insurgent groups in Myanmar.[127] Tamil Tiger rebels fighting for a homeland in Sri Lanka have shopped for weapons for years in Thailand, as have insurgent groups in Myanmar. The Thai military has close ties with military establishments in China and Myanmar that have been important conduits for weapons. The above-mentioned leader of the Malaysian KMM who was arrested in August 2001 was reported to have bought large quantities of weapons in Thailand.[128]

Second, Thailand has been trying to become an international banking center, despite its weak regulatory system. A lot of money flows between Thailand

and the Middle East and trade has grown significantly. Corruption is endemic in the government and police force. Because of Thailand's place in the international drug trade, there is a culture of money laundering, corruption, and operating in the shadows. According to the Thai government some 100 billion Thai baht (roughly $2.2 billion) in drug money is laundered annually through financial institutions in Thailand. An estimated 40 percent of Thailand's gross domestic product is underground, unregulated, and untaxed. Although in 1999 Thailand passed very stringent and retroactive anti–money laundering laws that have become a model for the region, corruption continues seemingly unabated. In March 2002, for example, Thai authorities arrested twenty-five Middle Eastern men suspected of laundering Al-Qaida funds in the kingdom. In addition, several of the suspects were charged with forging travel documents, passports, and visas for Al-Qaida members.[129] In 2002, intelligence officials noted that Thai immigration authorities had detained on average one person a day for traveling with forged documentation.[130]

Finally, Thailand is an international transport hub with easy international access. Thailand has relatively lax immigration requirements and tourist-friendly visa requirements. It is a convenient country in which to facilitate financial transactions, travel, and networking.

The Myanmar Connection

There is little information about the Al-Qaida network in Myanmar, but Myanmar nationals have been identified as Al-Qaida terrorists. Indeed, the largest Al-Qaida cell in Southeast Asia is said to be in Myanmar, though these links are much closer to Al-Qaida networks in South Asia.[131] Myanmar does not offer terrorists the infrastructure they need, especially the ability to set up front companies and nongovernmental organizations, nor is it a travel hub. Even so, there are a few disturbing signs.

Al-Qaida has been long established in neighboring Bangladesh, where thousands of Muslims have taken refuge from Myanmar's military government's systematic repression of its Muslim ethnic minorities, the Bengalis, Rohingas, and Kachin. Muslims account for roughly 4 percent of Myanmar's population. Whenever there are aggrieved people who are persecuted relentlessly, they will look to any means to fight back. Currently, there are three Muslim-based guerrilla movements in Myanmar: the Ommat Liberation Front, the Kawthoolei Muslim Liberation Front, and the Muslim Liberation Organization of Myanmar. The government has waged a harsh counterinsurgency against these groups and has at times tacitly supported local militias to engage in communal violence against Muslim communities. In Prone, for example, five people were reported to have been killed in state-supported communal clashes. In early 2001, there was a wave of anti-Muslim violence in central and northwest Myanmar near Bangladesh.[132]

Al-Qaida has recruited Myanmar Muslims from the border region and sent them for training in Afghanistan, but the number is thought to be quite small. In Bangladesh, the radical Harakat-ul-Jihad-al-Islami (HuJI), founded in 1992, is led by an associate of Osama bin Laden, Fazlul Rahman. The organization is closely tied to one of the Al-Qaida–linked groups in Pakistan/Kashmir. Several HuJI leaders are veterans of the Soviet-era mujahidin. Fazlul Rahman signed Osama bin Laden's February 23, 1998, declaration of holy war on the United States. HuJI has recruited from Bangladesh's 60,000 *madrasas* (thirty to forty of which are run by Afghan veterans) and is now believed to have more than 15,000 followers. HuJI was implicated in scores of bombings, including two attempted assassinations of then prime minister Shaikh Hasina in July 2000. HuJI has also been increasingly involved in politics in Bangladesh. Its slogan, "We will all be Taliban and Bangladesh will be Afghanistan," belies its political agenda. Though it is not a political party, many of its members are part of Islamic Oikya Jote, which was one of two Islamic parties (the other being Jamaat-e-Islami) that joined into a coalition government with Prime Minister Begum Khaleda Zia's Bangladesh Nationalist Party (BNP) in October 2001. Both Islamic parties have a history of links to terrorist organizations and openly supported the Taliban and Al-Qaida.[133]

HuJI also actively recruited Rohingas from Myanmar and sent them to fight in Kashmir, Afghanistan, and Chechnya.[134] There are about 200,000 Rohingas in Bangladesh. The largest Rohinga organization in Bangladesh is the Rohinga Solidarity Organization (RSO), established in the early 1980s, which has a large training camp in Ukhia, southeast of Cox's Bazaar. The militant group has actively recruited from among the destitute community and in the 1980s sent volunteers to Afghanistan to fight the Soviets. Bertil Lintner found that the RSO had maintained close links and received material support from other South Asian militant organizations including the Hizb-e-Islami in Afghanistan, the Hizb-ul-Mujahidin in Kashmir, and the Jamaat-e-Islami in Bangladesh.[135] More than 100 RSO fighters trained with the Hizb-e-Islami in Afghanistan, and Afghan trainers have come to RSO camps, which in the 1990s were taken over by Fazlul Rahman's HuJI. Most RSO weapons are Chinese-made and come from Cambodia, Thailand, and Myanmar's black markets. According to Lintner, Rohinga recruits who were sent to fight with the Taliban were well paid by Bangladeshi standards: 30,000 Bangladeshi taka ($525) upon joining and 10,000 taka ($175) per month. HuJI operates some nineteen training camps throughout the country that can accommodate more than 2,500 fighters and was listed by the U.S. Department of State as a terrorist organization on May 12, 2002. Among the sixty Al-Qaida videotapes that CNN acquired in Afghanistan, one was entitled "Myanmar"; moreover, John Walker Lindh, the "American Taliban," admitted that Al-Qaida's Arab brigade that fought alongside the Taliban was divided along linguistic lines with Bengali, Urdu, and Arabic units.[136] Many Al-Qaida and Taliban officials are thought to have fled to Bangladesh in 2002 following the defeat of the Taliban.

On December 21, 2001, a ship, the *MV Mecca,* offloaded some 150 Taliban and Al-Qaida fighters at the Bangladeshi port of Chittagong. "Portworkers that night said they saw five motor launches ferry in large groups of men from the boat wearing black turbans, long beards and traditional Islamic *salwar kameez*. Their towering height suggested these travelers were foreigners, and the boxes of ammunition and the AK-47s slung across their shoulders helped sketch a sinister picture."[137] HuJI officials later confirmed that the men were Al-Qaida fighters. On October 7, 2002, the Indian government arrested a HuJI operative, Fazle Karim (Abu Fuzi), who was born in Myanmar, as he arrived in Calcutta by train from Kashmir.

The government arrested four Yemenis, an Algerian, a Libyan, and a Sudanese, who were implicated in militant arms training at a *madrasa* in the capital run by the Saudi charity, Al Haramain, which was also raided by intelligence forces. They were all later released and the government stated that no incriminating evidence was found at the Al Haramain office, but concern remains that Bangladesh was increasingly important to Al-Qaida. Bangladesh's military intelligence service maintains very close ties with their counterparts in Pakistan's Inter-Service Intelligence and have a history of providing operational support for Kashmiri rebels. Indeed, the portworkers who saw the *Mecca* arrive claim that the man who greeted the militants was a major in the military intelligence service. There were also sporadic reports that Al-Qaida's second in command, Ayman al-Zawahiri, arrived in Dhaka in early March 2002, and stayed briefly in the compound of a local fundamentalist leader. Reports continue to emerge that he is based in the Chittagong region.

The RSO/HuJI is not the first time Muslims from Myanmar have been trained in Afghanistan. In the 1980s, there were Muslims from Myanmar in Afghanistan fighting with the mujahidin. Networks of people and groups already exist. According to Lintner, the foremost expert of insurgent politics in Myanmar, the Muslim Liberation Organization of Myanmar, "maintains some contact with Islamic circles in Pakistan."[138] On January 19, 1999, for example, police arrested seven Al-Qaida members (one of whom was a Myanmar national) who were plotting to blow up the U.S. Embassy in Delhi.[139] More recently, leaflets calling on Muslims to join the jihad against the Americans were reportedly found in Myanmar.[140]

As long as the Myanmar junta continues to repress the Muslim minority to the extent that it does, we should continue to expect them to reach out to any external group or state that will continue to provide them with some assistance. That said, to date most of the Al-Qaida activity in Myanmar is less oriented toward Southeast Asia than to the India-Pakistan-Kashmir region.

GAM: Al-Qaida's Link to Aceh?

Although GAM, the secessionist movement in Aceh formed in 1975, has never been publicly linked to Al-Qaida or other Middle Eastern–based Islamic terrorist organizations, it is suspected by U.S. officials of having some ties. Many GAM members fought with the mujahidin, so linkages are possible though none have ever been confirmed and the organization denies any: "We have never had any contact with Osama bin Laden. We don't want to have anything to do with an organization that plays the religious card like Al-Qaida," said a GAM spokesman. They are a nationalist, not an Islamic movement.

In June 2000, two of the most senior leaders of Al-Qaida, Mohammed Atef and Ayman al-Zawahiri, traveled to Indonesia, stopping in Aceh, where they reportedly met with Acehnese leaders. Hoping to establish a base area and training facilities in Indonesia, to complement Afghanistan, the two Al-Qaida leaders were favorably impressed by the lack of central government control, the Islamic fervor of the people, and GAM's local support. Despite their favorable impression, GAM resisted their overtures and Al-Qaida did not establish a base in Aceh. GAM leaders, according to a senior U.S. official, were extremely sensitive to the U.S. position on this issue and were courting U.S. support and recognitions. To date, only limited direct ties between GAM and Al-Qaida have been uncovered.

One Acehnese leader, a member of the splinter group GAM Administrative Council (MP-GAM), whom the Al-Qaida leaders met was Teuku Idris. Idris had already participated with Omar al-Faruq in a group called the Rabitatul Mujahidin. The Rabitatul Mujahidin was established in 1999 by Abu Bakar Ba'asyir and served as a focal point for coordinating activities between Al-Qaida, JI/MMI, and Al-Qaida cells in Myanmar, Aceh, and Thailand. According to GAM spokesman Soyfan Daud, Idris was formerly a GAM member but had "deserted" and became aligned with exiled GAM leader Hasan di Tiro in Europe, who had established MP-GAM. The spokesman denied that GAM was involved in the mujahidin.[141] As Al-Qaida seemed unable to co-opt or form an alliance with GAM, it may have turned to Tiro's splinter group or other defectors. Alternatively, the splinter group thesis could be a ruse to give GAM a degree of plausible deniability regarding its links to Al-Qaida.

GAM receives covert aid from several Middle Eastern countries, and links between GAM and Libya are well substantiated. The current head of GAM's military wing, Muzakkir Manaf, was trained in Libya between 1986 and 1989, and Libya continues to be GAM's main benefactor. For the most part, GAM purchases its weapons from illegal arms bazaars in Thailand and Cambodia, as well as from corrupt Indonesian military officials. GAM has also purchased weapons from the Philippines, a major bone of contention between Jakarta and Manila. GAM has approximately 1,800 guerrillas, though it claims to have 3,000, and has effectively fought government forces to a standstill. In mid-2002, national security officials requested an additional 8,000 troops to be deployed in Aceh. There are already 21,000 soldiers and 15,000 police, giving the government a ten to one advantage.

A peace accord between GAM and the Indonesian government was signed on December 9, 2002, giving the Acehnese greater autonomy. Elections are scheduled for 2004.

Jihad Down Under

The responsibility of the small Mantiqi 4 cell was to develop a terrorist network in Australia. Abu Bakar Ba'asyir and Abdullah Sungkar made eleven visits to Australia in the 1990s. Other JI members also traveled there for recruiting and fundraising. The leader of the JI Australian cell was Abdul Rahman Ayub, a Perth-based Islamic teacher and master of the Al Hidayah Islamic School and a five-year veteran of the mujahidin in Afghanistan before illegally emigrating to Australia in 1997. Ayub fled Australia soon after the October 12, 2002, attack in Bali with his twin brother, Abdul Rahim. Both are believed to be at large in Indonesia. Other Australian JI members include:

- Kusmir Nesirwan Nesirwan, a Sydney taxi driver, was a JI operative in the Malukus. He was implicated by Australian security forces for plotting attacks during the 2000 Sydney Olympics.
- Muksid bin Talib, a refugee from Indonesia, was Ba'asyir's host in Australia.
- Ali Basri, Azman, a Malaysian, is the head of the Sydney JI cell.
- Omar Batok, Abdillah, is the head of a Melbourne cell.
- Ahmed, the chief recruiter for Mantiqi 4.
- Nur Hakim, a warehouse worker and Ba'asyir's driver, had also videotaped the cleric's speeches and sent them back to Australia.
- Jack Roche, known in Australia as "Jihad Jack," a British convert to Islam who conspired to blow up the Israeli embassy and consulate in Canberra and Sydney and ran a training camp in the Blue Mountains outside of Perth.[142]
- Bilal Khazal, a Lebanese-born Australian, trained in Afghanistan with Al-Qaida in 1998. He worked as a baggage handler at Sydney airport and was believed to be involved in the plotting of attacks in Australia and the Philippines. Khazal was a leader of the Islamic Youth Movement in Sydney, which Australian intelligence believed to be a key recruiting ground for JI.

In conjunction with the Bali bombing investigation, the Australian Secret Intelligence Organization (ASIO) conducted raids on dozens of houses of Abu Bakar Ba'asyir's associates and suspected JI members.

The primary responsibility of Australian JI members was fundraising and recruiting among Australia's large Indonesian exile community. Yet not all their activities were so benign. Australian intelligence believed that in April 2003, JI leaders held a "high-level meeting in Indonesia" to identify new targets for Al-Qaida in Australia. The arrest of an Australian citizen in Egypt, suspected of ties to Al-Qaida, provided further evidence of Al-Qaida interest in attacking Australia. In a May 29 speech to Parliament, Australian Prime Minister stated, "I can now inform the House that new information has come to light very recently indicating that Al-Qaida explored possible targets in Australia in 2000 or 2001" that "predated the September 11, 2001, attacks in New York and Washington."[143]

Australia does feel vulnerable to Al-Qaida, and it has been mentioned by name on many occasions by Osama bin Laden and Ayman al-Zawahiri. In bin Laden's November 3, 2001, statement aired on Al-Jezeera, he warned that Australia was guilty of breaking apart a Muslim country: "The crusader Australian forces were on Indonesian shores, and in fact they landed to separate East Timor, which is part of the Islamic world." In November 2002, Bin Laden stated: "We warned Australia in advance about its involvement in Afghanistan, as well as about its reprehensible effort to separate East Timor, but it ignored the warning until it woke up to the sounds of the explosions in Bali—at which point its government slanderously and falsely claimed that they had not been targeted." In other statements he has justified attacking Australians because of their support for the Americans and their role in the invasion of Afghanistan. Ayman al-Zawahiri's May 21, 2003, statement called on all Muslims to attack Australian embassies and other targets to punish them for their role in the invasion of Iraq.

Australia is a close ally of the United States and has been one of the staunchest supporters of the war on terror. Its proximity to and interests in Southeast Asia, coupled with popular Indonesian antipathy toward Australia for its leading role in the East Timor peacekeeping operation ensures that it will be the target of Al-Qaida and Jemaah Islamiya wrath in the future.

Notes

1. Phil Hirschkorn, Rohan Gunaratna, Ed Blanche, and Stefan Leader, "Blowback: The Origins of Al Qaida," *Janes Intelligence Review* 13, no. 8 (August 2001).

2. After the meeting, Malaysian intelligence followed al-Mindhar and al-Hazmi, searched the hard drives of their computers, but did not have any evidence to arrest them. After the meeting, al-Mindhar and al-Hazmi left Malaysia, flew to Los Angeles via Bangkok, Thailand, and Hong Kong, respectively, on January 15, 2000. They lived openly, using their real names, and enrolled in a San Diego–area flight school. The

Malaysian intelligence service obviously shared the videotape and photos of the people who attended the meeting with the Central Intelligence Agency. The CIA knew that al-Mindhar had a multiple entry visa to the United States, but it did not put him on a terrorist watch list or inform the Immigration and Naturalization Service (INS) or State Department. Indeed al-Mindhar was able to leave the country for Frankfurt, Germany, on June 10, where he played a role in the October 12 attack on the USS *Cole*, and al-Hazmi applied to extend his visa on July 7, 2001. Following the attack on the USS *Cole*, Khallad was under intense investigation and on January 4 was named as a key planner of the attacks. In July 2001, a CIA officer assigned to the FBI rediscovered a CIA cable that detailed Khallad's presence at the Kuala Lumpur meeting and sent an e-mail to the CIA's counterterrorism center: "This is a major league killer, who orchestrated the Cole attack and possibly the [1998 East] Africa bombings." The FBI discovered al-Mindhar had reentered the country on July 4, 2001. The CIA put al-Mindhar and al-Hazmi on the terrorist watch list, but only on August 21, eighteen months after the Kuala Lumpur meeting, causing a huge scandal in the United States. According to recent congressional testimony, the CIA learned that the two men were in the United States in March 2000 but did not inform the FBI. According to Eleanor Hill, a staff director of the joint congressional inquiry, who testified on September 19, 2002, "Unfortunately, none of these things happened. The failure to watchlist al-Mindhar and al-Hazmi or, at a minimum, to advise the FBI of their travel to the United States, is perhaps even more puzzling because it occurred shortly after the peak of the intelligence community alertness to possible millennium-related terrorist attacks." When the INS was eventually informed, it was too late; the two were already in the United States. The FBI began looking for the two immediately but were unable to find them. A New York–based FBI agent requested his superiors on August 29, 2001, to allow "full criminal investigative resources" to find al-Mindhar. The request was denied because al-Mindhar was not under criminal investigation. The frustrated agent replied: "Someday someone will die—and wall or not—the public will not understand why we were not more effective and throwing every resource we had at certain 'problems.'" After the World Trade Center was struck, the FBI agent reviewed the passenger manifests from the four hijacked planes and told the joint congressional inquiry angrily: "This is the same al-Mindhar we've been talking about for three months!" His supervisor, replied: "We did everything by the book." Cited in Dan Eggen and Dana Priest, "FBI Agent Urged Search for Hijackers," *WP*, August 21, 2001; Tabassum Zakaria, "CIA Knew About 3 Hijackers in 2000—9/11 Inquiry," Reuters, September 20, 2002.

3. Tawfiq bin Attash was arrested on May 3, 2003. Ramzi bin al-Shibh, a Yemeni who was named as the missing twentieth hijacker, had tried to enter the United States four times but was denied a visa. Like his roommate, Mohammed Atta, bin al-Shibh attended Al-Quds Mosque in Hamburg, Germany, where he was recruited by a Syrian-German, Mohammed Haydar Zammar, then put in touch with Khalid Shaikh Mohammed, who came to Hamburg in early 1999 and sent al-Shibh to Afghanistan for training in 1999. Al-Shibh was related by marriage to one of the hijackers, Khalid al-Mindhar, the pilot of the hijacked plane that crashed in Pennsylvania; another 9/11 hijacker, Ziad al-Jarrah, tried to enroll bin al-Shibh into the Florida Flight Training Center in Venice. Between August and September 2000, bin al-Shibh was in his native Yemen, which investigators believe also links him to the October 2000 attack on the USS *Cole*. Unable to enter the United States, bin al-Shibh remained an important planner and financial backer of Atta. The two attended a meeting in Spain in July 2001 with a senior Al-Qaida official to go over the last details of the September 11 attacks before Atta left for the United States. Bin al-Shibh wired $6,200 to Marwan al-Shehhi and $14,000 to Zaccarias Moussaoui, the French Moroccan who was thought to be the

twentieth hijacker to pay for his flight training. Bin al-Shibh fled Germany on September 5, traveling via Spain to Pakistan. He was one of the most wanted terrorists, as he attended both the Kuala Lumpur and Madrid meetings and was captured in a shoot-out in Karachi, Pakistan, on September 11, 2002. For more on bin al-Shibh, see Douglas Frantz, "Search for Sept. 11 Suspect Focuses on a Visit to Spain," *NYT*, May 1, 2002; Peter Finn, "Al Qaeda's German Connections," *Washington Post Weekly*, June 17–23, 2002.

4. Edy Budiyarso, "Indonesia's Afghan-Trained Mujiheddin," *Tempo Weekly*, October 2–8, 2001.

5. Associated Press (AP), "Malaysia Uncovers Plots Against U.S.," December 9, 2001.

6. Patrick Sennyah, Ainon Mohd and Hayati Hayatudin, "KMM's Opposition Link," *New Straits Times* (*NST*), October 12, 2001.

7. Nelson Fernandez, "Police Have Videos, Pictures, Info on Afghan-Trained Students," *NST*, September 30, 2001.

8. Simon Elegant, "Getting Radical," *Time Asia*, September 10, 2001.

9. Edy Budiyarso, "Indonesia's Afghan-Trained Mujiheddin," *Tempo Weekly*, October 2–8, 2001.

10. Sungkar was born in 1937 in Solo, Central Java. Ba'asyir was born in 1938 in Jombang, East Java.

11. The land was donated by Kiai Haji Abu Amman, an ulama in Solo who was notable in the 1960s for his fervor to create an Islamic state.

12. For more on Al-Mukmin, see Bina Bektiati, Imron Rosyid, and L. N. Idayanie, "Exclusive and Secretive," *Tempo* 21 (January 29–February 4, 2002).

13. International Crisis Group (ICG), *Al-Qaeda in Southeast Asia: The Case of the Ngruki Network*. Asia Report (August 8, 2002), 7.

14. Baraja was also a part-time textile trader. He was related to Ba'asyir by marriage. Arrested in 1979, he was sentenced to five years in prison. In March 1985 he was again arrested for his role in the Borobudur bombing and sentenced to fifteen years in prison. He was released in 1999 and became a senior leader of the Council of Indonesia, heading its Fatwah Division.

15. Kadungga was born in Palopo, South Sulawesi, on May 20, 1940. He was the son-in-law of Kahar Muzakkar, who led the Darul Islam movement in Sulawesi from 1950 to 1965. Kadungga was active in student groups in the 1960s, and in Europe he was active in the World Assembly of Muslim Youth. He became a Dutch citizen but lived in Malaysia with Ba'asyir in the mid-1980s. He was arrested upon returning to Indonesia in December 2002 but was released after authorities ascertained that he had no role in the Bali bombing.

16. "Suharto's Detect, Defect, and Destroy Policy Towards the Islamic Movement," interview with Abdullah Sungkar, *Nida'ul Islam*, February–March 1997.

17. Ibid.

18. Ibid.

19. A transcript of Ba'asyir's sermon can be found at http://www.abc.net.au/4corners/stories/s711753.htm.

20. Mark Freeman and Richard C. Paddock, "Response to Terror: Indonesia Cleric Tied to '95 Anti-US Plot," *Los Angeles Times*, February 7, 2002.

21. Interview, Singapore, June 20, 2002.

22. Derwin Pereira, "A Potent Force with a Network in the Region," *Straits Times* (*ST*), January 20, 2002.

23. Interview with Abu Bakar Ba'asyir, Ngruki, Solo, June 11, 2002.

24. Rajiv Chandrasekaran, "Clerics Groomed Students for Terrorism," *Washington Post* (*WP*), February 7, 2002.

25. Cited in Alexa Olesen, "Singapore Terror Suspects Average," AP, September 27, 2002.

26. Simon Elegant, "The Family Behind the Bombing," *Time Asia*, November 25, 2002.

27. Wan Min Wan Mat fled Malaysia in early 2002 but returned from southern Thailand in September 2002, apparently missing his family. He was arrested in Kota Baru on September 27.

28. Ammonium nitrate, a common ingredient in chemical fertilizers, is not commonly found in Singapore, though it is readily available in Malaysia. There, one ton costs approximately S$400–500.

29. "Indictment Chronicles 'Overt Acts' That It Said Led to Sept. 11 Attacks," *New York Times (NYT),* December 12, 2001, B6.

30. Ministry of Home Affairs, *White Paper: The Jemaah Islamiyah Arrests and the Threat of Terrorism* (Singapore, 2003), 6.

31. Malaysiakini, "Ex-Army Officer Detained Under the ISA," February 25, 2003; Malaysiakini, "ISA Arrest of Ex-Colonel Must Be in Good Faith, Sukham," February 27, 2003; also http://abimjohor.org.my/kbi.htm.

32. The firm was capitalized with MR$300,000. The shares were distributed as follows: Abdul Manaf Kasmuri, 83,999 shares (24%); Faiz bin Abu Bakar Bafana, 83,999 shares (28%); Zulkifli Marzuki, 72,000 shares (28%); and Shaharudin Othman, 60,000 shares (20%). I have no evidence that Othman is a member of Jemaah Islamiya. There is evidence that the firm had been effectively dormant in 2001–2002.

33. Kavi Chongkittavorn, "Al Qaeda in Thailand: Fact or Fiction?" *The Nation*, January 13, 2003.

34. Ba'asyir traveled under the passport name Abu Samad, which means the "absolute one." In conjunction with the Bali bombing, the Australian Secret Intelligence Organization (ASIO) conducted raids on Ba'asyir's associates, including Nur Hakim, a warehouse worker and Ba'asyir's driver, who had also videotaped the cleric's speeches and sent the tapes back to Australia. The leader of the JI Australian cell seems to be Abdul Raha Ayub, a Perth-based Islamic teacher and master of the Al-Hidayah Islamic School. Another JI leader was Jack Roche, a British convert to Islam who conspired to blow up the Israeli Embassy and Consulate in Canberra and Sydney and ran a training camp in the Blue Mountains near Perth.

35. Four of the thirteen arrested JI operatives in Singapore identified al-Ghozi as their instructor in the Philippines.

36. Romesh Ratnesar, "Confessions of an Al Qaeda Terrorist," *Time*, September 16, 2002; BIN Interrogation Report of Omar al-Faruq (June 2002).

37. Fathur Rohman al-Ghozi, written deposition, July 2002.

38. The one ton of explosives purchased by al-Ghozi, as well as seventeen M-16s, detonating cord, and other bomb-making material, were to be hidden in two shipments of flour and nylon cord that were to be transferred to Bintam, Indonesia, an island off Singapore, via Poso, the port city where a JIN training camp was located. The deputy chief of the State Intelligence Agency, As'at Said, does not believe that there are any contacts between the Al-Qaida training camp in Poso (or its head, Parlindungan Siregar) and the Jemaah Islamiya network. See "The Jibril Document Was Fabricated: Interview with As'at Said," *Tempo* 25 (February 26–March 4, 2002).

39. Michael Lim Ubac, "Indon Terror Suspect Admits Planning Rizal Day Bombings," *Philippine Daily Inquirer* (*PDI*), February 27, 2002.

40. Jabarah was an ethnic Kuwaiti and naturalized Canadian citizen who traveled to Kuwait to study Islam. Unable to gain entrance in a university due to his poor Arabic, he moved to Pakistan sometime in 2000 and enrolled in an Islamic school. In Pakistan he was recruited into Al-Qaida.

41. Singapore-based fund-raisers and supporters of the MILF now under detention include: Husin Abdul Aziz, Sakahan Abdul Rahman, Habibullah Hameed, Faizal Khan Gulam Sarwar, and Mohamed Agus Ahmad Selani. The latter two were arrested in December 2001 but released and served with restriction orders. "Jemaah Islamiya Forged Links with Regional Groups," *ST*, September 20, 2001.

42. In April 2002, seventeen members of the Negara Islam Indonesia (NII), a radical Sufi sect, were arrested, though twelve were later released. The NII was established in 1949 by Sekarmaji Marijan Kartoswiryo, the founder of Darul Islam, and has remained active through its *pesentren,* the al-Zaetun School in the West Java town of Indramayu. The school is led by Abu Toto. See "Islamic Radicals Freed for Lack of Proof," *ST*, April 11, 2002.

43. Interview with Abu Bakar Ba'asyir, Ngruki, Solo, June 11, 2002.

44. Ibid.

45. Ibid.; interview with Drs. Prosetyo, Indonesian National Police Headquarters (MABISPOLRI), Jakarta, June 13, 2002; and interview with Drs. Bagus, director of the Office of Terrorism, Police Intelligence, MABISPOLRI, Jakarta, June 14, 2002.

46. BIN Interrogation Report of Omar al-Faruq (June 2002). The branch office was in Makassar.

47. Atef was the head of Al-Qaida's military operations and was responsible for the suicide attack on the USS *Cole*. Ayman was the head of Egyptian Islamic Jihad and was responsible for the murder of Egyptian president Anwar Sadat.

48. CNN, "Intel Report: Bin Laden Sought Indonesian Base," July 9, 2002.

49. Harold Crouch, "Qaida in Indonesia? The Evidence Doesn't Support Worries," *International Herald Tribune* (*IHT*), October 23, 2001.

50. ICG, "The Ngruki Network."

51. Lindsay Murdoch, "Bin Laden 'Funded Christian Haters,'" *Sydney Morning Herald* (*SMH*), September 28, 2001.

52. Interview with Abu Bakar Ba'asyir, Solo, June 11, 2002.

53. Dan Murphy, "Al Qaida's New Frontier: Indonesia," *Christian Science Monitor* (*CSM*), May 1, 2002.

54. It is important to note that Hadi Awang, a senior PAS official and minister of Terengganu, was a close associate of Agus Dwikarna and attended the founding meeting of Dwikarna's Committee for Upholding Sharia (Komite Pengerak Syariat Islam, KPSI) in South Sulawesi, the umbrella organization of the Laskar Jundullah.

55. "I don't have a history of violence. I am anti-violence. I am active in KOMPAK because that is a humanitarian organization. The activities of KPSI always avoid violence, such as minimizing protests and demonstrations." "I Don't Have a History of Violence," interview with Agus Dwikarna, *Tempo*, January 6, 2003, 38–41.

56. KOMPAK was founded on August 1, 1998, as an independent arm of the Dewan Dakwah Islam Indonesia (established February 1967). KOMPAK officials, while acknowledging that they operate in regions struck by sectarian conflict (Aceh, Poso, Malukus, and Bangunan Beton Sumatra), say they are there to alleviate the crises and provide necessary relief. They have denied any links to jihad activities. "We never give our money to the mujahidin or terrorists. We give our money to the needy, unemployed of the *ummah*." This assertion should be taken guardedly. Without a doubt KOMPAK has been involved in charitable work, especially food distribution. Yet the

former chairman of KOMPAK's South Sulawesi office was Agus Dwikarna, and the head of the Jakarta office was Tamsil Linrung. When asked about that, the secretary of KOMPAK stated, "What he does outside of KOMPAK is not our responsibility." Interview with H. Asep R. Jayanegara, secretary, Komite Penanggulangan Krisis, Dewan Dakwah Islam Indonesia, Jakarta, January 8, 2003.

57. "Indonesia: Overcoming Murder and Chaos in Maluku," ICG Asia Report No. 10 (December 2000).

58. Online at www.laskarjihad.org.

59. "Waiting for Osama's Blessing," *Tempo*, September 18–24, 2001.

60. Warren Caragata, "Radical Blasts," *Asiaweek,* October 5, 2001.

61. Romesh Ratnesar, "Confessions of an Al-Qaeda Terrorist," *Time*, September 16, 2002; BIN Interrogation Report of Omar al-Faruq (June 2002).

62. Ratnesar, "Confessions of an Al-Qaeda Terrorist."

63. Christopher Dickey, "New Faces in Al Qaeda Hierarchy," *Newsweek*, December 2001. Also see Giles Tremlett and John Hooper, "Eight Charged with Link to Sept. 11," *The Guardian*, November 19, 2001.

64. Personal correspondence, September 4, 2002.

65. Interview with Drs. Bagus, director of the Office of Terrorism, Police Intelligence, MABISPOLRI, Jakarta, June 14, 2002.

66. AP, "Thousands of Christians Flee Muslim Attacks," December 1, 2001.

67. Marianne Kearney, "Security Forces to Disarm Sulawesi Fighters," *ST*, December 6, 2001.

68. Fabiola Desy Unidjaja, "International Training Camp in Poso 'Empty,'" *Jakarta Post*, December 14, 2001.

69. *Al-Qaida's Infrastructure in Indonesia*, BIN, Jakarta, February 2002.

70. Unidjaja, "International Training Camp in Poso 'Empty.'"

71. Ratnesar, "Confessions of an Al-Qaeda Terrorist"; Central Intelligence Agency, "Terrorist Connections of Abubakar Bashir and Further Details on Terrorist Connections and Activities of Umar Faruq," September 2002.

72. The United States came across diagrams and blueprints detailing the U.S. Embassy and its security regimen from a terrorist suspect in the Middle East. When U.S. intelligence discovered that the six-member team was dispatched to Surabaya, U.S. ambassador Robert S. Gelbard went to the Indonesian intelligence services to arrest the six Yemenis. Indonesian military intelligence, however, brought in local police to do the arrest because it was a law enforcement issue. Although two CIA officials had already been flown in to assist in the arrest, along with a plane to take the Yemenis to the United States, the six were tipped off and fled the country.

73. Republic of Singapore, Ministry of Home Affairs, *White Paper: The Jemaah Islamiyah Arrests and the Threat of Terrorism* (Singapore, 2003), 27.

74. They are being held under the Internal Security Act that allows the government to detain them for up to two years without trial. On October 4, 2001, the high court rejected their appeal for habeas corpus. See AP, "Militant Suspects Jailed for 2 Years," September 27, 2001; and Manisah Usmail, "Nik Adli Stays Detained After Habeas Corpus Application Rejected," *NST*, October 4, 2001.

75. The May 18, 2001, Southern Bank robbery in Petaling Jaya led to the death of two of the robbers. One was captured and interrogated. On June 9 more KMM members were arrested and a cache of weapons was found in Puchong.

76. Taufik Abdul Halim was sentenced to death by a Jakarta court on May 7, 2002. His motive for the bombings was "revenge for the Christian slaughter of Muslims in Ambon," though he claims that he was coerced into delivering the bomb that exploded prematurely, taking his own leg in the process.

77. Rajiv Chandrasekaran, "Al Qaeda's Southeast Asian Reach," *WP*, February 3, 2002.

78. These four were Hussain bin Ismail, Mohammed Rashid bin Zainal Abidan, Ishak Mohammed Noohu, and Mohammed Hassan bin Saynudin.

79. Federal Bureau of Investigation, "Information Derived from Mohammed Mansour Jabarah," August 21, 2002.

80. The light weapons were destined for JI's paramilitary forces that were fighting in the Malukus and Poso. AP, "S'pore Tip-off Leads to Explosives Haul," *ST*, January 18, 2002.

81. Al-Ghozi was sentenced to ten to twelve years for possession of explosives and six years for possession of fake passports. Martin P. Marfil and T. J. Burgonio, "Hunt on for al-Qaida Men Tagged by Arrested Indon," *PDI*, January 10, 2001.

82. Several intercepted phone calls to Bafana from an individual known as "Freedom Fighter" on the evening of the bombings indicated to Philippine authorities that there were foreign liaisons to the MILF bombings. However, they did not know who Freedom Fighter was until they could match his cell phone number with al-Ghozi's.

83. By the end of 2001, there were twenty-three KMM members being detained under the ISA. Several were senior PAS functionaries or provincial religious leaders within PAS. Hazmi Ishak, for example, is a member of PAS, a former student in Pakistan who, between 1990 and 1995, underwent military training with the mujahidin. He is said to be a close aide of Nik Adli Nik Aziz. Other KMM members detained under the ISA included two PAS state youth chiefs. In early 2002, two additional KMM members were detained, bringing the total to twenty-five. Malaysian police are currently searching for up to 200 KMM and Jemaah Islamiya members. The forty-two-year-old religious teacher Ahmad Jinbaz Mukhlis Mokhtar Ghazali was detained on February 2, 2002. Another "religious official" was detained after being caught with a large cache of ammunition and Indonesian passports in Perak State on March 2, 2002.

84. "Suspected Terrorists Arrested at NAIA," *PDI*, March 15, 2002; "Jakarta Asks Manila to Clarify Arrests," *PDI*, March 17, 2002.

85. Dwikarna asserts that he was framed. See "I Don't Have a History of Violence," interview with Agus Dwikarna, *Tempo*, January 6, 2003, 38–41. Sidney Jones of the ICG, wrote that "the evidence in their suitcase in Manila was planted appears to be well founded" and that "no convincing evidence if involvement in terrorist activities has been made public against the suspects," including Dwikarna. See ICG, "The Ngruki Network," 20.

86. Tiarma Siboro and Yogita Tahilramani, "Back Room Deal Behind the Release of Two Indonesians," *JP*, April 22, 2002.

87. Ibid.

88. Irfan Budiman et al., "Islamic Organizations = Terrorists," *Tempo*, No. 29 (March 26–April 4, 2002).

89. Omar al-Faruq admitted during his interrogation in September 2002 that Linrung was a member of Jemaah Islamiya and participated in Rabitatul Mujahidin meetings from 1999 to 2000. BIN Interrogation Report of Omar al-Faruq (June 2002).

90. Personal correspondence with a senior Philippine intelligence official, March 2002.

91. Irfan Budiman and Darlis Muhammad, "Target: Agus Dwikarna," *Tempo*, No. 31 (April 9–15, 2002); Rajiv Chandrasekaran, "Indonesian Arrested in Manila Had Ties to Al Qaeda," *WP*, May 9, 2002.

92. Of the fourteen, twelve were Malaysian citizens and two were permanent residents from Indonesia. The arrests brought to a total of thirty-five people detained under the ISA.

93. "Islamic Group Had Designs on S'Pore Target," *ST*, September 20, 2002; "At Least 3 Detainees Went for Al Qaida Training," *ST*, September 20, 2002.

94. Ministry of Home Affairs, Singapore, press release, September 19, 2002.

95. AP, "KL Arrest Prime Terror Suspect," September 27, 2002.

96. Ba'asyir believes that this is a political act, as the original notice of the supreme court's verdict is dated February 6, 1985, and he has vowed not to serve the sentence. See "Jakarta Delays Cleric's Arrest to Review Old Case," *ST*, April 19, 2002; and Yogita Tahihramani, "Ba'asyir Mulls Challenging Court Verdict," *JP*, April 18, 2002.

97. Interview with Abu Bakar Ba'asyir, Solo, June 11, 2002.

98. "Four Tonnes of Explosives Go Missing in Manila," *ST*, March 19, 2002.

99. Central Intelligence Agency, "Terrorist Connections of Abu Bakar Bashir and Further Details on Terrorist Connections and Activities of Umar Faruq." Also see, Ratnesar, "Confessions of an Al-Qaeda Terrorist."

100. Ibid. The joint training operation lasted from May 30 to 3 June.

101. Central Intelligence Agency, "Terrorist Connections of Abu Bakar Bashir and Further Details on Terrorist Connections and Activities of Umar Faruq." Also see, Ratnesar, "Confessions of an Al-Qaeda Terrorist."

102. Ratnesar, "Confessions of an Al-Qaeda Terrorist"; Raymond Bonner, "Plan to Attack Embassies in South Asia Cited for Terror Alert," *NYT*, September 11, 2002.

103. See Robert Go, "Key Suspect Prepares to Face the Music," *ST*, September 20, 2002; Ellen Nakashima and Alan Sipress, "Arrests Provide Indonesia with New Al Qaeda Leads," *WP*, September 19, 2002; and Timothy Mapes, "Antiterror War Pressures Indonesia," *Wall Street Journal*, September 20, 2002.

104. "Government to Investigate Abu Bakar Ba'asyir's Alleged Involvement in Terrorist Network," *Tempo*, September 18, 2002.

105. Rajiv Chandrasekaran and Peter Finn, "U.S. Behind Secret Transfer of Terror Suspects," *WP*, March 11, 2002.

106. It is interesting that the operation to arrest al-Faruq was not led by the police but by Major Andika from Kopassus, the son-in-law of BIN chief lieutenant general A. M. Hendropriyono, one of the only Indonesian officials who immediately after the 9/11 attacks confirmed that there was an Al-Qaida and terrorist presence in the country.

107. Federal Bureau of Investigation, "Information Derived from Mohammed Mansour Jabarah," August 21, 2002.

108. See interview with Abu Bakar Ba'asyir in Joe Cochrane, "It Was Carried Out By America," *Newsweek*, October 22, 2002.

109. Interview with Drs. Bagus, MABISPOLRI, Jakarta, June 14, 2002.

110. A transcript of Ba'asyir's sermon can be found at http://www.abc.net.au/4corners/stories/s711753.htm.

111. Republic of Indonesia Police Headquarters, "Examination Report of Abdul Aziz, a.k.a. Imam Samudra," October 21, 2002.

112. A transcript of Ba'asyir's sermon can be found at http://www.abc.net.au/4corners/stories/s711753.htm.

113. Cited in Simon Elegant, "Cash Flowing," *Time Asia*, March 24, 2003.

114. Jane MacCartney and Simon Cameron-Moore, "US to Freeze 'Terror' Funds in SE Asia—Sources," Reuters, March 13, 2003. AFP, "FBI Watching al-Qaeda Funds in Southeast Asia," *Financial Times*, March 31, 2003.

115. The Egyptian is Esam Mohamid Khadir Ali, and the two Thai Muslims are Haji Thiming Abdul Azi and Muhammad Jalludin Mading. The teachers hailed from Yemen, Sudan, Egypt, Nigeria, Pakistan, and Thailand. See Ker Munthit, "3 Muslim

Foreigners Arrested in Cambodia," AP, May 28, 2003; Ek Madra., "Cambodia Cracks Down on Foreign Muslims," Reuters, May 28, 2003.

116. Ratnesar, "Confessions of an Al Qaida Terrorist"; Raymond Bonner, "Plan to Attack Embassies in South Asia Cited for Terror Alert," *NYT*, September 11, 2002.

117. In his initial interrogation, Imam Samudra admitted to pledging *bayat* to Abdullah Sungkar but not Ba'asyir. Indonesia National Police, Interrogation of Abdul Aziz aka Imam Samudra, October 21, 2003; BBC, "Bali Bomb Suspect Admits Role," May 28, 2003.

118. Ali Imron stated, "I don't know for sure, but my feeling is that after the previous leader of Jemaah Islamiya [Abdullah Sungkar] died, Abu Bakar Ba'asyir took over." Mathew Moore, "Bali Suspects Name Bashir as JI Head," *The Age*, May 29, 2003.

119. BIN Interrogation Report of Omar al-Faruq (June 2002).

120. Ibid.

121. The driver of the truck got into a traffic accident and fled the scene. The police towed the truck, unaware of the bomb in the back of the truck. It was only discovered three days later. An Iranian, Hossein Dastgiri, was arrested and convicted. On February 18, 1998, the Thai Supreme Court, under intense diplomatic pressure, acquitted him and allowed him to return to Iran. The court ruled that the eyewitness testimony failed beyond a reasonable doubt to show that he was the driver.

122. John McBeth, "The Danger Within," *Far Eastern Economic Review* (*FEER*), September 22–23, 2001.

123. Agence France Press (AFP), "Thailand Probes Local Groups for Terrorist Links," December 27, 2002.

124. "Muslim Group Linked to Attacks in Thailand," *ST*, March 25, 2002.

125. "Thailand Admits Presence of Militant Muslims," Reuters, May 29, 2003.

126. The three are Waema Hadi Wae Da-oh, a doctor; Bozoru Haji Abdullah, a master of a *madrasa;* and his son, Bozoru Muyai. Five additional JI suspects were being sought. "Terrorist Cell: 3 'JI Members' Arrested in the South," *The Nation*, June 11, 2003.

127. Pasuk Phongpaichit et al., *Girls, Guns, Gambling, Ganja: Thailand's Illegal Economy and Public Policy* (Bangkok: Silkworm, 1998), esp. 1127–1154.

128. AP, "Militant Suspects Jailed for 2 Years."

129. "Thailand a Transit Point for Terror Funds," *ST*, March 11, 2002.

130. "Canada Helps Thais Combat Terror," *FEER*, September 19, 2002.

131. Larry Jagan, "Bin Laden—The Asia Connection," BBC, September 27, 2001.

132. Maung Maung Oo, "Junta Hunting Down Muslim Extremists," *The Irawaddy*, October 15, 2001.

133. Alex Perry, "Deadly Cargo," *Time Asia*, October 21, 2002.

134. Bertil Lintner, "A Recipe for Trouble," *FEER*, April 4, 2002, 17; and Lintner, "A Cocoon of Terror," *FEER*, April 4, 2002, 14-17.

135. Bertil Lintner "Championing Islamist Extremism," *South Asia Intelligence Review* 1, no. 9 (September 16, 2002).

136. Ibid.

137. Perry, "Deadly Cargo."

138. Bertil Lintner, *Burma in Revolt: Opium and Insurgency Since 1948* (Bangkok: Silkworm Books, 1999), 489.

139. Yonah Alexander and Michael S. Swetnam, *Usama bin Laden's al-Qaida: Profile of a Terrorist Network* (Ardsley, N.Y.: Transnational Publishers, 2001), 43.

140. Oo, "Junta Hunting Down Muslim Extremists."
141. "GAM Denies Involved in Mujiheddin Network," *Tempo*, October 21, 2002.
142. Louise Perry, "Plotting Terror in a Beachside Flat," *The Australian*, May 31, 2003.
143. Patrick Walters, "Al-Qa'ida Plot to Hit Targets in Australia," *The Australian*, May 30, 2003.

CHAPTER 5

State Responses to the War on Terror

IN THE IMMEDIATE AFTERMATH OF THE SEPTEMBER 11 ATTACKS, ALL SOUTHEAST Asian governments expressed sympathy for the victims and their concern about terrorism in general. The Association of Southeast Asian Nations issued a brief statement of condolence and a vague call for "strengthening cooperation in combating terrorism around the world." While all the governments condemned terrorism and endorsed UN Security Council Resolution 1368, their individual responses have ranged from robust support for the United States to demands that the United States refrain from the use of force to an expressed fear that U.S. hegemony and arrogance will only lead to more terrorist attacks. Not surprisingly, the Muslim states of Malaysia and Indonesia were the most overtly critical of the U.S. war in Afghanistan. Southeast Asian governments responded in radically different ways, each according to their immediate political interests and foreign policy objectives. Indeed, each country's response was clearly aimed more toward their domestic constituencies, though there have been a few regional initiatives, the subject of Chapter 6.

We must be cognizant that the reactions of the Southeast Asian states are constrained by the growth of political Islam in their countries. The Islamic resurgence in the region has occurred because of long-standing disputes with the secular governments. Many of the Islamic movements in Southeast Asia have legitimate grievances, whether they were repressed, clamored for autonomy, or simply demanded greater religious freedom. Economically speaking, in all Southeast Asian countries, the *pribumi* (Indonesian native Muslim) and *bumiputra* (indigenous Muslim Malay) communities are less well off. Indeed, Malaysia had to implement a reverse affirmative action program in the early 1970s following race riots in 1969 to give the ethnic majority a greater share of the nation's wealth. There are considerable socioeconomic inequalities across the region between the different religious communities, and these have only been exacerbated by the Asian economic crisis since 1997.

But the fundamental point about the limits to how far the governments can go in supporting the U.S.-led war on terror is this: Southeast Asian Muslims, in general, believe that the war on terror is patently anti-Muslim. These sentiments only grew with the war in Iraq and added to a sense of humiliation and indignation on the part of Southeast Asian Muslims.

Indonesia

Indonesia has, perhaps, the most at stake of any Southeast Asian country. In the politically weak country's five-year experiment with democracy, radical Islamic forces have grown in strength and numbers, able to capitalize on the breakdown of law and order and central government control. As the world's largest Muslim country—its population exceeds 200 million people—much is at stake for the future of this 17,000-island nation. President Megawati Sukarnoputri has warned that Indonesia could easily disintegrate into a "Balkans of the Eastern Hemisphere." The economy is still not out of the crisis that hit the country in 1997–1998 and there are some 40 million unemployed people. Economic uncertainty has only driven more people to the mosque. The state of the economy has forced the government to appeal to the international community for assistance, in particular the International Monetary Fund (IMF) and major bilateral donors, such as Japan and the United States. Megawati had to choose between tackling her political vulnerability, namely Islamic-based parties, and her key economic vulnerability. Unfortunately, she wavered. One only has to look at the January 2003 price hikes that the government implemented at the urging of the IMF. These hikes, caused by the ending of subsidies, were a matter of principle, according to President Megawati. Yet after demonstrations erupted, fear of political instability forced her to back down. Rather than how she portrays herself, quiet but firm, she has acted silent and indecisive until the devastating bombing of a Bali nightclub on October 12, 2002.

Megawati was the first Muslim leader to visit the United States after the September 11 terrorist attacks, and she made a strong statement condemning the attacks, pledging to support the United States on September 19, 2001.[1] That the first visitor to the White House after the September 11 attacks was the president of the world's largest Muslim country was more than symbolic; it was crucial for the U.S. effort to assemble an international coalition to combat terrorism. Indonesia quickly signed an anti-terrorist act and agreed to freeze any assets of Osama bin Laden if found in Indonesia and investigate whether known terrorists reside there.[2] For this, Megawati was rewarded. President George W. Bush provided $400 million in economic aid to stimulate the Indonesian economy and asked the U.S. Congress to provide $130 million more in 2002. Bush also lifted bans on nonlethal military sales and direct contact with the Indonesian military imposed during the East Timor crisis. In addition, the United States pledged to support Indonesia's "territorial integrity," which many saw as a green light for Indonesia to continue coercive policies in Aceh.

Megawati seemed truly alarmed by the terrorist attacks, of which Indonesia has experienced in large numbers since 2000, and as a strict secularist she was very concerned that fundamentalists might take over the Muslim agenda. Megawati was a seemingly close ally of the United States, but her support was neither unconditional nor guaranteed. It is not that Megawati is basically opposed to U.S. goals or efforts but that she has considerable domestic opposition to guard against.

Islamic Opposition

There is a limit to how aggressive Megawati could be toward Islamic militants, as she has to contend with growing opposition in Parliament and from her vice president, Hamzah Haz. The head of the largest Muslim party and a staunch Islamist, not to mention a former opponent of Megawati who blocked her ascendancy to the presidency in 1999, Hamzah has gone out of his way to identify with leading radicals. He met several times with the Laskar Jihad chief, Jafar Umar Thalib, and was instrumental in behind-the-scenes politicking that got Thalib acquitted of all charges against him in January 2003. He has also met with Abu Bakar Ba'asyir on numerous occasions and even visited the Al-Mukmin boarding school in a show of support for the beleaguered cleric. Hamzah was instrumental in blocking the investigation of Ba'asyir's role in the Bali bombing despite considerable evidence to the contrary. Although Ba'asyir was detained in November 2002, and eventually put on trial in April 2003, he was tried under a post–September 11 counter-terrorism law for treason—a nebulous law that many in Indonesia equated with Suharto-era laws that were used to silence political opposition. Ba'asyir has a first-rate legal team that has run circles around the prosecution and by June 2003 he was poised to be acquitted, vindicating the Islamic opposition. Hamzah is also an outspoken opponent of the United States and any U.S. military action in the Middle East. Following the September 11 attack on the United States, he expressed his hope that it would "cleanse America of its sins." Megawati distanced herself from this remark, but Hamzah capitalized on popular sentiment that was increasingly anti-American.

Hamzah will be the leading candidate against Megawati in the 2004 presidential election and needs to shore up his electoral base. There is considerable pressure on him from his own constituency and party organization that want him to maintain a hard line. As the deputy leader of the United Development Party stated: "He has to follow the party line even more so because he's our leader."[3] This has not gone unnoticed. A senior official of the Democratic Party of Indonesia for Struggle (PDI-P) complained, "It is clear that Hamzah is exploiting this issue for his own political benefit." Indeed, the MMI (Mujahidin Council of Indonesia) has all but endorsed Hamzah. Although the attempt to enshrine the Jakarta Charter (*sharia* law) into the constitution in the fall of 2002 failed, that it even became an issue at all and garnered as much support as it did is noteworthy. Hamzah, of course, still has constraints. He is still a member of the administration and cannot be seen as always running interference in Megawati's policies. He also has to be guarded about his own party that is now taking a much more radical and anti-Megawati line than himself, the party leader.

As Laskar Jihad chief Thalib warned, if the government provided concrete assistance to the Americans in the war on terrorism, President Megawati "can start counting the days before she is pushed from power."[4] And parliamentary leaders called on her to take a firmer stance against the Americans and explicitly condemn the U.S. bombing of Afghanistan, which she did. As one member of her own party stated, "The president has pledged her support for the US but she can't openly back a war effort because of a domestic backlash that could be exploited by these groups to undermine her position."[5] On October 14, 2001, she met with Hamzah and expressed that he was being too inflammatory and inciting domestic unrest. She expressed concern that "things can get out of hand" and hinder the nation's fragile economic recovery. Yet the next day Megawati appeared to cave in to Hamzah and toughened her stance on the U.S. campaign in Afghanistan: "Terrorism deserves punishment," she said at a Jakarta mosque, but then added, "No individual, group or government has the right to catch terrorist perpetrators by attacking the territory of another country."[6]

Megawati's tepid support for the war on terror was brought on by political opposition. That said, she was able to withstand most of the pressure and demands for several reasons. First, the moderate Muslim organizations, the NU (Nahdlatul Ulama) and Muhammadiyah, have been fairly supportive of the war on terror and have explicitly criticized terrorism and Al-Qaida's interpretation of Islam. Although the influential but very conservative Indonesian Ulamas Council condemned the U.S. operation in Afghanistan and urged the government to sever diplomatic relations with the United States, the larger and more moderate NU did not, calling this a mistake: "We should not damage ourselves for the sake of solidarity. . . . Solidarity with the Muslims in Afghanistan must not sacrifice our national interests."[7] Second, Megawati has had the support of the military, which tends to be suspicious of radical Muslims, though they have used groups such as the Laskar Jihad in the past for short-term political gains. Third, the 2002 constitutional amendment making the president directly elected will help her candidacy in the 2004 election. Fourth, the Muslim parties are fraught with factionalism and contending egos, which makes cooperation on all but essential issues very difficult. As one commentator put it, "There's a lot of competition among radical groups. Even though they can never enter and influence the larger parties, these things ensure temporary fame."[8] Robert Heffner agreed: "Post-Suharto Indonesia is unlikely to see a single, dominant Islamic grouping any time soon; it is even less likely to see a clear Muslim consensus on the role of Islam in the state."[9]

Amien Rais, himself a presidential candidate, would not support Vice President Hamzah Haz, his longtime rival. Rais has made no secret of his presidential ambitions and was very supportive of the president's position after Bali, in glaring contrast to Hamzah Haz. A senior PAN (National Mandate Party) official was almost gushing: "It seems that President Megawati is already more capable of accepting the aspirations of the Islamic community."[10] Rais has recently been lobbying and campaigning hard. He is frequently on tour of the provinces. He has also been reaching out to NU leaders who are angered at him because of the leading role he played in Gus Dur's impeachment. "He is working the ground now with the knowledge of his opponents, most of whom are pre-occupied with political problems," said one political analyst.[11] Most important, he has tried to portray his political party, PAN, as a broad united front that is not decimated by internal wrangling.

Why, then, did Megawati not play up her secular nationalist credentials and crack down on the militants? Why did it take her until Bali to start to arrest terrorists? On the one hand, she painted herself into a corner by stonewalling the United States and her neighbors for over a year; she could not admit there was a terrorist problem in the country without losing a lot of face. On the other hand, there are still serious political constraints: Although her party, the PDI-P, still controls the single largest bloc in the parliament and most Indonesians are moderates who support secular rule, her party stands to lose the most in the 2004 election. First, the Islamic parties are increasing their share of the vote. The Laskar Jihad may not have had widespread political support, but they certainly did not have public opprobrium for their militant activities done in the name of holding the country together; most of their weaponry came from the army and police. Second, the other secular party, Golkar, was in disarray in 1999 and did not even field a presidential contender. By 2003, Golkar was in a much stronger position. Although the party leader, Akbar Tanjung, was convicted on corruption charges in late 2002, many see it as beneficial to the party, as it allows a new generation of leaders to emerge, not the same old crony politicos of the Suharto era. The reemergence of Golkar limits Megawati's course of action, for another reason. Golkar has been playing the nationalist card, appealing to Indonesians who resent the weakened status of their country in the world. Megawati simply cannot give in to the demands of other states without serious political repercussions. Her own party counseled against cracking down on the militants because, whereas Megawati does not have much to worry about in the polls (she will never win the support of the Islamists), local PDI-P parliamentarians do, and the Islamists are their major challenge. The PDI-P failed to improve the economy, they are perceived as being the most corrupt party, and they are bracing for a fierce campaign.

Half Steps

Until the Bali bombing, Indonesia took few constructive measures in the war on terrorism. The Singaporean, Malaysian, Philippine, and U.S. governments all expressed utter frustration with the Indonesian government, and despite many appeals, the Indonesians did not arrest any Indonesian suspects wanted abroad. The Indonesian police sent a high-ranking team to Kuala Lumpur and Singapore following the breakup of the Jemaah Islamiya network in January 2002 and were not convinced with the evidence against Ba'asyir. Although they brought Ba'asyir in for questioning, to all the other states' chagrin, they did not detain the cleric, and he continued to live freely until after the Bali attack. Indonesian officials completely denied the presence of JI and Al-Qaida within their country until October 2002. It is frustrating that only with the Bali attack, which had a devastating effect on Indonesia's $5.4-billion-a-year tourist industry, did it begin to do anything—yet there was a lot of pressure put on the radical parties and movements.

After organizing a mass demonstration in Jakarta, FPI (Defenders of Islam) chief Al Habib Muhammad Rizaq was detained by the police on the charge of "instigating mass hatred." He was sentenced to seven years imprisonment, but the charges were later changed to a loose house arrest in November 2002.[12] The police took the mass demonstrations that began after the U.S. bombing campaign in Afghanistan very seriously, fearful that the protests would spiral out of control and require the use of force to put down. Rizaq continued to organize mass demonstrations and violate his house arrest. Although many analysts and officials write him off as a potent political threat because of the goonish nature of his FPI members who went around Jakarta and destroyed bars and restaurants that remained open during Ramadan, Rizaq remains one of the most popular of the radical orators. In late 2002 to early 2003 he led the campaign against the U.S. war in Iraq, recruiting ten FPI members to go fight alongside Saddam Hussein's forces. Indeed, Rizaq himself, traveled to Iraq on a "humanitarian mission" in April 2003. Other Islamic groups also felt intense government pressure. Al-Chaidar, the spokesman for Darul Islam, admitted that rogue factions of his organization were responsible for a spate of bombings in the capital.[13] He began cooperating with police and was later put under protective custody while investigations of the Darul Islam faction continued. Seventeen members of the NII (Negara Islam Indonesia) were arrested in early April 2002.

However, the government failed to crack down on militant groups like the Laskar Jihad. In the immediate aftermath of the September 11 attacks, the

Indonesian government put an inordinate amount of pressure on the country's most visible Islamic extremist group, the Laskar Jihad, to not take advantage of the attacks and mobilize its supporters for a jihad against the Americans. The military increased its presence in the Maluku islands where Laskar Jihad–supported sectarian violence had killed some 9,000 people. And the Laskar Jihad leader, Jafar Umar Thalib, went to great pains to distance himself from bin Laden and the Al-Qaida network, though he had never previously done so.[14] Additionally, Thalib asserted that bin Laden was "very empty about the knowledge of religion."[15] While other groups such as the FPI and GPI (Islamic Youth Movement) waged large and public demonstrations against the United States and tried to recruit followers to join the jihad in Afghanistan, the Laskar Jihad was eerily silent. Obviously it was under intense political pressure, and it believed that any militant activities in the Malukus would be met with overwhelming force. Politically, Thalib may have just realized that the time was right to lay low.

In late November to mid-December 2001, the Laskar Jihad suddenly reentered the mainstream in three separate but alarming incidents. In the first, the Laskar Jihad renewed armed sectarian conflict in central Sulawesi Province, after infiltrating roughly 200 new fighters into the province, bringing its total to 1,000 in September 2001. The government never prevented the Laskar Jihad militia from coming, nor did it try to expel them. Muslim paramilitaries were reportedly armed with machine guns (including M-16s) and rocket-propelled grenades, forcing thousands of Christians to flee. The Laskar Jihad Web page had the title banner "Onward to Poso" and has called for more members to go to Sulawesi to fight, as the government is not standing up to protect the rights of the Muslim community.[16]

The military's initial response was critically lacking, its 500 troops were outnumbered. Twenty-six hundred additional troops and police were dispatched to the region, but Bambang Susilo Yudhono, the coordinating minister for political and security affairs, refused to declare either a civil or military emergency. Susilo stated that he was sending troops to "stop the conflict, conduct raids on firearms and on the presence of a *certain organization* that should not be allowed to stay in Poso."[17] Only after the central government became involved and dispatched additional troops did the Laskar Jihad disavow any role in the conflict, asserting that it was local Muslims fighting in self-defense.[18] Later it again backtracked, stating that it only had 700 militants in Poso. The government has since pledged to "conduct raids on groups in possession of firearms and then to deport all of the outsiders to their place of origin."[19] Government-sponsored peace talks began on December 20, 2001, and a tenuous peace ensued.

The second instance was an attack on members of President Megawati's PDI-P party in East Java. Laskar Jihad members were conducting sweeps and forcibly closing nightspots in Ngawi, which were operating during the holy month of Ramadan. Some PDI-P members retaliated and raided a house belonging to a Laskar Jihad leader, which also served as a headquarters for the group. The leader of that raid was abducted by Laskar Jihad militants, and fighting escalated. Within two days, Indonesian police had arrested almost thirty Laskar Jihad members in Ngawi and over eighty more who were traveling to Ngawi to fight.[20]

The third instance was the arrival of Laskar Jihad forces in Irian Jaya (Papua), where there is a small secessionist movement. Again, the government made no attempt to stop the Laskar Jihad from coming.

In the Maluku islands and Sulawesi, the government brokered fragile cease-fires and peace accords between the Christian and Muslim paramilitaries. Although a peace accord was signed in the Malukus on February 12, 2002, some 60,000 people remain displaced, neighborhoods have been ethnically cleansed, and approximately 8,000 weapons looted from a police armory are missing. The Laskar Jihad left 500 to 800 fighters in place, though the government has called on them to leave the area. The Laskar Jihad's leader, Umar Jafar Thalib, called the peace agreement a betrayal of Muslims and vowed to remain in the region to protect the rights of the Muslim community. The Laskar Jihad is believed to be behind a series of bombings in Ambon devised to break the peace process. In one attack, seven were killed and forty-two were wounded on a boat carrying mainly Christians.[21] In the other attack, nine were killed, again, mainly Christians. Another bombing occurred in April 2002.

Although the Laskar Jihad voluntarily disbanded following the Bali bombing, Thalib's assertion should be met by considerable suspicion. Only 300 paramilitary troops were withdrawn from Ambon, a fraction of their total forces. The parent organization, the Forum Komunikasi wal Sunnah wal Jamaah, was not disbanded. It has offices in seventy cities around the country. It operates several large *madrasas* (Islamic schools) and other organizations that espouse an intolerant brand of Salafi and Wahhabi Islam. It owns businesses, fund-raises, and publishes a weekly magazine. It is not going to relinquish this critical infrastructure even if it disbands some of its paramilitary. The group will lay low, rename itself, reemerge, bringing jihad, intolerance, and sectarian violence.

The reason why we have to examine the government's lack of political will to do anything about the Laskar Jihad is fourfold. First, Jafar Umar Thalib and the Laskar Jihad have considerable political support. Vice President Hamzah Haz has been a staunch defender of the organization and helped get Thalib acquitted in January 2003. Second, it is inimical to the development of Indonesian democracy to have vigilante groups wage sectarian conflict. Democracy is about the rule of law, not mob violence. Third, while the military has at times had to employ force against the Laskar Jihad, the reality is that the two organizations have the same goal in preventing secessionist movements from succeeding, as happened with East Timor. Therefore, we must expect that the military will turn a blind eye to many of the Laskar Jihad's activities. Fourth, no one appreciated the degree to which external forces, such as Al-Qaida, came in and manipulated sectarian conflicts in Ambon and Poso. Thus, such conflicts must be prevented, which is unlikely with Thalib's attitudes toward the peace process.

The second case of Indonesia's lack of political resolve to fight the war on terror centered on combating terrorist funding. Although the government pledged to freeze the accounts of any of the named individuals or organizations with suspected terrorist links that was issued by the Bush administration, Indonesia failed to implement that pledge. It did not ratify the UN Security Council Resolution 1373 on the suppression of the financing of terrorism, enacting its own law instead. But it took the government some six weeks to issue a presidential decree, enabling it to access and freeze bank accounts of suspected terrorists.[22] Until that point, the government was unable to freeze accounts unless the "owner [was] officially a suspect or proven guilty in a criminal case."[23] However, by May 2003 no assets have been frozen. Many blame not just a weak commitment but the unregulated and corrupt banking sector itself. That no assets are in Indonesia is unlikely. Indonesia, with its weak and unregulated banking sector, corruptible regulators, and endemic corruption has long been a haven for money laundering.

Although intelligence and some elite Kopassus forces under the leadership of the intelligence chief A. M. Hendropriyono's son-in-law attacked a terrorist training camp in the fall of 2001, political pressure was such that seven more JI training camps were discovered only after Bali in early 2003. There was ample evidence of Al-Qaida's role in these camps. Six foreigners (two Afghans, two Pakistanis, and two Arabs) were detained, yet Hendropriyono, who first acknowledged the existence of the camps, was overridden by his political superiors and later retracted his statement.

The Indonesian government was more helpful in dealing with non-Indonesian terrorist suspects. In several cases they detained Arabs, and on two occasions they rendered suspects to U.S. authorities. For example a Pakistani, Hafiz Mohammed Saad Iqbal, was rendered to Egypt where he was wanted in connection with the Richard Reid shoe-bombing investigation. Likewise, the Indonesians arrested a Kuwaiti, Omar al-Faruq, and rendered him to the Americans and detained a German-Egyptian, Reda Seyam.

Finally, the government drafted an anti-terrorism law, though it did not ratify any of the UN Security Council resolutions regarding the anti-terror war. The draft anti-terror law, however, has come under intense scrutiny for several provisions. These include the denial of suspects' rights to be represented by a lawyer, the right to remain silent, the right to be free on bail, and the right to communicate with family and friends. Many legislators have called the draft law unconstitutional and draconian and have announced that they will vote against it.[24] It was not until following the Bali attacks that Parliament passed the bill. Since then, there have been a number of attempts to water down the bill.

Since the Bali attack, Indonesia has been cooperating much more closely with the Americans, Australians, and its ASEAN neighbors. With the attack, a thorough investigation on the JI and Al-Qaida network was undertaken and over forty arrests were made. Most important, the Indonesian leadership finally acknowledged the presence of JI and Al-Qaida within its borders. The investigation and enhanced cooperation are positive steps, but they, too, are bound by politics. Vice President Hamzah Haz in mid-November 2002 came out and asserted that the scope of the investigations had already gone too far.

Restoring Bilateral Military Ties with the United States

The Laskar Jihad in many ways can be seen as a tactical ally of the TNI (Indonesian armed forces), especially in dealing with separatism. But the TNI has long prided itself on being a guardian of the secular state, and the military clearly has an institutional fear of Islamic fundamentalism, terrorism, secessionism, and instability in general. One could also make the argument that since 1998, the military's political influence has waned and that many are trying to once again dominate policymaking. Senior military leaders have been the most vocal advocates of waging a war on terrorism. A. M. Hendropriyono, the head of BIN (the State Intelligence Agency), and Matori Abdul Djali, the minister of defense, have both committed to start fighting the war on terror. "Of course there is Al-Qaida here," said Hendropriyono. The minister of defense went far ahead of the president and his other cabinet colleagues when he asserted: "We will wage war on terrorism. We must take firm and forceful steps."[25] Until that point, the government strenuously denied that there were any Al-Qaida cells operating in Indonesia. It seems that the military is trying to force the government's hand in the war on terrorism so that it has a freer hand in combating separatism. Indeed, there was a conspiracy theory in Indonesia that BIN tipped off the Philippine government to the presence of the three alleged terrorists in March 2002 to push their anti-terror agenda at home.[26]

There is one additional reason that the military is taking a more pro-U.S. position, and that has to be that the military is desperate to restore bilateral military relations with the United States that were severed in 1999 during the massacre in East Timor. Although President Bush lifted restrictions on the sale on nonlethal military items, the Indonesian armed forces, which for the most part is equipped with U.S. weapons, needs new equipment and spare parts. For example, half of Indonesia's fighter jets are currently grounded because of a lack of spare parts due to the embargo.

Admiral Dennis Blair, the former commander in chief of U.S. forces in the Pacific, was really concerned about the state of the Indonesian military and the long-term effects of the embargo. He counseled his counterparts in Jakarta that the only way that the United States would lift the embargo is if the military accounts for the violence in East Timor and punishes those responsible, especially for the killing of three UN workers. "We are ready to resume the full range of bilateral cooperation when the military reforms which the Indonesian armed forces (TNI) is undertaking reach maturity. The primary criterion is the completion of the actions regarding accountability of the TNI in East Timor following the referendum in 1999."[27] Blair testified on the Hill and called for the lifting of sanctions, arguing that current restrictions on U.S. interaction with the Indonesian armed forces limit U.S. effectiveness in combating terrorism.

To that end, the government began legal proceedings against the first four of eighteen military defendants on March 19, 2002. Little was expected of a trial of mid-level officers, as there was considerable popular support (let alone that from the government) for the defendants and the TNI's actions. Ultimately, all were acquitted. The trials of the TNI officials for the East Timor rights abuses, the sine qua non of the restoration of ties, were a mockery of justice.[28]

But the lifting of U.S. sanctions in itself is not enough to radically alter Indonesian behavior. In the end, it seemed that the United States was far keener to restore ties with the TNI than the other way around. Some TNI leaders express real concern about the operational status of their troops and equipment, as they have gone almost three years without new equipment and spare parts. Others will question the wisdom of close ties with the United States, citing conditionality and capricious moralistic policies that make the United States an unreliable ally.

Relations were further strained by U.S. assertions that Indonesia was dragging its feet in the war on terror, until Bali. The United States agreed to more intelligence sharing and greater cooperation in police investigations following FBI director Robert S. Muller III's visit in March 2002. In April 2002, the U.S. trade representative, Robert Zoellick, the third highest ranking trade official in the Bush administration, visited Jakarta and again appealed for greater cooperation in the war on terror. The United States also tried to induce cooperation from Jakarta by assisting to reschedule some $5.5 billion of Indonesia's sovereign debt at the Paris Club.[29] On April 25–26, 2002, senior-level officials from the Defense and State departments met their Indonesian counterparts to discuss security cooperation, including the possible lifting of all U.S. sanctions. Although the United States offered roughly $35 million in counterterrorism assistance, mainly earmarked for the police, sanctions against the TNI remained in place.

Megawati Walks a Tightrope

On the one hand, President Megawati is a secularist, fearful of the growing power of Islamic fundamentalism in Indonesia, committed to economic reform, and fearful of scaring away foreign investors who flee with every new day of angry anti-U.S. street protests. Her political base is Bali and she lacks a large base of support on Java, home to more than half of Indonesia's population. For political support she relies on the military, which is for the most part secular, and has fought a long war against Islamic fundamentalist secessionists in Aceh. On the other hand, she has to worry about the growth of the number of Islamic fundamentalists in Indonesia and, more important, their power in the parliament. Although elected in August 2001 with overwhelming bipartisan support, shifting coalitions dominated by fundamentalist parties led by her vice president, Hamzah Haz, and supporters of the ousted president Abdurrahman Wahid are already putting pressure on her. This is all the more important because constitutional reforms could make the president directly elected by the people in the 2004 election.

Economically Megawati cannot afford to go against the U.S.-led war on terrorism. The United States not only provides needed bilateral aid but is able to stall needed World Bank and IMF funding. Moreover, as will be discussed below, the United States was able to offer a wide range of economic stimulus incentives to countries that toed Washington's diplomatic line, as was the case in the Philippines.

Megawati has been concerned about the negative images that are being formed by foreign investors because of the mass anti-U.S. demonstrations.[30] As gross domestic product growth forecasts fell from 5 to 4 percent in 2002, inflation has now crept into the double digits, and the price of crude oil has fallen to $20/barrel, down from the estimated $22/barrel in the government budget. If economic recovery slows down, more people will be driven to join the protests against the government.

The minister of foreign affairs, Hassan Wirayuda, acknowledged that terrorism is a threat to Indonesia and that the presence of radical groups in the sprawling archipelago has grown tremendously. Yet he appealed to the international community to have patience: "We have limitations in legal infrastructure as we do not have an internal security act or laws on subversion. We also have problems in upholding human rights. So it is important for the international community to view the issues in the context that Indonesia is currently in a transitional period."[31]

For its part the U.S. government demonstrated patience, though not without frustration. Due to Indonesian protests, neither the United States nor the United Nations was able to designate the Jemaah Islamiya as a terrorist organization until October 23, 2002, eleven days after Bali, though it had been proposed for half a year already. Ironically, the Philippine New People's Army was designated as a terrorist group in August 2002, though it has no known ties to international terrorism. By early 2003, the U.S. government was full of praise for the Indonesian government's cooperation in the war on terror.

The Indonesian government, even after Bali, does not seem to be overly concerned with terrorism. One senior intelligence official told me that although they did not expect another major attack on Indonesian soil again, the country would be used as a base of terrorist operations for the region. A sense of complacency already existed by early 2003. Likewise, the government had not shifted more resources to Indonesia's beleaguered and understaffed police force, instead appealing on aid programs from the United States, Australia, and Japan. Although these programs will go a long way to improve the capabilities and professionalism of Indonesia's police, there needs to be a significant government commitment. The government has become immersed in the myriad of other domestic problems and the politics at hand as the 2004 presidential election nears.

Megawati should have the political courage to crack down on the militants. Radicals in the country have warned her to back off and not join the U.S. anti-terror bandwagon. As a senior MMI official said, "If security forces take action against the Muslim community, then I believe what will result will be major turmoil in Indonesia."[32] However, the radicals are a fringe minority; most Indonesians remain tolerant and moderate. Megawati should take heart in the fact that the largest Muslim organizations in the country have endorsed the war on terror. As the NU secretary general said, "We need to know just how big is the threat of terrorism existing here. The government of Megawati should not hesitate to search for terrorists' links."[33] He called for a "transparent and fair investigation." Yet Megawati has still not felt politically strong enough to embark on one. The economic costs of Bali should motivate her, as the costs of denial were too great to countenance, yet Megawati was one of Southeast Asia's most vociferous critics of the U.S.-led war in Iraq and did little to crack down on Islamic militants in early 2003.

Of concern is that the Pew Global Attitudes Project reported one of the most precipitous drops in support for the United States in the past three years among Indonesians. Whereas 75 and 61 percent of Indonesians had positive images of the United States in 2000 and 2002 respectively, only 15 percent did in 2003. Although 31 percent of Indonesians supported the global war on terror in 2002, only 23 percent supported it in 2003, despite the deadly terrorist attacks in Indonesia in October 2002. Moreover, there is a palpable sense of fear over U.S. unilateral action: 36 percent of Indonesians are worried about the potential U.S. military threat, and 38 percent are somewhat concerned. Regarding Iraq, 82 percent of the Indonesian respondents were upset that the Iraqi regime did not put up a stronger fight against U.S. forces, the third highest rate behind Moroccans (93 percent) and Jordan (91 percent) and tied with Lebanon and Turkey. The poll also demonstrated the heightened sense of nationalism and xenophobia among Indonesians: 87 percent believed that their way of life had to be defended against foreign influence; the highest rate in all of Asia, not just Southeast Asia.[34]

The Philippines

If Indonesia had the most to lose from the war on terrorism, then the Philippines had the most to gain. The Philippines gave the strongest response to U.S. appeals for assistance in the war on terrorism. Soon after September 11, President Gloria Macapagal Arroyo announced "14 Pillars of Policy and Action" to combat international terrorism and said that her administration will go "all out" to assist the United States and implement UN Security Council Resolution 1368. This included offering Philippine airspace and seaports to U.S. forces, including Subic Bay, the former U.S. naval base, intelligence sharing, and logistical support. The second form of assistance she has provided is the passage of an anti–money laundering law and "an intensified campaign to prevent the use of our financial institutions as conduits for the finances of international terrorists."[35] The third form of assistance was to step up the war on terrorism within the Philippines: "We must never lose sight of our immediate and overriding objective—identify the terrorists within our country, map out their networks, stop them and destroy their cause. In this war, as in any modern enterprise, we must think globally but act locally."[36] To that end, the Philippines allowed the deployment of more than 1,100 U.S. forces, including 160 special forces, to train and assist Philippine troops in their war against the Abu Sayyaf Group. This was the largest deployment of U.S. troops outside of Afghanistan in the war on terror.

What explains the robust response from the Arroyo administration? The Philippines does feel a close bond with the United States, yet President Arroyo clearly did this for domestic reasons. Politically, the "get tough" and "law and order" image played well in the Philippines. Second, the September 11 attacks gave the Arroyo administration both the domestic and foreign support that she needs to confront the ongoing Muslim insurgency in the south. Third, there were ongoing external factors in passing the anti–money laundering laws. Finally, she was greatly rewarded for her cooperation by the United States, which in November 2001 unveiled an aid program worth more than $1 billion. In short, Arroyo saw nothing but opportunity out of the crisis, and she made the most of it. Once the U.S. attacks began on Afghanistan, her support did not waver and she asked the Philippines to "pay a price" to eliminate terrorism.

> Our support is not only because of out strategic alliance with the US, which is leading the international coalition. We are obligated by all the values of humanity and civilized society to assist the global campaign to end the scourge of terrorism once and for all. We cannot be fence sitters nor should we be wishy-washy during this historic period when the civilized world has decided to annihilate by all means international terrorism. If we have to pay a price for our conviction against terrorism, so be it.

Arroyo had four interrelated goals: (1) To restore a close alliance and security relationship with the United States; (2) to defeat Muslim separatists in the south and to sign a durable autonomy agreement with groups who seek a political solution; (3) to end the use of the Philippines as a base of operations for international terrorist organizations; and (4) to consolidate her political position.

A Robust Response to Rebuild Relations

Immediately following the September 11 attacks, the Philippine government gave the Americans unconditional use of its two former military facilities, the Subic Bay Naval Base and the Clark Air Force Base, both of which were used by U.S. forces en route to the Gulf region. The loss of these bases in 1991 led to a sharp decline in bilateral relations, which the Arroyo administration wanted to reverse. The Philippine and U.S. governments worked to create a new legal framework for the use of Philippine bases by U.S. forces. High-level exchanges including a visit by Philippine president Arroyo to Washington and by Admiral Blair to Manila led to a draft agreement—the Mutual Logistics Support Agreement (MLSA), which provided short-term access to Philippine bases in exchange for military hardware and supplies.[37]

Some in the Philippines were angered by the treaty, arguing that it was simply going back to the pre-1991 era. They questioned why the Visiting Forces Agreement, the legal framework for U.S. military transit and joint exercises, was not sufficient. "The Arroyo government is colluding with the US government and using the anti-terrorist hysteria to underhandedly justify the heightened US military presence in the Philippines," complained one left-wing congressman.[38] The government was at pains to ensure the public that the MLSA would not lead to permanent U.S. bases in the Philippines, and it seemed pleased that there was considerable public support for improving ties with the United States, and certainly no sustained public outcry. The MLSA agreement was significant and warmly received in Washington. It went a long way in repairing defense ties that since 1991 had been all but moribund. The Philippine armed forces were confronted by a more aggressive China, which has seized a number of atolls in the South China Sea claimed by the Philippines. The Philippines tried to invoke the 1951 Mutual Defense Treaty, but to no avail. Fearful of a power vacuum if the United States became too engaged in the war on terrorism, Arroyo also wanted to keep the United States engaged in the region in order to check potential Chinese aggression.

President Arroyo was able to solidify her relationship with President Bush in her appeal for U.S. support to fight the Al-Qaida–linked Abu Sayyaf Group. That the ASG was immediately named by the United States as a terrorist organization with ties to Al-Qaida certainly bolstered her position. As the Philippine national security adviser Roilo Golez noted at the time, "Because the Abu Sayyaf is in [the United States] order of battle, maybe we will get an opportunity to ask for more assistance."[39]

The United States became steadily embroiled in the Philippines, culminating in the deployment of 1,300 troops, including 160 special operations forces. The U.S. and Philippine governments engaged incrementally, both testing the political waters. The United States first sent two teams of approximately twenty high-level military personnel to the Philippines to conduct a needs assessment and agreed to arm two 100-man light reaction companies and "give them special equipment for counter-terrorism operations."[40] Later the United States disclosed that it would also train the light reaction companies, though the Philippine military's chief of staff, Diomedio Villanueva, made it clear that U.S. forces "would not be participating actively" and that "any overt action will be done exclusively by Philippine troops."[41] President Arroyo stated, "It's very clear that I have told him [President Bush] that I draw the line on soldiers on the ground and he respects the line I have drawn." Yet as she said that, a third team of nineteen U.S. Army "advisers" arrived in Mindanao in December, equipped in full combat gear, seemingly ready to take casualties. Although the Philippine military spokesman claimed that they were there "to help train our troops," the commander of the AFP [Islamic armed forces] Southern Command, Lieutenant General Roy Cimatu, acknowledged that the U.S. advisers were part of the U.S.-trained light reaction company that had engaged the Abu Sayyaf in "very fierce fighting."[42]

In late January 2002, some 660 U.S. forces were deployed to Basilan to train Philippine troops and to provide operational assistance, including intelligence gathering and air support. Due to the Philippine Constitution, which explicitly forbids foreign forces fighting in the Philippines, the joint operation was called the Balikatan 02-1 (shoulder to shoulder) training exercise and lasted six months. Under the Terms of Reference, the legal document that governed the U.S. role in the Philippines, the Americans were not allowed to be directly involved in combat operations, but they could join front line troops to advise them and fight back in self-defense.[43] U.S. forces flew helicopter and Navy P-3 Orion reconnaissance planes, while special forces deployed ground sensors in the dense jungle. In April 2002, 340 additional troops were dispatched to Basilan, including 280 military engineers, to engage in civil works projects. That month both the Philippines and the United States announced that U.S. forces would continue their mission in Basilan beyond the six-month period. As one senior Bush administration official put it: "We're looking at prolonged training. It takes more to build up capabilities than saying 'Here are some night vision goggles.'"[44]

The expansion in both duration and the number of U.S. forces increased some political opposition. For the most part, however, the Balikatan exercise had the support of the majority of Filipinos, and one public opinion survey found 84 percent of those polled supported the U.S. presence.[45] With only ten deaths of U.S. soldiers, the exercises provoked no criticism in the United States. Both governments were adamant that the United States was not seeking to reestablish a permanent presence in the Philippines. That the Americans withdrew at the end of the six-month period assuaged many.

Yet Philippine armed forces failed to maintain the momentum generated by the joint exercises in the second half of 2002. A spate of bombings and a regrouping of rebel forces frustrated the United States. In February 2003, the two governments announced a second but expanded Balikatan exercise in the Sulu Archipelago against the Abu Sayyaf that would entail 1,750 U.S. troops, including more than 350 special forces and 1,000 marines. This time, though, Pentagon officials did not describe the mission as a training exercise but a combat operation. "This is different. This is an actual combined operation, and it is US forces accompanying and actively participating in Philippines-led offensive operations," a Pentagon spokesman said. This mission was also different in that it had no fixed period: "At this point, we're going into it saying the mission will go on until both sides agree it is finished."[46] The Americans were clearly frustrated with the Philippines and decided that they had to take a proactive role. However, President Arroyo, who announced in December 2002 that she would not run for reelection in 2004, felt that she could allow U.S. forces an expanded combat role without any significant potential political backlash. Yet the outcry was immediate, and the president backtracked, insisting that there would be no battlefield role for U.S. troops, except in self-defense and that the Terms of Reference would be the same as the 2002 Balikatan exercise.[47] As of June 2003, the Terms of Reference had not been signed and it remains to be seen whether Balikatan '03 will be held. There is considerable concern in the Pentagon that as campaigning for the 2004 presidential election in the Philippines gets under way, the window of opportunity for negotiating a second Balikatan exercise is closing.

Fruits of Her Labor

At President Arroyo's December 2001 meeting with President Bush, the U.S. president spoke warmly of the Philippines and announced a major aid package for the Philippines' support. "We're going to fight terror wherever it exists. And we will work with our allies and friends to use whatever resources we have to win the war." He announced a large military aid package worth $137 million. "I asked her point blank, what help do you need?" President Bush said.[48] The package included:

- $100 million in "security assistance" to help the Arroyo administration combat terrorism. This package included one C-130 cargo plane and

five UH-1 "Huey" helicopters for close combat support. Light arms included 30,000 M-16 rifles, 350 grenade launchers, 25 mortars, 50 sniper rifles, and night vision goggles and thermal imaging equipment.[49]
- $20 million to modernize the Philippine armed forces.
- Bush's request that Congress increase annual bilateral defense aid to the Philippines tenfold, starting in 2001, from $1.9 million to $19 million for FY 2002.
- $10 million in Defense Department goods and services—equipment from existing stockpiles.
- $1 billion in trade benefits.
- Up to $430 million in debt relief.
- Guarantees for up to $150 million in agricultural exports.
- $40 million in food aid.
- A $200 million line of credit through the Overseas Private Investment Corporations (OPIC).
- $29 million in poverty alleviation.
- A 27 percent increase in market access for textile exports.
- The allowance of imports of Philippine canned tuna and pineapples.
- Bush's pledge to double U.S. assistance to the island of Mindanao, which stood at $4.5 million, to train 13,000 former Moro National Liberation Front fighters to plant corn, breed fish, or grow seaweed.[50]

This economic and military aid package was significant. Although it did not make up for the steady decline in U.S. aid to the Philippines since 1987, it went a long way in starting to restore ties. In FY2001, for example, the United States only offered the Philippines $22 million in military aid, one-fifth of the amount it received after September 11. It clearly was needed both economically and militarily, and we should expect continued aid programs in the next few years.[51]

In addition to U.S. military training and aid that qualitatively improved the military, the Arroyo administration pledged to bolster the size of the army, which only had some 68,000 troops. Arroyo's request to Congress called for the financing of an additional 20,000 troops, almost a 30 percent increase in the size of the army. The military asserted that, confronted with 25,000 rebels from different groups, the army was understaffed and roughly forty new battalions would be required.[52]

Following President Arroyo's state visit to the United States in May 2003, only the third state visit during the George W. Bush administration, the United States again extended significant military and financial assistance to the person that Bush called a "friend of freedom" who's "tough when it comes to terror." The aid package included $95 million in military aid, tariff reductions, and expanded veteran benefits for Filipinos.[53]

Combating Muslim Separatism

The Arroyo administration clearly saw the September 11 events as an opportunity to deal with the Muslim separatists once and for all, knowing that the president had U.S. support. One of the most complicating factors in achieving this is dealing with not just the three different Muslim groups, the Morno National Liberation Front (MNLF), the Moro Islamic Liberation Front (MILF), and the Abu Sayyaf (ASG), but with factions in each of them. The military has been engaged in constant battle with the groups since September 11, deploying approximately 6,000 troops in the southern Philippines and, following Nur Misuari's revolt in mid-November, dispatching another 1,500. The government is pursuing different policies and has different goals for each of the groups.

Defeating the ASG. Unlike the MILF and MNLF, which the government believes to be legitimate organizations with real grievances, it labeled the ASG as a group of terrorists and bandits and has shown absolutely no willingness to negotiate a political settlement. "We know the enemy and we know that these are not people you talk to. These are people you fight," Arroyo told the United Nations, laying down her hard-line approach.[54] To that end, approximately 5,000 personnel were deployed in Jolo and Basilan and some 1,000 U.S. forces were deployed there to assist the Philippine military. In February 2003, an estimated 3,000 troops were deployed in a combat role for an open-ended period, until the Abu Sayyaf were eliminated.

Why with only 500 to 600 ASG fighters at its peak, and in 2003 between 250 and 500, was the Philippine military unable to defeat them? There are two answers. The AFP believes that their only deficiency was in their equipment. They were simply outgunned by the well-armed rebels. Moreover, they did not have the capability to operate at night. Thus, at the top of their request list to the Americans was a range of equipment that would allow them to better operate at night: night-vision goggles, thermal imagers, and helicopters that have night-flying capability.

The second explanation has to do with the rampant corruption within the Philippine police and military forces. Equipping a military with better counterinsurgency materiel is irrelevant when officers receive large bribes from the Abu Sayyaf rebels. In December 2001, the Philippine Senate reopened an investigation on alleged collusion between the military and the Abu Sayyaf, and the payment of kickbacks from ransom money in exchange for safe passage through military cordons. Senator Sergio Osmena led the attack on corruption and incompetence in the military. Osmena accused defense secretary Angelo Reyes and chief of staff General Diomedio Villanueva of not only condoning ransom payments to Abu Sayyaf (despite the government's pledge of "no ransom") but also of having taken 5 million pesos in kickbacks themselves. Although he later acknowledged that 17 million pesos in ransom was paid, Reyes denied that there were any kickbacks to himself or officers in Basilan.[55] There have been too many and too consistent reports of local-level collusion with the ASG.

Confident of external support, the Philippine military has intensified the fighting. The joint operations against the ASG progressed, though the ASG has not been eliminated and has still shown that it is a force than can inflict damage and terror. On October 29, 2002, it detonated a bomb in a Zamboanga food court, killing six and wounding almost sixty, in retaliation of increased military pressure on the group and the presence of twenty-three U.S. military advisers. ASG also claimed responsibility for a series of bombings in April 2002 in General Santos City, which killed fifteen people and wounded more than sixty. These attacks and reports of growing linkages between the Jemaah Islamiya and the Abu Sayyaf prompted the United States to call for renewed and expanded operations including a direct combat role in the Philippines beginning in February 2003. The Philippine government rejected this, following an outpouring of political opposition.

Negotiating autonomy with the MILF. Whereas a military solution was the only one being considered in the case of the ASG, it was not being contemplated against the large and well-armed MILF. The twenty-five-year-old Muslim MILF-led insurgency in the south has shown no signs of abating. With 12,000 to 15,000 men under arms who have fought the AFP to a standstill and a large amount of popular support in Mindanao, the government is still trying to get the MILF leadership to abandon their goal of independence and accept regional autonomy.

That the MILF has linkages to Al-Qaida and has received money in the past is of particular concern for the government. As mentioned in Chapter 3, Al Haj Murad, the vice chairman of military affairs for the MILF, admitted to receiving "substantial help and assistance for bin Laden including the training of his fighters in bin Laden's camps in Afghanistan." It was probably heartening for Arroyo's government to hear the MILF leadership reject bin Laden's October 8, 2001, call for a jihad against the United States and its allies and announce that it was respecting the cease-fire in preparation for the October 2001 peace talks. According to the MILF spokesman: "The MILF is far from the fighting and our efforts are directed towards the peace process in Mindanao."[56] The Arroyo administration, for its part, downplayed the MILF's connection to Al-Qaida and has prevented the Americans from designating the group a terrorist organization.

Peace talks that resumed in the fall of 2001 stalled over a number of issues. First, the MILF demanded an "East Timor Formula," that is, a referendum for independence under UN auspices. Second, the MILF demanded an economic rehabilitation program for Mindanao, as a good will gesture.[57] The

Philippine government refused as the MILF demanded that they run the projects, rather than joint management.

Talks were complicated by the introduction of U.S. forces in the southern Philippines. The MILF stated that it is against the United States interfering in the fight against the Abu Sayyaf, arguing that it would "complicate the peace talks with the government." Clearly the Abu Sayyaf is an embarrassment to the MILF. The leader of the MILF delegation to the peace talks, Murad Ebrahim, stated that the Abu Sayyaf's "link with the Osama bin Laden group is doubtful" and that there is "no clear link." But even if they are linked, "they are a small group" that did "not justify US military action."[58] "The claim is that [the United States] is going after the Abu Sayyaf," said Sharif Julabi, a regional commander of the MILF. "But we think they're looking for a justification to go to war with us."[59] To that end, a tri-lateral agreement was reached assuring the MILF that joint U.S.-Philippine patrols in Basilan would not enter MILF held zones, though the MILF only has a limited presence outside of Mindanao anyway. The Terms of Reference for the U.S. presence explicitly stated that Balikatan 02-1 "shall not in anyway contribute to an escalation of other conflicts in Mindanao, shall not adversely affect the progress of ongoing peace negotiations between the government of the Philippines and other parties."

The MILF also entered into some negotiations with their longtime rivals the MNLF. This concerned the government that the MNLF was considering breaking off the peace treaty that it negotiated with the government in September 1996. Suspicions were heightened in November 2001, when Nur Misuari led a group of MNLF members in armed rebellion against the government. Though the MILF may have enjoyed watching the Autonomous Region of Muslim Mindanao process fall apart, they pledged not to support Misuari.[60]

The MILF believes itself to be militarily strong enough and politically popular enough to continue its uncompromising demand for independence. It believes that MNLF members tacitly support MILF's efforts and are disgusted with the ARMM. The peace process must be seen in this context: It is a strategic interlude, as arms and funding from Al-Qaida and other external sources have dried up. Many in the Philippine government and military want to resume the war, believing they have U.S. backing. To that end, Philippine forces overran an important MILF base in January 2003. Among the things they found were significant quantities of documents that linked the MILF to Al-Qaida. This will complicate the peace process. The government is cognizant that the MILF has considerable popular support. Yet if the MILF is designated a terrorist organization by the United States or the United Nations, then it will be politically constrained in peace negotiations.

Although the MILF has to be given some of the blame for the breakdown in the Malaysian peace talks because of their intransigent position on development projects and independence, much of the blame should be focused on Minister of Defense Angelo Reyes. Under President Estrada, Reyes was the

AFP's chief of staff and he understood how politically popular the war against the MILF was. Now a presidential candidate for the 2004 election, Reyes seems to be using the war for his own political ends. The fact is that the AFP does not have the resources to continue the military campaign; nor can it count on U.S. support, as the Pentagon worries about being embroiled in a civil war. Although both sides have called on the Malaysian government to intervene and rekindle the peace talks, as of June 2003, they had not recommenced. The mistrust on both sides is palpable, and it is doubtful that they can even get back to the point that they were in before negotiations broke down.

For any durable political solution to be reached in the Muslim region there will have to be considerable improvements in the regional economy. There will never be lasting peace as long as the region has the highest rates of poverty in an already poor country. The government will have to allocate more resources to the ARMM, which currently receives the lowest budgetary allocations in the country. Of the sixteen regions, the ARMM had the lowest allocation in the 2002 budget, approximately $210 million, despite the fact that it accounts for nearly one-third of the total area of the country.[61] This is a paltry sum, and the government is going to have to rethink its budgetary allocations and development strategy. Without a brighter future, the local Muslim community will continue to turn to armed rebellion.

Routing Out Al-Qaida

The third goal of the Arroyo administration is to end the use of the Philippines as a base of operations by international terrorist organizations. The government has adopted a comprehensive strategy for achieving this. First, it has enhanced its police and intelligence-gathering mechanisms in order to rout out suspected sleeper agents and Al-Qaida cell members. The Philippine National Police arrested two individuals, a Jordanian and an Iraqi, in mid-November 2001. The Jordanian was found with a hand gun and detonating cords.[62] The Iraqi, Mohammad Sabri Selamah, had been a teacher in Mindanao and the director of the Islamic Quranic Memorization Center since 1998. He was in possession of explosives and forging equipment.[63] The al-Ghozi cell was broken up in January 2002, and in March 2002 three Indonesians were arrested for possession of bomb-making material. Yet Philippine police and intelligence services remain underfunded and poorly resourced. The government made no discernible attempts to bolster these arms, focusing along with the United States on a military solution against the Abu Sayyaf.

Second, the government has tried to improve its immigration system and has adopted computerized immigration checks at its international airports. Nevertheless, the Philippines remains a porous country of 7,000 islands.

Third, the government passed an anti–money laundering act to prevent the Philippines from being a safe haven for terrorist funding. Clearly, the

Philippines has an additional reason for passing an anti–money laundering law. This law was in the works for many years, and the Philippines was under threat of sanctions from the Office for Economic Cooperation and Development if it did not pass it by September 30, 2001.[64] This law, however, will have little efficacy for stemming terrorist uses of Filipino financial institutions. For one thing, the original bill was watered down by legislators. The committee that drafted the law proposed setting the threshold at $20,000, already two times the U.S. limit of $10,000. However, the Philippine Congress quadrupled the amount, making it a crime to transact amounts greater than $80,000 (4 million pesos), but most terrorist wire transfers are small amounts through the unregulated remittance systems.[65] Under U.S. and the OECD's Financial Action Task Force (FATF) pressure, the Philippines agreed to amend the law to a $10,000 limit. Yet even equipped with the new law, the Philippine government admits that it has no idea where the Abu Sayyaf and the MILF hide their assets. The law also does not regulate the *hawala* system of money transfers, which are the preferred financial mechanisms for terrorist cells that do not require vast sums of money for their operations. And since the passage of the law, many Philippine legislators have displayed anger that the FATF has not taken the Philippines off of its list of "non-cooperating countries who have made slow progress in fighting money laundering," and they have appealed to the United States to intercede on the Philippines' behalf.[66]

Rebuilding Ties and Reshaping Agendas

The Philippines responded quickly and enthusiastically to the U.S.-led efforts and assisted the United States on the diplomatic and political front in the region. The U.S. government was pleased by Arroyo's response and rewarded the Philippines generously. Arroyo won needed foreign aid to help with her own internal agenda, and she has done much to restore what were once very close ties between the United States and the Republic of the Philippines.

President Arroyo was not a lap dog of the Americans, and she used her good standing in Washington to help guide U.S. thinking on countering terrorism. Whereas she was committed to take the Philippines "every step of the way" with the Americans, she constantly reiterated the need for the first world to assist developing countries to eliminate poverty, what she referred to as the "spawning grounds" of terrorism. As she said during talks with Bush, the war on terrorism "should be fought in parallel with the war against poverty."[67] At the 2002 UN General Assembly meeting, she ominously warned of the increasing gap between first and third world countries: "It is this growing disparity between the ever fewer richer countries and ever more poor that has given terrorism the freedom of movement and impunity from accountability that it has enjoyed."[68] In her May 2003 press conference with President Bush, President Arroyo reiterated that "this trip is not just about fighting terrorism. It's about fighting poverty."[69] But she also held third world governments, including her own, accountable, arguing that economic development was not enough. Foreshadowing her own domestic economic agenda, she spoke of the need for societies "to adopt deliberate policies to ensure that the income levels of the poor rise faster than those of the rich."[70] Her surprise announcement that she would not run for reelection in 2004 freed her hands to embark on more radical social welfare programs, as well as sanction a combat role for U.S. forces; this was later retracted. The restoration of close security ties between the United States and the Philippines is also important for another reason. U.S. secretary of defense Donald Rumsfeld is shifting U.S. security policy from having several large overseas bases, "operational hubs," to the "lily pad" approach—whereby the United States establishes either small bases or "prearranged but unmaintained" staging areas around the world with an eye to rapid deployment.[71] In addition to the large U.S. bases in Guam, Hawaii, and Okinawa in the Pacific, the United States has expressed interest in prepositioning equipment in Australia and the Philippines.

Malaysia

The Malaysian response to the war on terror was robust, if not complex, owing to the fact that it is a predominantly Muslim country. Prime Minister Mahathir Mohammed, however, has used the war on terror adroitly to pursue four goals:

1. Eliminate Islamic militants operating in the country;
2. Consolidate his and the United Malays National Organization's political power and isolate his primary opposition party, the Islamic-oriented PAS;
3. Restore good relations with the United States; and
4. Enhance Malaysia's international standing, especially in the Organization of the Islamic Conference.

The prime minister has clearly succeeded in accomplishing the first three. The final goal of enhancing Malaysia's standing in the OIC has not been achieved. Although Malaysia hosted a major OIC conference to define terrorism in March 2002, there was no consensus, and Malaysia was decidedly out of step by being so moderate, as it was one of only two states that labeled Palestinian suicide bombings as acts of terrorism.

To understand the Malaysian response to the war on terror, one has to be aware that Malaysia, like its outspoken prime minister, operates at two levels: the rhetorical and the operational. On the one hand, Prime Minister Mahathir Mohammed, who is a bitter foe of nonsecular Islamic politics, condemned the September 11 attacks and pledged to fight terrorism within his own borders.

In a September 29, 2001, news conference, he stated that "we are uneasy with the Taliban and with Osama bin Laden." Later he further acknowledged, "We admit there are terrorists in the country, trained by the Taliban. . . . The only difference is that these terrorists are directing their attacks at us and we can take care of them, they are not attacking the United States."[72]

At the same time he was very critical of the U.S. military response. Malaysia was one of only a handful of countries among the fifty-six states that attended the October 10 OIC conference to explicitly condemn U.S. attacks on Afghanistan.[73] Mahathir was staunchly opposed to U.S. unilateralism and argued that the United Nations must lead any war on terrorism. He was also angry that the United States has done little to address the root causes of terrorism: "Our stand is that we feel efforts must be taken to find the reasons why these terrorists chose to resort to violence in the first place."[74]

Mahathir offered mixed support for U.S. investigations. The United States made a direct appeal to Malaysia to hand over several hundred people suspected of having links to terrorist organizations, though it was rebuffed. Mahathir announced that Malaysia would not turn over any suspected "terrorists" to the United States, unless the United States provided direct evidence that they committed a crime within the United States. He did acknowledge, however: "We do have Malaysian citizens who have shown that they want to use arms and other means to topple the government but they are Malaysians and we don't hand over Malaysians to other peoples. We will deal with them as we have sufficient laws to do so."[75] Yazid Sufaat, likewise, was not rendered or extradited despite U.S. requests. In other cases Malaysia was exceedingly cooperative with the United States. First, the Malaysian government shut down a website used by Al-Qaida (www.alneda.com), which was hosted on a Kuala Lumpur "server farm." In another instance, following the breakup of the Portland, Oregon, Al-Qaida cell in October 2002, Malaysia deported a leading member, Ahmed Ibrahim Bilal, who was discovered studying at Malaysia's International Islamic University. More important, Malaysia launched a thorough investigation and has detained more than seventy Kampulan Mujiheddin Malaysia and Jemaah Islamiya militants.

Anti-Terrorism Begins at Home

The clearest reaction of the Malaysian government to the September 11 attacks was at the domestic political level. While critical of the United States, Prime Minister Mahathir Mohammed has adroitly used the crisis to marginalize his domestic Malay opposition, win back wavering centrist Malay voters, and arrest dissidents.

UMNO, which steadily lost its core constituency of rural Malay voters to the Islamic PAS, tried to draw a clear line connecting PAS and the terrorists. Mahathir has made full light of the fact that an editorial in the PAS party paper, *Harakah*, asserted that "the coming war is a crusade against Islam," whereas PAS announced that it would continue to send humanitarian aid to Afghanistan while giving approval to its members to go to Pakistan to join in a jihad against U.S. and British forces.[76] The government announced that it would not stop PAS members from going to Afghanistan, instead capitalizing on their fanaticism and calling it a "cheap gimmick to score political points with the majority Muslim community." UMNO leaders took delight in the fact that few people joined the jihad, and they gloated that PAS leaders themselves "should lead the way" if they were going to incite their members.[77] Mahathir effectively portrayed PAS as extremists and linked them to the terrorists. And PAS was on the defensive, especially as National Front members demanded that PAS "state its stand on terrorism at the international and domestic levels. Its stand on the KMM must be made clear—is it for against the group? What's the use of condemning terrorism at the international level but cry foul when the government acts against KMM members in the country?"[78] PAS leaders blamed UMNO for using the issue to create a negative image of both PAS and Islam. "UMNO leaders . . . have succeeded in tarnishing the good name of PAS by their actions and conspiracy."[79]

Mahathir and UMNO milked this for all it was worth, linking Malaysians in Afghanistan and those detained under the Internal Security Act to PAS, which did much to discredit the party. This was played out, to a degree, in the polls. On September 27, 2001, for example, in elections in the largest of Malaysia's thirteen states, Sarawak, PAS suffered a crushing defeat. Mahathir's National Front won sixty out of the sixty-two contested seats, but not one seat was won by PAS. PAS has never been that strong in Sarawak, far from its stronghold in the northeast of the Malay Peninsula, but it was clearly a huge backlash. The PAS party paper afterward complained that Mahathir was "fear mongering."[80] Mahathir clearly hoped to increase the 60 percent of the Malay population who support UMNO.

PAS further alienated itself when the Chinese-dominated Democratic Action Party, which had joined PAS in an uneasy alliance for almost two years, quit because PAS would not surrender its goal of establishing an Islamic state. DAP leaders made it clear that they no longer saw PAS as simply an Islamic party but an organization connected to international terrorism: "We were alarmed by the calls of those who preach martyrdom and those who are prepared to die for an Islamic state."[81] It is a perception that the Malaysian government hopes to spread. It appears to be working. One young member of PAS told a U.S. journalist that "PAS is quite capable of ruling Taliban style."[82]

PAS suffered a huge defeat in November 2001, when the Angkatan Belia Islam Malaysia (Islamic Youth Movement, or ABIM), which had been founded in the 1970s by the jailed deputy prime minister Anwar Ibrahim, abandoned its pro–Berisan Alterntif (Alternative Front) position. The Islamic Youth Movement, with its 100,000 members, rallied against UMNO and

Mahathir when Anwar was sacked and arrested. Since 1998 it has backed the loose coalition of opposition parties, especially Keadilan and PAS. ABIM founded a network of nongovernmental organizations to seek justice for Anwar and became the precursor for Keadilan, founded by Anwar's wife, Wan Azizah Wan Ismail. The leaders of ABIM believe that their tilt toward the opposition parties, and PAS in particular "had weakened its ability to put forward a moderate position."[83]

The government has also been more aggressive in dealing with the extremist element of PAS. Mahathir announced that there would be increased surveillance and arrests of known Muslim fundamentalists who advocate nondemocratic means: "Once we identify them, we will definitely put them under arrest. We will not allow people with such ideas floating around."[84] By January 2003, the government had detained approximately seventy KMM and JI members under the draconian Internal Security Act for undisclosed "militant activities." Deputy Prime Minister and Home Minister Abdullah Ahmed Badawi announced that the government would continue to aggressively rout out terrorists: "We will use the ISA and other punitive measures to act against them [Muslim extremists] to protect national security," as well as establish a special investigative unit to deal with domestic terrorism. Unlike the Philippines, Malaysia invested more money and resources in the wake of September 11 into its internal security services.

On October 12, 2001, the government announced that they were implementing new regulations to make it compulsory for students to register with the Immigration Department if they study abroad, as it acknowledged that it has no information on self-financed students. Prime Minister Mahathir announced on October 15, 2001, that all schools run by PAS, from kindergarten to college, "will come under closer scrutiny." Mahathir expressed considerable alarm, for two-thirds of the 2,160 religious schools in Malaysia were linked to PAS. "What is being taught in these schools is not Islam," said Mahathir. "So we need to see what these people are doing."[85] As deputy prime minister Abdullah Badawi complained: "The majority of these schools contribute nothing to the educational stock."[86]

At the same time, Parliament passed an amendment to the 1959 Election Offenses Act, which stipulated harsh penalties for political party members who used violence during campaigns. This was clearly aimed at radical members of PAS who Mahathir contends "feel that the democratic way could never bring power to PAS. The only manner which can bring power to PAS is through militancy. And they also feel that democracy is not the way of Islam, because they reject democracy."[87] In November 2001, the government announced that it was planning to amend certain anti-terrorism laws to deal with the increased threat.

PAS leaders condemn these arrests and new policies as a political ploy. Even DAP officials have raised the alarm that these could be used as political tools to silence political opponents: "This could be an excuse to further stifle political dissent and retract the already limited democratic space in the country, especially for the opposition."[88]

The government also tried to preempt PAS by showing humanitarian concern for Afghans. The government responded to the U.S. campaign by sending ten medical teams to assist with the 2.5 million Afghan refugees in Pakistan and by establishing a $1 million fund for the refugees. Simultaneously, the semiofficial media launched a series of broadsides about what an Islamic state really is. Arguing that Malaysia is "already an Islamic state," Mahathir tried to get the Malay electorate to reembrace the secular, multicultural, and tolerant Islam of the ruling coalition government. UMNO believes that Malaysia is an Islamic state that still caters to the needs of its non-Muslim minorities. Mahathir wants to portray Malaysia as a modernist and democratic Islamic state that is focused on economic development and implements Islamic family law, while protecting women's and minorities' rights: a progressive rather than Orientalist Islamic state. To that end, Malaysia has two complementary legal codes, a civil code and *sharia*, whereas the constitution provides for freedom of religion. As one commentator put it: "Freedom of religion does not make [Malaysia] less Islamic. . . . Muslims here are more so thanks to a religious pluralism that places respect for other belief systems above all else."[89]

UMNO branded PAS as Taliban-like extremists who want to implement an extremist form of Islam. In the two states that PAS controls, for example, they have separate checkout lines in supermarkets for men and women, and separate hair stylists. PAS considers the National Front infidels because UMNO is always acceding to the needs of the Indian and Chinese communities. It demands that the civil code be scrapped and the nation be governed strictly by *sharia*. In short, Mahathir effectively used the war on terrorism to pursue his domestic political agenda, and the Malaysian response will be very much tailored to their domestic political situation—UMNO's need to regain the support of its core constituency, rural Muslim Malays, and draw a clear linkage in the public's eyes between PAS and terrorists. "We are here to run a country," Mahathir recently said, "and we will not hesitate to act against anyone who participates in terrorism or violence in this country irrespective of what they say against us. This is our responsibility to the people."[90] PAS is poised to not only retain control of Kelantan and Terengganu in the 2003 fall elections, but to make substantial inroads and possibly gain control of the BN-controlled states of Perlis, Perak, and Kedah. Tellingly, in a by-election in July 2002 in Prime Minister Mahathir's home state of Kedah, UMNO only won by 283 votes. There is also lingering doubt about Mahathir's successor, Abdullah Badawi. Although he has led the attack on militants, Badawi has little economic experience and there is concern that if the economy falters, PAS will benefit.

Other Measures to Fight Terrorism

Mahathir and UMNO are reacting in this way not only for their narrow and immediate political considerations. The Malaysian government has to be concerned that apart from some apparent linkages between the fringe elements of PAS and Al-Qaida, their country has been used as a base of operations, a transit point, and source of travel documents for terrorists in the past. This is something that the government truly has to take seriously and guard against. To that end, the Malaysian government has embarked on several other courses of action in their fight against terrorism.

The first government reaction involved cracking down on visa fraud and the use of Malaysia as a transit point for terrorists. Previously, Malaysia did not have stringent visa requirements for nationals of Muslim states. In November 2001, the government imposed visa regulations for Afghan, Irani, and Iraqi nationals. Although there was discussion of including other states on this list, the government decided against it, fearing a lack of tourism and investment. And for the most part, the government had ulterior motives, as Malaysia was used as a waypoint for Middle Eastern asylum seekers en route first to Indonesia and then to Australia. The Malaysian government believed that there were some 1,000 illegal immigrants, or "transient visitors," from Afghanistan alone. Although the ultimate goal was to crack down on human smuggling, there was clearly a national security component. Malaysia caused a firestorm of protests in the region in mid-2002 when it forced out nearly 100,000 undocumented workers from Indonesia and the Philippines.

The second government policy for combating terrorism has been to increase its intelligence capability. According to the deputy defense minister Datuk Shafie Afdal, "We have to strengthen our intelligence gathering mechanism so that we can neutralize the threats before innocent people are hurt."[91] This explicitly entails not just improving surveillance of dissidents and suspected extremists at home but also abroad. To that end, Afdal also called for greater intelligence sharing within ASEAN. Malaysian officials have expressed a desire to increase their capacity to counter terrorism. As a result, Malaysia has taken up a U.S. offer to host the Southeast Asian Regional Centre for Counter-Terrorism, an international organization intended to facilitate cooperation and conduct trainings for officials in all relevant government bureaucracies from around the region.

The government also sought to curb the independence of religious leaders and ensure a high degree of state control over religions. When the Ulama Association of Malaysia (UAM) issued a *fatwa* condemning the U.S. war in Afghanistan and forbidding Malaysia and any other Islamic nation to support the United States, the government reacted strongly, and Deputy Prime Minister Badawi asserted that only the government's Fatwa Committee had the right to issue a *fatwa*. Later, the UAM called for a boycott of U.S. goods and services. This upset the government because the United States is Malaysia's largest investor and trading partner, absorbing 20 percent of Malay exports.[92] The UAM is a private group that has always had poor relations with the government, especially over the role of the ulamas in shaping public policy. We should expect the UAM and supporters in PAS to continue to attack the government's control over nonsecular issues.

The final course of action undertaken by the Malaysian government has been to take a much harder line on the Mindanao conflict. Ever since the Philippines relinquished its claim to the Sabah, Malaysia has used its good offices to help broker a peace between Muslim rebels and the Philippine government. Malaysia is currently sponsoring the peace talks between the government and the MILF. Malaysia has some sympathy for the rebels, and it is hard for the government to publicly not support the right of fellow Muslims to have their own homeland or at least an autonomous region. Nonetheless, it is very concerned about Muslim rebels using Malaysia as a base of operations and their ability to link up with Muslim extremists in Malaysia. The establishment of trans-border linkages between different extremist groups alarmed Kuala Lumpur, which was victimized on several occasions by Abu Sayyaf guerrillas. "There is a possibility that Misuari's presence in the country is a threat to national security," said a senior Malaysian police official, as "we have received information that he is working closely with the Abu Sayyaf rebels."[93] Malaysia was angered by Misuari's revolt, especially after the Malaysian government had taken the diplomatic lead in brokering the 1996 accords. When the rebellion broke out, the government made it clear that it would neither support Misuari nor give him political asylum. Upon entering Malaysian waters, Misuari was arrested and eventually deported to the Philippines to stand trial.[94]

Malaysia and the United States

Malaysia is an important state in the war on terrorism, and the United States has worked to improve relations. Mahathir has long decried against U.S. hegemonism in the world, and bilateral relations between the two have been very poor since Vice President Al Gore's attendance at the 1998 Asia Pacific Economic Cooperation (APEC) summit, when he implicitly criticized Mahathir for crony capitalism and the jailing of his deputy prime minister, Anwar Ibrahim. Gore's speech, which called for "reformasi" in Malaysia, was labeled "disgusting" by one Malaysian cabinet member. Mahathir has clearly seen this as an opportunity to improve relations with the United States, and the Bush administration has given Mahathir very high marks. Malaysia seems out of the Anwar shadow.

Malaysia is important to the United States. It is an active member in the OIC, yet it is arguably the most successful—most industrialized and developed—Muslim state. As an editorial in the quasi-official *New Straits Times* put it: "We are a moderate Muslim nation and it may complement and even strengthen the American effort in building the coalition against terrorism."[95] Deputy Prime Minister Abdullah Badawi has stated, "We are committed, 100 percent committed to fight terrorism."[96] U.S. officials have noted "respect and admiration" for Mahathir's stand and cooperation. In unusually warm words, a senior State Department official said:

> He understood what the events of 11 September meant. His response to the terrorist incident, his recognition of the implication . . . was respected and admired. We have seen Malaysia has taken a number of steps to deal with the international terrorist threat. In that respect, the Malaysian response and the Prime Minister gets the credit.[97]

Despite past rhetoric, functional and economic ties between the two states are healthy. Malaysia is the United States's eleventh-largest trading partner and seventeenth-largest export market. Bilateral trade was worth $30 billion in 2001. The United States is the largest foreign investor in Malaysia. Defense ties have been low-key but stable: There have been seventy-five port visits by U.S. naval vessels since 2000 as well as biannual joint exercises with navy SEALs and jungle training with the U.S. Army.

Kuala Lumpur is clearly enjoying the rapprochement with the United States. There have been numerous exchanges of telephone calls and letters between President Bush and Prime Minister Mahathir, as well as a private conference at the APEC meeting in Shanghai. This is important, for Mahathir fancies himself a spokesman of the developing world and a statesman of international stature who deserves a place on the world stage. On May 15, 2002, Mahathir was a guest of President Bush's at the White House, where he met with other top administration officials. No mention of Anwar or other human rights abuses documented in the Department of State's annual human rights report were brought up.

Yet we should be aware that Mahathir likes to play the enfant terrible and will remain overtly critical of U.S. policies, especially as the United States has placed Malaysians on terrorist watch lists, making it harder for Malaysian men to get visas to the United States. Malaysia was deeply angered over the U.S. position on Iraq and contended that the hypocritical U.S. stance on North Korea reinforced the notion to Southeast Asians that the war on terror was patently anti-Muslim: "The blatant double standard is what infuriates Muslims, infuriates them to the extent of launching their own terror attacks," Mahathir warned. He went on to portend: "It is no longer just a war against terrorism. It is in fact a war to dominate the world."[98] However, Malaysia will remain a close ally of the United States at the operational level.[99] The fall 2003 transfer of power to Deputy Prime Minister Abdullah Badawi should also raise no concern as to Malaysia's continued commitment to the war on terror. He personally is very disturbed with the rise of Islamic militants and has led the attack on the KMM and the JI since mid-2001. As Badawi said in a September 2002 interview:

> We cannot allow extremism to take root in Malaysia. We have already started our battle against a trend towards extremism and potential terrorism through preventive detention. That action was absolutely necessary. We cannot wait until something serious has occurred. . . . We must thoroughly clean out our religious education establishment that has partly been responsible for the rise of extremism.[100]

Singapore

Singapore, the ethnic Chinese–dominated island wedged between Malaysia and Indonesia, has been alarmed at the spread of Islamic fundamentalism throughout Southeast Asia, and its response to the war on terror was robust. Its actions, in part, were due to the fact that there is little political opposition that the government has to worry about, but more important, the general public supported the government's efforts. The Singapore economy, still in a recession and experiencing the highest unemployment rates since 1986, would be devastated by a terrorist attack. The externally oriented economy is based on foreign investment, which would flee if security became an issue. Indeed, political stability and physical security tend to be the primary reasons multinational corporations base their regional headquarters in Singapore.

The Singapore government pledged to endorse all UN Security Council resolutions regarding counterterrorism. It also pledged to give its financial institutions even greater scrutiny. But as Singapore's financial sector is already the most regulated in the region, the chance that any large assets of Al-Qaida are there is slight.[101] Singapore signed the Convention for the Suppression of the Financing of Terrorism in December 2001, and in July 2002 its parliament ratified the convention, thereby criminalizing terrorist financing. As mentioned above, Singapore does have an extensive *hawala* system. Since September 11, the government has required all *hawala* to register and has shown an interest in regulating the system. This, however, is unlikely. Most *hawala* will continue to maintain a "don't ask, don't tell" approach to business. There is a sense among security officials that to crack down on *hawala* would simply drive it underground and make it harder to investigate.

Singapore's most robust contribution was in breaking up the Jemaah Islamiya cell that intended to target the U.S., British, and Israeli embassies in Singapore, as well as U.S. military personnel and commercial interests. The Singaporean response was swift and thorough. Thirty-one people were detained, four are free but restricted, and investigations are ongoing. Singapore security officials played important roles in the arrests of JI suspects in Malaysia, the Philippines, Indonesia, and Thailand. The existence of JI has thoroughly shaken the Singaporean elite who are still in utter shock that a group like that, made up of lower-middle-class individuals who had been through state schools and national service, was able to take hold in their society.

In the Singapore government's *White Paper*, issued in January 2003, the government outlined concrete measures it was taking to counter the terrorist threat, including enhancing its already efficient border security, customs, enhancing banking oversight, and improving the oversight of strategic goods (including chemical precursors for weapons of mass destruction). Singapore's security services are robust; they are well funded, staffed, and resourced.

The government also took measures to control the influence and reach of foreign religious teachers (such as Abu Bakar Ba'asyir) and called on the Islamic clergy in Singapore to implement a policy for self-regulation and identification of radical members of the *umah* (Muslim community). Finally the government realized that it had to readdress social cohesion and ethnoreligious harmony and implement new policies to rebuild trust between the communities.[102] Although the government noted that the majority of the country's Muslims were moderate and opposed to the JI or acts of terrorism, it did note the increasing trend of religiosity among the Muslim community.

The other form of support that Singapore provided the United States is military assistance, primarily the transit of U.S. ships and planes as well as a very high degree of intelligence sharing. Singapore, which has already begun construction of a naval facility that can serve U.S. aircraft carriers, is committed to maintaining the U.S. presence in the region.

In general the Singaporean government remained firmly behind the U.S. effort in both words and deeds. But in an editorial by Tommy Koh, the former ambassador to the United States who has become somewhat of an unofficial spokesman for the Singaporean government, he made clear that Singapore is insistent that the United States maintain its current multilateral approach, continue to consult closely with friends in the region so as to not lose the moral high ground, and maintain a degree of proportionality in its attacks.[103]

Thailand

The Thai response to the war on terror, in some ways, has been the most problematic and surprising. Thailand was slow to respond to the attacks on the United States, hiding behind the cloak of ASEAN's collective statement for several days. Prime Minister Thaksin Shinawatra showed hesitancy and contradiction, at first stating that Thailand would be neutral in the war on terror. The populist Thaksin, who is critical of the United States and especially the U.S. role in the Thai economic crisis, came under attack from his own government for not living up to his treaty commitments with the United States.[104] Thereafter, Thaksin was more supportive of the United States and stated that "Thailand will cooperate with the United States and the United Nations to eliminate terrorism." The Thai Foreign Ministry announced that as a "long-time friend and treaty ally," Thailand will "render all possible assistance to the United States as Thailand has done consistently in the past."[105] Thailand agreed to implement UN Security Council Resolution 1368, but its support of the U.S. campaign was half-hearted for a number of reasons.[106]

Thai legislators were more cautious and some were highly critical of the United States. There was considerable fear that the insurgency in southern Thailand would flair up as extremists become emboldened by the attacks and mobilized by the potential of war. While there was increased press coverage of the plight and socioeconomic conditions of the 3 million Muslims in Thailand, there were not any concrete government proposals as to how to ameliorate the poor economic conditions that give rise to radical secessionist sentiments. But anti-U.S. sentiments were also a factor. There was lingering resentment within Parliament about the tepid U.S. response to Thailand's economic crisis in 1997–1998. The head of the Senate Foreign Relations Committee, Kraisak Choonhavan, angrily remarked: "The US did nothing to help when the economic crisis started with Thailand."[107] He warned that the prime minister had to get parliamentary approval before "making any military commitment." One senator demanded that the government confirm whether U.S. forces are using the U-Tapao base and expressed outrage that Thailand "is being dragged into what could be a prolonged war."[108] One press report stated that some legislators even considered scrapping the 1996 Thai-U.S. acquisition and cross-servicing agreement, which expires in 2003.[109]

The Thai military was also surprisingly hesitant in their support of the United States. This probably had more to do with the fact that Minister of Defense Chavalit Yongchaiyudh, who was prime minister at the start of the economic crisis, was highly critical of the United States. But there was also real concern within the military about retaliation from Muslim fundamentalists in the south, whose insurgency had been more or less quelled. A bombing in early 2001 in Yala Province was a wake-up call for the military. The border with Malaysia is porous and Islamic fundamentalism is growing there.

Thai intelligence played a role in the country's tepid response, as they did not take the threat of terrorism that seriously. As one critic put it:

> Obviously the Thai intelligence agents had full knowledge of the presence of an al-Qaeda network in Thailand, even before the September 11 bombings. But they did not say so publicly as they believed that this network over

> here was a benign one: At the very least it did not target the Thai people. As such, the government was reluctant to adopt pro-active and tough countermeasures.[110]

Policy Responses

Unlike the Philippines, Thailand did little to tighten border security. Unlike Malaysia, Thailand did not impose any new visa restrictions. More troubling was evidence that JI and Al-Qaida operatives availed themselves of Thailand.

The United States was very critical of Thailand for failing to arrest Al-Qaida suspects that it identified. In response, Thailand claimed that the evidence in several cases was not sufficient enough to stand up in court. But U.S. officials, in particular FBI officials, were incensed that Hambali, the senior Jemaah Islamiya leader, was able to hold a major policy meeting in Bangkok in which the Bali attack was planned. Thai authorities, though they acknowledged that he and other JI officials transited the kingdom, assert that no such meeting took place: "The only plans they were making in Thailand were where to run next," asserted the top counterterrorism official, Major General Tritot Ronnaritivichai.[111] Although he asserted that the JI operatives were tracked by Thai officials, they were unable to arrest any, nor did they arrest any of their Thai liaisons. For its part, Thailand did tip off U.S. and Canadian officials about an Al-Qaida operative, Mohammed Mansour Jabarah, as he left Thailand for the United Arab Emirates.

The most significant operation occurred in March 2002, when Thailand and the United States broke up a ring of document forgers outside of Bangkok who were working for Al-Qaida. In all, thirteen people were arrested. Around the same time, Thailand began the investigations of three firms that were suspected of links to Al-Qaida in 2002. The Thais worked closely with Singaporean officials. Following the May 16, 2003, arrest of a senior JI leader from Singapore, Arifin bin Ali, Thai officials immediately rendered him to the republic. A follow-up joint operation between Thai and Singaporean officials led to the arrest on June 10, 2002, of three JI members in southern Thailand. Yet, the arrests, which coincided with Prime Minister Thaksin's visit to Washington and meeting with President Bush, led many to question the timing of the arrests and whether more arrests would be forthcoming.

In terms of support for curbing terrorist funding, Thailand did nothing additional after September 11, though it already had in place since 1999 one of the most thorough anti–money laundering laws and enforcement regimes in the region. The FBI also provided the Thai government with sophisticated computer software to assist in the tracking of assets. Ostensibly to combat domestic corruption, this law is also effective against terrorist organizations. Yet Thailand's financial sector remains weak and highly unregulated. Thai government officials acknowledged that more than $2 billion in illicit drug money gets laundered in Thailand each year. If this much is being laundered by drug syndicates, what is there to deter other criminal groups and terrorist organizations from doing the same? And there is little that the Thai government seems to be doing about this. There is now a law in the works that will make it illegal for individuals to bring in and take out more than $10,000 in cash.[112]

In short, Thailand offered support to the United States, but that support was qualified with a lot of "ifs," and in general, Thailand had no clear-cut strategy for dealing with the war on terrorism. Following the Bali attacks, it was in complete denial that Phuket or Pattaya were similar targets and its leaders rejected regional intelligence sources that asserted Hambali and other JI leaders held an important meeting in Bangkok in January 2002 to plan a wave of bombings against soft economic targets such as tourist venues.

Conclusion

The responses from the region have been very diverse, ranging from unconditional and full support from Singapore to a year of intransigence from Indonesia, until Indonesia itself became a victim of terrorism. To be sure, the threat posed by Islamic militants and terrorists to all the Southeast Asian states is real. Yet one must understand that every country in the region has responded to the war on terror in ways that serve their immediate political objectives. All, with the exception of Thailand, used the war on terrorism to improve their relations with the United States. However, as terrorism is an international crime, domestic responses are not enough, and effective multilateral solutions need to be implemented.

Notes

1. "Joint Statement Between the United States of America and the Republic of Indonesia," September 19, 2001.

2. "Govt to Freeze Assets of Osama bin Laden if Found: Hendropriyono," *Jakarta Post (JP)*, October 2, 2001.

3. Derwin Pereira, "Mega-Hamzah Honeymoon Over," *Straits Times* (*ST*), October 20, 2001; Gendur Sudarsono, Agus Hidayat, and Heru C. Nugroho, "Jumping the Gun," *Tempo*, October 23–29, 2001.

4. Warren Caragata, "Radical Blasts," *Asiaweek*, October 5, 2001.

5. "Government Urged to Issue Stronger Statement on Afghanistan," *JP*, October 13, 2001; Derwin Pereira, "Hamzah Meets Scholars to Defuse Crisis," *ST*, October 16, 2001.

6. Pereira, "Hamzah Meets Scholars to Defuse Crisis"; AFP, "Megawati Hits American Air Raids on Afghanistan Amid Protests," *Philippine Daily Inquirer* (*PDI*), October 15, 2001.

7. NU chairman Hasyim Muzadi, cited in "RI Ties with the US in Nation's Interest," *JP*, October 11, 2001.

8. Marianne Kearney, "Calls for Jihad in Indonesia Are All About 'Fame and Position,'" *ST*, October 18, 2001.

9. Robert W. Heffner, "Islam and the Nation in the Post-Suharto Era," in Adam Schwarz and Johnathan Paris, eds., *The Politics of Post-Suharto Indonesia* (New York: Council on Foreign Relations Press, 1999), 65–66.

10. Wicksono, Andari K. Annom, Agus Hidayat, and Kurie Suditomo, "Diplomatic Gloves Off," *Tempo*, October 23–29, 2001.

11. Cited in Derwin Pereira, "Amien: Quietly Cultivating Support from Muslims," *ST*, October 25, 2001.

12. Emay Fitri, "Police Question FPI Head Over Anti-US Protest," *JP*, October 23, 2001.

13. "Darul Islam Says Splinter Faction Behind Jakarta Bombings," *JP*, November 18, 2001.

14. Online at www.laskarjihad.org.

15. Caragata, "Radical Blasts."

16. See Ayip Syafruddin, "Why Is Laskar Jihad Heading to Poso?" at www.laskarjihad.org. In the article the author blames the success of Christian missionaries in converting locals and armed provocations by Christian mercenaries, aided by ministers, as the justification for the attacks. The author argues that the Laskar Jihad has no other choice but to fight in its own defense. Also AP, "Thousands of Christians Flee Muslim Attacks," *South China Morning Post* (*SCMP*), December 1, 2001; "Renewed Muslim-Christian Clashes in Sulawesi," *ST*, December 4, 2001; and Marianne Kearney, "Sulawesi Bloodletting a Result of Weak Leadership," *ST*, December 8, 2001.

17. Fabiola Desy Unidjaja, "Government Ready to Impose a State of Emergency in Poso Town," *JP*, December 5, 2001; Fabiola Desy Unidjaja, "State of Emergency in Poso on Hold: Police," *JP*, December 8, 2001.

18. Marianne Kearney, "Jakarta to Send 2,600 More Troops to Violence-Hit Sulawesi," *ST*, December 4, 2001.

19. Tiarma Siboro and Badri Djawara, "Troops Disarm Rivals, Expel Outsiders from Troubled Poso," *JP*, December 12, 2001.

20. "Police Arrest Over 100 Laskar Jihad Members, Seize Weapons," *JP*, December 2, 2001.

21. Novi Pinotoan, "Seven Killed, 42 Injured in Ambon Explosion," *JP*, December 12, 2001.

22. Tertiani Z. B. Simanjuntak and Tiarma Siboro, "Decree Readied to Freeze Terrorist Assets," *JP*, October 31, 2001. Many believe that there was a quid pro quo for Indonesian cooperation in issuing the presidential decree: In return for cooperation in investigating assets of suspected terrorists, the Federal Bureau of Investigation pledged to assist Indonesian investigators in tracing tainted money and, most likely Suharto family wealth, in U.S. financial institutions.

23. Bank Law No. 10/1998.

24. Yogita Tahilramani, "Definition of Terrorism Opens to Abuse: Experts," *JP*, April 2, 2002; "Legal Experts Criticize RI Anti-Terrorism Bill," *JP*, December 11, 2001.

25. AP, "Indonesia to Begin War on Terror," December 13, 2001.

26. "Vice President Denies Intelligence Role in Indonesians' Arrest in Manila," *Tempo*, March 26, 2002.

27. "US Official Outlines a Way Forward for Indonesia over Aceh," *ST*, December 4, 2001; Agence France Press (AFP), "Half of Indonesia's Jets Grounded," *ST*, December 5, 2001.

28. Moreover, there were severe conflicts of interest: One of the presiding judges had previously assisted one of the defendants prepare his case. Many of the Suharto family lawyers also served as counsel to the defendants. Jane Perlez, "Indonesia

Begins Trial of Military in East Timor Abuses," *New York Times* (*NYT*), March 20, 2002.

29. Berni K. Moestafa, "Antiterror Support Not Linked with Paris Club," *JP*, March 28, 2002. The Paris Club allowed Pakistan to reschedule over two-thirds of its debt over thirty-eight-year and twenty-three-year terms under the "Islamabad Terms."

30. "President Expresses Concern over Indonesia's Deteriorating Image," *JP*, October 24, 2001.

31. Cited in "Indonesia Asks for Patience in Dealing with Terrorism," *JP*, January 31, 2002.

32. Irfan Awwas, cited in Michael Richardson, "Indonesia Divided over Extremists," *International Herald Tribune* (*IHT*), January 23, 2002.

33. Masduki Baidowi, cited in Devi Asmarani, "Indonesia's Moderate Muslims Call for Probe on Terrorist Cells," *ST*, February 10, 2002.

34. Pew Global Attitudes Project, *Views of a Changing World* (Washington, DC: Pew Research Center, June 2003): 2, 4, 19, 28, and 94.

35. Presidential spokesman Rigoberto Tiglao, cited in Martin P. Marfil, "Macapagal Orders: Track Down Abu Sayyaf Assets," *PDI*, October 1, 2001.

36. Juliet Javellana, "President Announces '14-Pillar Policy' to Battle Terrorism," *PDI*, September 26, 2001.

37. Norman Bordadora, Tonette Orejas, and Dona Z. Pazzibugan, "Accord Allowing US Access to RP Bases in the Works," *PDI*, November 18, 2001.

38. Crispin Beltran, cited in James Hookway, "Just Say 'No' to U.S. Troops," *Far Eastern Economic Review* (*FEER*), December 6, 2001, 24.

39. Javellana, "President Announces '14-Pillar Policy' to Battle Terrorism."

40. Julie S. Alipala and Juliet L. Javellana, "US Pacific Chief Coming as Top Advisor," *PDI*, October 13, 2001.

41. AFP, "US Advisors to Visit Basilan, Says Military Chief," *PDI*, October 11, 2001; Alipala and Javellana, "US Pacific Chief Coming as Top Advisor," 41; Raissa Robles and Baraddan Koppusamy, "Southeast Asian Terror Links Under Pressure," *SCMP*, October 11, 2001.

42. See Julie S. Alipala, "11 Abus Slain in Clash, US Soldiers in Basilan," *PDI*, December 7, 2001; Julie S. Alipala and Armand W. Nocum, "US Offers Words—Not War Against Abu Sayyaf," *PDI*, December 8, 2001.

43. The Department of National Defense–AFP briefing paper on the Balikatan 02-1 exercises can be found in the *PDI*, February 1, 2002. The Philippine Supreme Court ruled in early 2003 that "to unleash American GIs to subdue (the Abu Sayyaf), even under the cover of expanding the U.S.-led war against global terror, is not only an unmitigated insult against the Filipino soldier, but a negation of our self-respect as a people and a mockery of the Philippine Constitution."

44. U.S. forces had already spent $3 million on public works in the island and expect to spend $4 million more. Infrastructure projects will include road building, well digging, and other construction projects. AFP, "340 US Military Engineers Coming with President's Nod," *PDI*, April 19, 2002; Julie S. Alipala, Martin P. Marfil, and Dona Pazzibugan, "US Military Studying Balikatan Extension," *PDI*, April 17, 2002; Jane Perlez, "U.S. Antiterror Forces May Extend Stay on Philippines Island," *NYT*, March 31, 2002.

45. Dan Murphy, "Filipinos Grow Divided over Return of US Military," *Christian Science Monitor* (*CSM*), February 8, 2002.

46. Bradley Graham, "US Bolsters Philippine Force," *Washington Post* (*WP*), February 20, 2003.

47. "These operations will be led by the Armed Forces of the Philippines with assistance by US forces," said a Pentagon official. The Philippine presidential spokesman Ignacio Bunye said the U.S. troops would only engage in training: "In other words, no combat troops. Everything will be for training and advice." When asked about the Terms of Reference, Secretary of National Defense Angelo Reyes commented, "As I said, we are going to discuss the details. . . . Nothing is final. The only thing that is final is that anything we will do will be within and in accordance with the Constitution, and we will not violate of any of our laws." Carlito Pablo and Martin P. Marfil, "Palace Insists No Combat Role for US Troops," *PDI*, February 22, 2002; AFP, "US Troops to Fight Abu: US Defense Official," February 22, 2002; Paul Alexander, "Philippines Faces Fallout on US Troops," AP, February 22, 2003.

48. James Hookway, "Just Say 'No' to US Troops," *FEER*, December 6, 2001, 24

49. "US to Supply Five Copters and C-130 to Philippines," *ST*, November 4, 2001.

50. Deidre Sheehan, "Swords into Ploughshares," *FEER*, September 20, 2001, 30–31.

51. The military aid was welcome by the Philippines but fell short of Arroyo's initial request. The original request included twelve UH-1 helicopters and four C-130s. The Philippine military has requested additional C-130s, three more UH-1 helicopters, a cyclone-class patrol craft, and an unmanned reconnaissance drone. "US to Supply Five Copters and C-130 to Philippines."

52. AFP, "Generals: 20,000 More Soldiers Needed," *PDI*, December 2, 2001. The 25,000 rebels include 12,000 communist New People's Army soldiers, 12,000 MILF soldiers, and 1,000 Abu Sayyaf gunmen. Of alarm to the military, the NPA has doubled in size since the mid-1990s. At the same time, Senator Sergio Osmena was highly critical of the military, which has an almost 100:1 advantage against the Abu Sayyaf. He has used his position as the chairman of the Senate Foreign Relations Committee to push for a 40 percent cut in the military's budget, from 10 billion pesos to 6 billion, contending that an increase was irresponsible and unnecessary with such significant aid from the United States. However, he supported increasing the size of the military by 5,000 troops and the police by 4,000.

53. Amy Goldstein and Vernon Loeb, "U.S. Offers Increase in Philippine Terror Aid," *WP*, May 20, 2003.

54. Reuters, "Manila: Fight Poverty to Wipe Out Terrorism," *SCMP,* November 17, 2001.

55. This was part of an alleged 17 million peso ransom to free three captives in June 2001. According to Osmena, the ransom was 10 million; 5 million went to Villanueva and Reyes, and 2 million went to local military commanders. The president has rejected the accusations. See Dona Z. Pazzibugan, Cynthia D. Balana, and Carlito Pabli, "President Stands by Defense, Military Chiefs," *PDI*, December 5, 2001; Dona Z. Pazzibugan, Cynthia D. Balana, and Martin Marfil, "Serge O: Gloria Knew of Ransom," *PDI*, December 4, 2001; and Martin Marfil, Rock Nazareno, and Ansbert Joaquin, "Defense Chief Admits Ransom 'Probably' Paid to Abus," *PDI*, March 12, 2002.

56. AFP, "MILF Ignores bin Laden Call for Holy War," *PDI*, October 8, 2001.

57. "Interview with Salamat Hashim: The Muslim Separatist Rebel Leader Wants the 'East Timor Formula,'" *Asiaweek*, March 31, 2000; AFP, "New Round of Talks with MILF Begins in Malaysia," *PDI*, October 15, 2001.

58. BBC, *East Asia Today*, October 18, 2001.

59. Cited in Dan Murphy, "US Troops Rile Filipino Separatists," *CSM*, February 20, 2002.

60. "MILF-GRP Ceasefire in Place amid Misuari Revolt: Kabalu," *PDI*, November 22, 2001.

61. "Misuari Rebellion Puts More Pressure on Peace Efforts," *PDI*, November 21, 2001.

62. AFP, "PNP Nabs Jordanian Terror Suspect," *PDI*, November 23, 2001.

63. AFP, "Iraqi Held in Sultan Kudarat on al-Qaida Suspicions," *PDI*, November 23, 2001.

64. Juliet L. Javellana, Armand Nocum, and Volt Conteras, "Bush Thanks RP for Passing Anti–Money Laundering Law," *PDI*, September 30, 2001; Mark Landler, "The Philippines Moves Against Bank Secrecy," *NYT*, October 13, 2001, C1, C2. The OECD's Financial Action Task Force was established in 1989 and was to impose sanctions on the Philippines.

65. Landler, "The Philippines Moves Against Bank Secrecy," C2.

66. The FATF asserts that the passage of anti-laundering laws does not automatically remove states from the watch list and that a government's implementation would be monitored. See Lira Dalangin, "FATF Slow to Remove RP from 'Laundering' Watchlist: Senator," *PDI*, December 13, 2001.

67. AFP, "Macapagal Reiterates Full Support for US War on Terror," *PDI*, November 20, 2001; "Arroyo Confronts Muslim Revolt After Securing US Aid," *SCMP*, November 24, 2001.

68. Juan V. Sarmiento, Jr., "Macapagal to UN: Help Poor Lick Terrorism," *PDI*, November 18, 2001.

69. Goldstein and Loeb, "U.S. Offers Increase in Philippine Terror Aid."

70. Reuters, "Manila: Fight Poverty to Wipe Out Terrorism."

71. Vernon Loeb, "New Bases Reflect Shift in Military," *WP*, June 9, 2003.

72. "Dr. M. Articulates the Taliban and Osama," *NST*, September 29, 2001; AFP, "Malaysia Pledges Cooperation with the US Over Anthrax Letter," *PDI*, October 14, 2001.

73. John Kifner, "56 Islamic Nations Avoid Condemning the US Attacks, but Warn of Civilian Casualties," *NYT*, October 11, 2001, B5.

74. Patrick Sennyah, "US-Led Bombings of Afghanistan Won't Resolve Terrorism: Dr M," *NST*, October 14, 2001.

75. Sarban Singh and Sharanjit Singh, "Local Terrorism Will Be Dealt with Internally: Dr. M," *NST*, September 29, 2001.

76. "Opposition, NGOs, Unions Condemn US Attacks on Afghanistan," *NST*, October 8, 2001.

77. Firdaus Abdullah, "Dr M Urges US to Stop Afghan Bombings," *NST*, October 12, 2001; Brendan Pereira, "PAS Backing for Jihad against US 'a Gimmick,'" *ST*, October 11, 2001; Joniston Bangkuai, "Malaysians Ignoring PAS Call to Fight for Taliban, *NST*, October 26, 2001.

78. Ainon Mohd, Ramlan Said, and Patrick Senneh, "Government on KMM," *NST*, October 24, 2001.

79. Zulkifli Sulong, the editor of the PAS party paper *Harakah*, cited in "PAS 'Hurt by Growing Anti-Muslim Sentiment,'" *ST*, December 13, 2001.

80. S. Jayasankaran and Lorien Holland, "Profiting from Fear," *FEER*, October 11, 2001, 34.

81. Ibid.

82. Simon Elegant, "Just What Dr. M Ordered," *Time Asia*, October 22, 2001.

83. Brendan Pereira, "Muslim Youth Body Deals Blow to Opposition," *ST*, November 30, 2001.

84. Tong Yee Siong, "More Arrests of 'Militants' to Come, Warns Dr. M," *Malasiakini*, September 29, 2001; Patrick Sennyah, Ainon Mohd, and Hayati Hayatudin, "KMM's Opposition Link," *NST*, October 12, 2001; Patrick Sennyah, "Special Probe Team to Beef Up Nation Defense Against Militants," *NST*, October 16, 2001.

85. "KL to Require Students Going Abroad to Register," *ST*, October 13, 2001; "Brendan Pereira, "KL to Keep Close Eye on Schools Run by PAS," *ST*, October 16, 2001.

86. Christopher Lockwood, "The Greening of Malaysia, the Changing of the Guard: A Survey of Malaysia," *The Economist*, April 5, 2003, 6.

87. Hamidah Atan, "New Election Act Amendment to Jail Trouble Makers," *NST*, September 29, 2001; "Dr. M. Articulates the Taliban and Osama."

88. AFP, "Malaysia May Amend Terrorism Laws, Opposition Fears Crackdown," November 30, 2001.

89. Askiah Adam, "Smashing the Orientalist Myth of Islam," *NST*, November 4, 2001.

90. Sennyah, "US-Led Bombings of Afghanistan Won't Resolve Terrorism: Dr M."

91. Azura Abbas, "Need to Improve Intelligence Gathering Machinery," *NST*, November 2, 2001.

92. Chea Chor Sooi and Manisah Ismail, "Ulama Association No Right to Issue Fatwah on Afghan War," *NST*, December 3, 2001; Reme Ahmad, "Boycott Call Unnerves American Investors," *ST*, December 7, 2001.

93. Lee Shi-Ian, "The Renegade Nur Misuari Arrested Off Sabah Waters," *NST*, November 24, 2001.

94. There was a diplomatic tussle between Malaysia and the Philippines over Misuari's extradition. President Arroyo feared his presence in the Philippines, especially as the elections in the ARMM were under way. She indicated that as he broke Malaysian law, he could be tried there. Malaysia worried about the implications of having and trying Misuari and pressured the Philippines to take him. Malaysia is home to approximately 100,000 refugees from the southern Philippines who fled over the course of nearly thirty years of war. The Malaysian government is also concerned about a public backlash if it tries Misuari—an Islamic freedom fighter in the eyes of many in the public—and appears to appease the Christian Philippine government. The open support that the government has shown the Philippines during the course of this crisis has already angered many Islamicists in the country. Malaysia gave the Philippines a December 24 deadline to take back Misuari, but the Philippines stalled. After Malaysia threatened to turn him over to a third country, Libya, the Philippines took possession of Misuari in January 2002. Carlito Pablo, "Macapagal Not Hot to Get Nur," *PDI*, November 25, 2001; AFP, "Malaysia Firm on Deporting Misuari," *PDI*, December 19, 2001.

95. Tan Sri Abdullah Ahmad, cited in Leslie Lau, "Malaysia Heralds 'New Era' in US Ties," *NST*, October 26, 2001.

96. Patvinder Singh, "Malaysia, Britain Reaffirm Commitment to Root Out Terrorism," *NST*, December 7, 2001.

97. Cited in "KL Ties Positive, Says Top US Official," *ST*, December 7, 2001.

98. Jasbant Singh, "Malaysian PM Says West Seeks to Dominate," AP, February 24, 2003.

99. "A Model Moslem?" Interview with Abdullah Badawi, *Far Eastern Economic Review*, September 5, 2002.

100. Mahathir was highly offended at the new visa restrictions imposed by the United States on males from twenty-six Muslim countries, including Malaysia, labeling them as racist. "US Slammed for Putting Malaysia on Visa-Restriction List," *ST*, November 12, 2001.

101. "Interview with Deputy Prime Minister Lee," *ST*, October 1, 2001.

102. Ministry of Home Affairs, *White Paper: The Jemaah Islamiyah Arrests and the Treat of Terrorism* (Singapore, 2003), 21–23.

103. Tommy Koh, "America with Its Friends on the Moral High Road," *IHT*, September 26, 2001.

104. Thailand and the United States are bound by two agreements, the 1954 Manila Pact and the 1962 Communiqué. In addition, Thailand and the United States hold the annual Cobra Gold military exercises, the largest bilateral exercises in the region.

105. "Thailand Gives Support to War on Terrorism," *Bangkok Post* (*BP*), September 17, 2001.

106. Publicly the United States did not request Thai military facilities as it did during the 1991 Gulf War when U.S. bombers used Thai airfields, yet there were reports that since the bombings on Afghanistan began on October 8, 2001, the U-Tapao airfield was used by U.S. forces.

107. "Senators Say PM Too Quick to Side with the US," *BP*, September 29, 2001.

108. "Utapao Explanation Demanded," *BP*, October 10, 2001.

109. Wassana Nanuam, "US Military Pact Could Be Scrapped Before Expiry Date," *BP*, October 13, 2001. The agreement obligates Thailand to provide bases, refueling services, communication equipment, repair and maintenance facilities, and warehouses. In return, the United States provides weapons and training for Thai military personnel through the Foreign Military Sales Project.

110. Kavi Chongkittavorn, "Al-Qaeda in Thailand: Fact or Fiction?" *The Nation,* January 13, 2003.

111. Shawn W. Crispin, "Thais Clash with the FBI," *FEER*, February 13, 2003, 16–17; Crispin, "Thailand Tracked Terrorists, Official Reveals," *FEER*, February 13, 2003, 16.

112. "$4b in Drug Money Laundered Annually," *ST*, November 10, 2001.

CHAPTER 6

Fighting Terrorism in Southeast Asia: The Future of Militant Islam

WHAT DOES THE RISE OF RADICAL ISLAM AND THE ONGOING WAR ON TERROR mean for Southeast Asia? How will the war be fought? What are the pitfalls and obstacles in defeating terrorism in the region? There are six points that should be raised in answering this question. The first is that despite considerable success in dismantling the Al-Qaida organization, it is still far from defeated. It is a fluid organization with an uncanny ability to recruit, indoctrinate, and reconstitute itself, and Southeast Asia will be an important theater of operation for it in the coming years. The arrests of key Al-Qaida operatives such as Abu Zubaidah, Khalid Shaikh Mohammed, Abdullah al Rahim al-Nishiri, and Ramzi bin Al Shibh were significant losses for Al-Qaida. Yet the organization has shown a high degree of operational flexibility and leadership selection. Dispersed, it is a more formidable adversary. Moreover, the war in Iraq has angered many, especially Muslims in Southeast Asia, who already viewed the war on terror as being patently anti-Muslim. The United States is no longer perceived in the region as a benign hegemon, but as an aggressive and imperialist state. People are angry at U.S. hypocrisy and unilateral actions. The swift victory over Iraq instilled a greater sense of humiliation on the part of Muslims. The lesson, for Muslim militants the world over, is this: No state can confront the United States with any chance of winning. The only way that the United States can be made to "taste" the humiliation and injustice that Muslims the world over feel is through terrorism.

Second, despite the ongoing threat posed by terrorism in the region, there are uni-, bi-, and multilateral obstacles to effectively fighting terrorist groups. In addition to resource issues and bureaucratic competition, states will continue to react and cooperate only in their immediate short-term political, economic, and diplomatic interests. Third, the Association of Southeast Asian Nations, although the appropriate venue for a multilateral effort to fight terrorism, is a much weakened organization, and its efficacy in combating terrorism will be limited. Multilateral institutions are simply too weak to make any meaningful contribution to the war on terror in Southeast Asia. Fourth, the war on terror is important in that it has reengaged the United States in the region. After more than a decade of attaching little to no importance on the region, the United States is finally cognizant of the fact that the consequences of disengagement are too great. Fifth, the war on terror cannot come at the expense of human rights in the region. The war on terror cannot be carte blanche for states to arrest and imprison bona fide political opponents. Terrorism results from a lack of political freedom. If anything, we must foster the development of law-governed democracies and assist these countries in building durable political and legal institutions. As *New York Times* columnist Thomas Friedman put it, we should not be afraid of the "Arab street" but of the "Arab basement."[1] The same holds true for Southeast Asia. Related to the conundrum of human rights is a final issue: how to engage the secular nationalists and moderates who can project a viable alternative to the radical Islamists.

The Continued Threat of Al-Qaida

Al-Qaida suffered serious setbacks following the U.S. invasion of Afghanistan in the fall of 2001. With the loss of its training camps and its rear base area, Al-Qaida was forced to diversify its operations. Throughout 2002, attacks (both planned and executed) were spread around the world. Command and control, likewise, was diversified following the arrest of senior Al-Qaida leaders. Individuals such as the Indonesian Hambali and Khalid Shaikh Mohammed became key leaders of the organization. In October 2002, Ayman al-Zawahiri, the second in command of Al-Qaida, announced that Al-Qaida would begin to strike U.S. economic interests. Al-Qaida, always believing in guilt by association, was responsible for the bombing of a French-leased but Malaysian-owned oil tanker and the October 2002 attack on a Balinese nightclub, in which 202 people, mainly foreign tourists, were killed. Hambali, at a January 2002 meeting, directed Jemaah Islamiya cells to attack tourist sites and other soft economic targets. Clearly the goal of Al-Qaida is to cause a substantial economic downturn in the region. Poverty does not cause terrorism, but it does create the conditions in which it thrives, in which radicals and militants are able to indoctrinate and recruit. As Ayman al-Zawahiri explained in a May 21 broadcast on al-Jazeera, "The crusaders and the Jews do not understand but the language of killing and blood. They do not become convinced unless they see coffins returning to them, their interests being destroyed, their towers being torched, and their economy collapsing."[2]

Al-Qaida is far from defeated. Although by the end of 2002, some 3,000 Al-Qaida members and suspects were detained around the world, the organization is still able to plan and execute attacks and recruit new members. If anything, a more diffused and decentralized organization is a far more lethal enemy. In many ways the security forces are the victims of their success: they did such an effective job in arresting first- and second-tier leaders, that they simply do not know who the third- and forth-tier leaders are, who now are in charge of the organization. There is some question over why Al-Qaida did not launch an attack during the Iraq war when it would have been able to take advantage of popular animosity toward the United States and capture the hearts and minds of Muslims watching their own governments unable to stop the United States. On February 11, 2003, Osama bin Laden issued a solidarity statement with the people of Iraq and called on Muslims to rise up "incite and mobilize the Islamic nation . . . to break free from the slavery of these regimes who are slaves of America." Bin Laden clearly sought to assume the moral leadership of the Muslim world. By not retaliating against the United States, Al-Qaida may have shown the world that it is defeated and currently unable to launch an attack. Yet Al-Qaida has never been event driven. The hallmark of Al-Qaida attacks is that they are meticulously planned and executed. Al-Qaida only attacks when they have the resources to execute and attack with a high probability of success. The organization is biding its time, rebuilding its network. Al-Qaida does not view the current situation as a defeat. The organization is structured on Abdullah Azzam's concept that the jihadist organization must be built along the lines of the life of the Prophet Mohammed. To that end, the strategic retreat (i.e., the withdrawal from Mecca to Medina) is an integral and acceptable part of the struggle.[3] Al-Qaida is down but not out.

Clearly Southeast Asia has become one of its key theaters of operation, and we should expect continued attacks and operations in the region. This will have a profound economic impact on the region. The attacks on Bali, for example, were estimated to result in the loss of nearly $5 billion a year in tourist receipts—approximately 2 to 3 percent of gross domestic product. The ripple effects, such as the loss of tourism in all the countries in the region, are acutely felt. Could one imagine the impact on the region of a terrorist bombing in Singapore?

Al-Qaida in many ways has been transformed from an organization to an ideology, especially in Southeast Asia. The first place we should start is for security specialists, journalists, and academics to go back and revisit the sectarian conflicts in the Malukus and Sulawesi. This was a generation's Afghanistan. Although it will never have the religious and political symbolism of the Afghan jihad, it was their jihad, their first taste of blood, of war in God's name. It was the formative experience of their life. There were some 4,000 people who fought in the Malukus and Poso (3,000 Laskar Jihad and approximately 1,000 Laskar Mujahidin and Laskar Jundullah). That is four times the number of all Southeast Asians who fought against the Soviets.

Where are they now? Are they setting up their own radical *madrasas* (Islamic schools)? Recruiting? Preparing for their next jihad? Forming networks and trans-border alliances? This group of individuals is a potential time bomb. It is disturbing that the Mujahidin Council of Indonesia, an overt civil society organization, is distributing books on guerrilla warfare and translations of Shaikh Abdullah Azzam's memoir of the Afghan jihad.

But Al-Qaida can be an ideology for individuals in the region as a whole. Osama bin Laden has become a romanticized figure. Although few Indonesians support his means, or even his ends, most believe that he is a brave man, a defender of Muslim causes. Moreover, with the economies in the region still not fully recovered from the Asian economic crisis, the socioeconomic conditions for recruitment into radical groups exist. Poverty does not cause terrorism, but it does provide the conditions for it to spread. With some 40 million unemployed Indonesians alone, not to mention all the underemployed persons, radical groups will find fertile ground for recruiting.

The ongoing crisis in the Middle East, a world away from Southeast Asia, has become a metaphor for injustice in the region and has led to virulent anti-Americanism by some strata. War in Iraq, likewise, was the final confirmation for many Muslims in Southeast Asia that the Americans really are fighting Islam, not terrorism or proliferation, especially as they juxtapose Washington's response to North Korea's admission that it has a nuclear weapons program. War against Iraq put hundreds of thousands of people on the streets across the region. Though the demonstrations were not as large, sustained, or violent as anticipated, the protests put inordinate political pressure on their governments to curtail cooperation with the United States in the war on terror. War against Iraq, in other words, has led to a growth in popular support for radical Muslim causes, diminished support on behalf of secular nationalists for the United States, and potentially less cooperation by regional governments in counterterrorism efforts. The United States is portrayed as an arrogant and aggressive hegemon with no concern for international law or public opinion.

The Limits of Regional Cooperation

As terrorism is truly an international threat, states are unable to combat terrorism alone and must engage in both bi- and multilateral cooperation. Despite a common threat, the reactions by the individual states in Southeast Asia were varied, especially their willingness to work closely with the United States. More important is regional cooperation to deal with the flow of individuals, financial transfers, and the flow of explosives and weapons. Here cooperation has been, and will continue to be, mixed due to bureaucratic politics and character, historical legacies, and lingering mistrust as well as the weakness of multilateral institutions in the region. There are a number of problems that make counterterror operations difficult at the uni-, bi-, and multilateral levels. At each level, the same problems are multiplied in complexity.

At the unilateral level, counterterrorist operations first require the attention of the security services. This sounds nonsensical, but many governments in the region did not consider international terrorism to be on their list of threats facing their countries. Although there are cases in which Malaysia and Thailand knew that both foreign terrorist and paramilitary organizations were operating within their borders, the security services deemed these groups to be of no threat to them or their nationals. They were simply banking, purchasing weapons, transiting, disseminating propaganda, and providing other back office functions, not threatening the host regime. If a state considers the likelihood that it will be the target of an international terrorist attack low, then it will direct its scarce resources elsewhere. Even Singapore's robust and well-funded security apparatus was taken aback by the scope of the network of Islamic militants because it has always focused its attention on other threats.

In some cases, the security services are simply spread too thin with greater and more pressing security threats, even if they know that they are a potential terrorist target. For example, in the Philippines, the security services must focus on the revived threat posed by the communist New People's Army, the Moro Islamic Liberation Front, the Abu Sayyaf Group, the Moro National Liberation Front, and all the factions thereof, in addition to Al-Qaida, Jemaah Islamiya, and other transnational terrorist groups. In Thailand, security forces are preoccupied with Myanmar and their Indochinese neighbors. In Indonesia, government forces focus their efforts on secessionist movements, especially in Aceh, the greatest threat to the Indonesian state. In Malaysia and Singapore, more attention was paid to domestic security threats.

Despite large intelligence and internal security apparati in the region, in general there does not seem to be much understanding of their neighbors and a dearth of internal analytical capabilities. In Southeast Asia, most intelligence budgets are directed toward internal security. Thus, resources for external intelligence gathering are also prioritized. Southeast Asian states, as all states do, spy on one another. It is a matter of course. But they tend to direct their limited intelligence resources to the country or countries that they consider to be the most immediate threat to them. For example, the Singaporeans focused their resources on Malaysia, and in the post-Suharto era they began focusing more on Indonesia. The Malaysians focus on Singapore. The Thais focus on Myanmar and Indochina. The Philippines and Indonesia tend to be more inwardly focused due to their internal difficulties. In sum, all of these states have limited resources that they concentrate on their immediate "threat," and then they rely on an ally to help fill in the pieces with regards to the others. It is absolutely appalling how little each state knows about one another, even basic political situations, political actors, and trends, with the exception of an immediate neighbor, their traditional threat. States were not focused enough on the repercussions of changes in the internal political situations of neighboring states.

The second problem at the unilateral level is that counterterrorist operations require the cooperation of the security and police forces, first within their own border. The failure in the United States for information to be shared between the Federal Bureau of Investigation and Central Intelligence Agency led to devastating consequences, as two of the September 11 hijackers were in the United States months before the attacks. There may be fairly legitimate reasons for a lack of coordination. For example, intelligence gathering is different than building up a police case and using all of the garnered information in a court proceeding with the goal of incarcerating a terrorist for a crime. Yet often the lack of cooperation is driven by personal rivalries and bureaucratic competition.

Such bureaucratic competition and lack of coordination gets exacerbated in conditions of resource scarcity. This is true in most Southeast Asian states where intelligence and security is housed in a number of different ministries and competing bureaucracies. It is not uncommon in any of the countries to have an external intelligence service, military intelligence service, a domestic intelligence service, as well as police intelligence. Police forces are hampered by center-provincial competition. In developing countries, this leads to intense competition over resources and funding and a lack of cooperation between the services. For example, in the Philippines, there are more than ten intelligence and security services spread across numerous ministries and cabinet offices, making coordination and information sharing all but impossible.

The Indonesian situation is even more troubling. Even in Indonesia, where the nonmilitary intelligence services are ostensibly under one cabinet minister, the coordinating minister for state security, there is intense competition between BIN (the State Intelligence Agency), the National Police, and a small intelligence office housed in the Ministry of Justice.

During the Suharto era, military intelligence was the most powerful and best-funded security apparatus. Owing to their political role in the New Order era, they suffered acute cuts in their funding, and their operations and networks of informers became more concentrated in hot spots such as Aceh and Papua. The organization has lost in prestige and resources to the newly organized intelligence service, BIN.

BIN is the largest intelligence arm, and it is the one to which the Americans have turned since the September 11 attacks on the United States, but not without some reservation. The head of BIN, Lieutenant General (retired) A. M. Hendropriyono, was implicated in a 1989 attack in which some 100 civilians, now characterized as Muslim extremists, were killed. But Hendropriyono was also the most outspoken official on both the threat of Muslim militants in Indonesia as well as Al-Qaida's penetration of the country. Hendropriyono was infuriated by the TNI's (Indonesian armed forces') support of the Laskar

Jihad, which was founded by Jafar Umar Thalib, a veteran of the mujahidin's war against the Soviets, who raised a 3,000-man army that waged sectarian violence against Christians in the Malukus in May 2000. He was also the first and only Indonesian official to publicly assert that Al-Qaida was active in Indonesia and tried to force the government's hand in declaring a war on terrorism by acknowledging the existence of an Al-Qaida camp in Sulawesi: "Poso has been used by international terrorist groups to support activities they plan from outside the country."[4] Despite cooperation with the United States, BIN has its own problems, including intense factionalism. Like the Pakistani Intelligence Service, which for years supported Islamic militants in Kashmir as well as the Taliban, there are many in BIN who support the growing number of Islamists in Indonesia.

The police intelligence force is small and severely underfunded. Competition over resources is legion. Competition is also intense between the military and police, which were separated only in 1999. Both services rely on legal businesses, government positions, and illegal businesses to generate income for themselves. In Indonesia, the military receives $3.2 billion, or only one-third of its operating budget, from the state. It earns the rest, more than $6 billion, through legal and illegal activities, sixty-four companies that include logging and natural resource exploitation, an airline, and "charitable" organizations. Its illegal activities include people smuggling, gambling, drug running, prostitution, and extortion. One of its key sources of revenue is selling protection to Western gas and mining firms, such as ExxonMobil, in the troubled provinces of Aceh and Freeport-McMoRan in Papua (both provinces beset by their own secessionist insurgencies). In the past few years, Freeport paid the regional Kopassus command in Papua some $10 million to $11 million annually for protection from insurgents. Like the TNI, the police rely on both legal and illegal activities to augment its budget, and oftentimes the turf wars are not over investigations but over illegal business competition. In September 2002, TNI troops attacked a police station in northern Sumatra Province with rocket-propelled grenades, killing eight—all over a marijuana smuggling racket.

The military was unhappy that I Made Mangku Patika, himself a Balinese and the head of Papua's police who originally implicated them in the Freeport killings, was in charge of the Bali bombing investigations. The military also mistrusted his close working relations with Australian investigators, owing to Australia's lead role in the UN peacekeeping operation in East Timor. Additionally, the police and military resented Hendropriyono's close ties with President Megawati Sukarnoputri and the steady budget his agency received, especially the bulk of $50 million in counterterrorism aid provided by the United States. There is also intense resentment over his close ties with the Americans, relations and financial support long enjoyed by the TNI. Until there is an accounting for East Timor, the United States will continue to improve ties with BIN and the police, only serving to add to the rivalries among Indonesia's security services, hampering the war on terror on Al-Qaida's new battlefront.

In short, competition over budgets and resources led to a significant lack of professionalism. But even with greater resources, where one would anticipate higher levels of technology that would facilitate communication and information sharing, often intelligence coordination is poor.

Finally, intelligence services in Southeast Asia are often overly politicized and used for regime maintenance. Too frequently they are focused on domestic political opponents to the regime, and not to bona fide threats. For example, in the Philippines under the Joseph Ejercito Estrada administration, most intelligence officers were reassigned, and many ongoing investigations were dropped because Estrada believed the intelligence services were too close to the former president Fidel Ramos.[5] If intelligence services are too political they lose the trust of the people and government, making their job that much more difficult.

At the bilateral level, coordination and information sharing are even more complex. The war on terror has led to many states calling for the need for greater police cooperation and intelligence sharing. Yet the nature of intelligence agencies, which tend to be secretive and suspicious, makes information sharing difficult. As they tend to hoard information at home, why would they be likely to share it with outsiders?

In some instances, states have cooperated well, especially among the police forces. There is a long history, for example, of cooperation between the Malaysian, Singaporean, and Bruneian internal security departments. All three states shared similar threats, especially of the Malaysian Communist Party, which they worked together to suppress. All were developed on the British model, thus their similar organizational model facilitates cooperation. Singapore and Malaysia worked closely in breaking up the Jemaah Islamiya network, though there was still some friction. Singapore, for instance, decided to begin arresting suspects in December 2001, before the Malaysians were informed, thus several of the Malaysian suspects had time to flee.

Whereas the Singaporean intelligence service was able to provide operational assistance to Philippine authorities during the arrest of Fathur Rohman al-Ghozi, this has been more the exception than the rule. The Philippines and Singapore have no history of animosity (with the exception of a diplomatic row over Singapore's execution of a Filipina maid for murder). Thailand did not arrest any of the JI suspects who fled from Malaysia in December to January 2002, until June 2003 when it arrested three people in a joint operation with Singapore.

We also cannot lose sight of the fact that often the largest foreign intelligence gathering organs in each state is housed in its respective Ministry of Defense, which consider one another to be their greatest security threat and hence direct the majority of their resources at each other. It is, therefore, unlikely that there is close coordination of intelligence.

History plays a very important role. Philippine intelligence officials, whom I interviewed, were still mistrustful over Malaysia's former assistance to the MILF and MNLF, not to mention the Sabah territorial dispute. Due to Malaysia's long history of supporting the MNLF and the MILF from the late 1960s to 1980s, there is little belief among Philippine intelligence officials that Malaysia has washed its hands of these secessionist groups. However, this flies in the face of all the evidence. There is no proof that Malaysia continues to aid Muslim secessionists in the Philippines. By the 1980s, Kuala Lumpur came to the understanding that closer ties with Manila far outweighed the foreign policy benefits of such support to the rebels. It is the avowed public policy of Malaysia that the Philippines' territorial integrity be maintained, and it does not support the secessionist aims of the MILF. Indeed, the Malaysians shocked everyone in the region, including the Moro peoples, by returning Nur Misuari to Manila after his November 2001 revolt.

In another instance, throughout 2002 Malaysia and Singapore repeatedly approached the Indonesians to arrest suspected terrorists. Until the Bali bombing, they were repeatedly frustrated by Indonesian intransigence and an unwillingness to arrest militants or render suspects. Indeed, whereas Indonesian officials acknowledged Jemaah Islamiya's existence in Singapore, Malaysia, and the Philippines, they thoroughly denied the organization's existence in Indonesia. Much of the reason for Indonesia's intransigence had to do with lingering anger toward the two states over past security issues. Indonesian security officials are still unhappy with the Singaporeans after uncovering a huge spy ring there in the mid-1990s. Likewise, for years the primary security threat in Indonesia was that of the Acehnese rebels, yet the Malaysians did little to curtail GAM's (Free Aceh Movement's) activities, including fund-raising, gun running, and transit, within their borders. Kuala Lumpur could have offered considerable assistance to Jakarta in their three-decade war with the GAM; yet, for the most part, the Malaysians turned a blind eye to their activities in Malaysia.

Abu Bakar Ba'asyir and Abdullah Sungkar are another case in point. The two were convicted criminals (albeit for political crimes at the time) who fled to Malaysia where they lived openly for fourteen years. There is no evidence that the Indonesian government sought their extradition, nor did the Malaysian government seek to curtail their anti-Indonesian activities. Even JI leader Hambali, who was first indicted in Indonesia, returned to Malaysia but was not arrested.

The Philippine government, likewise, appealed to the Indonesian government to crack down on the Jemaah Islamiya. But President Megawati was unwilling to offer any assistance to President Gloria Macapagal Arroyo until the Philippine government could crack down on the illegal but steady flow of light arms into Indonesia, which fueled much of the militant and secessionist activity.

The government that seemed the most intransigent and uncooperative was Indonesia's. However, the investigation into the Bali attack had a profound effect on police officials about the benefits of cooperation. Clearly without international cooperation—especially of the Australian Federal Police, but also of Britain's Scotland Yard, the FBI, and regional police forces—the Bali investigation would not have progressed as quickly or as thoroughly as it did. As I Made Mangku Pastika, who led the Balinese investigation, said in his speech before the ASEAN Workshop on Combating Terrorism on January 20, 2003, the Indonesian National Police "need mutual cooperation," especially in the fields of forensics, computer technology, cellular intercepts, ballistics, money launderings, and chemistry.[6] Pastika was concerned about a backlash from international cooperation: "Although the cooperation with the foreign agencies has been very beneficial, it has been interpreted as a form of intervention by foreign governments towards the sovereignty of Republic of Indonesia [sic], particularly by some observers and politicians."[7]

There is no doubt that intelligence sharing and police cooperation in Southeast Asia have dramatically improved in the course of the war on terror. It is not overstating it to say that such cooperation has reached new heights; but they also started from a low point. The successful investigations that led to the breakup of the JI cells around the region and the uncovering of the Bali attack are certain to reinforce the understanding that international cooperation is not just beneficial but necessary in combating international terrorism.

There also has to be greater bilateral cooperation with their U.S. counterparts. The United States itself has only limited intelligence capabilities in Southeast Asia. Although it enjoys the most advanced technical means, it has not been a focus in terms of human intelligence or analysis since the 1980s. The United States, however, does have vast resources at its disposal and can serve as a bridge between the different security forces in the region. Southeast Asian security forces will also have to improve their ties with European, Middle Eastern, South Asian, and Israeli counterparts.

The sharing of information and holding dialogues is only the first step in improving bilateral coordination, and it must be institutionalized and regularized. One way of doing this, and clearly a politically sensitive one, is the opening of liaison offices in embassies. There is a push, for instance, from both Washington and Canberra, to expand the number of liaison offices and police officials of the FBI and AFP, respectively, in the countries throughout the region.

Second, more bilateral extradition treaties are needed in the region to facilitate better law enforcement and counterterrorism. No state in ASEAN has extradition treaties with all other members. Most have only one or two extradition treaties. In the coming years, a series of extradition treaties must be signed.

It is essential to further develop a strong foundation of bilateral cooperation. Without such a foundation, it will be impossible to develop a multilateral framework for combating terrorism and transnational crime.

ASEAN's Growing Pains

What does the war on terror mean for ASEAN? Is there an effective role the organization can play in combating transnational terrorism? Bringing ASEAN back into the fray is not a bad idea if our expectations are low. The United States forced the anti-terror treaty on ASEAN in May 2002, not the other way around. It was only with considerable U.S. diplomatic arm-twisting that ASEAN accepted the agreement.

ASEAN is a much weakened organization since expansion in the mid-1990s, for four interconnected reasons that stem from the groups expansion.

Expansion

Since Vietnam's membership into ASEAN in 1995, the organization grew to include Laos, Myanmar, and Cambodia. While this fulfilled the organization's desire to become a regional organization rather than a subregional organization, it led to significant changes in the policy orientation, decisionmaking process, and norm-setting. There were several important outcomes due to expansion.

First, the degree to which ASEAN believed it could socialize its new members into the "ASEAN way" was overstated; the new members, xenophobic and authoritarian regimes, did not alter their modus operandi and adopt foreign norms. According to one ASEAN official, "ASEAN would be in a better position to influence the two countries [Myanmar and Cambodia] once they become members as there are norms and practices in conducting intra-ASEAN relations."[8] These are countries known for their fierce diplomatic unilateralism, who now had to work on the basis of consensus in a multilateral setting.[9] ASEAN, for its part, was confident that it could socialize its new members to its established norms and codes of conduct. If anything, increased membership has gone to dilute core organizational values. As Kay Moeller noted, the Myanmar junta did not see ASEAN as a constraint on its behavior.[10] The new members of ASEAN have discovered that membership in ASEAN actually protected them and their preexisting diplomatic agendas. They used the cloak of consensus to shield themselves from international criticism. Rather than adapting to ASEAN's norms, they used ASEAN to forestall exogenous pressures to reform themselves.

The second outcome, the degree to which ASEAN believed that enlargement would lead it to become an even more effective dispute resolution organization, as it included all states in the region, again proved overstated.

ASEAN's underlying assumption was that a subregional organization that did not seat all the players at the table could not resolve regional disputes. With expansion, there were more conflicts in the organization, as more members had a greater diversity of interests. That is troubling as "ASEAN is fundamentally about the convergence of its members' narrowly defined interests."[11] The new members brought a host of new issues and concerns that were often at odds with or exacerbated existing tensions within the organization.

Enlarged, the organization was more legitimate; yet since its expansion to ASEAN-10, the organization has been unable to take on any major issues that divide them. For example, whereas alone Vietnam could not change ASEAN, the bloc of four has significantly altered the organization's composition. Although they are the poorest and least developed members, they form a caucus, which was very apparent in 1998. The significance of Hanoi hosting a pre-Manila summit meeting of Laos, Cambodia, and Myanmar to coordinate policy was lost on no one. It is not that these states are authoritarian in an organization dominated by democracies—Malaysia, Brunei, and Singapore are all soft authoritarian states. But the four new member states are hard authoritarian regimes that utilize all the resources at their disposal, including overwhelming force and systematic and widespread human rights abuses and terror to maintain their monopoly of power. They also actively seek to curtail the growth and development of civil society. Whereas there are other one-party or soft authoritarian states in ASEAN, there is political dialogue, compromise, accommodation, a quasi free press, and a civil society in which alternative interests can be articulated. In Myanmar, Laos, Vietnam, and Cambodia, there is no tradition of political compromise. Indeed, in all of these authoritarian political cultures, compromise is equated with weakness.

Consensus

Even without membership expansion, ASEAN was weakened by the principles that made it possible: consultation and consensus. ASEAN did not take on controversial issues, deferring instead to issues upon which it could build consensus. Differences, when they arose, were papered over and confrontation was avoided in deference to the ASEAN way. As the former Filipino national security adviser Jose Almonte put it, "Divisive issues are simply passed over for later resolution—or until they have been made either irrelevant or innocuous by time and events."[12] ASEAN eschewed formal legalistic sanctions, relying instead on persuasion and informal discussion. The ASEAN way employed the lowest common denominator approach of consultation and consensus that ensured that the organization takes incremental and nonconfrontational steps to security.

ASEAN simply managed conflicts, it did not resolve them. It built an informal community of elites that allowed diplomatic coordination on a number of issues. Trust and healing were the immediate goals. As Michael Leifer, the foremost scholar of ASEAN, put it, "ASEAN was established in order to locate post-conflict intra-regional reconciliation within an institutionalized structure of relations."[13] This was only possible because of the shared threat each state had from externally sponsored communist insurgencies. "Without that threat," according to Shaun Narine, "the ASEAN states would not have had the incentive to put aside their own conflicts and learn to cooperate. ASEAN never developed the skill of resolving conflicts, however, just avoiding them."[14]

As long as all states were prospering, there was little reason or incentive for conflict. But with the region's dramatic economic reversal in the summer of 1997, many lingering disputes surfaced. The organization showed a lot of strains in the late 1990s, but because of a commitment to consensus-style decisionmaking and strict noninterference policies, ASEAN was unable to deal with a number of issues that confronted the members:

- The pollution and smog caused by Indonesia's clear-cutting and burning of tropical forests, some 750,000 hectares in 1997 alone, rankled Singapore and Malaysia, which estimated that the fires cost some $1.38 billion in health care for 200,000 affected people and lost tourism revenue. There was nothing Malaysia and Singapore could do to force Indonesia to stop the fires; all that ASEAN provided for was the establishment of a regional smog monitoring station.
- The Asian economic crisis really pushed the limits of the organization, which was not able to respond collectively in any way. There was a paltry degree of economic coordination to resolve the crisis multilaterally through the organization; each state tried to cope as best it could alone, or with external bi- or multilateral partners such as the International Monetary Fund. Although ASEAN has since then gone on to create a regional economic surveillance mechanism, "given the divisions within ASEAN on how to run economic matters, such a mechanism is only going to be a 'talk shop.'"[15]
- The use of territory by insurgents caused numerous conflicts between neighboring states. For example, Islamic rebels operating in the southern Philippines kidnapped tourists in Malaysia, while ethnic insurgents fighting the Myanmar regime have used Thailand as sanctuary. Hot pursuit of rebels into the host states, such as the Tatmadaw's pursuit of Karen rebels into Thailand, led to armed clashes between Thailand's and Myanmar's armies.
- The sharing of water resources has severely strained relations between Singapore and Malaysia, the latter of which recently announced that it would not extend a water sharing agreement past 2061. Restrictions on Singapore's use of Malaysian airspace have also caused tensions.

- The flow of refugees and illegal immigrants due to political instability, especially from Indonesia, Myanmar, and Cambodia, constantly strains relations with their neighbors.
- The failure of collective engagement with Myanmar and its underlying assumptions has also strained the organization's unity. Myanmar's membership creates annual diplomatic crises with the European Union and the United States. The organization's current policy on Myanmar has become absolutely untenable and is causing deep rifts in the organization. The regime's continued use of forced labor, the resignation of UN human rights observer Rajsoomer Lallah, and the continued frustration of the UN special rapporteur, Razili Ismail, to broker an accord between Aung San Suu Kyi and the junta will only cause greater diplomatic tensions.
- The unabated flow of drugs into Thailand from ethnic groups in Myanmar, notably the United Wa State Army, has infuriated the Thai government. Yet the government's complaints have fallen on deaf ears in Yangon, whose leaders in the State Peace and Development Council continue to cut deals with the insurgents, allowing them to control the lucrative drug trade in return for ending the civil war and a portion of the proceeds.
- ASEAN's involvement in East Timor, including the presence of Thai and Malaysian peacekeepers, now under the command of a Thai general, infuriated many within the Indonesian government and military. East Timor's proposed membership into ASEAN will also be a sticking point.

The Thais, in particular, were frustrated by the Myanmar junta and have since questioned the wisdom of allowing Myanmar to join the organization. The uncontrollable flow of drugs across the border into Thailand has created an enormous social crisis and forced Thailand to speak out and cast doubt on the wisdom of the organization's existing Myanmar policy; a policy that failed on all counts to resolve the political stalemate, resume the dialogue between the junta and Suu Kyi's National League for Democracy, end the civil war and ethnic insurgencies, stem the flow of drugs and refugees, and prevent the egregious violations of human rights.

As a result, the former Thai foreign minister, Surin Pitsuwan, called for the end to the organization's long-standing policy of noninterference in the internal affairs of other states. Surin proposed that when events in one country affected other states, than there were grounds for interference, what he terms "enhanced interaction": "It is time that ASEAN's cherished principle of non-intervention is modified to play a constructive role on preventing or resolving domestic issues with regional implications."[16]

Only the Philippines came out and publicly supported the Thai proposal for increased interference in the internal affairs of other states or the reevaluation of the Myanmar policy. The Thai proposal infuriated the xenophobic new members who were drawn to the organization's key principle of noninterference, and the Thai proposal was soundly rejected. Then at the July 2000 ASEAN meeting, Thailand proposed establishing a troika, comprising Indonesia, Thailand, and Singapore, to address regional concerns. The idea was met with hostility and rejected. As a result, leaders of other states became emboldened to pursue their own interests without any concern of condemnation or sanction by the grouping.

Finally, the one attempt to really institutionalize conflict resolution, the ASEAN Regional Forum (ARF), has been a failure. Launched in 1994, the organization now includes twenty-one member states. However, it remains unable to take on any serious conflict because the core operating principle of the ARF is the "ASEAN way," namely, it tries to reach consensus but tends to only be able to achieve consensus on the lowest common denominator. The ARF will become irrelevant if ASEAN continues to steer it, and if the ARF does assume a greater role in regional security, it will only be because great powers (the United States or China) are able to influence the agenda. Although the ARF is working on confidence-building measures, it has not even begun to delve into the realms on preventative diplomacy, much less conflict resolution.

Preoccupation and Leadership

Since 1997, ASEAN member states have turned inward, focusing on their immediate political and economic troubles. There was considerable political turnover since 1998, particularly with the resignation of Indonesian strongman Suharto, and the rapid succession of three leaders who were much more concerned with consolidating the country's political situation. Indonesia, always primus inter pares, has abdicated its leadership role without any obvious successor. Thailand is unacceptable to many because of its proposals to reform the organization and its standard operating principles. There is a leadership vacuum that has benefited the new members. Vietnam, which was a very passive member of ASEAN for the first four to five years of its membership, became the rotating president at a critical time. The Philippines, Indonesia, Malaysia, and Thailand were preoccupied with internal problems, which allowed Hanoi to actively push its own agenda including Cambodian membership and noninterference in the internal affairs of other states.

The leadership transition was important for another reason. Despite the myriad of meetings and working groups that the organization hosts each year, ASEAN is less institutionalized than it likes to believe and remains very much a club of individual leaders. As Michael Leifer put it, ASEAN is a "culture of intramural dialogue and consultation based on close working relationships between ministers and officials."[17] This is not entirely a bad thing. What ASEAN did so successfully was that it forced regional leaders and ministers to get to know one another: It personalized diplomacy through the some 230 to 250 different annual ASEAN meetings. But there are limits to a personalized rather than institutionalized system as leaders change. Whereas intraelite understanding was possible in the relatively staid era of the 1970s–1980s, the current weakness of the organization can be seen in the recent turnover of leaders—as only the Malaysian prime minister remained in office of the original ASEAN-5 members. The organization could barely withstand the nearly simultaneous and rapid turnover of key leaders within the original ASEAN-5 states. Conflict resolution in ASEAN was too much based on personalities, not institutions.

Loss of U.S. Support

For all the reasons above, ASEAN suffered an additional hit: External partners, such as the United States, became frustrated with ASEAN's seeming inability to deal with any of those problems and the least common denominator approach to security and conflict resolution. The United States continued to support the organization, if for no other reason than there was no other organization to deal with in the region.

ASEAN was always a cornerstone of U.S.-Asia policy, but there has been little policy consideration on how the organization's evolution would affect U.S. policy. The original members of ASEAN always asserted in their desire to expand that regime type did not matter. Yet all of the original five members were virulently anticommunist and at least nominally pro–United States (clearly supportive of U.S, continued military presence in the region). These factors simply were not true by the late 1990s. Moreover, ASEAN always worked in concord with U.S. foreign policy. When ASEAN made the collective decision to enlarge, the organization was at the peak of a decade-long economic boom that gave the members inordinate self-confidence. They saw the Europeans and Americans who counseled against increasing membership to pariah states such as Cambodia and Myanmar as blatant interference in their internal affairs, and they rushed to admit the new members to prove a point, especially in time for the organization's thirtieth anniversary. As one respected Thai academic stated: "ASEAN's decision was made, to no small degree, in a show of determination not to bow to external pressure, though there were reservations by some members on the admission of Myanmar and Cambodia."[18]

The go-slow style of consensus seeking, even if it meant that a single state or minority of states could affect policy, infuriated U.S. officials, who considered ASEAN and the ARF to be nothing more than talk shops.

If ASEAN is to remain a dynamic and viable international organization, it will have to reassess its policy of consensus-style decisionmaking—the so-called ASEAN way—and its policies of nonintervention. Counterterrorism provides the organization with such an opportunity.

The United States can no longer distance itself from the region much less abandon it as they were accused of doing during the Asian economic crisis. There is a growing realization that the continued economic slide in this region will have dire national security implications for the United States. As Michael Armacost put it, "Now no one in Washington can ignore Southeast Asia because there are large Muslim populations in Indonesia and the Philippines, and these countries are taking a real hit in the global downturn."[19] Though for a shortsighted reason, Washington became reengaged. Yet it has to understand that the war on terror was its priority, not the region's, and that it would have to give consideration to their political and economic contexts when formulating policy.

ASEAN's Counterterrorism Platform

In the face of continued terrorist threats, the states of the region are going to have to work hard to overcome these lingering senses of animosity. Bilateral cooperation must be enhanced. But any significant improvement will have to be at the multilateral level.

What had ASEAN done prior to September 11, 2001, to combat terrorism? The short answer is very little. Since December 1997, ASEAN held biennial meetings on transnational crime, in which the issues of drug trafficking, human smuggling, arms smuggling, terrorism, money laundering, and piracy were discussed. The result of the first two meetings, held in December 1997 and June 1999, were paltry. States were "encourage[d] to expand their efforts in combating transnational crime." States pledged to increase cooperation without any legal commitments to do so. At the 1999 meeting, the Plan of Action to Combat Transnational Crime was raised to "enhance coordination" and facilitate the enactment of bilateral extradition treaties between states. At the 1999 meeting, the Senior Officials Meeting on Transnational Crime was established to coordinate the various laws of states. This annual meeting would be held in conjunction with the annual ASEAN Senior Law Officials' Meeting, the ASEAN Attorney Generals' Meeting, and ASEAN Chief of Military Staff Meeting. In sum, these meetings have been talk shops that have resulted in little meaningful policies and transnational cooperation.

In the immediate aftermath of the September 11 attacks, all governments in the region expressed sympathy for the victims and their concern about terrorism in general. ASEAN issued a very brief statement of condolence and a vague call for "strengthening cooperation in combating terrorism around the world," and all the governments endorsed UN Security Council Resolution

1368. Yet their individual responses varied greatly according to their immediate domestic political considerations.

On November 5, 2001, the ASEAN heads of state signed the Declaration on Joint Action to Counter Terrorism, in which they pledged to enhance cooperation in combating terrorism and abide by other UN decisions. In particular, the declaration pledged to "deepen cooperation among our front-line law enforcement agencies in combating terrorism and sharing 'best practices.'" It also committed member states to "enhance information/intelligence exchange to facilitate the flow of information, in particular, on terrorists and terrorist organizations, their movement and funding, and any other information needed to protect lives, property, and the security of all modes of travel." By May 2002, the ASEAN states had reached an agreement to try to standardize their criminal laws regarding transnational crimes.

ASEAN's importance will diminish if it cannot respond to the war on terror in a meaningful way. Unilaterally, several ASEAN states have done much to combat terrorism within their borders. There is clearly a lot of skepticism in the region whether ASEAN as an organization can rise to the challenge and effectively cooperate on the terrorist threat. ASEAN was clearly divided throughout the fall 2001 and winter 2002 over the U.S.-led operation in Afghanistan, with the Philippines and Singapore giving full endorsement to the operations, while Malaysia and Indonesia, majority Muslim states, were highly critical of the war. With such divisions, not to mention suspicion by the authoritarian members (Myanmar, Vietnam, Laos, and Cambodia) over police and intelligence sharing and noninterference, was it possible to expect any more than lip service from ASEAN? Admiral Dennis Blair, the former U.S. commander in chief of Pacific forces, implored the states of the region to engage multilaterally as the challenge "is beyond the resources of any single country and its armed forces."[20]

ASEAN army chiefs also met in November 2001, the second time that they had ever met, to discuss ways in which they could fight terrorism. At this meeting they pledged to share intelligence and assist one another in combating terrorism. Again, certain signatories were more willing to share information and cooperate. There are considerable limits to what ASEAN can accomplish simply because of the different views of the member states on the degree to which they will cede a portion of the sovereignty to multilateral institutions and the consensus-style decisionmaking that leads to the least common denominator decisions for the organization. As one commentator noted, ASEAN is still a "sovereignty enhancing rather than a sovereignty reducing" body.[21]

At the Special ASEAN Ministerial Meeting from May 20 to May 21, 2002, in Kuala Lumpur, the ASEAN foreign ministers gave full support to the organization's role in addressing the issue of combating terrorism. Yet it took several more months, until the July–August ASEAN summit, before a consensus on an anti-terror joint declaration was reached, and then only with intense pressure from the United States. In short, vast differences of opinion led to nominal support, but little in the way of concrete policies.

The limits to ASEAN's role in counterterrorism led to two interesting developments. The first was the proliferation of more bilateral arrangements, such as the Joint Malaysian-Indonesian General Border Committee that coordinated maritime and land-border policing; this led to Nur Misuari's capture in November 2001. Philippine and Indonesian governments pledged to increase intelligence sharing and in particular stem the illegal flow of small arms. Singapore and Indonesia met to discuss piracy and bilateral defense cooperation. U.S. naval patrols through the Straits of Malacca increased in 2001–2002. Bilateral meetings and arrangements increased throughout 2002.

The second development was the establishment of a subregional multilateral counterterrorism agreement that included the Philippines, Malaysia, and Indonesia. Both Singapore and Thailand expressed interest in joining the May 2002 agreement. It is interesting that these states decided to work outside of the ASEAN framework. Though the Philippine undersecretary of foreign affairs said, "The initiative is meant to complement the ASEAN process,"[22] it is clear that these states, the most affected by international terrorism, but also the original ASEAN members, were concerned that the new members of ASEAN would undermine any new policies that would allow other states to interfere in their internal affairs. The trilateral anti-terrorism agreement covered terrorism, money laundering, smuggling, drug trafficking, hijacking, people smuggling, and piracy.

These two points are really important, because multilateralism is more successful when it is built upon a firm foundation of bilateral treaties and agreements. ASEAN is the appropriate organization to take the lead on counterterrorism. Institutionally, the mechanisms and processes are already in place, with, for example, the annual meetings of heads of state, foreign ministers, military chiefs, intelligence chiefs, and police chiefs.

The most concrete step ASEAN took toward combating terrorism was not the result of their own efforts but the result of concerted diplomatic pressure from the United States. The ASEAN-U.S. Joint Declaration for Cooperation to Combat International Terrorism was the result of mixed support for the U.S. effort on the war on terror. Whereas the Philippines, Singapore, and Malaysia had given the United States significant support, the Thais did less so, while little at all had come from Indonesia. The joint declaration was a watered down version of the bilateral U.S.-Malaysian pact that was reached in the spring of 2002. Many of the ASEAN states, in particular Vietnam, were concerned about the implications of the treaty on their national sovereignty and demanded a softer version of the treaty.

The U.S.-ASEAN counterterror treaty did a number of things. First, it boosted U.S. law enforcement and intelligence cooperation with states in the region. In return for cooperation, the United States pledged technical and logistical aid to "prevent, disrupt and combat" terrorism.[23] Second, the counterterror pact provided a way for the traditional leaders of ASEAN to reexert themselves, to find a way to retake the agenda of the organization. Third, the treaty committed the United States to the region:

> The participants stress their commitment to seek to implement the principles laid out in this Declaration, in accordance with their respective domestic laws and their specific circumstances, in any or all of the following activities:
>
> I. Continue and improve intelligence and terrorist financing information sharing on counter-terrorism measures, including the development of more effective counter-terrorism policies and legal, regulatory and administrative counter-terrorism regimes.
>
> II. Enhance liaison relationships amongst their law enforcement agencies to engender practical counter-terrorism regimes.
>
> III. Strengthen capacity-building efforts through training and education; consultations between officials, analysts and field operators; and seminars, conferences and joint operations as appropriate.
>
> IV. Provide assistance on transportation, border and immigration control challenges, including document and identity fraud to stem effectively the flow of terrorist-related material, money and people.
>
> V. Comply with United Nations Security Council Resolutions 1373, 1267, 1390 and other United Nations resolutions or declarations on international terrorism.
>
> VI. Explore on a mutual basis additional areas of cooperation.[24]

Finally, Malaysia, with U.S. support and encouragement has agreed to host the Southeast Asia Regional Centre for Counter-Terrorism. Though it is in its early stages, this center hopes to become a forum for capacity building for the various relevant bureaucracies across the region. It is unlikely that it will become an operational coordinating center for intelligence services.

Keeping the United States Engaged

Clearly not everyone in ASEAN supported the ASEAN-U.S. Joint Declaration for Cooperation to Combat International Terrorism, and it was only accepted following the intense diplomatic maneuverings of the United States, which had used every multilateral forum in the Asia Pacific region since October 2001 to push its anti-terror agenda. For some states, notably Vietnam and Myanmar, the agreement posed too much of a challenge to their traditional notion of sovereignty. But ASEAN states themselves understood the threat that terrorism posed to themselves. Even Indonesia, which had been highly critical of the U.S. war on terror and had chafed at U.S. criticism of its own handling of domestic militants, signed the agreement, nearly three months before the attack on Bali.

The agreement was important in symbolic if not substantive terms. For the United States, it was certainly important to get the ASEAN states, in particular Malaysia and Indonesia, to endorse the war on terror, so that the United States could continue to rely on an international coalition that included Muslim states. President George W. Bush asserted that the war on terror was not a war on Islam, but only with the support of Muslim states could he say this with any confidence. Indeed, Southeast Asian Muslims believe the war on terror to be patently anti-Muslim. In a speech delivered to the ASEAN summit in late July 2002, the sultan of Brunei warned the Americans to be prudent about offending Muslim sensibilities in the region, though he did endorse the joint declaration. For the ASEAN states, it was important because it signaled the return of the United States to the region. The war on terror might not have been the top priority of every state in the region, but they knew it was the priority of the United States and they used it to reengage the Americans. As U.S. secretary of state Colin Powell stated, the anti-terror accord would build a "more intimate relationship" between the United States and ASEAN.[25]

This is important. The United States ignored the region since the end of the Cold War. With the conclusion of the Cambodian civil war, the loss of U.S. bases in the Philippines, and the shutdown of the Soviet naval base in Vietnam, there was little to keep the United States engaged in the region. Differences over human rights and Asian values, not to mention ASEAN's hubris in accepting Myanmar for membership, only distanced the United States from the region. ASEAN's resentment of the U.S. reaction to the Asian economic crisis certainly soured its perceptions of the United States. The lack of support by the United States toward the Australians who took the lead in the East Timorese peacekeeping operation again angered many in the region. In short, Southeast Asian states felt abandoned. There were close business ties and trade flows, but these were driven by market concerns, not state intervention.

The only two states that truly sought to maintain a serious security relationship with the United States were Thailand and Singapore. Singapore went to great lengths to provide the United States with the critical infrastructure and strong bilateral defense ties to keep the United States engaged in the region. Singapore, though the only state in the region with an offensive military capability, relies on the U.S. presence in the region to maintain the status quo. Malaysia and the United States have much closer ties at the working level than appears due to the rhetoric at the political level. Thailand never made the mistake that the Philippines made, and when the United States shut down its bases in the kingdom in the 1970s, the Thais went to great lengths to continue to engage the United States in regional security, through the Cobra Gold and other training exercises and weapons sales.

The war on terror has other important effects on international relations in the region. First, it allowed the states in the region to have good relations with both China and the United States, an opportunity that does not avail itself often. All states in the region acknowledge the U.S. dominant "hard" power position, but China's "soft" power is considerable. Since 1991, when the United States began to disengage itself from the region, as China's military spending and modernization began to soar and assertive nationalist foreign policy took hold, states have been tailoring their policies with China's consideration in mind; what I call the "China test." All states remain concerned about whether the United States will become bogged down in nationbuilding in Iraq: Will China take advantage of U.S. preoccupation and attack Taiwan? Will it become more assertive in the South China Sea? The fact is all the states see the United States as the balancer in the region and China as the disaffected revisionist state. Currently the U.S. relationship with China is good, but this is a short-term phenomenon, and competition and enmity will soon shape bilateral ties.

Will the United States stay engaged in the region? Is the war on terror a passing thing? How engaged will the United States be in the region in the long term? Will this be another case of typical U.S. shortsightedness? The United States cannot afford to ignore the region the way it did since the Philippine Senate voted to not renew the leases for the two military bases, which were shut down in 1991. Even if you make the case that the United States never completely withdrew from the region, the popular perception is that the United States did. The United States failed to deter Chinese aggression in the South China Sea throughout the 1990s, and it failed to come to the aid of its allies in their time of economic need, in 1998–2001, while China played the role of a hegemon, providing a collective good (not devaluing its currency) that while costly and detrimental to its own economy, enhanced its soft power throughout the region. Is it any wonder that states began to consider relations with China as a greater priority than ties to United States? Perhaps the U.S. government, both the executive and legislative branches, learned how important it is to stay engaged in the region, to keep tabs on political developments, and not be caught by surprise again. Colin Powell announced that the United States did not seek bases in the region, but that it was committed to staying engaged in the region.

Whereas the Singaporeans and Thais continued to engage the United States in the 1990s and armed themselves with U.S. weapons, the Philippines did neither. Although the United States and the Philippines came a long way to restoring their bilateral defense ties, which was clearly one of President Arroyo's goals, the Philippines probably overestimated the U.S. commitment to them. To allay fears that the United States was not seeking to regain a permanent base in the Philippines, U.S. troops withdrew when the six-month Operation Balikatan exercises came to an end in July 2002. When the Philippine armed forces failed to continue the intense operations against the Abu Sayyaf in the latter half of the year, the United States expressed frustration. The Abu Sayyaf regrouped, and four bombings in the Philippines in October

2002 demonstrate their continued commitment. In February 2003, a second Balikatan exercise was announced, only this time, the United States announced that their 1,750-strong force would be engaged in combat. This provoked a firestorm of criticism in the Philippines, as the constitution explicitly bans foreign forces. If the United States is constrained in its operations, the relationship will be weakened.

Indonesia is, once again, the question mark. At this point, they are so inward focusing that it does not seem like they have any concern or interest in engaging the United States. The trials of the TNI officials for the East Timor rights abuses, the sine qua non of the restoration of ties, have been a mockery of justice. President Bush pledged to support Indonesia's territorial integrity, which many saw as a green light for Indonesia to increase coercive policies in Aceh. It is unlikely that the U.S. Congress will authorize military sales, military aid, or repeal the Leahy Amendment, though it did offer $50 million in counterterrorism assistance, mainly to the Indonesian police. The Bush administration, for its part, repeatedly tried to get the Indonesian government to punish the perpetrators of the East Timorese violence, so they can get Congress to lift the Leahy Amendment. As Secretary of State Colin Powell said at a press conference with his Indonesian counterpart, Hassan Wirajuda:

> [W]e are starting down a path to a more normal relationship with respect to military-to-military. We're not there yet, but we're starting. And we believe that programs such as international military education and training and fellowship programs, that expose Indonesian military personnel to United States training and to United States personnel, help with respect to human rights issues and we should not cut off that opportunity. This is a position I think that we have been able to successfully present to our Congress, but at the same time the American Congress is watching carefully and is expecting action to be taken with respect to past abuses that might have occurred. And so this is just the beginning of a process. We are not at the end of the road yet, but I think it's a very strong and positive start to a more normal military-to-military relationship.[26]

Clearly these are cases where interests between the United States and its ASEAN allies converged. But what happens when interests diverge? The United States has the capability and the resources to stay engaged in the region. Whether it has the will to remain engaged over the long term is another question. Powell tried to allay concerns and stated that "President Bush is determined to keep US troops in this region as friends, not as foes, not as aggressors, seeking nothing but to help our friends feel secure in their own countries as part of [an] alliance or just partners with the United States of America."[27] There also seems to be a growing sense in the United States that it could not afford to lose sight of a region that is very dynamic and increasingly volatile again. For Southeast Asia, the greatest outcome of the war on terror would be a United States that is committed to more durable ties and a greater understanding of the region. The reality is that a myriad of other crises will distract the United States and that, once again, the region will be of secondary importance to Washington.

There is also great concern over what the war in Iraq means for the region. On the one hand, all the ASEAN states were concerned about the impact of the war on their economies. Rising oil prices would hurt the economies of every state in the region. Even Malaysia, a net exporter of petroleum products, was hurt as they suffered a decline in manufactured exports, especially electronics. Of greater concern to the governments of the region is growing popular antipathy for the United States. Already the Muslims in Southeast Asia believe that the war on terror is really a war on Islam. Second, they are infuriated with the hypocrisy of U.S. foreign policy, as the United States embarked on a diplomatic course of action against North Korea. As Malaysian prime minister Mahathir Mohammed remarked: "The fact that North Korea's open admission that it has weapons of mass destruction has met only with mild admonishment by the West seems to prove that indeed it is a war against Muslims and not against the fear of possession of weapons of mass destruction by the so-called rogue countries."[28] He warned that "the attack against Iraq will simply anger more Muslims who see this as being anti-Muslim rather than anti-terror." As prone to rhetoric as Mahathir is, he was accurately reflecting the sentiments of the majority of Southeast Asians. The day before he spoke, around 100,000 people gathered in a Kuala Lumpur stadium in an officially sanctioned show of opposition to war on Iraq. The war in Iraq has made the war on terror in Southeast Asia more difficult to fight. Antiwar demonstrations, which quickly turned into anti-U.S. demonstrations, erupted across the region beginning in the fall of 2002. The mood of mistrust and antipathy toward the United States is palpable.

On the one hand, it will be effectively manipulated by terrorist groups such as Jemaah Islamiya and the MILF, as well as radical-clerics in the mosques. These groups, which hold anti-U.S. sentiments, will attract new members. In addition to more radicals, combating them will become more difficult. War has increased animosity toward the United States and its policies. A surge in antipathy will put pressure on governments to no longer cooperate with the Unites States in the war on terror. One Indonesian intelligence official, who himself is deeply troubled by the rise of radical groups and terrorists, complained to me that war in Iraq would put such intense political pressure on the government, that his investigations into radical elements would come to a near standstill.

The Human Rights Conundrum

There is another difficulty in fighting the war on terror in Southeast Asia: balancing human rights and legitimate security concerns. This is a very fine line, but one that is essential. Amnesty International already sounded the alarm in a report entitled, "Rights at Risk," in which it stated: "The 'war on terror' may be degenerating into a global 'dirty war' of torture, detentions, and executions." The report singles out Malaysia for its draconian Internal Security Act, which allows for detention without trial for up to two years, the systematic use of torture, and "a series of progressively restrictive legislative amendments, paralleled by judicial rulings interpreting these laws, [which] have rendered the writ of habeas corpus essentially meaningless."[29] Many critics of the war on terror in the region saw their government's support of it as simply an attempt to crackdown on political opponents at home. The threat of terrorism in the region is real, but governments need to be cognizant that one of the key causes of terrorism is coercive policies and the lack of democratization. Repression against the Muslim communities only serves to drive them deeper underground. We cannot allow our allies to use the war on terror to arrest and imprison bona fide political opponents. Terrorism often results from a lack of political freedom and "space" in civil society. As a member of the Kampulan Mujahidin Malaysia quipped, "We stopped believing in the democratic process. So we felt that *jihad* was the only way to change the government."[30]

States need tools to effectively counter terrorism. One such tool that Singapore and Malaysia have is the draconian Internal Security Act, which allows them to detain suspects up to two years without trial. The use of the ISA is always politically charged. For decades it was used against not just communist and other militants but against bona fide political opponents who threatened the regimes' monopoly of power. The systematic use of the Internal Security Act led to poor relations with the United States, which was highly critical of Malaysia's detention and imprisonment of former deputy prime minister Anwar Ibrahim, whom they termed a "political prisoner." One would hope that the approximately 110 people currently detained in the two states under their respective ISAs will soon be brought to trial and not detained indefinitely; though for intelligence purposes (not wanting to reveal intelligence information in an open court to the suspect) it is unlikely to happen.

The United States lost the moral high ground with regards to human rights with the establishment of the internment camp at Guantanamo Bay, where Al-Qaida suspects have been detained without due process, any legal rights, or trial in sight.

Secretary of State Powell reiterated at the ASEAN summit on July 31, 2002, that human rights would remain a key foreign policy objective in the region: "I made the point to all of my interlocutors that we still believe strongly in human tights, and that everything we do has to be consistent with universal standards of human rights."[31] He went on to say, the following day, "The United States feels strongly about these sorts of issues and believes that if we're really going to prevail over this plague on the face of mankind, then we have to do it in a way that respects human dignity. Human rights have to be protected."[32]

But clearly U.S. priorities changed. In Malaysia, the day before the ASEAN summit began, Powell sidestepped a question about the comparison between the ISA and the treatment of Al-Qaida detainees in Guantanamo Bay. For the first time, a U.S. secretary of state did not attack the ISA:

> We did discuss human rights in each meeting in the context of our counter terrorism efforts. I made the point to all my interlocutors that we still believe strongly in human rights and that everything we do has to be consistent with universal standards of human rights. We talked about the ISA which the Malaysians have used for purposes I am sure that Minister would be better able to explain.[33]

Powell also mentioned that he and the foreign minister "touched on the case of Mr. Anwar Ibrahim."[34] During Prime Minister Mahathir Mohammed's April 2002 meeting with President Bush at the White House, the U.S. president evaded all questions regarding Anwar. To his credit, Powell did not. When asked if the United States still considered Anwar Ibrahim a political prisoner, Powell replied:

> Yes, as you know, we believe the [trial] was flawed. The Appeals Court has acted on the first charge and that is the end of the process as it is envisioned in the Malaysian law. But we have always felt that the [trial] was flawed, and we had a candid discussion about this matter. One of my associates met with his wife this morning as well, to express our interest and concern.[35]

Yet the Americans seemed to go no further than this pro forma statement. Malaysia's cooperation in the war on terror was too important.

Another troubling issue has to do with the rendering of suspects to third countries. In one case, a Pakistani and Egyptian national, Hafiz Mohammed Saad Iqbal, who was detained in Indonesia, was rendered to U.S. authorities without trial, who then transferred him to Egypt in January 2002 where he was wanted in connection with the Richard Reid shoe-bombing incident.[36] A suspected Al-Qaida operative, it is unknown why Iqbal came to Indonesia, whether escaping a Pakistani police dragnet or to lay the foundation for other escaping Al-Qaida operatives. He was later reported to have died during a rigorous interrogation.

The issues of human rights are very complex, and there are no easy answers. Most intelligence and police services in the region, at various times in their history, have been highly politicized and have systematically abused human rights. However, we are now relying on these same security services to assist us in rounding up suspected militants and terrorists. The case of Indonesia is an interesting one and it shows how difficult it will be to reconcile human rights with the war on terror.

At a press conference with the Singapore prime minister Goh Chok Tong, Secretary Powell stated his support for the full resumption of bilateral military ties with the Indonesian army, including weapons sales and training. Such ties were suspended by the Leahy Amendment due to the Indonesian armed forces' egregious human rights record in East Timor. Yet Powell was outspokenly in defense of restoring these ties.

> [T]here is not an inconsistency between military-to-military cooperation and abuse of human rights . . . if you get young officers, expose them to a military organization that is within a democratic political institution, such as the United States, then that rubs off on them. You can enhance human rights, you can improve human rights, by exposing them to the best examples of military organizations that are under civilian political control and have a commitment to the people and a commitment to human rights, and also a commitment to defend their nation. These are not inconsistent objectives or values.[37]

But the TNI has a long way to go to improve its human rights record. There is one instance that perfectly highlights the contradictions of what the United States is up against. On August 31, 2002, three employees of the U.S.-owned Freeport-McMoRan Copper and Gold, two Americans and an Indonesian, were ambushed and killed on a remote road near the mining giant's Indonesian headquarters on the remote island province of Papua. The initial investigation led by the commander of the Papuan provincial police, I Made Pastika—the same man who led the Bali bombing investigation—implicated the Indonesian military. Signals intelligence gathered by both the Australians and the Americans has led to the same conclusion. Four FBI officials who investigated the Papua murders in January reached the same conclusion.

The FBI was in a bind. On the one hand, U.S. citizens were killed by members of another country's armed force in order to send a signal to the corporation that it needed to continue to pay it for "security." In the past few years, Freeport paid the regional TNI command in Papua some $10 million to $11 million annually for "protection" from insurgents. When Freeport balked at the rising cost, the local Kopassus commander reminded the mining giant that Papua remained a dangerous place and the threat of insurgents remained great. U.S. legislators, already hostile toward the TNI, put pressure on the FBI to resolve the murder. On the other hand, it is the same organization, whose head has made counterterrorism the top of the FBI's agenda. The TNI, and in particular the elite force Kopassus and the military intelligence service were charged by Indonesian president Megawati Sukarnoputri to be lead counterterror forces. Already implicated in human rights abuses in East Timor and for its brutal "security approach" in Aceh, the TNI's implication in the Freeport slayings is only going to add fuel to the U.S. congressional fire to not restore ties to the TNI.

A commitment to human rights needs to be at the forefront of any country's counter-terrorist strategy. Indeed, one of the goals of terrorists is to provoke a heavy-handed government response against their constituency in order to win more sympathizers and supporters to convince the fence sitters that the government is oppressive. Maintaining the moral high ground is essential to isolating terrorists who resort to extralegal behavior.

Courting the Secular Nationalists and Moderates

The threat posed by governments systematically violating human rights of their citizens is enormous. States cannot use the war on terror to curtail press and legal freedoms or hamper the development of democracy. Terrorism results from a lack of political freedom. If anything we must foster the development of law-governed democracies and assist these countries in building durable political and legal institutions.

This book has tried to look at the question of why secular nationalists have not been more vociferous in speaking out against the militants and providing a more moderate set of policy options. One of the reasons that secular nationalists in the region, and especially in Indonesia, have been so loath to support a government crackdown on Muslim militants, people whom they should decry, is that they are afraid that the same draconian laws could be imposed on themselves. In Indonesia, it was only in 1999 that the post-Suharto regime repealed the draconian antisubversion laws and many were resistant to implementing new counter-terrorism measures. Likewise, in Malaysia and Singapore many advocates of democratization and political liberalization condemn the use of the ISA.

The moderates and secular nationalists must begin to promote alternatives to the radical Islamists. They must play a proactive role in developing civil society. To that end they will need the political space and democratic freedoms to operate. Their contribution is essential to the efforts to eradicate terrorism. The war on terror cannot be won through military means, alone. It relies on the active support of the silent majority of moderates, whose support will be lost if we turn a blind eye to the crackdowns and systematic violations of human rights perpetrated by their governments. Only with the active support of this group of individuals will Islam in Southeast Asia, once again, become equated with moderation, tolerance, and secularism.

Notes

1. Thomas Friedman, "Under the Arab Street," *New York Times* (*NYT*), October 23, 2002.
2. "Transcript of Ayman al-Zawahri Tape," Reuters, May 22, 2003.
3. Elena Pavlova, "An Ideological Response."
4. Fabiola Desy Unidjaja, "International Training Camp in Poso 'Empty,'" *JP*, December 14, 2001.
5. Interview with a colonel of the PNP-IS, Makate, Philippines, January 17, 2002.

6. I Made Mangku Pastika, "The Uncovering of the Bali Blast Cases" (paper delivered at the ASEAN Workshop on Combating Terrorism), January 20–22, 2003, Jakarta.

7. Ibid.

8. Kusuma Snitwongse, "Thailand and ASEAN: Thirty Years On," *Asian Journal of Political Science* 5, no. 1 (June 1997): 87–101.

9. For example, in the mid- to late 1990s, there were concerns that Vietnam would not be able to grasp the subtleties of ASEAN's consensus-style diplomacy. Arguing that Vietnam's diplomacy has been guided by confrontation with adversaries, there was concern whether Hanoi would be able to understand the "unwritten rules" of the grouping. One Thai commentator, a former deputy foreign minister, noted a fear that after Vietnam's membership, "posturing and bargaining will replace consultation and consensus building as the predominant form of conducting intra-mural affairs." Some in Vietnam policymaking circles were cognizant of the subtleties of intra-ASEAN diplomacy. Acknowledging that due to Vietnam's four decades of war, "the tendency to settle disputes and conflicts by military means is understandably rooted in the thinking of Vietnamese leaders," Tuan urged that Vietnam must therefore "accept ASEAN's rules of the game." Sukhumbhand Paribatra, "From ASEAN Six to ASEAN Ten: Issues and Prospects," *Contemporary Southeast Asia* 16, no. 3 (December 1994): 253; Hoang Anh Tuan, "ASEAN Dispute Management: Implications for Vietnam and Expanded ASEAN," *Contemporary Southeast Asia,* 18, no. 2 (June 1996): 61–81.

10. Kay Moeller, "Cambodia and Burma: The ASEAN Way Ends Here," *Asian Survey* 38, no. 12 (December 1998): 1087–1104.

11. Shaun Narine, "ASEAN in the 21st Century: Problems and Prospects," *The Pacific Review* 12, no. 3 (1999): 357–380.

12. Jose Almonte, "Ensuring Security the 'ASEAN Way,'" *Survival* 39 (Winter 1997–1998): 80–92.

13. Michael Leifer, "The ASEAN Peace Process: A Category Mistake," *The Pacific Review* 12, no. 1 (1999): 25–38.

14. Narine, "ASEAN in the 21st Century," 374.

15. Anthony Smith, "Indonesia's Role in ASEAN: The End of Leadership," *Contemporary Southeast Asia* 21, no. 3 (August 1999): 2238–2260.

16. Cited in Raphael Pura, "Asean Adds Diversity to Its Myriad Strains," *Wall Street Journal,* December 17, 1998.

17. Leiffer, "The ASEAN Peace Process," 28.

18. Kusuma Snitwongse, "Thailand and the ASEAN."

19. James Hookway, "Just Say 'No' to U.S. Troops," *Far Eastern Economic Review (FEER)*, December 6, 2001, 24.

20. Speech by Admiral Dennis Blair, commander in chief of U.S. Pacific Command, to the Asia-Pacific Parliamentary Forum, January 8, 2002.

21. Philips J. Vermonte, "ASEAN Needs to Address Illegal Trade in Small Arms," *Jakarta Post*, April 16, 2002.

22. Agence France Press (AFP), "RP, Malaysia, Indonesia Start Counter-Terror Talks," *Philippine Daily Inquirer* (*PDI*), December 27, 2002.

23. Slobodan Lekic, "Powell, Asian Leaders Sign Anti-Terror Pact," Associated Press (AP), August 1, 2002.

24. The U.S.-ASEAN Joint Declaration on Combating Terrorism, August 1, 2002, can be found at http://www.state.gov/p/eap/rls/ot/12428.htm.

25. Ibid.

26. U.S. Department of State Press Release, "Remarks with Indonesian Foreign Minister Hassan Wirajuda," August 2, 2002, Jakarta.

27. U.S. Department of State Press Release, "Remarks with Singaporean Prime Minister Goh Chok Tong," July 30, 2002, Singapore.

28. Jalil Hamid, "Malaysia's Mahathir Says World in State of Terror," Reuters, February 23, 2003.

29. The report, "Rights at Risk," January 18, 2002, can be found at: http://web.amnesty.org/library/index/ENGACT300012002.

30. Rajiv Chandrasekaran, "Clerics Groomed Students for Terrorism," *Washington Post* (*WP*), February 7, 2002.

31. Todd S. Purdham. "Powell Treading a Thin Line in Rallying Antiterror Support," *NYT*, July 31, 2002.

32. Peter Maass, "Dirty War," *The New Republic*, November 11, 2002, 18; Lekic, "Powell, Asian Leaders Sign Anti-Terror Pact."

33. U.S. Department of State Press Release, "Press Briefing with Malaysian Foreign Minister Datuk Seri Syed Hamid Albar," July 30, 2002, Kuala Lumpur.

34. Ibid.

35. Press Briefing with Foreign Minister Datuk Seri Syed Hamid Albar of Malaysia, July 30, 2002, can be found at http://www.state.gov/secretary/rm/2002/12275.htm.

36. Rajiv Chandrasekaran and Peter Finn, "U.S. Behind Secret Transfer of Terror Suspects," *WP*, March 11, 2002.

37. U.S. Department of State Press Release, "Remarks with Singaporean Prime Minister Goh Chok Tong.

Acronyms and Abbreviations

ABIM	Muslim Youth Movement of Malaysia (Angkatan Belia Islam Malaysia)
ADB	Asian Development Bank
AFP	Philippine armed forces
APEC	Asia Pacific Economic Council
ARF	ASEAN Regional Forum
ARMM	Autonomous Region of Muslim Mindanao
ASG	Abu Sayyaf Group
ASEAN	Association of Southeast Asian Nations
BIN	State Intelligence Agency
BPCA	Bangsamoro People's Consultative Assembly
BN	Berisan Nasional
CIA	Central Intelligence Agency
CPP	Communist Party of the Philippines
DAP	Democrative Action Party
DI	Darul Islam
DPR	Parliament
FATF	Financial Action Task Force
FBI	Federal Bureau of Investigation
FPI	Defenders of Islam
GAM	Gerakan Aceh Mederka (Free Aceh Movement)
GAM-MP	GAM Administrative Council
GIA	Algerian Armed Islamic Group
GDP	gross domestic product
GPI	Islamic Youth Movement
HuJI	Harkat-ul-Jihad-al-Islami
ICB	Islamic Consultative Body
ICG	International Crisis Group
ICS	Islamic Call Society

IIRO	Islamic International Relief Organization
INS	Immigration and Naturalization Service
IRIC	International Relations and Information Center
ISA	Internal Security Act
ISCAG	Islamic Studies Call and Guidance
ISI	Pakistani Intelligence Service
IWWM	Islamic Wisdom Worldwide Mission
JI	Jemaah Islamiya
KISDI	Indonesian Committee for Solidarity with the Islamic World
KMM	Kampulan Mujahidin Malaysia
KPSI	Komite Pengerak Syariat Islam
LTTE	Tamil Tigers
MaK	Maktab al Khidmat lil-Mujahidin al-Arab
MCA	Malaysian Chinese Association
MCP	Malaysian Communist Party
MER-C	Medical Emergency Relief Charity
MIC	Malaysian Indian Congress
MILF	Moro Islamic Liberation Front
MIM	Moro Islamic Movement
MLSA	Mutual Logistics Support Agreement
MMI	Mujahidin Council of Indonesia
MNLF	Moro National Liberation Front
NEP	New Economic Policy
NGOs	nongovernmental organizations
NII	Negara Islam Indonesia
NU	Nahdlatul Ulama
NPA	New People's Army
OECD	Office for Economic Coorperation and Development
OIC	Organization of the Islamic Conference
OFW	overseas foreign workers
PAN	National Mandate Party
PAS	Parti Islam SeMalaysia
PDI	Democratic Party of Indonesia
PDI-P	Democratic Party of Indonesia for Struggle
PKI	Communist Party
PNP	Philippine National Police
PPP	United Development Party
RM	Rabitatu Mujahidin
RSO	Rohinga Solidarity Organization
TNI	Indonesian armed forces
UAM	Ulama Association of Malaysia
UMNO	United Malays National Organization
UTM	Universiti Tecknologi Malaysia
WKR	Wae Ka Raeh

Bibliography

Abat, General Fortunato U. *The Day We Nearly Lost Mindanao: The CEMCON Story*. 3rd ed. Manila: FCA Publishers, 1999.

Abuza, Zachary. "Tentacles of Terror: Al Qaeda's Southeast Asian Network." *Contemporary Southeast Asia* 24, no. 3 (December 2002): 427–465.

———. "Funding Terrorism in Southeast Asia: The Financial Network of Al Qaeda and Jemaah Islamiya." Unpublished manuscript (June 3, 2003).

Adkin, Mark, and Muhammed Yousaf. *Afghanistan—The Bear Trap: Defeat of a Superpower.* London: Casemate Publishers, 2001.

Alexander, Yonah, and Michael S. Swetnam. *Usama bin Laden's* al-Qaida*: Profile of a Terrorist Network.* Ardsley, N.Y.: Transnational Publishers, 2001.

Almonte, Jose. "Ensuring Security the 'ASEAN Way.'" *Survival* 39 (Winter 1997–1998): 80–92.

Andaya, Barbara Watson, and Leonard Y. Andaya. *A History of Malaysia.* 2nd ed. Honolulu: University of Hawaii Press, 2001.

Arquilla, John, David Ronfeldt, and Michele Zanini. "Networks, Netwar, and Information-Age Terrorism," in Ian O. Lesser et al., *Countering the New Terrorism.* Washington: Rand Corporation, 1999, 39–84.

Baden Intellijen Negara. *Al-Qaida's Infrastructure in Indonesia.* Jakarta, February 2002.

———. "Interrogation Report of Omar al-Faruq." Jakarta, June 2002.

Baker, Richard W., and Hadi M Soesastro, et al., eds. *Indonesia: The Challenge of Change*. Singapore: Institute of Southeast Asian Studies, 1999.

Benjamin, Daniel, and Steven Simon. *The Age of Sacred Terror*. New York: Random House, 2002.

Bergen, Peter. *Holy War Inc.: Inside the Secret World of Osama bin Laden*. New York: The Free Press, 2001.

Brown, David. *The State and Ethnic Politics in Southeast Asia*. New York: Routledge, 1994.

Cheong, Yong Mun. "The Political Structures of the Independent States," in Nicholas Tarling, ed., *The Cambridge History of Southeast Asia, Vol. 2, Part 2, From World War II to the Present*. New York: Cambridge University Press, 1999, 59–138.

Council on Foreign Relations. *Terrorist Financing: Report of an Independent Task Force Sponsored by the Council on Foreign Relations*. New York: The Council on Foreign Relations, October 2002.

Crouch, Harold. *Government and Society in Malaysia*. Ithaca, N.Y.: Cornell University Press, 1996.

Davis, Michael. "Laskar Jihad and the Political Position of Conservative Islam in Indonesia." *Contemporary Southeast Asia* 24, no. 1 (April 2002): 12–32.

Department of the Interior and Local Government. "Country Report of Republic of the Philippines." Paper presented to the International Conference on Counter Terrorism, Baguio City, Philippines, February 18–21, 1996.

Department of National Defense. *The Philippine Campaign Against Terrorism*. Camp Aguinaldo, Quezon City, 2001.

Djadijono, M. "Economic Growth and the Performance of Political Parties," in Richard W. Baker, Hadi, Soesastro, et al., eds., *Indonesia: The Challenge of Change*. Singapore: Institute of Southeast Asian Studies, 1999, 126–128.

Dupont, Alan. *East Asia Imperilled: Transnational Challenges to Security*. New York: Cambridge University Press, 2001.

Emmerson, Donald. "Whose Eleventh? Indonesia and the United States Since 11 September." *Brown Journal of International Affairs* 9, no. 1 (Spring 2002): 115–126.

Gomez, Edmund Terence, and K. S. Jomo. *Malaysia's Political Economy: Politics, Patronage and Profits*. New York: Cambridge University Press, 1997.

Gunaratna, Rohan. *Inside Al Qaeda*. New York: Columbia University Press, 2002.

———. "The Evolution and Tactics of the Abu Sayyaf Group." *Jane's Intelligence Review* (July 2001).

Hamilton-Paterson, James. *America's Boy: A Century of Colonialism in the Philippines*. New York: Henry Holt, 1998.

Haneef, Mohamed A. "Islam and Economic Development in Malaysia: A Reappraisal." *Journal of Islamic Studies* 13, no. 3 (2001): 269–290.

Hedman Eva-Lotta E., and John T. Sidel. *Philippine Politics and Society in the Twentieth Century*. New York: Routledge, 2000.

Heffner, Robert W. *Civil Islam*. Princeton: Princeton University Press, 2000.

———. "Islam and the Nation in the Post-Suharto Era," in Adam Schwarz and Johnathan Paris, eds., *The Politics of Post-Suharto Indonesia*. New York: Council on Foreign Relations Press, 1999, 40–72.

Heffner, Robert W., and Patricia Horvatich, eds. *Islam in the Era of Nation States*. Manoa: University of Hawaii Press, 1997.

Hirschkorn, Phil, Rohan Gunaratna, Ed Blanche, and Stefan Leader. "Blowback: The Origins of Al Qaida." *Jane's Intelligence Review* 13, no. 8 (August 2001).

Huxley, Tim. *Defending the Lion City: The Armed Forces of Singapore*. Crows Nest: Allen and Unwin, 2000.

Indonesia National Police. "Examination Report of Abdul Aziz, aka Imam Samudra." October 21, 2002.

International Crisis Group (ICG). *The Megawati Presidency*. Asia Report No. 9. September 10, 2000.

———. *Indonesia: Overcoming Murder and Chaos in Maluku*. Asia Report No. 10. December 2000.

———. *Indonesia: Violence and Radical Muslims*. Indonesia Briefing. October 10, 2001.

———. *Al-Qaeda in Southeast Asia: The Case of the Ngruki Network*. Asia Report. August 8, 2002.

———. *How the Jemaah Islamiyah Terrorist Network Operates*. Asia Report No. 43. December 11, 2002.

Islam, Syed Serajul. "The Islamic Independence Movements in Patani in Thailand and Mindanao of the Philippines." *Asian Survey* 38, no. 5 (May 1998): 441–456.

Krause, Keith, ed. *Small Arms Survey 2001: Profiling the Problem*. New York: Oxford University Press, 2001.

Leifer, Michael. "The ASEAN Peace Process: A Category Mistake." *The Pacific Review* 12, no. 1 (1999): 25–38.

Lesser, Ian O. et al. *Countering the New Terrorism*. Washington: Rand Corporation, 1999.

Levitt, Matthew. "Combating Terrorist Financing, Despite the Saudis." Washington Institute for Near East Policy. Policy Watch No. 673. November 1, 2002.

———. "Saudi Financial Counter-Terrorism Measures (Part II): Smokescreen or Substance." Washington Institute for Near East Policy. Policy Watch No. 687. December 10, 2002.

———. "The Political Economy of Middle East Terrorism." *Middle East Review of International Affairs* 6, no. 4 (December 2002).

Lintner, Bertil. *Burma in Revolt: Opium and Insurgency Since 1948*. Bangkok: Silkworm Books, 1999.

———. "Religious Extremism and Nationalism in Bangladesh," paper presented at Religion and Security in South Asia, Asia Pacific Center for Security Studies, Honolulu, Hawaii, August 19–22, 2002.

Made Mangku Pastika. "The Uncovering of the Bali Bomb Blast Case." Paper delivered at the ASEAN Workshop on Combating Terrorism, January 20–22, 2003, Jakarta.

Man, W. K. Che. *Muslim Separatism: The Moros of the Southern Philippines and the Malays of Southern Thailand*. Quezon City: Attaeneo de Manila University Press, 1990.

Martinez, Patricia. "The Islamic State or the State of Islam in Malaysia." *Contemporary Southeast Asia* 23, no 3 (December 2001): 474–503.

McKenna, Thomas M. *Muslim Rulers and Rebels: Everyday Politics and Armed Separatism in the Southern Philippines*. Berkeley: University of California Press, 1998.

Moeller, Kay. "Cambodia and Burma: The ASEAN Way Ends Here." *Asian Survey* 38, no. 12 (December 1998): 1087–1104.

Muzaffar, Chandra. *Islamic Resurgence in Malaysia*. Selangor: Penerbit Fajar Bakti, 1987.

Nair, Shanti. *Islam in Malaysian Foreign Policy*. New York: Routledge, 1997.

Nakamura, Mitsuo, Sharon Siddique, and Bajunid, *Islam and Civil Society in Southeast Asia*. Singapore: Institute of Southeast Asian Studies, 2001.

Narine, Shaun. "ASEAN in the 21st Century: Problems and Prospects." *The Pacific Review* 12, no. 3 (1999): 357–380.

O'Rourke, Kevin. *Reformasi: The Struggle for Power in Post-Soeharto Indonesia*. Crows Nest, NSW: Allen and Unwin, 2002.

Paribatra, Sukhumbhand. "From ASEAN Six to ASEAN Ten: Issues and Prospects." *Contemporary Southeast Asia* 16, no. 3 (December 1994): 253.

Pavlova, Elena. "An Ideological Response to Islamist Terrorism: Theoretical and Operational Overview," in Rohan Gunaratna, ed., *Terrorism in the Asia Pacific: Threat and Response*. Singapore: Eastern Universities Press, 2003, 30–46.

Philippine National Police. *After Intelligence Operations Report*. Camp Crame, Quezon City, Philippines. February 27, 1995.

Rabasa, Angel, and John Haseman. *The Military and Democracy in Indonesia*. Washington, D.C.: Rand Corporation, 2002.

Rais, Amien. "Islam and Politics in Contemporary Indonesia," in Geoff Forrester, ed., *Post-Soeharto Indonesia: Renewal or Chaos?* Singapore: Institute of Southeast Asian Studies, 1999, 198–202.

Ramage, Douglas E. "Social Organizations: Nahdlatul Ulama and Pembangunan," in Richard W. Baker, M. Hadi Soesastro, et al., eds. *Indonesia: The Challenge of Change*. Singapore: Institute of Southeast Asian Studies, 1999, 201–216.

Rashid, Ahmed. *Taliban: Militant Islam, Oil, and Fundamentalism in Central Asia*. New Haven: Yale University Press, 2000.

Reeve, Simon. *The New Jackals: Ramzi Yousef, Osama bin Laden, and the Future of Terrorism*. Boston: Northeastern University Press, 1999.

Republic of the Philippines, National Intelligence Coordinating Agency. "An Update on the Recent Bombings in Mindanao and Metro Manila." Quezon City. November 25, 2002.

———. "Summary of Information: Kalid Shaykh Mohammad." Quezon City. November 5, 2002.

———. "Summary of Information: Umar Al-Faruq." Quezon City. November 2002.

Republic of Singapore, Ministry of Home Affairs. *White Paper: The Jemaah Islamiyah Arrests and the Treat of Terrorism*. Singapore, 2003.

Rhode, David. "Indonesia Unraveling?" *Foreign Affairs* (July/August 2001): 110–124.

Riddell, Peter R. "Arab Migrants and Islamization in the Malay World During the Colonial Period." *Indonesia and the Malay World* 29, no. 84 (July 2001).

Schwarz, Adam. *A Nation in Waiting: Indonesia in the 1990s*. Boulder, Colo.: Westview Press, 1994.

Schwarz, Adam, and Johnathan Paris, eds. *The Politics of Post-Suharto Indonesia*. New York: Council on Foreign Relations Press, 1999.

Simon, Sheldon W. *Southeast Asia and the US War on Terrorism*. NBR Analysis 13, no. 4 (July 2002).

Smith, Anthony. "Indonesia's Role in ASEAN: The End of Leadership." *Contemporary Southeast Asia* 21, no. 3 (August 1999): 2238–2260.

Snitwongse, Kusuma. "Thailand and ASEAN: Thirty Years On." *Asian Journal of Political Science* 5, no. 1 (June 1997): 87–101.

Stange, Paul. "Religious Change in Contemporary Southeast Asia," in Nicholas Tarling, ed., *The Cambridge History of Southeast Asia, Vol. 2, Part 2, From World War II to the Present*. New York: Cambridge University Press, 1999.

Tarling, Nicholas, ed. *The Cambridge History of Southeast Asia, Vol. 2, Part 2, From World War II to the Present*. New York: Cambridge University Press, 1999.

———. "The Establishment of the Colonial Regimes," in Nicholas Tarling, ed., *The Cambridge History of Southeast Asia, Vol. 2, Part 1, From c. 1800 to the 1930s*. New York: Cambridge University Press, 1999, 201–256.

Torres, Jose, Jr. *Into the Mountain: Hostaged by the Abu Sayyaf*. Quezon City: Claretian Publications, 2001.

Tuan, Hoang Anh. "ASEAN Dispute Management: Implications for Vietnam and Expanded ASEAN." *Contemporary Southeast Asia* 18, no. 2 (June 1996): 61–81.

Van der Kroef, J. M. "The Indonesian Arabs." *Civilisations* 5, no. 13 (1955): 15–23.

Vitug, Marites Danguilan, and Glenda M. Gloria. *Under the Crescent Moon: Rebellion in Mindanao*. Quezon City: Ateno Center for Social Policy and Public Affairs, 2000.

Index

About the Book

ISLAMIC EXTREMISM IN SOUTHEAST ASIA HAS MOVED BEYOND A MATTER OF LOCAL concern to one of global significance—as the events of the past decade have so clearly demonstrated. Drawing on intensive on-the-ground investigation and interviews with key militants, Zachary Abuza explains the emergence of radical Islamist groups in the region, examines Al-Qaida's role as organizational catalyst, and explores individual and multilateral state responses to the growing—and increasingly violent—Islamic political consciousness.

Abuza also analyzes state strategies for combating, co-opting, or coping with militant Islamist groups. A key question here is whether state actors are trying to resolve the root causes of Muslim disaffection—or merely using the "war on terrorism" to suppress the symptoms.

Zachary Abuza is associate professor of international politics at Simmons College. He is author of *Renovating Politics in Contemporary Vietnam* (Lynne Rienner, 2001).